STRANGE FRUIT AND BITTER ROOTS

STRANGE FRUIT AND BITTER ROOTS

Black History in Contemporary Graphic Narrative

DANIEL STEIN

University Press of Mississippi / Jackson

The University Press of Mississippi is the scholarly publishing agency of the Mississippi Institutions of Higher Learning: Alcorn State University, Delta State University, Jackson State University, Mississippi State University, Mississippi University for Women, Mississippi Valley State University, University of Mississippi, and University of Southern Mississippi.

www.upress.state.ms.us

Cover and front matter illustration by John Jennings

The University Press of Mississippi is a member
of the Association of University Presses.

Any discriminatory or derogatory language or hate speech regarding race, ethnicity, religion, sex, gender, class, national origin, age, or disability that has been retained or appears in elided form is in no way an endorsement of the use of such language outside a scholarly context.

Copyright © 2026 by University Press of Mississippi
All rights reserved
Manufactured in the United States of America

∞

Publisher: University Press of Mississippi, Jackson, USA
Authorised GPSR Safety Representative: Easy Access System Europe - Mustamäe tee 50, 10621 Tallinn, Estonia, *gpsr.requests@easproject.com*

Library of Congress Cataloging-in-Publication Data available

LCCN 2025035798 (print) | ISBN 9781496860583 (hardback)
ISBN 9781496860590 (trade paperback) | ISBN 9781496860606 (EPUB single)
ISBN 9781496860613 (EPUB institutional) | ISBN 9781496860620 (PDF single)
ISBN 9781496860637 (PDF institutional)

British Library Cataloging-in-Publication Data available

CONTENTS

Acknowledgments vii

INTRODUCTION. Strange Fruit and Bitter Roots 3

CHAPTER 1. Middle Passage Epistemologies 19

CHAPTER 2. Legacies of Lynching 57

CHAPTER 3. Civil Rights Pedagogy 94

CHAPTER 4. Afrodiasporic Archives 136

CHAPTER 5. Monstrous Pasts 168

CODA 217

Notes 229
Works Cited 265
Index 299

ACKS.

ACKNOWLEDGMENTS

Many people have influenced the gestation of this project, but four colleagues and friends stand out. During my student exchange year (1998–99) at Austin College in Texas, Truett Cates drove me around Sherman and told me about the 1930 lynching of George Hughes. Page Laws and Geoffroy de Laforcade reminded me during one of our many encounters that Nat Turner's 1831 rebellion took place within earshot of Hampton Roads, where Norfolk State University is based. When I visited the University of Tulsa for the first time in 2018, Kristen Oertel introduced me to the events of the 1921 Tulsa Race Massacre and talked about how the city was grappling with this part of its history. I thank all of these friends for sparking my interest in these historical places, figures, and events.

I also thank everyone who invited me to speak at their institutions and allowed me to present earlier versions of some of the chapters from this book: Laura Bieger and Florian Sedlmeier at Ruhr-Universität Bochum; Zuleica Romay Guerra at Casa de las Américas, Havana; Pia Wiegmink at the Bonn Center for Dependency and Slavery Studies at Universität Bonn; Kerstin Schmidt and Nicole Schneider at Katholische Universität Eichstätt-Ingolstadt; Alfred Hornung, Oliver Scheiding, and Mita Banerjee of the Obama Institute for Transnational American Studies at Johannes Gutenberg Universität-Mainz; Irmela Krüger-Fürhoff, Nina Schmidt, Jasmin Wrobel, and Dustin Breitenwischer at Freie Universität Berlin; the members of the African Atlantic Research Group at the FU Berlin and the Graduate Center, City University of New York (Martin Lüthe, Frank Kelleter, Robert Reid-Pharr, Herman Bennett, and many more); Walter Grünzweig, Iris-Aya Laemmerhirt, and Julia Sattler at Technische Universität Dortmund; and Catrin Gersdorf and Maria Eisenmann at Julius-Maximilians-Universität Würzburg. I appreciate all their questions and critical feedback, much of which has found its way into the final version of this book.

When I spent some time at the University of Tulsa in 2024 as part of a delegation from my home institution, the University of Siegen, I was privileged to access materials from the Eddie Faye Gates Tulsa Race Massacre Collection.

Jana Gowan, the reference and outreach librarian at the Helmerich Center for American Research, Gilcrease Museum, was tremendously helpful in making my stay a rewarding experience. In Tulsa, I also had the opportunity to visit the Greenwood Rising Museum and meet Raymond Doswell, its executive director, whom I thank for taking the time to discuss the history of Black Tulsa with me.

A few more people have shaped my thinking in this book. I am grateful for Julie Buckner Armstrong of the University of South Florida, who carefully reviewed the essay that forms the basis of a chapter, and I admire—and have learned greatly from—her research on the civil rights movement and on Mary Turner. It has been a great honor to have sponsored her and Thomas Hallock (also of the University of South Florida) as Georg Bollenbeck Fellows at the University of Siegen. Mirko Petricevic suggested James H. Cone's powerful *The Cross and the Lynching Tree* (2011), which helped shape my thinking about lynching iconography in chapter 2. Many thanks go to the Isamu Noguchi Foundation and Garden Museum, New York/Artists Rights Society for granting permission to reproduce the photograph of Noguchi's "Death" in chapter 2.

I am particularly thankful for the two highly detailed, greatly insightful, and stimulating anonymous reviews and for the time and care the reviewers invested in making this a better book. I have tried to accommodate their comments and suggestions and hope that the final product satisfies their critical concerns.

I am still stunned by John Jennings's brilliance and generosity. Not only is he a key figure in chapter 5, both as a creator of hard-hitting horror comics and as a critical commentator of comics and US history, but he also very generously allowed me to use his drawing of his creature The Murder on the cover of the volume. He also shared his comic *The Mighty Struggle: A Town Called Miracle*, which features The Murder, with me.

Kudos go to the folks at University Press of Mississippi who wonderfully supported all steps in the submission, review, copyediting, and production process: Amy Atwood, Joey Brown, Ellen Goldlust, Pete Halverson, Courtney McCreary, Lisa McMurtray, Valerie Jones, and Katie Turner. And a special shout-out to Cassie Winship for the fantastic cover design!

Earlier versions of some of the chapters were published as "Ta-Nehisi Coates's *Black Panther* and Afrodiasporic Archives," *Amerikastudien/American Studies* 67.2 (2022): 127–43; "Black Bodies Swinging: Superheroes and the Shadow Archive of Lynching," *Closure: Kieler e-Journal für Comicforschung* 7.5 (2021): 54–78; "Lessons in Graphic Nonfiction: John Lewis, Andrew Aydin, and Nate Powell's *March* Trilogy and Civil Rights Pedagogy," *Journal of American Studies* 55.3 (2021): 620–56; "Recuperating the Black Family in Graphic Narrative: Tom Feelings's *The Middle Passage* and Kyle Baker's *Nat Turner*," *Migration, Diaspora, Exile: Narratives of Affiliation and Escape*, edited by Daniel Stein, Cathy C. Waegner, Geoffroy de Laforcade, and Page R. Laws (Rowman & Littlefield and

Lexington, 2020), 21–41. I thank the editors and reviewers of these publications for accepting my work as well as the journals and publishers for the permission to feature revised and extended versions of these works in this book.

Last but not least, I want to thank my student assistant Ann-Katrin Limper for creating the elaborate index at the end of this volume.

A NOTE ON IMAGES

I do not reproduce photographs of racist violence in this book, but I do include depictions of violence, often horrific ones, from the comics I discuss. Viewer discretion is advised.

A NOTE ON LANGUAGE

I include quotations featuring the N-word only when they are essential for my argument. I retain only the first letter and change all other letters to asterisks to avoid perpetuating racist language.

A NOTE ON POSITIONALITY

I am aware that my personality—German, male, white, cis—puts me in a difficult position vis-à-vis the historical events and their graphic revisions studied in this book. I have tried to read, look for, and listen to the arguments of a wide range of scholars and critics who write about these issues from an inside perspective and to incorporate their concerns and suggestions. Ultimately, the graphic narratives in my corpus guide the scope of my analysis, as I focus on anti-Black violence when these works depict it and aim to bring scholarship from African American and diaspora studies into conversation with research and scholarship from comics studies. I hope that my perspective as an outsider—which, as a German professor of American studies, I am by default—allows for valid insights to the study of a medium that still deserves more critical attention.

A NOTE ON QUOTATIONS AND CITATIONS

Many of the graphic narratives discussed in the book are not paginated. To increase readability, I use chapter numbers or contextual clues to pinpoint the passage where a quotation/scene appears instead of the usual "n.p." The same applies to quotations from unpaginated online sources. I indicate my own omissions from quotations with bracketed ellipses [. . .]; all other ellipses appear in the source.

STRANGE FRUIT AND BITTER ROOTS

INTRO.

Introduction

STRANGE FRUIT AND BITTER ROOTS

This book takes as its starting point the heightened visibility of Black history in contemporary graphic narratives produced by mostly African American creators since the mid-1990s. Working in a medium that is still somewhat notorious for marginalizing Black voices and that has a long tradition of racist representation, these creators not only have developed innovative visualizations of central events from Black history but also engage in processes of graphic recuperation to excavate buried narratives and foreground otherwise excluded perspectives. The main question this book seeks to answer is how these creators grapple with what Michael A. Chaney has called "the archive of racist visualization" ("Is There" 73). How do they tease out established and entrenched notions of Black history that carry inbuilt racialized assumptions to revise those ideas and project more complex, more inclusive, and more affirmative visions of Black life, art, and culture?

Rebecca Hall, Hugo Martínez, and Sarula Bao's *Wake: The Hidden History of Women-Led Slave Revolts* (2021), a graphic account of Hall's historical research on the agency of Black women in the Middle Passage, provides some first and tentative answers to this question. The book's final chapter features a remarkable double splash page that provides the beginning for my investigation of Black history in graphic narrative.[1] The image shows Hall's graphic avatar walking across the main concourse of New York's Grand Central Station. She has almost crossed the concourse, with her back turned to its massive windows, the golden terminal clock standing on its pedestal, and sunlight flooding the building. Her front is in shadow as she is about to exit the scene, marching forward into the future, the past lying behind her. Dispersed across the page are six captions that reveal Hall's thoughts as she is traversing this urban space. "We are haunted. Haunted by slavery and its legacy. Our country lives in the afterlife of slavery," three captions on the left page state. Three captions on the right page continue: "It is in the legacy of the slave patrol, where not just police but white people in general see themselves as responsible for monitoring everything we do 'while Black.' It is in the way that Black men and often women are seen as always already dangerous. Or how Black women, who as slaves legally gave birth to property, not children, are still seen as less sensate, subhuman." In these captions, *Wake* proposes a historical continuum of racialized and gendered violence that reaches back to slavery and extends to the present, where dispossession and discrimination still shape the lives of many African Americans (and other racialized groups) and where police brutality cases and the Black Lives Matter (BLM) movement, referenced a few pages later, remain important forces in US culture.[2] Avoiding utopian sentiment, Hall's lament on this double splash page works toward the anticlimactic and starkly dissonant words of Thomas Jefferson, whose *Notes on the State of Virginia* (1785) the narrative quotes: "A black, after hard labor through the day, will be induced by the slightest amusements to sit up till midnight, or later, though knowing he must be out with the first dawn of morning," the passage begins, recalling the third US president's notorious remarks about the enslaved as a supposedly happy race. Comparing African Americans to white Americans, Jefferson discerned "a want of forethought, which prevents their seeing a danger till it be present . . . Their griefs are transient . . . In general, their existence appears to participate more of sensation than reflection." Jefferson's assessment clashes sharply with Hall's revisionary perspective, which suggests that slavery continues to haunt Black Americans more than a century and a half after official abolition and alleges that the sensations and perceptions of white supremacy ("Black men and often women are seen as always already dangerous") burden the reflections of historians turned graphic novelists like Hall. (Note the collective and communal *We* vs. Jefferson's generic *A black* and *They are*.) As *Wake* forcefully shows, the grief caused by slavery and its legacies is anything but transient: it transcends generations, spans continents, and shapes *Wake* as well as the other graphic narratives analyzed in this book.

Hall, Martínez, and Bao's phrase *often [. . .] seen as* contests Jefferson's allegation of an inability to see danger by disputing the claim of an absence of vision in Black life, historical or contemporary. In fact, the three snippets from US history that are brought to light by the sunbeams streaming through the windows of the concourse undermine everything Jefferson claims. In addition, these snippets ground the narrative in a visual discourse that haunts marginalized writers and artists who (re)imagine history. The first of these images (panels with a frame made up by the reflection of the light against the dark shadow of the rest of the concourse) conjures up the sundown towns that barred African Americans after dark (either legally fortified or sanctioned by segregationist practice). The image graphically remediates a popular photograph of a sign: "Whites Only / within city limits / After Dark."[3] The second panel shows the bottom half of Lawrence Beitler's well-known photograph of the lynched Thomas Shipp and Abram Smith, who were murdered and hanged from a tree by a white mob in Marion, Indiana, on 7 August 1930.[4] The remediated and curtailed version of the photograph in *Wake* foregrounds the amused and amazed onlookers, including only parts of the victims' legs and feet, an arrangement that other African American graphic artists have also used to avoid replicating the brutality of the scene and preserve the dignity of the dead men. It is ironic that Jefferson's description of Black Americans (many of whom were legally not Americans in 1785 but property owned by Americans), especially the phrase *will be induced by the slightest amusements to sit up till midnight, or later*, captures the morbid enjoyment of the white crowd instead of the experience of the lynched and those forced to live under the threat of lynching. In a similar vein, Jefferson's remark about Black Americans' lack of forethought is undermined by the lynching, whose cause was certainly not the victims' "adventuresome" behavior (they were accused of robbing a white man and raping his female companion) but a white vigilante mob violating the constitutional rights of the accused. In passages like these, *Wake* models the workings of archival retrieval and remediation as I conceive them in this book: as practices of superscribing images and narratives from the racist archive with new renditions that keep the old racism visible as a reminder of its entrenchment and longevity in US culture but refuse to submit to its logic by providing critical counterimages and alternative narratives.

The third image remediates a photograph held by the McFarlin Library at the University of Tulsa. It shows two men armed with rifles walking away from the burning buildings of Tulsa's Greenwood District, also known as Black Wall Street, during the 31 May–1 June 1921 Tulsa Race Massacre.[5] The image—both in its original photographic form and its remediation in *Wake*—is striking because of the casualness with which the two men walk away from the massacre in open daylight, obviously unafraid of any legal consequences of their actions. Moreover, three finely dressed women and one man are strolling toward the burning district, perhaps to enjoy the spectacle and revel in the destruction of the city's most visible signs of Black prosperity. The cars parked on the side of the road suggest that many other people have already arrived, either to watch or to participate in the carnage.

The remediations of historical photographs in *Wake* mesh with a deeper understanding of the forms and functions of archives and with our engagement with what they hold or exclude. "When we shift our emphasis from historical recovery to rigorous and responsible creativity," Vincent Brown suggests, "we recognize that archives are not just the records bequeathed to us by the past;

archives also consist of the tools we use to explore it, the vision that allows us to read its signs, and the design decisions that communicate our sense of history's possibilities" (134). Brown's observations are a useful frame for my analysis of contemporary graphic narratives, where this history is not merely recovered from the archives but creatively re-visioned and redesigned. These narratives utilize medium-specific tools to uncover hidden parts of Black history and activate comics' affective affordances to imagine more adequate pasts, presents, and futures. These narratives subscribe to a notion of "race as design" as developed by scholar, author, and graphic artist John Jennings, whose efforts to "undesign" race and expose the "fallacy that [Black] identity is connected to this made up thing" (Evans 111, 112) inform the analyses in this book.[6]

As my close reading of the ending of *Wake* shows, contemporary graphic narratives of Black history utilize existing archives and the histories of racial discrimination they contain as prompts for proposing new visions that acknowledge the continuing power of racist images and narratives yet superscribe them with critical and aesthetically challenging visuals. They dig deep and go far in their investment with historical hurt and their critiques of present failures to address the racisms of the past and the present. These narratives are more than educational and entertaining works of graphic storytelling, and they have much to offer to ongoing debates about how to reconcile racist pasts with current injustices and the possibilities for better futures—both on the comic book page and in real life.

Following Toni Morrison's observations about memorializing slavery, the remainder of this introduction explores the universe of (Black) modernity, which is shaped and bounded by "dark matter" (a term introduced by Howard Winant and further developed by Simone Browne) that threatens to render Black perspectives invisible but is countered by the creative historical revisions of the graphic narratives studied in this book. I also elaborate on processes of building new graphic archives that are aware of the pitfalls of filling in the gaps of historical documentation but nonetheless mobilize these gaps as creative spaces to imagine different pasts that make possible better futures. I then historicize and contextualize the two organizing metaphors from the book's title—strange fruit and bitter roots—and close with a summary of my argument and a preview of the chapters.

DARK MATTER IN THE UNIVERSE OF BLACK MODERNITY

The graphic narratives discussed in this book, which were produced primarily by authors and artists identifying as African American, are invested not only in the history of Black representation in comics but also—and perhaps even more—in the histories of the Black diaspora.[7] They wrestle with the powerful legacies of racial depiction in comics as well as in the broader US visual culture as they strive to create new images of Black life.[8]

Lance Tooks's *Narcissa* (2002) is a fitting example in this regard. Tooks calls forth these legacies not only to underscore their continuing power over representations of blackness but also to overcome the creative and cultural limitations inscribed in racist visual culture by satirizing Black stereotypes. *Narcissa* tells the story of the young Black film director Narcissa who wants to shoot an art movie, *Shadows Have I*, about an activist theater company. Her plan is thwarted by her white producer, who wants to rename the movie *Keepin' It Real* and who installs an ensemble of characters straight from the blackface repertoire: Baadass Blackie da Buck; Nurturin' Negro Mammy; Da Mystikal Magic Negro; Slappy, the Sexless Sidekick; Self-Sacrificin' Sambo Sucka; and Methuselah's Mama. The continuing presence of such figures in American racial iconography reveals them as the stereotypical foil against which Tooks and other graphic authors and creators develop new images and visual aesthetics.[9]

In doing so, these narratives offer sweeping criticisms of "the overweening, defining event of the modern world" that, according to Toni Morrison, "is the mass movement of raced populations, beginning with the largest forced transfer of people in the history of the world: slavery" ("Home" 10). As La Marr Jurelle Bruce writes in *How to Go Mad Without Losing Your Mind* (2021), his study of "madness and radical black creativity" (4), these works acknowledge "the depth of the wound that the Middle Passage inflicts on modernity" (3) and acknowledge that "the Atlantic slave trade, and the antiblack modernity it inaugurated, framed black people as always already wild, subrational, pathological, mentally unsound, mad" (4).[10] As such, they produce a sense of historical recognition that serves as a launching pad for creative transformations and means of reframing blackness, even though it is clear that the violence of the past will never completely subside and that its traumatic effects will always remain. If, as Howard Winant suggests, "race remains the *dark matter*, the often invisible substance that in many ways structures the universe of modernity" (605), the question is how contemporary graphic narratives make this dark matter visible and how they transform what Michele Wallace terms the "dark designs" of the past into more adequate visions for the present and the future.[11]

This is not a simple question, as Morrison's "perfect dilemma" (or what chapter 1 calls Morrison's paradox) of memorializing slavery indicates: "Forgetting is unacceptable. Remembering is unacceptable" (qtd. in Chassot 197). This dilemma is particularly vexing in the case of graphic narratives, where the genealogy of comics as a lowbrow medium and its reputation as a form of escapist, even frivolous, entertainment complicate attempts to overcome the exclusion of dark matter, including efforts to redress the traumas inflicted by centuries of anti-Black violence. Rebecca Wanzo has a point when she argues, in view of entrenched forms of racist caricature and other forms of visual abuse (e.g., blackface minstrelsy), "The rehabilitation of black representations is foundational to African American cultural production, so much so that we must understand the shadow of black racial caricature as haunting all African American representations" (*Content* 211; see also Tim Brooks; Michael D. Harris; Pieterse; Whitted, *Desegregating*). The graphic narratives considered in this book acknowledge the dark shadows of history, but they also offer more illuminating images of Black resilience and survival.

These narratives cannot simply ignore the violent parts of Black history and cannot create new images and narratives without registering, recognizing, and reconfiguring the archive of modernity's racist visualizations.[12] As Simone Browne holds, these violent parts are not always accessible, and new images and narratives are not always within reach. Elaborating on Winant's work, Browne suggests that "dark matter"

> might bring to mind opacity, the color black, limitlessness and the limitations imposed on blackness, the dark, antimatter, that which is not optically available, black holes, the Big Bang theory, and other concerns of cosmology where dark matter is that nonluminous component of the universe that is said to exist but cannot be observed. [. . .] Its distribution cannot be measured; its properties cannot be determined; and so it remains undetectable. The gravitational pull of this unseen matter is said to move galaxies. Invisible and unknowable, yet somehow still there, dark matter, in this planetary sense, is theoretical. (9)

Unobservable and unseen, undetectable and unknowable: "dark matter" is a constitutive component of the universe of (Black) modernity, nonluminous but somehow still there, its gravitational pull shaping the cosmology of a modern world in which Black characters were powerfully stereotyped in the newspaper comic strips of the 1890s and 1900s (see Stein, "Racialines") and have become more complex and broader in historical scope in graphic narratives since the 1990s.

In such a world, to register, recognize, and reconfigure images of blackness while laboring within the orbit of black holes and in the shadow of racial caricature (to continue the metaphor of absent illumination) is more than a reactionary endeavor.[13] In fact, as Darieck Scott proposes, graphic narratives can tap into the powers of the fantastic to open up new ways of thinking and seeing race. "Fantasy's activity is partly the recovery of the possible, the *action* [. . .] of forging some kind of *realization of the possible*," Scott argues in *Keeping it Unreal* (33); "in fantasy lies, inherently, resistance," while "thinking blackness in relation to fantasy" (35) means rethinking blackness "as an invention of the fantasy that there are races" (12; see also Ebony Elizabeth Thomas). Ironically, then, the fantasy of racial difference that undergirded and legitimized slavery as a defining event of the modern world also provides the critical impulse for comics authors and graphic illustrators to face this history and embrace Morrison's "perfect dilemma" of forgetting/remembering. How these authors and illustrators approach this dilemma—what histories they tell and how they tell them—is the key question addressed in this book.

BUILDING A RADICAL GRAPHIC ARCHIVE

The back cover description of Tina M. Campt's *Listening to Images* presents her study as an effort to listen "closely to photography, engaging with lost archives of historically dismissed photographs of black subjects taken throughout the black diaspora." What is needed, the description continues, is "a radical graphic archive of the African Diaspora that grapples with the recalcitrant and the disaffected, the unruly and the dispossessed." Campt's claims are an important reminder that the new visions of race that contemporary graphic narratives derive from the archive of racist visualization are indeed radical in terms of both their subject matter and their ways of depicting it on the comics page.

Campt asks a series of questions about archival practices that inform my approach to the contemporary graphic narratives in my corpus: "How do we contend with images intended not to figure black subjects, but to delineate instead differential or degraded forms of personhood or subjection—images produced with the purpose of tracking, cataloging, and constraining the movement of blacks in and out of diaspora? What are the technologies of capture and what are the stakes of the forms of accounting that engendered the archives?" (3). The graphic narratives discussed here ask these questions, albeit not always as explicitly, and provide answers as well. Perhaps the most productive means of contention—of registering and recognizing degrading and constraining archives of blackness—in these works is the creative reconfiguration or remediation of existing images into visuals that resist the racist logic inscribed in and prescribed by these images. Take the archive of lynching photography, which at once captures the suffering of the Black victims and provides African American creators with material they can graphically redesign (or undesign) and creatively reimagine (or unimagine): chapters 2 and 5 analyze this process in works such as Kyle Baker's *Nat Turner* (2008); Jeremy Love and Patrick Morgan's *Bayou* (2009–10); Derek McCulloch, Shepherd Hendrix, et al.'s *Stagger Lee* (2006); Mat Johnson and Warren Pleece's *Incognegro: A Graphic Mystery* (2008); David F. Walker, Chuck Brown, and Sanford Greene's *Bitter Root* (2019–21); Rob Guillory's *Farmhand* (2019–); John Jennings's *Blue Hand Mojo: Hard Times Road* (2017); and Ayize Jama-Everett and Jennings's *Box of*

Bones (2021).¹⁴ Another example, discussed in chapter 1, concerns the creation of a comic-specific Middle Passage iconography in Baker's *Nat Turner* and Hall, Martínez, and Bao's *Wake: The Hidden History of Women-Led Slave Revolts*. Here, Campt's practices of "tracking, cataloging, and constraining the movement of blacks in and out of diaspora" become instruments of recuperation and restoration, of ensuring that the otherwise invisible dark matter of modern racist regimes is conjured up on and through the comic book page.

The narratives I study are aware of the dangers inherent in this endeavor: they all negotiate the tension between recovering archival traces of the past (remembering) and redressing the loss of Black life recorded in the archive as an alternative to willful forgetting. Yet to register, recognize, and reconfigure images of blackness from the archives of racist modernity comes with additional risks. Saidiya Hartman warns that "the loss of stories" in these archives and from cultural memory "sharpens the hunger for them. So it is tempting to fill in the gaps and to provide closure where there is none. To create a space for mourning where it is prohibited. To fabricate a witness to a death not much noticed" ("Venus" 8). This warning is echoed by Laura Helton and her coauthors, who observe that Lisa Lowe's essay "History Hesitant" "urges scholars to pause before attempting to fill in gaps in the archive, so as to invite the past to exceed what is 'visible within current epistemological orthodoxy.' Such hesitation offers a space to ask what histories we are yet unable to imagine, and what pasts have been 'forcibly assimilated, or forgotten,' because they escape the frames of reference we find most familiar" (9). Frames and framing are central processes of comics storytelling that become particularly relevant in graphic narratives whose main objectives include reframing Black history and its attending notions of blackness to escape the epistemological orthodoxy questioned by Lowe.¹⁵

One of the central conundrums I confront in this book, therefore, is one of the key challenges faced by the creators whose work I examine: the difficulty of producing graphic narratives of Black history that are grounded in recorded facts even though these facts are scarce or slanted toward an anti-Black perspective. This includes the problem of having to imagine a different history (and thus to potentially fill in gaps in the archive, convert absences into presences, and speculate about the historically uncertain) to imagine a more adequate past as the basis for a better future. "To focus the inquiry on *recovery* mobilizes the different valences of the term," Lowe writes, "a sense of retrieval of archival evidence and the restoration of historical presence, on the one hand, and the ontological and political sense of reparation, on the other, that is, the possibility of recuperation, or the repossession of a full humanity and freedom, after its ultimate theft or obliteration" (85). Recuperation and repossessing are useful concepts for understanding graphic narratives that interrogate and revise stereotypical notions of Black history.

To make this tension productive, the graphic narratives I analyze conjure up America's violent past and reference the troubled present yet hesitate to fantasize radically utopian futures. They are strongest when they wrestle with the racist visual archive and struggle to expunge from it familiar narratives of degradation and discrimination. I am reminded in this context of Bruce's rethinking of Hortense Spillers's notion of the "American Grammar Book," which she defines as the "symbolic order" that continues to shape how "African-American life in the United States" is considered: as an outcome "under the pressure of those events" (68) and as a history whose initial rupture (the Atlantic slave trade) remains largely invisible dark matter even to the present day.[16] For Bruce, this American Grammar Book contains "a complex assemblage of symbols, discourses, archetypes, themes, and recursive dramas reflecting and reproducing America's racial and sexual regimes" (33), but its focus is largely language, or text, which comes with an inevitable muting of the visual elements of this history. Bruce thus envisions "an American Picture Book, a repertoire of images that lately abound in American public spheres," that evokes "scenes of state-sanctioned black wounding and death that saturate our information age: black people fleeing, charging, hands up, hands clenched, battered, throttled, shot, kneeling, flailing, staggering, convulsing, slumped over, prostrate on asphalt or grass, then photographed or video-recorded, then bandied about endlessly on social media timelines and network news broadcasts" (33). If Bruce's enumeration sounds overly passive, figuring victims of anti-Black violence mostly as raw material for the production and circulation of media images, the point is to imagine a response that moves from reaction to action, or, as Sara Clarke Kaplan puts it, transforms "grief into the articulation of grievances that traverse continents and cross time" (513). We can understand this American Picture Book as a serialized affair, an ongoing, open-ended narrative or an archive that, like many comic books, is less a stable and finite storage space than a constantly evolving assemblage of images emerging from the practice of "resisting closure" (Chassot 197).

The graphic narratives I analyze combine elements of Spillers's American Grammar Book with Bruce's American Picture Book. They register both the history of Black modernity and the "rupture" that stands at the "beginning" of the modern Black diaspora (Spillers 68) as well as the politics of the current moment, which I define as the years between 1995, when Tom Feelings's *The Middle Passage: White Ships/Black Cargo* was published, and 2025, when Guillory's *Farmhand* series and Walker, Brown, and Greene's *Bitter Root* continue to be serialized and when the #BlackLivesMatter movement has turned into a more enduring Movement for Black Lives (cf. Christopher Paul Harris 8).[17] While I hesitate to call these narratives "Afrofuturist" (I prefer to speak of "Afrodiasporic archives" in connection with the *Black Panther* and *Shuri* series in chapter 4), they share with Afrofuturism a sense of the speculative as well as an interest in the past as a gateway to a different future.[18]

This speculative encapsulation of the past and the present finds figurative expression in the character Major Sankofa, developed by graphic artist and scholar John Jennings as a kind of Black diasporic Captain America (depicted in Donna-lyn Washington, *John Jennings* 31) who embodies the basic idea of Afrofuturist speculation with a historical twist: "Usually people who are minorities are stereotyped and forced to live inside of that tiny little box of identity," Jennings observes. "Then, historically, public policies have been put into place to police that box. The speculative space allows minorities to imagine another self that is in another space and by doing so provides a release from that box." He continues, "Afrofuturism has always been about the idea of 'sankofa,' reaching back and getting the past and bringing it forward" (Chambliss, "Soul" 23). Jennings elaborates elsewhere that Sankofa is "a West African term; it literally means 'go back and get it.' [. . .] A lot of things around Afrofuturism and Black speculative culture is going back and trying to show new generations the power of the narrative, the power of the types of things that have come before" (Watt 76, 77).[19] Going back and getting it: What may sound like a simple endeavor emerges, on closer inspection, as a series of complex practices that range from registering, recognizing, and reconfiguring the past to retrieving, reconstructing, recuperating, restoring, recreating, and revisioning a different kind of Black history.

STRANGE FRUIT AND BITTER ROOTS

This book's two-part title finds its inspiration in the long history of antiracist interventions in US culture. The first part, "Strange Fruit," comes from the Jewish high school teacher Abel Meeropol's 1937 antilynching poem immortalized by Billie Holiday's Café Society renditions and 1939 recording of the song as well as by several later recordings and live performances.[20] As one of the most consequential encapsulations of the horrors of race-based lynching, the poem is central to my argument, and this centrality is further emphasized by the fact that Holiday's musical rendition adds interracial and intersectional components (a Black woman singing the lyrics of a white Jewish man) that complicate readings of Black history either as an account of white atrocities or as a story limited to Black (male) suffering. Moreover, the poem underscores my argument that contemporary graphic narratives remediate and revision a history filled with anti-Black violence because the poem is already a remediation of lynching photographs Meeropol had seen, while Holiday's vocals rearticulate the written words through her Black voice.

"Strange Fruit" offers an ekphrastic encapsulation of lynching photographs. It uses nature imagery as a central metaphor—the magnolia tree as the gallows of the "gallant" South and the Black bodies hanging from these trees as "strange fruit" and specimens of a "strange and bitter crop." The natural imagery evokes both farming and agriculture and thus Jefferson's agrarian ideal as well as the slavery-based cotton economy and the system of sharecropping after the Civil War. The poem's main metaphor, the fruit-bearing tree ("poplar trees," "root," "magnolias," fruit "for the tree to drop") not only dramatizes lynching as an unnatural—*strange*—act, as a crime against humanity, and as an atrocity rooted in the South but also offers a poetic transformation of lynching's horrors, visualized so starkly in photographs, by turning atrocity into an aesthetic form and thereby offering a different kind of annotation to the photographs.[21] These photographs were initially wordless, yet whenever they were printed and disseminated as postcards, they were inscribed by the sender. Meeropol's poem thus offers a counternarrative, and the Barthesian grain of Holiday's remarkable voice adds a sonic dimension to the violence and suffering that the photographs record.

"Strange Fruit," both poem and song, thus indicates that the murder of Black Americans can produce an aesthetic response beyond the gloating of white spectators and racist commentators. Many African American writers and artists acknowledge the bitter parts of Black history, including lynching, to document atrocities seldom included in official narratives, making the dark matter of race visible by reimagining its nature and impact. In doing so, these creators endorse a different reading of this history, offering new visions that move beyond documenting violence and trauma toward a more productive and potentially even redemptive form. Accepting the tree as a metaphor for American history, they acknowledge its atrocious uses—as an apparatus of lynching and a locus of Black bodies as "strange fruit"—as well as its life-sustaining powers, from the nourishing fruit it can produce to the shade it can provide.[22]

Moreover, trees conjure up family lineages and kinship genealogies. They suggest familial stability where it seems impossible, especially for Black families (see chap. 1). Think of the notion of the family tree and the ancestry it records, visualized in several graphic narratives—Walker, Brown, and Greene's *Bitter Root*, Guillory's *Farmhand* series, and John Jennings and David Brame's *The Mighty Struggle: A Town Called Miracle*, whose prologue speaks of an old tree on which "a fearless Black man who spoke truth to power" was lynched in Mississippi. This "echo tree" has a magical branch that the man's wife, a conjure woman, turns into a time-traveling and universe-transcending megascope and that helps its bearer to carry "the burden of justice and the stories [and] rage [. . .] of the ancestors." We may also think of the roots and routes that Paul Gilroy theorizes in *The Black Atlantic* (1993), a concept that reconciles notions of movement (often forced and involuntarily, in the sense of an uprooting) with a sense of longevity, as is exemplified in the works I examine through depictions of black sharecropping and other forms of connecting with the land (mainly in the US South).[23] While trees are rooted in one particular place, their seeds can travel and produce new life in different places and climates, suggesting the possibility of escape from the violence of the past and from the threats of the present as well as raising hope for a better future (see chap. 5).[24]

The connection between the traveling of tree seeds and the notion of the Black diaspora—diaspora being etymologically tied to the Ancient Greek διασπορά, "scattering"—is central to my argument. I understand the graphic archive as a collection of images and visual narratives that have historically sought to determine—and thus fix—concepts of blackness in the modern imagination, propagating unanimous visions of race while aiming to prevent their scattering beyond the stereotypical mold. The graphic narratives analyzed in this book work against such delimitations and toward the diversification of the archive and do so not by proposing a wholly new visual discourse but by making material from the archive productive through remediation and counterdepiction.

Finally, the notion of bitterness in Meeropol's "Strange Fruit" is a bittersweet affair, as the *Bitter Root* series also suggests. The roots may be bitter, evoking the notion of forced uprooting through the Atlantic slave trade and the Middle Passage as well as the fear, during slavery, of being "sold down the river" and losing family members, but these roots nonetheless ground Black experience.[25] This bittersweet history places Walker, Brown, and Greene's narrative in a tradition of African American literature exemplified by Langston Hughes's poem "The Bitter River" (1942), indicating a level of literariness and intertextual awareness seldom recognized in comics. The poem is "dedicated to the memory of Charlie Lang and Ernest Green, each fourteen years old when lynched together beneath the Shubuta Bridge over the Chicasawhay River in Mississippi, October 12, 1942," and some of its most haunting moments include the opening lines about a "bitter river" that is "flowing through the South" whose water, filled with "filth and mud," has left a bitter taste in the speaker's mouth: "Too long has its evil poison / Poisoned my blood." In a variety of areas, Hughes's poetics correspond with the graphic narratives I study: watery imagery (see chap. 1 and 5), which calls forth both the Middle Passage depicted in Baker's *Nat Turner* and Hall, Martínez, and Bao's *Wake* and the Southern swamps and bayous imagined in Love and Morgan's *Bayou*; filth and mud, which conjure up the Mississippi (the muddy river) and its devastating force, including the flood in Love and Morgan's *Bayou* and the monsters chased by Jennings's hoodoo detective Half-Dead Johnson in *Blue Hand Mojo* (see chap. 5).[26] Toward the end, Hughes reads the river as a "tragic" space "where the lynched boys hung": "The gall of your bitter water / Coats my tongue." Here, the bitterness of racial violence has a visceral feel (it can be tasted), and a coated tongue will have a hard time speaking out. The poem can be read as an appeal to bear witness through poetry and other forms of creative expression that reject anti-Black violence and racial oppression and strain to leave behind the bitterness.

BLACK HISTORY IN CONTEMPORARY GRAPHIC NARRATIVE

The chapters that follow focus on racist violence from the Middle Passage and US slavery to lynching, Jim Crow racial segregation, and the struggle for civil rights. They engage with the ways in which, according to the graphic narratives examined, historical violence continues to exert power on Black lives in the present. These works seek to recover a Black past, in Lowe's understanding, by retrieving, restoring, recuperating, and repossessing narratives and images of Black history to challenge conventional conceptions of national history. In addition, these works strive to create new visions of a more inclusive and more nuanced sense of Black life in the United States, including hopeful and joyful aspects as well as pedagogical impulses (see especially chap. 3 and the coda).

While the book covers a succession of historical periods and events, it purposely avoids a linear trajectory (or epistemology, in Michelle M. Wright's nomenclature).[27] It covers publications from 1995 to 2025 but favors thematic clusters—Middle Passage Epistemologies, Lynching Legacies, Civil Rights Pedagogy, Afrodiasporic Archives, Monstrous Pasts—instead of an overly creator- or work-focused approach, which also means that several graphic narratives appear in multiple chapters.[28]

I have chosen works that offer critical takes on the African American past while aiming for a broader overall scope that reads these works vis-à-vis literary and photographic representations of Black history. Thus, I excluded works with more subdued, subtle, or implied historical elements, such as Ebony Flowers's *Hot Comb* (2019), whose treatment of Black hair evokes a long history of Black hairstyles and their social, cultural, and political implications, or Tananarive Due, Steven Barnes, and Marco Finnegan's *The Keeper* (2022), which deals with intense personal trauma. I selected works of graphic nonfiction (Baker's *Nat Turner*; Hall, Martínez, and Bao's *Wake*; Ho Che Anderson's *King*; and John Lewis, Andrew Aydin, and Nate Powell's *March* books) as well as works of graphic fiction (Love and Morgan's *Bayou*, Ta-Nehisi Coates, Roxane Gay, Yona Harvey, and Nnedi Okorafor's *Black Panther* and *Shuri*, Jama-Everett and Jennings's *Box of Bones*, Jennings's *Blue Hand Mojo*, Guillory's *Farmhand* series, and Walker, Brown, and Greene's *Bitter Root*) but had to exclude several interesting publications.

Documentary or historical comics discussed only marginally include Roland Laird, Tanesha Nash Laird, and Elihu "Adofo" Bay's *Still I Rise: A Graphic*

History of African Americans (2009); Blair Imani's *Making Our Way Home: The Great Migration and the Black American Dream* (2020); and David F. Walker and Marcus Kwame Anderson's *The Black Panther Party: A Graphic Novel History* (2021). I turn to Joel Christian Gill's *Uncelebrated Narratives from Black History* (*Strange Fruit* vol. 1, 2014), *More Uncelebrated Narratives from Black History* (*Strange Fruit* vol. 2, 2018), and *Tales of the Talented Tenth* series (2014–) in the coda, and I draw occasionally on his graphic adaptation of Ibram X. Kendi's *Stamped from the Beginning: A Graphic History of Racist Ideas in America* (2023). However, I have not considered Bill Campbell and Bizhan Khodabandeh's *The Day the Klan Came to Town* (2021) and Tony Medina, Stacey Robinson, and John Jennings's *I Am Alfonso Jones* (2017) as well as biographies such as Frank "Big Black" Smith, Jared Reinmuth, and Améziane's *Big Black: Stand at Attica* (2020), Whit Taylor and Kazimir Lee's *Harriet Tubman: Toward Freedom* (2021), and Elizabeth Colomba and Aurélie Levy's *Queenie: Godmother of Harlem* (2023). I also excluded adaptations of sociological or literary works such as Paul Peart-Smith's *W. E. B. Du Bois: The Souls of Black Folk: A Graphic Interpretation* (2023) and John Jennings and Damian Duffy's graphic renditions of Octavia Butler's works (e.g., *Kindred* [2017], *The Parable of the Sower* [2020], and *Parable of the Talents* [2025]) even though they certainly deserve extended study.

Chapter 1, "Middle Passage Epistemologies," focuses on depictions of the Middle Passage in three publications: Feelings's *The Middle Passage: White Ships/Black Cargo*, Baker's *Nat Turner*, and Hall, Martínez, and Bao's *Wake: The Hidden History of Women-Led Slave Revolts*. I read these works as graphic interventions into what Michelle M. Wright defines as the "narratives of knowledge that are taught, learned, relayed, exchanged, and debated in discussions of the 'fact' of Blackness" (*Physics* 7–8). They aim at broadening the scope and increasing the depth of Black history by daring to reconstruct, recuperate, and represent a past that can never be fully reconstructed, recuperated, and represented (Morrison's "perfect dilemma") as they attempt to move beyond established epistemologies of the Middle Passage through innovative stylistic decisions (Feelings's silent tableaus, Baker's separation of text and images, and Hall, Martínez, and Bao's palimpsestic confluence of past and present as well as recurring visual tropes in all three works). I historicize and contextualize these works with scholarship on the Middle Passage and confront them with literary attempts to create a poetics of the transatlantic slave trade.

Chapter 2, "Legacies of Lynching," returns to Baker's *Nat Turner* and adds Love and Morgan's *Bayou*; McCulloch, Hendrix, et al.'s *Stagger Lee*; and Johnson and Pleece's *Incognegro: A Graphic Mystery* to study how these works treat lynching imagery, especially by remediating photographs. Suggesting that the figure of the American superhero emerged from an ethos of hooded violence that constitutes the genre's unacknowledged premise, the chapter examines the intriguing connections between this popular serial figure and what Jacqueline Goldsby calls "lynching's cultural logic" (5). Rather than searching the archive of superhero comics for (scarce) depictions of racially motivated lynchings, I look at graphic narratives about Black history that evoke a sense of superheroism to renegotiate the genre's lynching roots and use these narratives' storyworlds to creatively revise and thus lay claim to the archive of lynching photography. The chapter ends with an explorative section that juxtaposes (sensu Teju Cole's approach to photographic images) a lynching photograph from 1930 with a commemorative sculpture from 1934 and ponders the visual echoes that emerge when they are placed vis-à-vis the appearance of Miles Morales as an African American and Afro-Latinx Spider-Man.

Chapter 3, "Civil Rights Pedagogy," revolves around the civil rights movement as it is portrayed in Lewis, Aydin, and Powell's *March* (2013, 2015, 2016) trilogy, as well as in Ho Che Anderson's *King: A Comics Biography*, with glances at Mark Long, Jim Demonakos, and Nate Powell's *The Silence of Our Friends* (2012) and Lila Quintero Weaver's *Darkroom: A Memoir in Black and White* (2012). These narratives reiterate as well as complicate the master narrative of the movement (with its focus on a few male figures, on the South, and on the limited time span of the 1950s and 1960s) not so much by extending what Waldo E. Martin Jr. and Patricia A. Sullivan criticize as "a limited, all-too-familiar repertoire of events, places, and people" (xiv) but by negotiating the many layers of mediation and remediation that constitute what has come to be understood as the civil rights movement—that is, by remediating what Leigh Raiford calls the "media-mediated events" ("Come" 1150) that shape mainstream narratives of the movement. Another central element of the chapter is its emphasis on the need to develop and embrace a "metacritical pedagogy" (Santos, *Graphic* 8) that recognizes the graphic narratives' didactic impulses and considers these impulses for classroom use.

Chapter 4, "Afrodiasporic Archives," deals more specifically with superhero comics, taking Ta-Nehisi Coates's *Black Panther* run (illustrated by Brian Stelfreeze and others) as a starting point for investigating absences in Afrodiasporic archives and thinking about popular narratives' potential to revise and reimagine these absences into fuller accounts of Black history. Coates and his illustrators utilize the suggestiveness of the archive as a critical lens through which ongoing superhero narratives like *Black Panther* can reflect on and reckon with the propagation of imperial fantasies and myths of national exceptionalism, creating what Teju Cole calls a sense of "global diasporic blackness" that strains to venture beyond "that colonial hangover" in addition to "the

American experiences of slavery, slave rebellion, Jim Crow, and contemporary racism, as well as the connective tissue that bound the Black Atlantic into a single territory of pain" ("On the Blackness").[29] The chapter further distinguishes between the depiction of archives in the storyworld and a reading of the comics as an intervention into comic book history as well as into the colonial past that created the African diaspora. It traces Coates's revisioning of African historical memory (the Djalia, which holds Wakanda's collected memories) and his technodystopian treatment of a neocolonial intergalactic space empire that mines the memories of the enslaved to secure and increase its political power. The chapter ends with a consideration of Nnedi Okorafor et al.'s *Shuri* (2019) and the spin-offs *World of Wakanda* (Roxane Gay, Coates, et al., 2017) and *Black Panther & the Crew* (Coates et al., 2017), pondering how these series question conventional depictions of women in superhero comics.

Chapter 5, "Monstrous Pasts," picks up historical associations of the Black Other as a monstrous figure and considers how images of monstrosity take on different functions in recent graphic narratives. Looking closely at Love and Morgan's *Bayou*, Jennings's *Blue Hand Mojo: Hard Times Road*, Jennings and Brame's *The Mighty Struggle: A Town Called Miracle* (2024), Walker, Brown, and Greene's *Bitter Root*, Jama-Everett and Jennings's *Box of Bones: Book One*, and Guillory's *Farmhand* series, I consider the ways in which historically entrenched and racist images of monstrous Otherness are refigured in these narratives as African American visions inspired by Black folklore, conjure women, hoodoo characters, and swamp monsters.

The coda turns to a visual trope that runs through many of these works and that reappears as a variation in Joel Christian Gill's *Uncelebrated Narratives from Black History* (*Strange Fruit* vol. 1): a frayed and severed rope that is miraculously still, upheld by an unknown force. This image and several others that evoke escape from ropes and chains encapsulate the idea that by absenting the tortured and tormented Black body from the depiction and by uprooting the tree that traditionally bears lynching's iconic "strange fruit," Gill and other contemporary creators acknowledge centuries of aggression, violence, and abuse without showing them, conjuring up familiar images of anti-Black violence while daring to imagine history differently.

Chapter 1

MIDDLE PASSAGE EPISTEMOLOGIES

Attempts to memorialize the Middle Passage—the western route of the transatlantic slave trade that brought millions of Africans into a life of enslavement on the American continents and caused the deaths of many millions more during the voyage—appear relatively frequently in African American literature. Poems and poetry collections like Robert Hayden's "Middle Passage" (1945), Kamau Brathwaite's *Middle Passages* (1992), Kwame Dawes's "Requiem" (1996), James A. Emanuel's "The Middle Passage Blues" (1999), and Lucille Clifton's "Slaveships" (2000); plays like Amiri Baraka's *Slave Ship: An Historical Pageant* (1967); and novels like Charles Johnson's *Middle Passage* (1990) strain to "render speakable what was formerly unspoken," as Toni Morrison observed in "Unspeakable Things Unspoken" (132).[1] Yet as the doubly negated neologism in Morrison's title indicates, these works confront the problem of representing a historical event whose transgenerational and transnational magnitude calls into question literature's capacity to express the sense of traumatic loss that stands at the beginning of the African presence in the New World.[2] If the Middle Passage is indeed "the ground zero of signification" (88), as Simon Gikandi remarks, and if, as Rutherford Calhoun, the Black narrator of Charles Johnson's *Middle Passage*, asserts, "none of it made sense after the Middle Passage" (188), then the challenge for authors is to use literature to imagine a historical experience that defies existing epistemologies—that is, to acknowledge "the impossibility that conditions our knowledge of the past" (Hartman, "Venus" 13) and to recognize the difficult "parameters for knowing, reading, and making legible the conditions of slavery and its aftermath" (Lowe 87). In fact, literary authors and comics creators alike have accepted the representational and ethical challenges of historical depiction by venturing into the past as a means of recovering, reconstructing, and reimagining Black history.[3]

If the Middle Passage eradicated Black life and reduced it to the inhumane mechanics of enslaved labor, the graphic narratives discussed in this chapter seek to recuperate it in comic form, seeking the kind of "symbolic possession of the past" that Cheryl Finley locates in the works of "contemporary African American and African diaspora artists [who] have found it necessary to reach back in time to reclaim important emblems and icons of history as a way of understanding their relationships to the present" (10–11).

Africans were forced onto ships and discharged on the shores of the Americas after a horrendous journey during which they were stripped of their humanity and reduced to the status of commodities. Gikandi thus speaks of the Middle Passage as the "Atlantic crypt" and "a place of pure negativity" (92, 86), while Saidiya Hartman characterizes her archival work as "entering a mortuary; it permits one final viewing and allows for a last glimpse of persons about to disappear into the slave hold" (*Lose* 17). As historical documents indicate, the captured Africans were often shaved as well as branded with their new owner's initials, thereby marking their property status—as "cargo," in the brutally technocratic language of the day—on their skin. All three graphic narratives analyzed in this chapter foreground the moment of branding in disturbing visuals that underscore the transformation of the newly enslaved from human beings to property that could lawfully be treated like cattle (or worse). This stigma, physically imprinted on the skin of the newly enslaved and enforced on their minds as their "blackness" was abused as evidence of inhumanity, features prominently in graphic narratives of the Middle Passage, thereby indicating a profound concern among contemporary creators not only with current forms of racial repression but also with the history and genealogy of white supremacy and anti-Black violence as constitutive forces of Western modernity.

Tom Feelings's *The Middle Passage: White Ships/Black Cargo* (1995) shows two white crew members as one of them is holding down a chained Black man and the other is pressing a branding iron onto the man's left arm as he writhes in pain. Choosing sequential depiction over Feelings's tableau-like still images, Kyle Baker's *Nat Turner* (2008) devotes five panels spread over two pages to depict the process of shaving (first panel), the heating of the iron (panels 2 and 3), and the painful application of the hot metal to the chained Black man's skin (panels 4 and 5) (37–38). Rebecca Hall, Hugo Martínez, and Sarula Bao's *Wake: The Hidden History of Women-Led Slave Revolts* (2021) imagines a scene at the Whydah (or Ouidah) slave trading port in present-day Benin, where the newly enslaved are undressed before undergoing shaving and physical inspection. They are then branded, as the final panel on the page shows a steaming branding iron and the stern face of the woman about to undergo the humiliating procedure.[4] Beyond eliciting a sense of revulsion and disgust at such systemic instances of degradation and torture, scenes such as these also have a metahistorical function as they showcase the making of race as a process of white domination over Black bodies that must be unmade in the effort to create a more equitable and just world—an effort in which graphic narratives are increasingly claiming a substantial role.

These newly enslaved men and women—"no longer Africans, yet not American either" (125), as the narrator of Johnson's *Middle Passage* puts it—could be traded and sold at their enslavers' will after arriving in the New World, a practice that was designed not only to create leverage for buyers and sellers but also to sever family relations and cut tribal affiliations. Enslaved women were often abused as "breeders" to increase their owners' human property through routine acts of sexual exploitation and rape.[5] The traumatic effects of this epochal dehumanization through which Africans became "Black" (and thus publicly marked as racially inferior) and Europeans and Americans became "white" (and thus elevated to a status of racial superiority) "locked [them] symbiotically" in what Paul Gilroy calls "an antagonistic relationship marked out by the symbolism of colors which adds to the conspicuous cultural power of their Manichean dynamic" (1).[6] This racially charged symbolism continued long after slavery, as Morrison's "Unspeakable Things Unspoken," seminal nonfiction writings (see Morrison, *Playing*; Morrison, *Origins*; Morrison, *Source*), and fiction, especially *Beloved* (1987), indicate. Morrison's oeuvre serves as an important intertext for contemporary graphic narratives that engage in a type of reverse ekphrasis: the visualization of historical events only scarcely documented in the archives but already variously narrated in literary texts.[7]

Morrison's Pulitzer Prize–winning novel centers on the formerly enslaved Sethe, a woman haunted by the ghostly return of her dead baby daughter, whom Sethe killed to spare her the burdens of (re)enslavement. In the postbellum era, Sethe wants to achieve a kind of "family relationship" (31) that was never fully available during her time as an enslaved woman, when she was raped by her owner's sons and when her husband, Halle, went mad as he watched the abuse. Sethe's eventual lover and surrogate father to her children, Paul D, recalls his childhood in slavery: "Mother. Father. Didn't remember the one. Never saw the other" (258). Baby Suggs, Halle's mother and Sethe's mother-in-law, remembers that Sethe "barely glanced at [the last of her children] when he was born because it wasn't worth the trouble to try to learn features you would never see change into adulthood anyway" (163).[8] The destruction of Black families through centuries of racist violence and the struggles to preserve familial relations and establish alternative forms of kinship is a central theme in the comics as well.

Since *Beloved* can be categorized as a neoslave narrative, it is not surprising that Morrison's fictional characters echo the openings of seminal slave narratives and postslavery autobiographies, which constitute another significant referential framework for graphic narratives.[9] While Frederick Douglass remembers and names his enslaved mother in *Narrative of the Life of Frederick Douglass* (1845), he writes that his father "was admitted to be" a white man "by all I ever heard speak of my parentage. The opinion was also whispered that my master was my father; but of the correctness of this opinion, I know nothing" (12). Writing more than half a century later, Booker T. Washington declared in *Up from Slavery* (1901),

> Of my ancestry I know almost nothing. In the slave quarters, and even later, I heard whispered conversations among the coloured people of the tortures which the slaves, including, no doubt, my ancestors on my mother's side, suffered in the middle passage of the slave ship while being conveyed from Africa to America. I have been unsuccessful in securing any information that would throw any accurate light upon the history of my family beyond my mother. [. . .] In the days of slavery not very much attention was given to family history and family records—that is, black family records. (7)

As *Beloved* and Douglass's and Washington's autobiographies indicate, Black history is often marked by an absence of stable families and ancestry, an absence that Feelings, Baker, and Hall, Martínez, and Bao seek to overcome by imagining alternative origin stories, both familial and communal, for their protagonists and their ancestors and descendants.

Such alternative stories are not confined to narratives about slavery and the Middle Passage. While I turn to John Jennings's *Blue Hand Mojo* in more depth in chapter 5, the story's protagonist, the conjure man Half-Dead Johnson, who is the only survivor of a lynching that killed his wife and two children, tells an impertinent underling threatening to harm his family, "My family? The fuck you know about my family, muthafucka?" (interlude). In David F. Walker, Chuck Brown, and Sanford Greene's *Bitter Root*, there is Ford Sangerye, who lost family members in a race massacre in Chicago. When the young white Southerner Jonnie-Ray asks Ford about his family, he responds, "Don't wanna talk about my family" (169). Thinking and speaking about family is hard for characters whose families have been murdered in cases of anti-Black violence, but their struggles make up a significant part of their lives and shape their appearance in the comics.

David F. Walker, Damon Smyth, and Marissa Louise's graphic biography *The Life of Frederick Douglass* (2018) even suggests a direct lineage from Douglass's autobiography to contemporary graphic narratives, thus connecting comics with the slave narrative as a foundational genre of African American writing. The biography emphasizes Douglass's roles as a husband and father—roles that are certainly not the norm in comic book depictions of Black masculinity. It begins with a gallery that features his maternal family members (his grandmother, Betsy Bailey, and his mother, Harriet Bailey) but excludes his paternal (white) lineage, perhaps because of the uncertainty about who his father was as well as because the authors do not want to afford the white enslaver any formative space in Douglass's life. Moreover, the opening chapter follows Douglass's *Narrative* by documenting his early life as an attack on his family and the families of all the enslaved. Douglass wrote, "Slavery cares not for the family. The relationship between a slave mother and her child is no different from that of a cow and her calf—all are property and subject to their master's whims" (7). This depiction resonates with the later scene in which Douglass recalls eating cornmeal from a wooden trough with the other enslaved children on the plantation. Walker, Smyth, and Louise include this passage (16), and Baker's *Nat Turner* (70) shows children eating from a trough as a stark image of slavery's inhumanity.

Writing at the tail end of the Harlem Renaissance, almost a century after Douglass but decades before Morrison, the poet Sterling Brown thematized attempts to eradicate Black families and the erasure of the products of Black labor in his poem "Bitter Fruit of the Tree" (1939). This title recalls Abel Meeropol's "Strange Fruit," which had been published as "Bitter Fruit" two years earlier and which contains the line "Strange fruit hanging from the poplar trees." (Billie Holiday recorded it in the same year Brown published his poem.) "Bitter Fruit of the Tree" consists of two stanzas, the first of which considers the fate of the speaker's grandmother during slavery, the second of which that of his father during the Jim Crow era's system of Black sharecropping. The poem begins,

> They said to my grandmother: "Please do not be bitter,"
> When they sold her first-born and let the second die,
> When they drove her husband till he took to the swamplands,
> And they brought him home bloody and beaten at last.[10]

The poem ends with white supremacists (identified in the poem as a generic "they") advising his father, "You must not be bitter." Brown connects the lives of Black Americans with the practice of lynching only through the title of the poem and through suggestive phrases such as "they brought him home bloody and beaten at last," leaving readers to make the connection to Meeropol's poem and Holiday's recording. Black children are either sold or allowed to die, the poem suggests, and if their parents rise against their oppression, they will be driven to the swamplands and beaten or lynched.

Struggling to address the historical magnitude of such lasting attacks on Black lives and Black families and the urge to revere Black ancestry, Morrison, Hayden, Baraka, Brathwaite, Dawes, Emanuel, Clifton, Johnson, Brown, and other writers have sought to creatively imagine the pain and anguish of the murdered, enslaved, and oppressed. They have tried to bear literary witness to centuries of onslaught on the lives of Black Americans while acknowledging that there is no escape from the pitfalls of representing the unspeakable, of turning historical "absences [into] vital presences" and "implying a full descriptive apparatus (identity) to a presence-that-is-assumed-not-to-exist," as Morrison puts it ("Unspeakable" 139, 145), or of mining "the violence of the archive" of transatlantic slavery and of "writing at the limits of the unspeakable and the unknown," as Hartman suggests ("Venus" 1).[11] The graphic narratives examined in this book both write and draw at the limits of the unspeakable and the undrawable, referencing and reframing a deeply troubling historical imaginary that has already found aesthetic form in poetry and literary prose but becomes reimagined anew in the medium of comics.

VISUAL-VERBAL REPRESENTATION: GRAPHIC NARRATIVES OF THE MIDDLE PASSAGE

The pitfalls of representation run especially deep in the medium of graphic narrative, which burdens creators with the additional task of confronting not only a centuries-long history of racist speech and writing but also an equally trenchant visual culture of racist depiction. Traditionally, graphic narratives, from caricatures and single-image cartoons to comic strips and comic books, were complicit in the broader visual culture's racist ridicule and misrepresentation of Black lives and experiences. Yet if African American literature can trace its roots to the narratives of the formerly enslaved, popularly known as slave narratives, of the eighteenth and nineteenth centuries, the "coloring of America" in graphic narrative that Derek Parker Royal diagnosed in 2007 is a much more recent phenomenon. As such, it draws its historical material not only from recorded history, revealing an awareness of the blind spots, distortions, and misrepresentations that for centuries have shaped this history. This coloring also builds on literary attempts to rectify these oversights and find suitable aesthetics for the creative recuperation of Black history.

Given the still-common association of graphic narratives (or comics) with the lighthearted, funny, and hilarious, it is not surprising that the horrors of the Middle Passage rarely surface in this medium. While Black history has been gaining traction as a subject matter in comics since the 1990s—Ho Che Anderson's initial work on *King* (1993) being an early example and Joel Christian Gill's *Uncelebrated Narratives from Black History* (*Strange Fruit* vol. 1, 2014) and *More Uncelebrated Narratives from Black History* (*Strange Fruit* vol. 2, 2018) indicating a continuing interest—only three graphic narratives have addressed the Middle Passage in substantial detail: Feelings's *The Middle Passage*, described in its peritexts as a "visual narrative" or series of "narrative paintings"; Baker's *Nat Turner*, advertised on the cover of the Abrams edition as a "graphic novel" about the 1831 rebellion that shook Southampton County, Virginia; and Hall, Martínez, and Bao's *Wake*, labeled "part graphic novel, part memoir" on the inside flap of the hardcover edition and described as "an imaginative tour de force" that chronicles "efforts to uncover the truth about these warriors who, until now, have been left out of the historical record."[12] These revisionary works of Black diasporic historiography approach the impossible task of picturing the Middle Passage—"it seems that the Middle Passage resists narrative form," as Joanne Chassot puts it (37)—by diverging in various ways from conventional modes of visual storytelling. In doing so, they constitute "not so much histories as epistemologies," or "chosen arrangement[s] of historical events [. . .] perceived to be the defining moments of collective Blackness," as Michelle M. Wright observes in *Physics of Blackness: Beyond the Middle Passage Epistemology* (7). They function as graphic interventions into what Wright defines as the "narratives of knowledge that are taught, learned, relayed, exchanged, and debated in discussions of the 'facts' of Blackness" (8). They broaden the scope and increase the depth of more conventionally and more widely endorsed notions of Black history by reconstructing, recuperating, and graphically representing a history that ultimately cannot be fully reconstructed, recuperated, and represented—by accepting "Morrison's paradox."[13]

All three works discussed in this chapter announce their attempts to complicate and move beyond established epistemologies of the Middle Passage through far-reaching stylistic decisions. Feelings, whose earlier historically conscious work includes the comic strip *Tommy Traveler in the World of Negro History* (1958–59), *Crispus Attucks and the Minutemen* (1967), as well as illustrations for children's books such as *To Be a Slave* by Julius Lester (1968), selects a silent black-white-gray depiction, banning words and color from his visual account of the events.[14] In *Nat Turner*, Baker largely excludes language from his images except for a few strategically placed speech balloons, and he uses a grayscale color scheme with a hint of sepia to communicate a sense of historicity. He also cites sporadically from *The Confessions of Nat Turner* (1831), the initial as-told-to Thomas Ruffin Gray account of Turner's life, but sets these quotations apart from the images, in a separate space where they cannot sully the graphic rendition of this life story. Hall, Martínez, and Bao's black-and-white drawings may seem more conventional at first sight since they incorporate language into the standard format of captions and balloons, yet they too revert to moments of speechlessness where language is unable to grasp what the images struggle to illustrate. "Like invisible forces have shaped everything around you . . . . . . but you've lost the words to describe them," one sequence of captions in *Wake* declares, with the second part of the statement superimposed over an image of chained and near-naked or naked enslaved Africans being led from a ship into New York City in the 1700s. "This is what it means to live in the wake of slavery," the caption continues, completing the statement. These words extend across three panels, with the right and left ones picturing a portion of Wall Street's New York Stock Exchange, which was the epicenter of the eighteenth-century trade in enslaved persons and which is bifurcated by the middle image showing the ship, an overseer, and the enslaved Africans. It is as if the curtain is being pulled aside to reveal the hideous history behind the building's iconic facade and everything for which it still typically stands.[15]

An earlier scene in *Wake* depicts Hall walking through the streets of New York when a man bumps into her, not seeming to see her. The way the man is drawn represents both present-day forms of misrecognition of Black lives and the historical roots and trajectory of this predisposition (his reflection in the window reveals an eighteenth-century colonist). In imagining the physical friction inherent in the collision of Black and white bodies, the scene evokes the opening sentences of Ralph Ellison's *Invisible Man* (1952): "You're constantly being bumped against by those of poor vision. [. . .] You wonder whether you aren't simply a phantom in other people's minds. [. . .] It's when you feel like this that, out of resentment, you begin to bump people back" (3).[16] Considering the prominence of mirror-like surfaces that project scenes from the racist past onto the modern cityscapes depicted in *Wake*, it makes sense to continue this Ellisonian reading: "I am invisible, understand, simply because people refuse to see me," Ellison's narrator proclaims. "It is as though I have been surrounded by mirrors of hard, distorting glass. When they approach me they see only my surroundings, themselves, or figments of their imagination—indeed, everything and anything except me" (3). To visualize such invisible histories, then, is the task that the creators of graphic narratives face. That Ellison ties his narrator's notion of racial nonrecognition explicitly to the field of the visual—"That invisibility to which I refer occurs because of a peculiar disposition of the eyes of those with whom I come into contact. A matter of the construction of their *inner* eyes, those eyes with which they look through their physical eyes upon reality" (3)—adds to the pertinence of his central metaphor for graphic narratives of Black history, including those that seek to rescue the Middle Passage from its dominant state of graphic invisibility.

Thus, rather than simply "drawing the unspeakable," as Consuela Francis maintains, *Middle Passage*, *Nat Turner*, and *Wake* can be read as answers to Morrison's call to unspeak the unspeakable and to Ellison's mandate to bump back against those who refuse to recognize blackness by exploring ways to *undraw* the unimaginable. This endeavor does not simply entail the invention of new imaginaries but necessitates profound encounters with archivally solidified constructions of Black invisibility—constructions that are so deeply entrenched in the visual vocabulary of Western culture that they must be excavated to be exposed, expunged, and exchanged with more self-determined and adequately complex visions of Black life. John Jennings's understanding of "race as design" and his recognition of "the culpability of design in actually pushing particular notions about what race is and how it functions" (Evans 112) come to mind in this context, as they necessitate recuperative and revisionary techniques to "undesign" the power of racial exclusion vested in the archives and suffusing the Western cultural imaginary (111).[17]

These three works undesign such exclusion by envisioning images of the Black family and recovering ancestral relations as nodes in the African Atlantic diaspora, veering back and forth between historical verisimilitude and visual hyperbole to negotiate the complex legacies of racial representation.[18] As such, they mobilize the means of their chosen medium to practice a graphic variant of Hartman's "critical fabulation," which she defines as "straining against the limits of the archive to write a cultural history of the captive, and, at the same time, enacting the impossibility of representing the lives of the captives precisely through the process of narration" ("Venus" 11). Feelings, Baker, and Hall, Martínez, and Bao fabulate graphic visions of an otherwise unspeakable and unrepresentable experience.[19] They certainly "expand the limits of the archive through attentive reading amplified by speculative narrative" (Hartman, "Dead" 211), as in Hartman's critical practice. But as works that engage existing elements of visual culture, they combine speculative amplification with archival resuscitation through the mechanisms of graphic narrative.

This combination is crucial because colonial archives contain extensive documentation and justification of transatlantic slavery yet provide little testimony of the enslaved and thus hardly any information on which graphic artists could base their imagery. "Of the twelve or fifteen or twenty million or more who endured the Middle Passage," Hartman observes, "the few who went on to write about it emphasized the terror of the unknown that characterized life in the hold, the grief and despair, the regular course of sexual violation and brutality, the disease and abjection created by living in waste, and the daily routine of death" ("Dead" 211). Olaudah Equiano and Ottobah Cugoano are survivors of the Middle Passage who wrote about their experiences; both describe the misery on the ships but ultimately acknowledge the unspeakability of what they endured. While Equiano notes that the enslaved on board "continued to undergo more hardships than I can now relate" (59), Cugoano is even more explicit: "It would be needless to give a description of all the horrible scenes which we saw, and the base treatment which we met with in this dreadful captive situation" (15).

Building on such written testimony, including its expression of inexplicability, and confronting a dearth of visual information, Feelings, Baker, and

Hall, Martínez, and Bao face additional challenges peculiar to their chosen medium. If Cugoano cannot even provide a description of the horrible scenes he witnessed, how are graphic artists supposed to visualize the events? And how does their work compare to the long history of visualizing what Finley calls "the *slave ship icon*, the most enduring image from the history of transatlantic slavery" (5) and its function "as a template for the historical memory of the Middle Passage for visual artists around the black Atlantic" (9)?[20] These creators incorporate bits and pieces from this past as a means of extending the referential frame from history and literature to visual art but do so with a particular agenda: to make the world of comics more cognizant of Black history by drawing such iconic images into the scope of graphic depiction as well as to signal that contemporary graphic narratives are very much willing and able to develop their own historical aesthetics.

Feelings, Baker, and Hall, Martínez, and Bao confront challenges that include the need to avoid the visual codes that continue to shape depictions of racial difference while acknowledging the pervasive politics of racialized graphic representation. These creators emphasize the violent actions of the enslavers as well as the counterviolence of the enslaved, drawing on visual conventions from other genres, including superhero comics and the horror genre, thus offering important additions to the "mnemonic aesthetics" that underlie "contemporary presentations of the art of slavery" (Finley 5). Baker's account of Turner's rebellion, which left fifty-five enslavers and members of their families dead and ended with Turner's public execution (covered at length), gloats in guts-and-gore scenarios of righteous Black retaliation, but it also portrays the enslaver violence that *The Confessions of Nat Turner*, white Southern lawyer Thomas Gray's treatment of Turner's life and the rebellion composed on the basis of interviews conducted shortly before his execution, excised from his account.[21] Hall, Martínez, and Bao contrast the often sexually charged violence on ships during the Middle Passage and the actions of American colonial "rapists" in New York City in 1712 with the communal solidarity of the enslaved who rise up against their oppressors. Feelings's tableaus depict the enslaved variously as a dehumanized mass of bodies, both dead and alive, or as representative but unnamed Black characters, often forced to bend into the most uncomfortable poses by the horrendously confined spaces of the hold. In so doing, he evokes the "eyeless contortionists emerging from a dark shadowy Platonic cave" (120) that Johnson's narrator imagines in the *Middle Passage* through a visceral discourse of bodily disfiguration that is highly suggestive in terms of its graphic potential.[22] Looking at the painful positions of these chained beings, the narrator's question about the ship captain becomes even more pressing: "Who else could twist the body so terribly?" (120). He thus foregrounds the discrepancy between the captain's white uncontorted body and the violently twisted Black bodies of the enslaved.[23]

Portraying the Middle Passage through a succession of "narrative paintings" instead of Johnson's literary means or even a more conventional comic-like sequential narrative with panels and speech balloons, Feelings accounts for what Britt Rusert calls "the alternative temporalities of the trade" (277) in enslaved persons. Rusert asserts, "Given the high mortality rates on the ships, the regimes of violence and terror found there, and the conditions for enslaved people, it's not clear how we can even begin to visualize the subjective experience of 'captive time' on the slave ship: the fear, anxiety, confusion, illness, despair, and death that necessarily shaped the experience of time on the slave ship" (277). Largely voiding the visuals of language and choosing a hybrid format anchored in the aesthetic space between individual painting and moving image—between J. M. W. Turner's *The Slave Ship: Slavers Throwing Overboard the Dead and Dying—Typhon Coming On* (1840) and Steven Spielberg's *Amistad* (1997)—Feelings approximates a sense of "captive time" by complicating any attempt at simply consuming the images.[24] Readers—or rather, viewers—of the narrative must make difficult decisions, page after page, about how much time to spend with the individual images of pain and torture, how long to devote to witnessing the depicted atrocities. Yet these creators also contrast the violence of the trade with more harmonious and occasionally sentimental scenes of Black family life, seeking to re-create a sense of Black futurity and wholesomeness that survived slavery and continues into present imaginations of Black life and culture. For Francis, it is in the "hyperbolic imagery that Baker comes closest to recreating the sentimentality of nineteenth-century slave narratives" (122). Instead of merely replicating this sentimentality, however, Baker utilizes its rhetorical and aesthetic power to revise conventional images of blackness on the comic book page.

MIDDLE PASSAGE MEMORY

Michael A. Chaney discerns a significant discrepancy between Eurocentric notions of traumatic memory as allusive and discursive and an African American sense of "a different kind of trauma, one tied to racial community" ("Slave" 280). Feelings's foreword to *The Middle Passage* underscores this distinction by imagining a "race memory" that is shared, "consciously or unconsciously," by members of the African diaspora. Directing his remarks to a Black readership, Feelings connects "those shackles that physically bound us together against our wills" in the past with the emergence of "spiritual links that willingly bind us together now and into the future."[25] He proposes turning the Middle Passage into "a positive connecting line to all of us living inside or outside of the continent of Africa." However we gauge this racially exclusive understanding of transhistorical diasporic affiliation, Feelings undoubtedly negotiates the

Fig. 1.1: Rebecca Hall is haunted by the historical evidence she finds in the archives in *Wake*.

Fig. 1.2: A white slave catcher shooting an African villager from behind in *The Middle Passage*.

discrepancy between the suffering of the individuals who survived the journey and the faceless and nameless corpses on the bottom of the Atlantic Ocean. His foreword and his illustrations commemorate those who were "locked in the belly of each of these ships, chained together like animals throughout the long voyage from Africa toward unknown destinations, millions dying from the awful conditions in the bowels of the filthy slave galleys."[26]

Wake also acknowledges the significance of such links—for instance, when Hall (the character) researches her family history and, in a moment of desperation, seeks spiritual guidance from her grandmother, Harriet Thorpe: "As I grew older," the caption explains, "and learned more about you and about life, I have felt your indomitable spirit and the spirit of all my ancestors, including those in slavery." However, the narrative ultimately focuses on Hall's professional experience with the archives of slavery, an experience that invades her personal space and well-being. A double-page sequence (fig. 1.1) shows the women who jumped off the ships to resist their enslavement and thus chose death before capture as well as Hall in the archive, shocked by the evidence of these suicides she finds there and literally touched by the past: "I am a historian. And I am haunted," Hall's avatar confesses. She does not foreground a Black communal *we* until near the end of the narrative, after she has connected her story to the civil rights and Black Lives Matter movements, when she is lecturing to her students about using "our haunting to see how Black life truly is and see how it could be otherwise" and reminding them that "we must live in an alternative Black temporality where we reach into the past to 'reimagine a future otherwise.'"

Both Feelings's *Middle Passage* and Hall, Martínez, and Bao's *Wake* detail historical memory as a process of "unmaking" (Chaney, "Slave" 286) that leads to a condition Hortense J. Spillers calls the "sameness of anonymous portrayal that adheres tenaciously across the division of gender" and that registers "anonymity/anomie in various public documents of European-American mal(e)venture" (73). *Wake* pushes back against this process by contrasting the anonymity/anomie of the archive with creative fabulations of specifically female experiences.[27] Feelings's and Baker's narratives, in turn, foreground this unmaking (undrawing the undrawable) by grappling "with transnational racial discourses that have historically marked and muted blackness as other" (Whitted, "And the Negro" 80). They interrogate this Otherness by depicting the Black body as a sign of spectacular erasure (Chaney, "Drawing" 176), filling page after page (in Feelings's case) with near-naked or naked Black bodies as they are chained and beaten, lashed and whipped, tortured and terrorized, mutilated and killed by the pale, ghostlike whites who control the ship.[28] By connecting "spectacle and spectatorship" (Whitted, "And the Negro" 80), both authors force moments of recognition by triggering "readers' awareness of their own subject positions as observers" (81) and by refusing them "the passivity of the spectator" (Chaney, "Slave" 284). *Wake* also forces such moments but does so mainly through Hall's avatar, who serves as readers' guide through the archival maze and is touched and haunted by her findings.[29]

Early in the narrative, Feelings's *Middle Passage* displays a multilayered image of a white enslaver shooting an African villager from behind, with other chained villagers in the background forced at gunpoint to walk toward the ship (fig. 1.2).[30] The composition of the image means that the shooter points his rifle not only at the villager but also at readers, who are positioned in the crosshairs and thus compelled to consider their role in and historical culpability for the transatlantic trade in human beings. This consideration hinges on the onlookers' racial affiliation: readers identified and/or identifying as white might be compelled to acknowledge their privileged position as descendants of the invaders, while readers socially constructed and/or understanding themselves as Black or otherwise nonwhite might imagine themselves in the role of Black villagers, recognizing centuries of dispossession and murder as part of the historical conditions that still impact race relations across the globe.[31] Without suggesting an essentialist sense of racial affiliation, this image invites us to think about our personal relation to the atrocities of Western imperialism and colonialism.[32] The fact that the pained face of the Black victim is placed at the lower left corner of the image heightens this effect. It is as if he is about to stumble into our hands, fatally wounded by the bullet that might just as well have killed us. His eyes are closed and his mouth is agape in agony, preventing any overly romantic identification. The man's death is simultaneously intimate, since he is stumbling toward us, and anonymous, as he has no other discernable identity beyond that of a victim of the slave trade.

The tension between mass anonymity and individual pain is emblematized by the diverging foci of Feelings's, Baker's, and Hall, Martínez, and Bao's narratives. Feelings emphasizes the scope of the Middle Passage and the dehumanization of the enslaved and the monstrousness of their enslavers through his title. The main part, *The Middle Passage*, names the event, while the subtitle, *White Ships/Black Cargo*, evokes the inhumanity of the slave trade by reducing the enslaved to the status of cargo and equating the merchants and their helpers with the vessels of their trade.[33] Feelings graphically counteracts this dehumanization toward the end of the narrative with a double page on which he places a two-tiered succession of small rectangular close-up portraits of alternating Black and white faces, insinuating a back-and-forth between the enslaver and the enslaved and contrasting the white men's stern and unmoved faces with the more expressive and pained expressions of the Black men. Strangely, the ten images that make up the upper tier are the same images that constitute the second tier, but they appear in a different order. The page ends with an upright image of a beaten Black man lying face down on the deck with an armed white enslaver looking down on him and four other Black men being strung up by the neck or feet on one of the ship's masts, evoking lynching imagery. In the middle of the image, additional crew members restrain and attack the enslaved.

Choosing a different focus, Baker cites as one of his historical sources a passage from the memoirs of captain Theodore Canot that speaks of the enslaved Africans as "cargo belong[ing] to several owners" (*Nat Turner* 36). Baker centers the narrative on Turner, for whom the Middle Passage provides a kind of origin story or transgenerational justification for his leadership in the Southampton revolt. Baker announces his concentration on the life and motivations of this historical figure through the narrative's title, whose brevity is telling because it refuses to evoke the moral framework imposed on Turner's experiences in *The Confessions of Nat Turner* (there is nothing to confess, according to Baker). That title had marked the narrative as a religiously grounded as-told-to confession. Gray judged Turner according to the legal codes of the white antebellum South, but Baker does not replicate that judgment. Gray also characterized the insurrection as a fight between "these barbarous villains" and his "fellow citizens" (258) and contrasted the "fearful tragedy" and the "bravery" of one of the enslavers with the "diabolical actors," "band of savages," and "remorseless murderers" involved in "this dreadful conspiracy" (245, 263, 246, 245). Gray further sought to contain Turner's life story within the Western mode of written confessional autobiography, which is at odds with the visual emphasis of Baker's graphic narrative and leaves no room for what Baker imagines as Turner's ancestral yearnings.

Using the affordances of verbal narration and commentary in a predominantly visual medium, *Wake* is the most specific of the three works about the status of the enslaved as dehumanized cargo. Allotting six full pages to "the four-hundred-year sweep of Atlantic slave trade history" and the archived documentation of the trade (including business records and information on the technicalities of insuring the "cargo"), Hall, Martínez, and Bao cite entries from a captain's log that "keep track of each slave's death" and contain "some of the most disturbing material a historian of slavery has to think through."[34] They replicate a much-cited image of a tightly packed slave ship, the *Brookes* (which Feelings and Baker also include in their narratives) but complicate this replication first by affording the otherwise tiny Black stick figures individualized faces and varying body types and second by verbally foregrounding the contrast between the brutalizing language of the traders ("cargo") and the brutalized conditions of the enslaved: "Do the shareholders in this particular ship subscribe to the 'tight-packing' method? Where more people die, like cargo spoiling, but more arrive who can in turn be sold in the Americas," the caption reads. "Or are they 'loose packers,' believing that profit is maximized by less mortality, thereby giving their cargo more room to breathe? It is a complex business turning people into things. Things that can be stored, shipped, and sold."[35] Recalling Harriet Ann Jacobs's description of her status as an enslaved woman in *Incidents in the Life of a Slave Girl* (1861) and her blissful ignorance as a child—"I was so fondly shielded that I never dreamed I was a piece of merchandise, trusted to" her parents "for safe keeping, and liable to be demanded of them at any moment" (751)—and evoking Dawes's "Requiem," which commemorates "the dead, caught in that / mercantilistic madness" (21) of the Middle Passage, *Wake* enters into a conversation with a foundational text of the so-called slave narrative genre and with contemporary poetry, suggesting that comics will have a say in constructions of Black (literary) history.

Earlier in *Wake*, captions inform readers about the entrenchment of slavery in the British economy and legal system, including the creation of the "infamous Brookes Diagram" on which the images of the ships in the graphic narratives are based. "The slave trade was central to England's economy, and regulated and managed at every level," we learn, and the royally backed African Company included John Locke as one of its stockholders. The archival document, the actual *Brookes* diagram, is headed "Stowage of the British Slave Ship Brookes under the REGULATED SLAVE TRADE Act of 1788," indicating "the maximum number of slaves allowed under" the act and thereby reducing enslaved Africans to the status of cargo. Baker, Feelings, and Hall, Martínez, and Bao seek to undo/undraw this reduction.[36]

NAT TURNER

Baker's *Nat Turner* was published about a decade after *The Middle Passage*, and it borrowed from Feelings the conceit that the visual depiction of the voyage and the subsequent life in slavery would largely be devoid of language. Feelings had explained in his foreword, "I should try to tell this story with as few words as possible, if any. Callous indifference or outright brutal characterizations of Africans are embedded in the language of the Western World. It is a language so infused with direct and indirect racism that it would be difficult, if not impossible, using this language in my book, to project anything black as positive." Feelings's shift from language to vision can be read as a response to the Enlightenment's privileging of writing over orality that Henry Louis Gates Jr. criticized in *The Signifying Monkey: A Theory of African-American Literary Criticism* (1988), even though the case could be made that Western visual culture is equally infused with direct and indirect forms of racism. *Nat Turner* foregrounds this infusion by evoking the Sambo stereotype of nineteenth-century blackface minstrelsy, depicting the characters who betray Turner and his followers by informing the enslavers of the looming rebellion with bulging eyes, sheepish grins, and exaggerated gestures (130, 132, 136).[37] In addition, he presents one of these followers, Will, as "a hulking golem, a visual crystallization of the Big, Black Buck figure used to justify slavery" (Fisher 265), creating a graphic embodiment of Gray's pro-slavery semantics (murderers, savages, monsters). Yet Baker also includes a scene in which young Nat is reading the Bible and, when caught by an overseer, flips the book upside down and flashes a grin, utilizing the Sambo mask as a performative strategy through which the enslaved can resist his enslaver.[38] The scene suggests that literacy—and by implication visual literacy—can serve as a weapon in the arsenal of antiracist resistance and as such also works on a metalevel by priming readers for the counternarrative to conventional historiography that *Nat Turner* proposes.

Hall, Martínez, and Bao's *Wake* illustrates a variation on this theme of (il)literacy in a wordless segment that traces Hall's grandmother Harriet Thorpe's life in Omaha, Nebraska, at the beginning of the twentieth century. She is portrayed as a hardworking woman, loving mother, and devoted churchgoer. Sitting next to her husband and children in church, she holds the Bible upside down, pretending to be able to read, when her oldest son, Otto, turns the book around for her. Directly afterward, we see her mimicking her white employer's stern admonition (symbolized by a raised index finger) behind her back, performing her own little act of resistance, which makes the other Black maids laugh. On the next page, we see her learning to read with the help of her son: "Squire Sweeney didn't let any of us learn on his plantation," she recalls, "and after slavery, all my time was spent working and earning money." Martínez visualizes these aftereffects of slavery by placing Harriet and Otto behind a window that looks like the iron bars of a prison window. In the next scene, Otto's father tells him not to aspire to become an architect but "to set your sights on something more realistic," like postal clerk. The page is framed with Booker T. Washington's *Up from Slavery*, which appears in both the first and last panels on the page; in the bottom panel, it is ironically placed upside down from the reader's perspective, as if to suggest that Washington's ideology is holding aspiring young Black men down rather than lifting them up. This is at once a nod to the narratives of the enslaved as a foundational genre for graphic narratives on Black history and a reminder that readers need to acquire graphic literacy to properly decode the critical discourse of comics like *Wake*.

Resisting the notion of literacy as a prerequisite for humanity or citizenship, Baker rarely incorporates sound words and speech bubbles into the images, avoiding an overly comic-like feel of his "primarily imagistic" (Neary 171) narrative.[39] He relegates selections from *The Confessions of Nat Turner* outside of the panel frame. Qiana Whitted finds a "defiance of (black) pictures in a society dominated by the objectification of (white) words" ("And the Negro" 81), which is foregrounded through the division of the narrative into Baker's "black" images and Gray's "white" words, which are not allowed to intrude on the visual account. This becomes especially apparent in the contrast between the intimacy of the horrified look on Turner's mother's face as an enslaver threatens her with a razor and the detached account of this practice ("The head of every male and female is neatly shaved") that appears in Canot's memoir, *Captain Canot; or, Twenty Years of an African Slaver* (1854), cited below the image (Baker, *Nat Turner* 36) as a reminder of the "callous indifference" and "outright brutal characterizations of Africans" that Feelings described as "embedded in the language of the Western World."[40]

Baker takes Turner's enigmatic character as the starting point for a graphic revision of American history. In the preface to the book edition, Baker wonders, "Who was this man who was important enough to be mentioned in *all* the history books, yet is never spoken about at length?" He then reimagines the protagonist as a husband and father whose early childhood memories include his mother's report of an infanticide on board the ship that brought her to America.[41] In Baker's account, Turner's use of violence against the enslavers is motivated by the separation of his family at a Southern auction. By devoting a quarter of his narrative to Turner's mother's life in Africa and voyage to America, Baker creates a teleological plot that moves from the African "home" to Turner's childhood "education" in the antebellum South and then toward "freedom" (the rebellion) and "triumph" (the lynching that turns him into a Christlike figure of Black rebellion, a powerful counterimage to Harriet Beecher Stowe's obedient Uncle Tom). This plot provides the backstory—and thus a rationale—for Turner's messianic violence, the religious fanaticism that, in contrast to Stowe's piously passive evangelicalism, propels him to lead the uprising against the enslavers.[42] Jonathan Gray calls the "home" section "early speculative pages" that "establish a genealogical continuity between events in Africa and those in the Americas that both the act of enslavement and the archive of slavery attempted to eradicate" ("Commence" 187).[43] Moreover, proposing an "imaginative expansion" of the archive by depicting events that "have no counterpoint in" the original *Confessions*, the story these images tell "is not dependent on literacy for its legibility" (Neary 167). Imagining Turner's mother's African origins emphasizes the diasporic affiliation of the enslaved with their homelands and ancestry, insinuating that America can never fully be home (cf. 187). While Turner's deeds appear as the efforts of a remarkable individual, they are presented as the direct result of the subjugation and attempted eradication of Black families and their lives as cargo belowdecks and as chattel on Southern plantations (cf. Francis 114). Turner's actions underscore Orlando Patterson's observation that "slaves differed from other human beings in that they were not allowed freely to integrate the experience of their ancestors into their lives, to inform their understanding of social reality with the inherited meanings of their natural forebears, or to anchor the living present in any conscious community of memory" (5).

Baker's narrative begins with the disruption of life in an African village by Black invaders intent on enslaving the residents (another parallel to Feelings's *Middle Passage*). Baker depicts the raid as an attack on the Black family by complicit Africans, following historical accounts and evoking Cudjoe Lewis's recollections about his capture by Dahomey warriors:

> I try to make it to de bush, but all soldiers overtake me befo' I git dere. O Lor', Lor'! When I think 'bout dat time I try not to cry no mo'. My eyes dey stop cryin' but de tears runnee down inside me all de time. When de men pull me wid dem I call my mama name. I doan know where she is. I no see none my family. I doan know where dey is. I beg de men to let me go findee my folks. De soldiers say dey got no ears for cryin'. De king of Dahomey come to hunt slave to sell. So dey tie me in de line wid de rest. (Hurston, *Barracoon* 47)

In Baker's graphic depiction of such events, we see mothers grabbing their children to protect them from the aggressors; we later witness a young woman's attempted leap to death to evade capture in a sequence that (p)refigures D. W. Griffith's Klan-inspired depiction of Flora's suicide in *The Birth of a Nation* (1915) from an African American perspective.[44] The woman emerges as a fierce fighter who does everything to resist her pursuers but is ultimately overpowered. This places Turner, popularly labeled the "rebel slave," in a line of Black resistance and counterviolence and makes him a representative rather than aberrational figure. On a metalevel, banning written language from the "home" segment except for a few sound words "has the effect of linking the violence of colonial intrusion with the violence of white narrative control" (Neary 167), which Baker's narrative seeks to escape by visualizing a near-Edenic, precolonial life devoid of "white" discourse.[45]

Yet even in the decidedly non-Edenic space of the hold of the ship, new life emerges. A baby is birthed by a mother who dies after the delivery, acknowledging bell hooks's assertion that "the numbers of black women who died during childbirth or the number of stillborn children" during the Middle Passage "will never be known" (*Ain't* 18–19). The baby is picked up by two of the other enslaved, one of whom cradles its head to protect it from harm and averts its eyes from the surrounding physical abuse. Chaney reads these enslaved people as "the equivalent of the nuclear African family during the Middle Passage" and finds "these visual cues of family" to be "an odd imposition [...] onto otherwise ungendered figures" ("Slave" 286). Recalling Spillers's point about the anonymity/anomie of the Black subject, he suggests that "sameness is rendered, but it is also partly undone by the illustration," as the scene "ascribes a normative heterosexual coupling to figures who may just as easily be read as same sex strangers" (286). We can read this sequence as a response to the destruction of the Black family, as the instantiation of an "ethic of surrogacy" (Wells-Oghoghomeh 81) or an "ethics of care" (Christopher Paul Harris 14): the absent family is replaced by a makeshift parental unit, albeit a traditionally gendered one, that—like Morrison's Sethe and the real-life Margaret Garner on whose experiences *Beloved* builds—chooses infanticide as a moral imperative.[46]

Fig. 1.3: The enslaved baby as death-bound subject in *Nat Turner*.

After recognizing the horrors that lie ahead, the surrogate father tries to throw the baby overboard and into the gaping mouth of a shark (fig. 1.3). Seeking to protect the cargo, a crewman clasps the baby by the hand, stopping its fall toward death only to release it when the surrogate father bites his arm. Baker's image, however, arrests the baby's fall in midair, fixing its tiny body in a position that allegorizes the enslaved person's precarious status as a death-bound subject.[47] Here, too, Baker seems inspired by Feelings or at least invested in a similar visual vocabulary, if we are willing to acknowledge the resonance between Baker's falling baby and Feelings's depiction of a baby hovering above the head of a grieving African woman and boxed in by the sharp blades of two spears.

Sharks appear prominently throughout the three graphic narratives discussed in this chapter, already figuring as a poetic trope in Hayden's "Middle Passage" ("Sails flashing to the wind like weapons, / sharks following the moans the fever and the dying" [48]) but attaining visual form here. In one of Feelings's images, sharks encircle the bodies of the deceased men and women who have fallen victim to the inhumane conditions belowdecks, trailing in the ship's wake. In a later image, sharks roam the bottom of the Atlantic Ocean, which is covered with the bones of the dead, in search of fresh flesh as some of the enslaved jump overboard, preferring death to a life in slavery. "I see the bones / picked clean in the belly / of the implacable sea," Dawes writes in "Requiem" (21), a poem inspired by *Middle Passage* that features an image from the book on the cover. *Wake* uses the shark motif only once, toward the end of the story, when they attack the boats carrying the enslaved to another ship, the *Unity*.[48] Evoking this motif integrates all three narratives into a network of intertextual and interpictorial portrayals, inscribing these comics into Middle Passage historiography while introducing this historiography and its attendant iconography into the space of the comics medium.

Moreover, infanticide is a powerful topos in Baker's and Feelings's narratives, forestalling Black futurity by ending the possibility of new Black families. The "death of the slave child," Chaney suggests, "comes to stand for a negated African American future" ("Slave" 295). Baker is building on literary depictions such as Johnson's *The Middle Passage*, in which narrator and protagonist Rutherford Calhoun must witness scenes that make him wonder "how in God's name I could go on after this" (66–67) and that turn his hair white: "A woman pitched her baby overboard into the waters below us. At least two men tried to follow, straining against their chains" (66). Yet the forestalling of Black futurity also delivers the critical impetus for Black rebellion. The scene of the baby thrown to the sharks in Baker's *Nat Turner* has a discursive and visual afterlife, reappearing two pages later in a speech balloon through which young Nat relates the event to fellow enslaved children (fig. 1.4). This visually mediated, transgenerational moment of oral historiography—an example of Marianne Hirsch's notion of postmemory—connects the Middle Passage with American slavery and extends the story of the makeshift family's mercy killing into a mechanism for kinship affiliation and community-building, as Nat begins to rally his enslaved brethren in preparation for his role as a self-declared prophet.[49] When Henry and Will, two members of Turner's posse, later kill the baby of the enslavers who are the first victims of the rebellion, we are spared the depiction of the final blow. But the killing emerges as the consequence of Turner's recollection of his own children's sale at auction; images of the auction appear as inserts next to Turner's face, reiterating the separation of Turner's family as the event that motivates the rebellion.[50] Moreover, the baby's death is foreshadowed through its visual appearance in another speech balloon when one of Turner's accomplices realizes that they have forgotten to kill the child.

Baker's narrative is filled with such visual resonances. An earlier scene in which Will grins at his enslaver's toddler culminates in the depiction of the boy's beheading by Will's merciless axe. In such scenes, Baker "refuses respectability politics" (Wanzo, *Content* 72) and makes it difficult for readers to root for the rebels, even as his depiction counters the many references in *The*

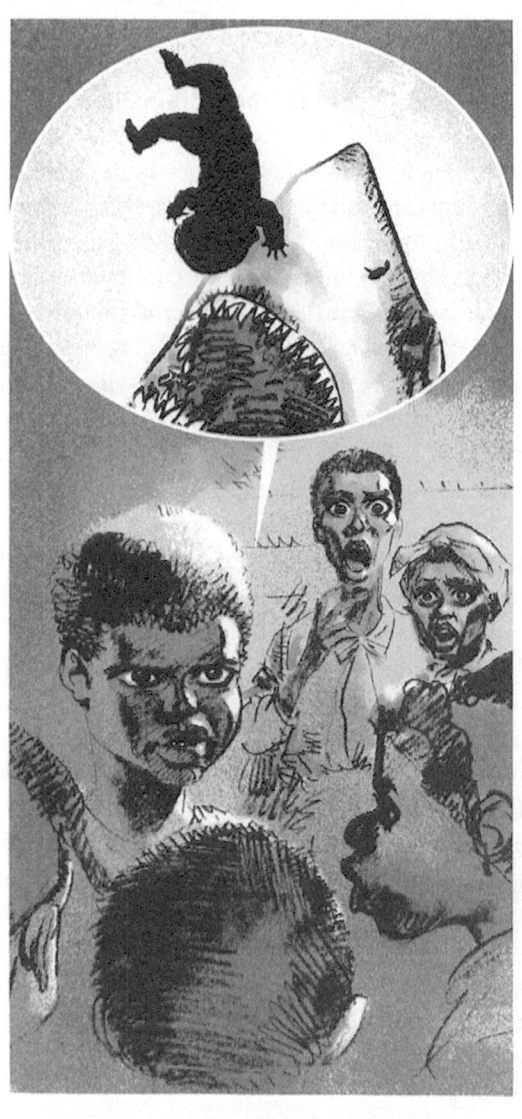

Fig. 1.4: Young Nat relating an incident from the Middle Passage in *Nat Turner*.

Confessions of Nat Turner to the poor white families killed by the rebel and his followers.[51] As Francis suggests, Baker offers "no euphemisms" and "forces the reader to look directly at what it would mean, what it would *look like*, to kill 55 men, women, and children" (134). In fact, Baker (re)inserts the "retributive justice" (Chaney, "Slave" 293) that is largely absent from the slave narrative, which can imagine such justice only from the perspective of Southampton's white population, as Gray's final comments on Turner's confession indicate, into the medium of graphic narrative. Here, the enslaved person's exertion of retributive justice, so common in superhero comics, is met with the extralegal violence of lynching as a means of protecting antebellum power relations.[52]

Baker's emphasis on Turner as a family man and the narrative's return to scenes of child-killing revise *The Confessions of Nat Turner*, which withholds the fact that Turner is married and has children.[53] Baker devotes ten pages to Nat's love for his children and his son's frantic attempt to save his father from corporal punishment. In the passage that follows the auction scene, Baker contrasts an image of the happy enslavers as they tuck one of their children into bed and embrace their baby, with a stick drawing on the floor of Turner's cabin. This drawing marks the absence of his children and complicates Gray's distinction between the enslaved as "diabolical actors" and the brave enslaver and "his lovely and amiable wife" (245, 263). While the excessive violence of Baker's narrative may force some readers out of their comfort zone—by making them witness the cruel punishment of an enslaved man who is whipped, has salt rubbed into his wounds, and has his hands chopped off—these quieter moments utilize the affective wounding power of sentimental depiction as analyzed in Marianne Noble's *The Masochistic Pleasures of Sentimental Literature* (2000). Baker achieves many of these effects through the specificities of graphic narrative, structuring his images and the passages he cites from Turner's *Confessions* into an "'ironic' relationship" (Francis 120) that contrasts an emotionless and detached written discourse with confrontational and disturbing images (cf. Francis 114). We can thus connect the "dichotomy" and "disconnect" between images and words that Tim Bruno finds in *Nat Turner* (cf. 933, 934) with what Marc Singer labels the "friction between Baker's narrative and his source material" (*Breaking* 200). Singer notes that Baker either visualizes events that do not occur in *The Confessions of Nat Turner* (and are often also not documented anywhere else) and thereby creatively intervenes in the representation of Turner as a figure of the (popular) historical imagination or illustrates scenes from *Confessions* "to rationalize his own contributions to the story" (201) rather than flat-out contradicting Gray's version of the events (203–4).

In that sense, the absence of color in *Nat Turner* emerges as a gesture toward the historicity of the material and the reduction of the world of slavery into a black, white, and gray life devoid of happiness. A more thorough analysis of the narrative, however, would have to address its status as a "mixed media adaptation" (Whitted, "And the Negro" 92) that remediates images from the historical archive and defamiliarizes them through Baker's "stylistic promiscuity" (Bruno 931). In the preface to the Abrams edition, Baker provocatively names "compelling graphics," "action and suspense," and "superhuman abilities" (6) as his ingredients, and some critics have noted the visual reverberations between Baker's images and those of superhero comics, such as when character drawings recall Marvel's Incredible Hulk or when the graphic design evokes Frank Miller's silhouette style (cf. Chaney, "Slave" 281; Fisher 266). Singer is especially critical of what he identifies as Baker's mixture of "fantasy, mythology, and pop-cultural cliché" with "the paratextual conventions of historiography" (*Breaking* 199, 211), such as endnotes, photographic reproductions, and bibliographic references. This mixture, Singer suggests, cannot cover the "lapses, shortcuts, creative distortions, and outright errors" that turn the narrative into "a shoddy simulacrum of the past" (218), a form of "historical fiction of a particularly dishonest kind, one that freely invents and reshapes history while declaring its accuracy and objectivity" (216).

However, Singer's notion of Black diasporic history as something that can be shown accurately and objectively through the procedures of established historiography—through established Middle Passage epistemologies—may not be appropriate. Where Singer identifies the "visual and narrative vocabulary [...] from the fantasies of popular cinema" (*Breaking* 192) and criticizes Baker's Turner "not just as a heroic figure but as a victorious one" (188), William Murray sees "a world where it is hard to find villains and heroes" (330). Moreover, when Singer faults *Nat Turner* for proposing an argument that "is primarily dramatic rather than historical in nature" and is interested in "novelty and spectacle" rather than in "historical fidelity" (*Breaking* 195), he fails to connect Baker's version with Gray's already overly dramatic and spectacular presentation of the events: "It will be long remembered in the annals of our country, and many a mother as she presses her infant darling to her bosom, will shudder at the recollection of Nat Turner, and his band of ferocious miscreants" (247). Rebecca Wanzo thus reads Baker's "temporal mash-up of the twentieth-century superhero and action-hero comic with the drawings that evoke nineteenth-century representations of slaves" as a way of unsettling "the complex relationship contemporary readers have to representations of slavery" (*Content* 75).

If Baker's goal is to illustrate the fallibility of the written (white) archive and insist on a Black re-visioning, the bifurcation of his images and Gray's narrative makes sense on both formal and ideological levels. Jonathan Gray suggests that *Nat Turner* "seeks to broaden the canon(s) in which it participates" ("Commence" 185), and the narrative does so in part by evoking centuries of writing about literacy as a step toward freedom by opening with an image of a Black reader holding a white book, completely enveloped in darkness. Baker ends the narrative with an enslaved woman retreating with *The Confessions of Nat Turner* into another completely blackened space, which can now be viewed as an incubator in which Turner's rebellion, though officially terminated through the lynching depicted a few pages earlier, might grow into new acts of resistance (cf. Neary 171).[54] A less affirmative reading of this ending might hold that the girl reading *Confessions* will have to see through the account's ideological framing of the rebel's life to recuperate some sense of Turner's political significance.

THE MIDDLE PASSAGE: WHITE SHIPS/BLACK CARGO

Feelings's *The Middle Passage* anticipates motifs as well as the focus on the Black family in Baker's narrative. Like *Nat Turner*, the story begins with enslavers raiding an African village. The enslavers capture women, men, and children, but the illustrations repeatedly portray mothers holding babies and young children as victims of the raid. One illustration shows a man being shot in the back as he is running away from the attackers, leaving behind his wife and baby. A few images later, we see the same woman herded together with others in front of huts set ablaze by the white captors, and in another illustration, a family is torn apart: two women, perhaps mother and grandmother, trying to save a baby, a crying child, and a man restrained by the enslavers. The two double-page illustrations that follow the man's death present the villagers as they are driven by the white enslavers and their African helpers toward their ultimate destiny: the seashore, the ship, and, should they survive the ordeal, life in American slavery.

Feelings's depiction does not allow his readers to lose sight of the fact that enslavement destroyed African families, whose members are tied up and prepared for the transatlantic journey. While the mother with the infant constitutes a recurring trope, two naked boys foreground slavery's demand for Black bodies regardless of their gender in a scene that evokes a passage from a ship log by captain James Barbot (1770) cited in *Wake*. This passage records the crew's sexual assault on the enslaved women, describing them in brutally pleasurable terms ("sprightly maidens, full of jollity and good humour, afforded us abundance of recreation"), as well as homosexual pedophilia ("as did several little fine boys, which we mostly kept to attend on us about the ship"). This passage makes Hall's avatar cry, shutting out all background imagery and presenting her before a black void, her tears matching those shed by one of the enslaved women on the bottom of the preceding page. The passage is especially cruel since it pretends that the women were enjoying their abuse—"Toward the evening the women slaves diverted themselves on the deck, as they thought fit, some conversing together, others dancing, singing, and sporting after their manner, which pleased them highly"—and because of the pedophilia, a theme that Johnson's *Middle Passage* also explores.

The two boys in Feelings's image are shown behind bars in a barracoon, with chains around their necks, one of them wearing an ankle shackle. This

Fig. 1.5: A transhistorical emblem of the Black family in times of transatlantic slavery in *The Middle Passage*.

depiction again recalls Lewis's recollections of his African enslavement and connects with a more detailed and elaborate illustration of the barracoon where *Wake*'s Alele, Adono, and their fellow captives are held before they are brought on board the *Unity*. The double splash page that depicts the barracoon holding a group of naked and chained people clearly remediates an 1849 illustration, "Slave Barracoon," that depicts an almost identical scene from Sierra Leone. Missing from *Wake* is the flogging scene on the right of the 1849 illustration; another difference is that the Africans in the illustration wear loincloths, perhaps to adhere to visual codes of decency in the mid-nineteenth-century press. According to a prefatory note in Zora Neale Hurston's *Barracoon*, "The Spanish word *barracoon* translates as 'barracks' and is derived from *barraca*, which means 'hut.' The term 'barracoon' describes the structures used to detain Africans who would be sold and exported to Europe or the Americas. These structures, sometimes also referred to as factories, stockades, corrals, and holding pens, were built near the coast. They could be as insubstantial as a 'slave shed' or as fortified as a 'slave house' or 'slave castle,' wherein Africans were forced into the cells of dungeons beneath the upper quarters of European administrators" (iii). While *Wake* represents a shed-like structure, Feelings's

Middle Passage imagines a castle-like building with a dungeon. Both narratives base their depiction of the African side of the slave trade on archival documents, signaling a sense of historical veracity and verisimilitude.⁵⁵

Such attacks on the Black family—and on the future of Black communities—also occur in Feelings's *Middle Passage*, where they are encapsulated in the iconic image of a family that presents the half-naked chained mother leaning forward and holding her head in pain, the father's disembodied face turned upward with the eyes closed in resignation, and a baby hovering over his head between two spears pointed at its head and feet (fig. 1.5). In the background, we see another chain of enslaved men and women and the notorious enslavers as well as, on another representational layer, the oversized heads of two Africans looking down at the scene. This illustration collapses centuries of abuse into a transhistorical emblem that speaks to the past, present, and future of Black suffering.

Feelings employs this type of condensed representation repeatedly, for instance when he shows a mother holding her infant, her hands in chains and a drawing of the hold of a ship superimposed on her torso. This drawing is positioned between two images of an analogous visual structure: two faces screaming in pain as they carry the white ship forward and a Black figure in chains rushing through the sea covered by a historical drawing of a tight-packing ship. The two faces in the first image depict a man and a woman as a *pars pro toto* for the enslaved Africans, whose offspring, as shown in the second image, will either die or live a life of subjection. The hold of the ship separates the baby from its mother's breasts and thus from the nourishment and sustenance necessary for physical and spiritual survival.⁵⁶ The third image subsumes the symbolic African family into the anonymous mass of Africans in the ship's hold, connecting the practice of tight packing and the resulting misery (depicted throughout the book, sometimes in images that anachronistically recall the inhuman living conditions in Nazi death camps and the tortured bodies of their inmates) with the loss of African identities on the voyage.⁵⁷

That the illustration of the hold remediates the eighteenth-century Brookes diagram underscores Feelings's grappling with the archives of slavery that fail to convey the atrocities unleashed on generations of Africans and African Americans.⁵⁸ In these archives, suicides and other forms of rebellion appear only as irritations to the supposed order on the ship, as threats to be averted, as resistance to be quelled, as deaths marked in the logbooks as losses of cargo. *Middle Passage*, *Nat Turner*, *Wake*, and other graphic narratives contextualize and historicize these records by imagining the sense of anger and despair that the conditions on the ships must have caused the enslaved Africans. While Feelings does not depict infanticide, he includes scenes of suicide in which some of the enslaved jump overboard, perishing amid sharks and joining other corpses on the bottom of the Atlantic. There is also resistance against the all-male white crew as the enslaved are forced into the hold, including a man and woman who may be husband and wife as well as women and children. Instead of recording the loss of cargo, Feelings's images offer a sense of self-determination and liberation, as acts of resistance and jumping into the ocean attain a dimension of heroic sacrifice. As the elderly female narrator of Roland Laird, Taneshia Nash Laird, and Elihu "Adofo" Bey's *Still I Rise* notes alongside an image of Africans leaping off a ship, "Now there's a lot of confusion about why some of the Africans jumped off those ships. A lot of folks have said those Africans would rather die than stay on those ships. But if you ask me, some of those jumpers planned to hook up with the ancestors and ask them to help their descendants survive. If you ask me, those weren't suicides, but sacrifices" (29).

It makes sense, then, to speak of a particular Middle Passage iconography these graphic narratives share despite their stylistic differences. In addition to the sharks, the shared elements include the rats that pester the enslaved in the hold of the ship, thereby expressing a double notion of dejection and abjection.[59] In Feelings's *Middle Passage*, the rats gnaw on the bodies of dead or near-dead captives and, on one page, scuttle across the hold in an arrangement that evokes the gilded frames of historical paintings, perhaps to foreground the discrepancy between the high-art pretensions of Western culture and the culture of exploitation and death that finances art for the rich. In Baker's *Nat Turner*, the rats climb over the bodies of the enslaved in search of food; in *Wake*, the rats run around on the bottom of the ship beneath a female captive reaching out of the hold to attract the attention of the archive-bound Hall.[60] Rats also symbolize abjection beyond the medium of graphic narrative—for instance, in Richard Wright's *Native Son* (1940)—showing that depictions of Black history in comics frequently draw on inspirations from literature to escape the visual stereotypes and iconographic traditions that have marred the medium since its inception. Rats also appear in Johnson's *Middle Passage*, where the hold of the ship is a "squalid pit that would house" the enslaved "sardined belly-to-buttocks in the orlop, with its dead air and razor-teethed bilge rats" (65).

Yet Feelings does more than visualize literary predecessors and witness what Hartman calls "the intimacy with death that was first experienced in the hold" and that "continues to determine black existence" ("Dead" 208). Despite the barrage of horrifying images with which the book confronts its readers, not all is hopeless, as Feelings seeks creative answers for Hartman's harrowing questions: "How do we attend to black death? How do we find life where only the traces of destruction remain?" ("Dead" 208). Into a dark scene of human degradation and agony, Feelings inserts a pregnant woman who seems oblivious to the carnage around her, placing her hand over her belly and feeling the new life growing inside her. Her nakedness in this image and elsewhere throughout the narrative is problematic because it reiterates the fact "that processes of black maternal longing limit the ability of black women to self-possess" (Kimberly Juanita Brown, *Repeating* 15) in many accounts of slavery. But it is not easily classified among the "pornotropic representations that eroticized black suffering" (Wanzo, *Content* 88) challenged by critics like Spillers and Hartman, mainly because it positions the woman as a nurturing and thoughtful figure, insisting that she is not merely "flesh," in Spillers's theoretical vocabulary, but a "body" whose presumed "physical powerlessness" (67) as an enslaved woman is shown here as a physical and spiritual force focused on the unborn baby. She is portrayed not as merely "a thing, becoming *being for* the captor" nor simply as a degendered "territory of cultural and political maneuver" (67) but as an ancestral figure whose depiction exposes the brutalities of enslavement and reclaims visually what ship captains like Canot had stated (in vaguely Christian terms aimed perhaps at a sense of self-absolution) about the newly enslaved: "They are entirely stripped, so that women as well as men go out of Africa as they came into it—naked" (qtd. in Baker, *Nat Turner* 36).[61]

Nonetheless, Feelings's *Middle Passage* remains ambiguous in its depiction of gender. The pregnant women and mothers shown throughout the narrative are not completely reduced to giving "birth without female subjectivity," where "the gendered body is one of total and complete physical (and violent) utility" (Kimberly Juanita Brown, *Repeating* 7). Rather, Feelings's narrative condenses individual experiences into emblematic still images that suggest subjectivity without succumbing to the utilitarian gaze of the crew and the dehumanizing logic of the system of enslavement at large. For Alexis Wells-Oghoghomeh, the logic behind this system lies in "the reduction of the womb and its (re)productions to machinery for the production of human capital in a global economy" that "extended the violent, mercenary apparatuses of slavery into the intimate spaces of women's bodies and sexual lives, radically altering the meanings of their bodies and relationships" (5). When Feelings portrays the thoughtful woman, he at least allows for the possibility that she is pondering the implications of these altered corporeal and relational meanings.

The woman reappears as an insert image in the narrative's penultimate illustration, which shows the American arrival of the enslaved and the sale of the new Black family in a scene that visualizes the final lines of Hayden's "Middle Passage": "Voyage through death / to life upon these shores" (54). The pregnant woman thus memorializes the Middle Passage and at the same time instills a sense of futurity despite slavery's attempts to erase Black life and ancestry—a sense that is complicated by the possibility that this new life may have resulted from the acts of rape that were common on the ships, as the naval officer Robert Shufeldt revealed when he noted that many of the mothers with infants arriving in the New World had been "impregnated by someone of the demonic crew that brought" them over (qtd. in hooks, *Ain't* 18).[62] As the new life in the wombs of the enslaved survivors indicates, "invisible things are not necessarily 'not-there,'" because "a void may be empty but not be a vacuum" (Morrison, "Unspeakable" 136). Moving from vacuum to void is exactly what Hartman's critical fabulation seeks to achieve: "not to *give voice* to the slave, but rather to imagine what cannot be verified [. . .] and to reckon with the precarious lives which are visible only in the moment of their disappearance" ("Venus" 12).[63] The scene of the pregnant woman may thus be read as an iconic visualization of these unavailable voices, a graphic instantiation of the dream of liberating the enslaved "from the obscene descriptions that first introduced them" in the archives of slavery (6).

Hurston had already lamented the absence of the survivor's voice in accounts of the Middle Passage: "Those who justified slaving on various grounds have had their say. Among these are several slave runners who have boasted of their exploits in the contraband flesh. Those who stood aloof in loathing have cried out against it in lengthy volumes. [. . .] All these words from the seller, but not one word from the sold. The Kings and Captains whose words moved ships. But not one word from the cargo" (5–6). As Hurston's remarks and Feelings's depiction of the pregnant woman show, the Middle Passage does not constitute "a clean break between past and present, but a spatial continuum between Africa and the Americas, the ship's deck and the hold, the Great House and the slave quarters" (Diedrich, Gates, and Pedersen 8). Feelings conjures up this continuum when he evokes the power of the enslaved family, a largely invisible and unstable institution within the system of chattel slavery, in an image that turns historical absence into presence, the vacuum of the Middle Passage into a "spatial and temporal continuum" (Diedrich, Gates, and Pedersen 8), by featuring the survivors or descendants of the journey as they look toward the future with resilience and determination.

WAKE: THE HIDDEN HISTORY OF WOMEN-LED SLAVE REVOLTS

Wake details Hall's quest for the lost stories of enslaved African and African American women and her attempts to imagine their acts of resistance and revolt against centuries of systemic oppression and abuse. Like Feelings and Baker, Hall, Martínez, and Bao investigate the historical impact of slavery on the (im)possibilities of Black family life, casting the narrative as an act of ancestral recuperation and familial consolidation centered not only on the Middle Passage but also on life in Africa and in the American colonies. In doing so, they follow hooks's seminal observation that "a devaluation of Black womanhood occurred as a result of the sexual exploitation of black women during slavery that has not altered in the course of hundreds of years" (*Ain't* 53).

Wake proposes a notion of "ancestry in progress," a phrase the creators borrow from the title of an album by the Belgian Afro-Pop band Zap Mama. Hall, Martínez, and Bao introduce this phrase toward the end of the story to foreground the need for descendants of enslavement and other members of the African diaspora to actively claim and reclaim their ancestry as a means of coming to terms with life in the present. The phrase appears as a chapter title above a visually striking image that recalls elements from the graphic narrative's cover illustration. Hall stands on one of the iconic eagle ornaments on the sixty-first floor of New York City's Chrysler Building, looking over the cityscape while accompanied by a group of seven African women depicted as ancestors emancipated from the shackles of the past and now claiming their rightful place at the heart of the African slave trade in the United States. The image evokes comic book superheroes but also differs from this imagery. Hall may be positioned, like Batman, on a gargoyle, but unlike the Dark Knight, she is not crouched on Gotham's rooftops overlooking the cityscape in search of criminal activity. Rather, she is supported by her ancestors, who appear as time-traveling warriors leaping not over tall buildings (as Superman would) but over generations to break from the past into the present. Her mission is not to save Gotham or Metropolis from evil but to uncover hidden parts of the past—sometimes literally buried beneath the cityscape—to imagine a Black future.[64]

The upper right corner of the image features two lines from Maya Angelou's poem "Still I Rise" (1978) that add meaning by casting Hall as the fulfillment of the enslaved people's hopes and dreams: "Bringing the gifts that my ancestors gave, / I am the dream and the hope of the slave."[65] Prefiguring these lines, Hall's avatar recognizes toward the end of the narrative's opening sequence that "for hundreds of years, our ancestors were brutally silenced. I wasn't supposed to find their voices. But sometimes, when you think you're hunting down the past . . . the past is hunting you . . . I was born to tell these stories."[66] As an attorney who became a historian because she "felt the need to see underneath the 'justice system'—to get at the root of what was warping the world," Hall is haunted by the urge to confront the legacies of four hundred years of slavery, as she is seeking to come to terms with her own family history (reconstructing the life story of her grandmother, Harriet Thorpe) and with the impact of a historical archive that has largely buried the experiences especially of her female ancestors—sometimes literally, as in a splash panel that shows the 1990s construction of what would become Manhattan's Ted Weiss Federal Building, which unearthed a burial ground holding the bodies of approximately fifteen thousand free and enslaved African Americans. The panel depicts a digger about to sink its shovel into the ground as the bones of an arm and hand are reaching out of the ground. "New York City was built on slavery and the slave trade," the caption on the preceding page explains, "and as I dug into the history of my hometown . . . . . . I began to see it everywhere."[67]

The labor-intensive and frustrating task of retrieving ancestral experiences or specters of the past through archival traces in documents whose main purpose was to eradicate these experiences and reduce the enslaved to mere property makes up the bulk of Hall, Martínez, and Bao's narrative.[68] But these segments are interspersed with more private scenes of family life that show Hall and her female partner raising their young son, spending time on the beach, and talking on the phone whenever Hall is traveling in pursuit of historical information.[69] In detailing this pursuit, Hall, Martínez, and Bao focus especially on the role of women in revolts against enslavement, finding archival echoes of female-led uprisings in New York City in 1708 and 1712 and on the ship *Unity* in 1700.[70] Forced to read between the lines and against the grain of the archival documents, *Wake*'s creators follow Hartman's practice of critical fabulation in a process that involves finding traces of the voices of ancestors and using the historical imagination to envision their life stories in search of "an alternative Black temporality where we reach into the past to 'reimagine a future otherwise'" (Hall, Martínez, and Bao quoting van Veen 79).

Hall, Martínez, and Bao repeatedly speak of the "afterlife of slavery" (a phrase they take from Hartman ["Dead" 210]) and of "living in the wake of slavery" (a phrase coined by Christina Sharpe [*In the Wake* 15]) as a way of grasping this alternative temporality. These creators make connections between what the narrative unmasks as the West's systematic exploitation of Black lives and labor from the late fifteenth to the late nineteenth centuries and the narrative present, which is variously the late 1990s, when Hall did her research, or the late 2010s and the early 2020s, when police shootings of Black Americans have revealed the lasting fallout of slavery and when the Black Lives Matter movement has tied the revolts of the past to a more recent tradition of civil rights protest. One double splash page in the second chapter shows Hall walking through New York City as the captions recall details about the 1712 revolt. Key elements of the story are visualized behind the shop windows Hall passes on her way to an archive. The right side of the page shows a parked police car with the letters NYPD clearly visible. Inside the car, we see a scaffold filled with empty nooses, suggesting a continuum spanning the early revolts against enslavement, the lynchings of the postbellum era, and the police killings of Black citizens. Responding to Audre Lorde's saying "We were never meant to survive" ("Litany") with a note of resilience—"But we have"—Hall, Martínez, and Bao compel readers to listen to the voices silenced by the archive and made to resound in this graphic narrative through acts of defending the dead against "the historical archive that violently erased our past [and] continues its violence against us."[71]

Conceptually, *Wake* begins where most history books end and where archives fail to provide the information necessary to reconstruct the stories of female-led revolts. Dissatisfied with the scarce material she finds in historical accounts of the 1712 revolt, one of which mentions that twenty-seven of the rebels were "condemned, whereof twenty-one were executed, one being a woman with child, her execution by that means suspended," Hall decides to "look at the original court records" at the New York City Municipal Archives and finds the names of four women who were tried for their actions (Sarah, Abigail, Lily, Amba).[72] But the trial records reveal next to nothing about their motivations, containing only circular statements ("Having nothing to say for herself than what she had previously said . . .") without yielding further insight. For Hall, this archival absence bears a significance that goes beyond the historian's frustration with incomplete sources, opening space for creative speculation. "The answers to my questions can't be found here. They can't be found in the historical record at all," her avatar notes, concluding that the only way to "honor these ancestors and the sacrifices they made" is to "make some educated guesses about what happened" and "tell their story, using everything I know to be true about their lives, and add the parts we don't know but could be true."

Earlier in the narrative, when we read about Hall's decision to pursue a doctorate in history, the captions recall, "I dove straight into the erased, the unspoken, the blank spaces in the documents. I felt compelled to uncover the stories of other Black women who fought for justice. Those women warriors who fought their enslavement."[73] This is essentially Hartman's notion of critical fabulation, and it is presented as a mixture of historical fact-finding mission, imaginative recovery, and ancestral veneration. What distinguishes Hall, Martínez, and Bao's approach from Hartman's concept is its graphic nature, the fact that the educated guesses and imaginative fabulations take visual form. For instance, the creators suffuse scenes of current New York City with images of the past, which creep into the crevices of the postmodern cityscape, most often through watery spaces, such as puddles and rivers, that recall the Atlantic Ocean as the passageway to America, and underpin the contemporary metropolis with a historical subtext that constitutes a palimpsestic rather than chronological relationship between the past and the present.

Adding to this palimpsestic depiction of New York City is Hall's recovery of her grandmother's life story. Harriet Thorpe is shown as a loving mother, hardworking wife, and activist on behalf of women's and civil rights. She appears as what Morrison, whose *Beloved* features prominently in *Wake*, calls "the advising, benevolent, protective, wise Black ancestor" ("City Limits" 39), one of those "timeless people whose relationships to [other] characters are

Fig. 1.6: The ascending woman warrior at the end of *Wake*.

benevolent, instructive, and protective" and who "provide a certain kind of wisdom" ("Rootedness" 343). Hall, Martínez, and Bao add a second ancestral figure to the mix: the Black woman warrior who graces the title page of the book and constitutes its final image—emerging from the ocean with a spear in her raised hand as a counterimage to the bodies of the enslaved Africans who are jumping off the ship or the corpses of those who died in the hold and were thrown overboard like waste (fig. 1.6).[74]

This image claims an African diasporic futurity (the woman in the final image yells, "For the Future!") that was never meant to be. If "history written by the victors always erases resistance," as a caption at the beginning of the second chapter explains, and if "those of us who live in the wake/ruins learn that we were inferior and needed to be conquered and enslaved," one way of overcoming this erasure, according to Hall, Martínez, and Bao, is to tell a different story, one that is invested in history but also able and willing to read between the lines, to see interpretive possibilities where others only see the dead ends of documentation. Exploring these possibilities by calling the enslaved humans leaping off the ships "Flying Africans," La Marr Jurelle Bruce imagines their acts as "a mode of radical dreaming, an urge to escape to a distant elsewhere in an afterlife, otherworld, ancestral gathering place, heaven, or home" as well as "an act of radical self-care" (16). Bruce continues, "Sometimes the leap was not a plummet to doom, but a launch into flight;

not an outcome of self-abnegation, but an act of self-assertion; not a bog of hopelessness, but an outburst of radical hope hurled into another world" (16).

With such alternative imaginings in mind, the word *wake* acquires multiple implications throughout the narrative. For one, it suggests that rather than having overcome slavery, we continue to live in a postslavery world shaped by structures of racism that have evolved from the centuries-long exploitation and erasure of Black life (i.e., living in the wake of slavery). "Living in the wake means living the history and present of terror, from slavery to the present, as the ground of our everyday Black existence," Sharpe holds. "Living the historically and geographically dis/continuous but always present and endlessly reinvigorated brutality in, and on, our bodies while even as that terror is visited on our bodies the realities of that terror are erased" (*In the Wake* 15). Second, the phrase implies a sense of mourning and defending the dead, issuing an ethical imperative to remember those who suffered from and perished during slavery and its aftermath: accordingly, Sharpe asks, "What does it look like, entail, and mean to attend to, care for, comfort, and defend, those already dead, those dying, and those living lives consigned to the possibility of always-imminent death, life lived in the presence of death; to live this imminence and immanence as and in the 'wake'?"(38). Third, Hall, Martínez, and Bao repeatedly refer to the burials of the enslaved, from the drowned bodies during the Middle Passage (sea burials in the literal wake of the ship, what Dawes calls "the watery tomb" in "Requiem" [21]) to the lengthy depiction of the enslaved Ekua at New York's African burial ground. Here, Hall, Martínez, and Bao embrace Sharpe's understanding of the "multiple registers of 'wake'—the path behind a ship, keeping watch with the dead, coming to consciousness" and use it to illustrate "how Black lives are swept up and animated by the afterlives of slavery" (*In the Wake* description). Like Sharpe, these creators understand "the wake as the conceptual frame of and for living blackness in the diaspora in the still unfolding aftermaths of Atlantic chattel slavery" (Sharpe, *In the Wake* 2).

Hall, Martínez, and Bao's defense of the dead is visually striking, recalling elements from both Feelings and Baker but adding new insights and affects. One particularly noteworthy splash page of *Wake*'s opening scene squeezes the narrative sequence into the sails, deck, and hold of a ship whose outlines frame the action instead of the conventional comic book panels, asking readers to make sense of the different temporalities displayed in the image: the symbolically charged *Unity* on its long journey to the New World versus the initial resolve of the enslaved to wait for the right moment to revolt. "They wait . . . ," reads the single speech balloon on the preceding page, which shows the *Unity* sailing in the Atlantic; the statement is completed as we turn the page: " . . . for our signal." The Africans realize that they "will die here" and are in fact "dead already," but they nonetheless rise up against their confinement. Stasis and action are welded into a single image as we know it from Feeling's elongated tableaus, but Hall, Martínez, and Bao employ a wider range of page designs to cover the unfolding action. The splash panel on the next page depicts the two female protagonists of the book's critical fabulation, Adono and Alele, hugging and swearing "unity" with each other. These women are positioned in the hold, with ethereal daylight streaming down through the iron grate separating them from the deck. By naming these two women, Hall, Martínez, and Bao symbolically counter the loss instantiated by the archive, where ship's logs record only the number of enslaved who have died: "Died a Man Slave No. 8"; "died a girl Slave No. 9"; "died a Woman No. 10. Of Captain Moneypenny's purchase" (see also Teutsch, "Layouts"; Teutsch, "Retrieving").[75] While the next two pages use midsized panels to show the enslaved in the act of breaking their chains and beating drums, the following two pages create a double splash page in the form of a polyptych that illustrates the fighting on deck between enslavers and enslaved, with Adono and Adele diving off the ship to their deaths (as shown on the next page). While graphically remarkable, this polyptych is much less gruesome and brutal than the literary depiction of the slave revolt in Johnson's *Middle Passage*, which describes the shipboard violence in stark detail and narrates the tossing overboard of the corpses of the enslaved with a sensory precision that evokes Feelings's most horrifying images of dead men and women belowdecks rather than Hall, Martínez, and Bao's more subdued depiction of violence.[76]

As this passage draws to a close, the diving warrior's hands grab Hall's arm while she sleeps on a desk in an archive, revealing the previous pages as a figment of the historian's fever dreams, a series of images triggered by her effort to picture the lives of the enslaved that continue to haunt her. These images reemerge at the end of the narrative, in the ironically titled chapter "The Insurrection of Cargo," which connects Hall's language-driven research on women-led slave revolts (as the archives contain mostly written documents) with an alternative attempt to recall history. "They say that sound travels differently in water," the captions state in a splash panel that shows an injured woman (perhaps Adono or Adele, whose lives in the kingdom of Dahomey were related in chapter 9) diving off the ship while yelling "In Unity." The image shows the woman's bleeding body (the result of a shotgun wound inflicted in one of the panels of the earlier polyptych) submerged in the water, sinking toward the bottom of the Atlantic. "Sound waves travel so slowly in water and the ocean is so vast, the sound can last centuries under water," the captions continue. "Maybe, if we listen carefully, we can hear them."[77]

Hall, Martínez, and Bao are again referencing Ellison's *Invisible Man*, translating the narrator's question in the novel's final sentence—"Who knows but that, on the lower frequencies, I speak for you?" (439)—into a notion of listening to the drowned voices of the past. In addition, by beginning the graphic narrative with the revolt on the *Unity*, providing a critically and creatively fabulated backstory, and ending with the visual and discursive recovery of the deceased women warriors come back to life, *Wake*'s creators underscore Ellison's speaker's circular remarks in the prologue that "the end is in the beginning and lies far ahead" (5).

RISKING REPRESENTATION

The Middle Passage, *Wake*, and *Nat Turner* construct sites "in which the very meaning of US blackness becomes contested and defined" (Bruno 925). The creators' "historiographic pedagogy" (Chaney, "Slave" 280) exposes the historical archive's inability to preserve traces of Black family life and ancestry as one of the most consequential elements of what Hartman terms "the afterlife of slavery" ("Dead" 210) and Kimberly Juanita Brown labels its "corporeal afterimage" (*Repeating* 18) in the present. Feelings, Baker, and Hall, Martínez, and Bao transform this archive into stories of resilience and resistance but also return to a heteronormative notion of the family as the backbone of African American culture and life in the diaspora (though Hall's family is the exception). If their narratives amend the historical record and insert new interpretive possibilities into the popular "image bank" (Chaney, "Drawing" 188) of transatlantic diasporic blackness, they graphically fabulate "the recuperation of a usable history of slavery for contemporary African Americans" (Chaney, "Slave" 283). They do not propose what James Braxton Peterson terms a "graphic black nationalism" but rather understand archival documents and archival absences "as dynamic, dialogic units of communication available for recombination and interpretation" (Chaney, "Drawing" 199). They accomplish this by creating a bulwark against the historical amnesia and denial that dominate much of the present discourse. These works urge readers to consider their entanglement in the contemporary world, its history, and its future.

Undrawing the unspeakable, then, becomes a balancing act, a constant negotiation between grounding these narratives in the scarce archival traces of Black life in the Middle Passage as they become available through scholarship and imagining Black life beyond the racial hierarchies sanctioned by archival silence. Referencing Naomi Mandel's *Against the Unspeakable: Complicity, the Holocaust, and Slavery in America* (2006), Singer proposes that "the unspeakable doesn't simply describe acts of atrocity; it makes claims on how such atrocities should be represented while declaring the limits of representability itself" (*Breaking* 229–30). This proposition amends Morrison's notion of unspeakability as the marked absence of African Americans from US history ("Unspeakable" 139) with a more epistemologically minded understanding of it as "a capacity to deny comprehension and to compel silence not in the name of avoiding the unspoken but, ostensibly, of respecting it" (Singer, *Breaking* 230). As a peculiar form of storytelling dependent on visually foregrounding the historiographic process through drawn and often framed and sequenced images that self-reflexively put their acts of framing on constant display (Chute 18), graphic narratives diverge from this deference. *Middle Passage*, *Nat Turner*, and *Wake* accept "the risk of representation" (Chute 5) by refusing "to follow the protocols of unspeakability, rendering trauma visible while recognizing the challenges it poses to representation" (Singer, *Breaking* 230). These processes inform the double resonance of the term *recuperation* as it emerges in Feelings's, Baker's, and Hall, Martínez, and Bao's work: to accept the risk of representation by reconstructing a history that frustrates our capacity to capture the past in words and images and to heal historical wounds by reopening the pains of the past for contemporary consideration.

Chapter 2 turns to the ways in which contemporary graphic narratives revise images of lynching. Moving from the Middle Passage and slavery to the post-Reconstruction period, I examine how Kyle Baker, Jeremy Love, Derek McCulloch and Shepherd Hendrix, and Mat Johnson and Warren Pleece, among others, remediate the vast archive of lynching narratives, especially photographs, to foreground a history of anti-Black violence that constituted a new system of racial subjugation after Reconstruction. These authors and artists accept the risk of representing lynching as an unspeakable crime by engaging with the lynching origins of the superhero genre while straining to undraw the racist legacies of lynching imagery and insisting on the potential to wrench from it a sense of beauty and creative self-determination.

CH. 2

Chapter 2

LEGACIES OF LYNCHING

Writing in the *Chicago Daily News* on 8 May 1940, author and literary critic Sterling North minced no words when he described comics as "lurid publications [that] depend for their appeal upon mayhem, murder, torture and abduction" and complained about their "Superman heroics, voluptuous females in scanty attire, blazing machine guns, [and] hooded 'justice.'" Mobilizing a similar discourse in the *American Journal of Psychology* at the end of the decade, cultural critic Gershon Legman attacked the "aggressive content of comics," suggesting that even in educational comics, "murder is rewarded" and that the "Superman formula is essentially lynching."[1] Both midcentury salvos against the medium evoke images of lynching—Legman claiming its centrality to the concept of the comic book superhero, North speaking of "hooded justice"—while failing to associate it with the white mobs that murdered thousands of African Americans between the mid-nineteenth and mid-twentieth centuries.[2]

This failure is not surprising. As Amy Louise Wood and Susan Donaldson have argued in a US context, "lynching haunts our social memories, but we are reluctant to grasp it or hold it carefully up for view" (10). Ashraf Rushdy even speaks of a "collective American amnesia about the history and practice of lynching" (*End* x–xi). This haunted reluctance or collective amnesia registers in the convoluted wording of North's sentiments. Once we decode the pulp ingredients in his enumeration—the "voluptuous females" and "blazing machine guns"—as potential references to the racist weaponization of white femininity and shift the acts of violence into a more systematic sequence ("mayhem, abduction, torture, murder, hooded justice"), we arrive at a fitting description of the "spectacle lynchings" (Wood's term) that terrorized African Americans after Reconstruction and far into the twentieth century.

Despite their hostile attitude toward comics, North and Gershon were not entirely misguided in associating the medium with lynching. Chris Gavaler has shown that the figure of the comic book superhero emerged from a history of popular lynching narratives, represented most prominently by Thomas Dixon Jr.'s *The Clansman: An Historical Romance of the Ku Klux Klan* (1905) and D. W. Griffith's blockbuster film adaptation of the novel, *The Birth of a Nation* (1915). Gavaler suggests that the "masked vigilantes" glorified in the novel and onscreen "entered the American consciousness" as admired figures and that "the Klansmen's characteristics—as introduced by Dixon, adapted by Griffith and emulated by actual Ku Klux Klan members across the United States—continue to shape present-day superheroes" (191). Thus, an eerie echo exists between a sentiment expressed in Harry Haywood and Milton Howard's 1932 pamphlet *Lynching: A Weapon of National Oppression*, published as part of their work for the Communist Party of the United States, and Bruce Wayne's resolution to dress up as a bat to fight crime in Gotham. The "ruling class savagery" of race-based lynching "has a purpose," Haywood and Howard argue, "to strike terror into the hearts of oppressed Negro people so that they dare not strike out for liberation" (5). In Bob Kane and Bill Finger's "The Legend of the Batman—Who He Is and How He Came to Be!" Bruce Wayne muses, "Criminals are a superstitious cowardly lot. So my disguise must be able to strike terror into their hearts. I must be a creature of the night, black, terrible, . . . a . . . a . . . A bat! That's it! It's an omen. I shall become a bat!" And the narrator declares, "And thus is born this weird figure of the dark . . . This avenger of evil: The Batman." Gavaler is therefore right to note that by the mid-1930s, "Ku Klux Klan hero tropes had been absorbed into popular culture, distanced from their white supremacist roots and reproduced as generic formula in pulp adventure fiction" (192). The comic book superhero thus "originated from an oppressive, racist impulse in American culture" (192).

According to the formula, superheroes are "champions of the oppressed" (to use Christopher Murray's phrase) but rarely grasp oppression in explicitly racial terms. Superheroes serve as defenders of the status quo rather than as regime-changing revolutionaries: "The superhero is a white—and overwhelmingly cisgender, male, straight, and middle-class—ideological formation and has been so since its inception," Sean Guynes and Martin Lund note, identifying a hegemonic narrative rooted in the "racist basis of the genre's ingrained whiteness" (7, 11; see also Benson and Singsen). "What is the black superhero without imagining the white hero as its Other?," Rebecca Wanzo wonders accordingly (*Content* 210).[3] The Black superheroes that started to appear in the 1960s and 1970s (Black Panther, Falcon, Luke Cage, Storm) are paradoxical figures, as protecting the status quo has historically meant preserving "a racialized regime of power that extends social control over those deemed both white and those marked as nonwhite" (Guynes and Lund 5).[4] If the superhero is a vigilante acting self-righteously as judge, jury, and executioner, the figure aligns more with the actions of the white lynch mob than with its victims. The genre's lynching origins remain the superhero's most "spectacular secret," as Jacqueline Goldsby terms it.[5]

Taking up the notion that lynching and vigilante violence constitute the superhero's unacknowledged roots, this chapter examines the intriguing connections between this popular serial figure and what Goldsby calls "lynching's cultural logic" (5). I have yet to find substantial scenes in superhero comics that remediate the kind of spectacularly staged mob executions investigated by scholars like Goldsby, Dora Apel, Sandy Alexandre, Julie Buckner Armstrong, Amy Kate Bailey and Stewart E. Tolnay, W. Fitzhugh Brundage, Susan V. Donaldson, Jonathan Markovitz, Michael J. Pfeifer, Leigh Raiford, Ashraf H. A. Rushdy, Evelyn M. Simien, Shawn Michelle Smith, and Amy Louise Wood, so rather than searching the archive of superhero comics for depictions of racially motivated lynchings, I assess the genre's lynching roots via graphic narratives about Black history that evoke a sense of superheroism. One candidate for analysis is David F. Walker, Chuck Brown, and Sanford Greene's *Bitter Root*, which is examined in detail in chapter 5. The series's first issue ends with the near-lynching of a Black man by hooded henchmen. Issue 6 offers a more elaborate depiction of a lynching, including a representation of a Black body hanging from a tree that recalls the conventions of lynching photographs but is presented from a worm's-eye perspective that complicates what might otherwise constitute a reality effect. The comic also spends a few pages showing the grief and suffering of the victim's family members, which are usually excised from historical representation. Issue 11 features an evil tree in southwestern Tennessee, outside of Memphis, that devours its victims and leaves their dead bodies hanging from its branches; in issue 13, members of the Sangerye family come across another such tree in central Tennessee with an empty noose hanging from it and note that "this tree is the only one we've seen with nothing. No bodies hanging from it. No bones scattered all around it. Nothing."

References to lynching appear repeatedly in *Bitter Root*. In conjunction with stories such as John Jennings and David Brame's *The Midnight Struggle: A Town Called Miracle*, where a Black man is lynched and his wife uses her conjuring powers to take revenge on the murderers, these references indicate an ongoing interest in addressing anti-Black violence and its visual archive in comics. This chapter focuses on Derek McCulloch, Shepherd Hendrix, et al.'s *Stagger Lee* (2006), Kyle Baker's *Nat Turner* (2008), Jeremy Love and Patrick Morgan's *Bayou* (2009–10), and Mat Johnson and Warren Pleece's *Incognegro* (2008), with cursory references to Ho Che Anderson's *King* (2010) and John Lewis, Andrew Aydin, and Nate Powell's *March: Book One* (2013).[6] These narratives perform crucial memory work as they offer alternative frameworks for understanding the comic book superhero by investing this figure with images of the lynched (and usually male) Black body. My focus on predominantly male victims and male superheroes is meant neither to marginalize the existence of lynched Black women nor to downplay the significance of Black female superheroines.[7] Black women were indeed victims of lynching, albeit in much smaller numbers than Black men. One example is nineteen-year-old Mary Turner, who was killed in Brooks County, Georgia, in May 1918, when she was eight months pregnant, and whose murder is memorialized in Rachel Marie-Crane Williams's *Elegy for Mary Turner: An Illustrated Account of a Lynching* (2021).[8]

BLACK BODIES, SUPERHERO BODIES

Lynching and superheroes share a deep investment in public displays of the (super)human body. From the wealth of research on superhero bodies, I take three insights as starting points for my investigation of the visual and cultural confluences between the exposed bodies of the victims of lynching and the extraordinary corporeality of comic book superheroes. First, I am intrigued by José Alaniz's attestation of the superhero's "decades-long iconography" of "hyper-masculinized vigor" (5) and his interest in narratives of death and disability that posit the potential fragility of the seemingly invulnerable superbody. Following Alaniz's lead, I read the superhero as a popular figure with a particular ability to incarnate "the anxieties and desires of the age," and I consider "the *super-body* as a site of elaborate, overdetermined signification" (*Death* 5–6, 18), attributes that may well be associated with Black bodies in the American racial imaginary. Second, I am struck by Scott Bukatman's observation that "superhero bodies, despite their plasticity, are armored bodies, rigid against the chaos of surrounding disorder" and that they facilitate a corporeal "mapping of the subject into a cultural system" (*Matters* 56, 49). Bukatman further suggests that "superhero bodies are mysterious, invested with magical abilities and a metamorphic pliability" (49). Third, I wonder about Ramzi Fawaz's assertion that "bodily vulnerability [. . .] constituted the postwar superhero as a figure in continual *flux*, visualized on the comic book page as constantly moving among different identities, embodiments, social allegiances, and psychic states." Noting "the monstrous powers and bodies of postwar superheroes," Fawaz suggests that they "exhibited a form of *fluxability*, a state of material and psychic *becoming* characterized by constant transition or change that consequently orients one toward cultivating skills for *negotiating* [. . .] multiple, contradictory identities and affiliations" (10–11).

Instead of armored yet flexible or pliable bodies, the graphic narratives investigated in this chapter offer "representations of the wounded black male body" and "display[s] of black bodily disfiguration" (Jackson 5, 3). Here, Bukatman's "chaos of surrounding disorder" morphs into the lynch mob, which creates temporary disorder to secure white rule over the allegedly transgressive Black body, sometimes accused of violating the sexual boundaries between Black men and white women. Cassandra Jackson emphasizes the gendered implications of lynching, asserting that "the lynching of black men is inseparable from the policing of white women's bodies and the sexual exploitation of black women's bodies by white men" (3). Along similar lines, Robyn Wiegman concentrates on "questions of the visible" in her analysis of "the sexual economy that underlies lynching's emergence as a disciplinary practice for racial control" in which "the de-commodification of the African-American body that accompanies the transformation from chattel to citizenry is mediated through a complicated process of sexualization and engendering." As part of this process, "not only does lynching enact a grotesquely symbolic, if not literal, sexual encounter between the white mob and its victim, but the increasing use of castration as a preferred form of mutilation for African-American men demonstrates lynching's connection to the socio-symbolic realm of sexual difference" (82). How contemporary graphic narratives visualize the grotesque symbolism of racially charged sexual difference without reiterating the violence and public degradation of the lynchings is a major question in this chapter and is complicated by Raiford's understanding of a "triangulated presence of the black male victim, white male mob members, and white female mob members." Raiford argues that "black women were confined to the periphery of this narrative, and unless they themselves were the victim of a lynching, absent from the picture's frame. [. . .] If black men are enframed—fixed and entrapped—within the lynching photograph, then black women are utterly expunged" (*Imprisoned* 52–53). As a medium that conventionally consists of framed sequential images, comics are uniquely positioned to critically foreground and revise processes of racist (en)framing, and Baker; Love and Morgan; McCulloch, Hendrix, et al.; and Johnson and Pleece mobilize the grammar of comics to reframe images from the lynching archive. The choice of a girl protagonist, Lee Wagstaff, in Love and Morgan's *Bayou*; McCulloch, Hendrix, et al.'s investigation of Stagger Lee's raced masculinity; and Johnson and Pleece's inclusion of a castration scene indicate that sexual difference plays a major role in these recent graphic encounters with the lynching archive.[9]

Graphic narratives of lynching reveal the limits of Fawaz's claims by showing Black bodies whose destruction and public desecration deny them the possibility to flux. On rare occasions, such as in Don McGregor and Billy Graham's Black Panther story "A Cross Burning Darkly Blackening the Night!" the Black superhero escapes a lynching, flexing his muscles to break away from the cross to which Klan members have tied him and turning against his tormentors. But this is clearly marked as a fantasy that accomplishes in a comic what was almost unthinkable in real life (see Peppard; Alaniz, "Wakanda"). The only viable transition for the victim of a lynch mob is to become, in Abel Meeropol's words, "strange fruit hanging from the poplar trees," a "strange and bitter crop." As Shawn Michelle Smith observes, "The corpse functions as the negated other that frames, supports, and *defines* a white supremacist community" (127). Flux, if possible at all, may come only after the murder, when the sight of the corpse enters the realm of mediation and eventually what Raiford calls "the shadow archive" of lynching (*Imprisoned* 48) through photographs taken as souvenirs and circulated as postcards, through newspaper reports and magazine articles, and through a variety of literary representations.[10]

Part of a larger project of anti-Black "thanatopolitical disposability," these photographs functioned as "a prosthetic to a historically implanted gaze applied to the black body rendered generic by its defacement" (Feldman 372, 373). Walter White lamented this widespread mediatization of lynching (a phenomenon he called mobbism) in his antilynching treatise *Rope and Faggot* (1929), juxtaposing lynching narratives with comics: "An uncomfortably large percentage of American citizens can read in their newspapers of the slow roasting alive of a human being in Mississippi and turn, promptly and with little thought, to the comic strip or sporting page. Thus has lynching become an almost integral part of our national folkways" (viii). Lynching's representation on postcards and related graphic forms worked as a type of tourism "that furthered the conjugation of the black body as a circulating and pleasure-generating consumable mass article" (Feldman 373).

The 1901 lynching of twenty-seven-year-old George Ward in Terre Haute, Indiana, was a particularly horrific event, according to a *New York Times* report ("Negro Hanged"). Beaten and shot, Ward most likely was already dead when he was hanged from a bridge. His body was then burned as approximately two thousand spectators watched the scene unfold: "The east bank of the river, the bridges up and down the stream, and hundreds of housetops were black with spectators, from whom not a word of pity escaped, although many deprecated the burning of the body. [. . .] Souvenir hunters were on hand in force and fragments of the body are now scattered broadcast." The report continues with a detailed description of men and women desecrating the body, enacting a kind of journalistic voyeurism only superficially masked by a slight exculpatory rhetoric ("many deprecated the burning"). The article concludes by noting that the crime will most likely go unpunished but refrains from demanding legal or political change: "As public sentiment upholds the lynching no prosecutions are expected."[11] These souvenirs (as well as postcards featuring photographs of the event) initially kept the Black body "frozen as a wounded subject" (Wanzo, *Content* 82), rendering it fixed, mute, and still even as they publicly dispersed its photographic reproduction. "Taken after death, lynching photographs may technically qualify as postmortem images, but they generally do not seek to memorialize the dead," Goldsby maintains. In most cases, "lynching photographs figure the dead as signs of pure abjection who radiate no thought, no speech, no action, no will; who, through their appearance in the picture's field of vision, become invisible" (231).

Public displays of a lynching victim's body parts were common. W. E. B. Du Bois recalled writing to *The Atlanta Constitution* about "a poor Negro in central Georgia, Sam Hose," who had killed his landlord, Alfred Cranford, on 12 April 1899, and been accused of raping Cranford's wife, though she denied having been attacked (*Dusk* 34). Du Bois laid out a detailed defense of Hose, but on his way to deliver the letter, he learned that the man had been lynched, "and they said that his knuckles were on exhibition at a grocery store farther down on Mitchell Street" (34). Writing in the *New York Times* on 27 April 1899, Northern commentator Harry Luther Sears complained about the "outrageous brutality," "barbaric cruelty," and "disgraceful travesty" of Hose's lynching. Sears decried the lynch mob's disregard of the rule of law and accused Southerners of "degenerating into brutes" who "calmly and deliberately torture a human being and gloat over it." Yet he displayed little empathy for Hose, whom he called "a brute of the lowest order" (6; for more on this lynching, see Arnold).

The photographs and written commentary that encapsulated such public atrocities depicted the mutilated Black bodies as proof of white power rather than as memento mori but could not prevent other uses and other narratives. Apel and Smith speak of "the malleable nature of lynching photographs" (18), noting their reappropriation by antilynching activists who sought to reframe the images as evidence of white violence and employed them to protest racial injustice. This meant changing "the received narrative of black savagery" to "one of black vulnerability" and that of "white victimization" to that of "white terrorization" (Raiford, *Imprisoned* 40). It also implied transforming "those photographs from icons of white pride to emblems of American shame" (Rushdy, *End* 68). Here, "the black body in the center of the photograph—which had been cast as a criminal and an animal—now became a victim, and a victim not only of a crime against an individual, but a victim of a crime against law and order, against the nation, against civilization" (72). Love and Morgan; McCulloch, Hendrix, et al.; and Johnson and Pleece add yet another transformation to this reception history, rejecting the impulse to use lynching imagery as emblematic of shame and offering more critical and confrontational visions instead.

A leaflet from the NAACP verbally reframed a photograph of the 19 July 1935 lynching of Rubin Stacy in Fort Lauderdale, Florida, in an attempt to direct the viewer's gaze away from the victim and toward lynching's function as an instrument of racist indoctrination: "Do not look at the Negro. His earthly problems are ended. Instead, look at the seven WHITE children who gaze at this gruesome spectacle" (qtd. in Apel and Smith 59).[12] Rushdy maintains, "Even in the moment when they were most unashamedly used to celebrate lynchings as communal acts, those photographs remained unstable entities, public artifacts that contained all the elements of their own undoing. The death at the very center of those photographs—the corpse that the mob and photographers thought they had contained and fixed—would take on a haunting afterlife when those photographs became subject to a considerably more critical set of editors and readers" (*End* 67).

Like the bodies of comic book superheroes, the bodies depicted in these lynching photographs and their contested remediations serve as sites of overdetermination. "Black bodies are overburdened by a history of representation that can somewhat overdetermine readings of them," Wanzo notes (*Content* 141). This includes the Black bodies exposed in the photographs as well as the drawn images of lynched Black men and women in contemporary graphic narratives. "Black bodies are already stories, mythological beasts with epic powers and tragic presaged endings in the faulty perspectivalism of the white supremacist world," Anna Beatrice Scott suggests (312). Lynching photographs therefore did not so much document a particular form of white terrorism as draw on and feed into a widely established, thoroughly racialized visual culture that inscribed Black bodies with predetermined meanings.[13] "Photography documented lynching but also played a role in orchestrating it," Shawn Michelle Smith rightly concludes. "Making a photograph became part of the ritual, helping to objectify and dehumanize the victims and, for some, increasing the hideous pleasure" (Apel and Smith 16).[14] These photographs continue to serve as ambivalent incarnations of the anxieties of their age, "occlud[ing] more about black existence in the United States" than they expose (Raiford, *Imprisoned* 33–34). Staging "a pageant of excessive violence and torture situated in, on, and about the black body, lynching masks these anxieties" (39–40). That depictions of lynching occur across a wide range of contemporary graphic narratives indicates that these anxieties are not confined to the past but continue their violence into the present.

In an essay on Kyle Baker's *Nat Turner*, Darieck Scott speaks of a "surfeit of signification [that] attends the *image* of black bodies" to acknowledge "the challenge of the always-spectacular black body: nowhere more readily a spectacle than in scenes [. . .] of the black person suffering" ("Not-Yet" 337). Images of Black bodies, he concludes, are always "enmeshed within the various overdeterminations which produce [them] as replete with readable meanings." They are "always bearing a story, an explanation" (341). Which stories and explanations these images may yield and to whom is an altogether different issue that involves both ethical and aesthetic questions.

THE ETHICS AND AESTHETICS OF LOOKING AT BLACK BODIES

Recognizing a genealogy of racialized overdetermination and surfeit signification ascribed to Black bodies, Harvey Young observes, "The black body, whether on the auction block, the American plantation, hanged from a lightpole as part of a lynching ritual, attacked by police dogs within the Civil Rights era, or staged as a 'criminal body' by contemporary law enforcement and criminal systems, is a body that has been forced into the public spotlight and given a compulsory visibility. It has been *made to be given to be seen*" (12). Young's observations remind us that the overdetermination of the Black body, its compulsory visibility, has always depended on a public eager to draw it into the spotlight and subject it to intense and perverse scrutiny. This is particularly relevant in the context of the ritualized spectacle lynchings Young mentions in his list of corporeal abuses, which, as Wiegman notes, "function as a panoptic mode of surveillance" that issues the "threat of always being seen" (13).[15] This panoptic mode entails a convolution of gazes: of those who attended the lynchings and often explicitly posed for the camera; of the camera as a humanly operated technical apparatus that captured the mutilated Black body and the onlookers at the scene; and of those who decide to look at or are involuntarily confronted with photographic, drawn, or moving images of lynching. Not to be forgotten are those who could not and cannot (bear to) look—the people whose murdered bodies the photographs contain as well as viewers who still find themselves under constant surveillance and subjected to harmful forms of compulsory visibility.[16] "If lynching photographs were meant for white consumption, to reaffirm the authority and certainty of whiteness through an identification with powerful and empowered whites who enframe the black body, what then did black looking affirm?" Raiford asks, raising an issue that graphic narratives address in various ways before continuing, "What concept of the black self could emerge from an identification with the corpse in the picture?" (*Imprisoned* 35).[17]

Taking this convolution of gazes into account, Bettina M. Carbonell urges us to "analyze the ethics and aesthetics of our encounters with the afterlife of lynching" (198). *Afterlife of lynching* possesses semantic proximity to *afterimages* and the *wake of slavery*, and the phrase indicates that thinking and writing about lynching images should not concern solely the visual material and its retrospective representations or reframings, nor should it exclusively address ethical questions at the expense of the aesthetic dimension. Wood and Donaldson therefore ask, "How does one go about trying to represent what initially appears beyond description, and how does one do so without reimposing upon those victims of past atrocities the utter debasement and abjection they experienced in ritualistic acts of violence and murder? Who has the right to tell their stories, and how should one respond to them?" (7). I understand Wood and Donaldson's questions as an obligation to take seriously the ethical implications and the aesthetic appeal of lynching images, a demand Apel shares when she wonders, "Who has the right to look at such photos?" and concludes that it "inevitably" depends on "who is doing the shooting and the looking, and thus it matters how and where the pictures are presented" (Apel and Smith 43). Trying to bury these images in the archive would render invisible one particularly atrocious instrument of white supremacy as well as nullify a particularly violent part of Black history. Wood and Donaldson nonetheless make us aware of the risk that comes with engaging with these images: "Because lynching was so often perpetrated through spectacle and sensationalism, any attempt to represent it risks re-engaging in that spectacle or exploiting the sensationalism once again." Furthermore, "any public representation of lynching renders an individual's most excruciating moment—excruciating not only because he suffered physical pain, but because others watched and enjoyed the suffering publicly—public once again. [. . .] But to represent or denote lynching without using direct imagery or description also risks diluting or sanitizing the atrocity and its effects" (16–17).

I agree with Wood and Donaldson and Apel as well as with Hartman's question, "How does one revisit the scene of subjection without replicating the grammar of violence?" ("Venus" 4), and join them in acknowledging that there is no easy way out of the ethical conundrum with which lynching images have confronted generations of viewers. Wanzo, for instance, notes that some scholars argue "that the replication of lynching photographs produced and circulated by whites only replicates the politics of white supremacy that produced the lynching itself" (*Content* 67; see also Koritha Mitchell). Faced with this dilemma—the problem of erasing lynching from American history by rejecting its photographic afterlife; the danger of replicating the tools of white supremacy and inflicting new hurt on those who are routinely targeted by racist images; the potential anesthetizing of "audiences to black pain and suffering" and the "increasing desire for more and more graphic accounts" (Raiford, *Imprisoned* 65)—I follow Jackson's and Wanzo's suggestions for how to treat these images.[18] When selecting images for her analysis of wounded Black bodies, Jackson excluded those that simply reinscribed "the imagery of woundedness without illuminating it" (10). Acknowledging the devastating powers of "visual imperialism," Wanzo holds that "the ethics and possible consequences of replication push us to think about how we might defamiliarize the treatment of the body in ways that may call attention to the horror as opposed to routinizing it" (*Content* 67).[19] The graphic narratives assessed in this chapter do not routinize the body horrors associated with lynching. They defamiliarize the treatment of the Black body by remediating lynching imagery in a medium that invites readers to "impart significance, through affect, to otherwise inert, insensible images" (Chaney, *Reading* 146) and that shares an ethical imperative with lynching photography: "Photographic meaning results from what we *do* with photographic evidence. Lynching photographs, finally, do not deliver testimony so much as they call us to it" (Apel and Smith 41).[20]

Instead of reopening wounds by replicating images of mutilated and murdered Black bodies, I focus on images that illuminate the long history of visual degradation as a means of gaining an alternative perspective on a past that is too often mainstreamed into a narrative of national greatness (enlisted to express US exceptionalism) or pressed into a story of racial progress that ignores Ralph Ellison's forceful reminder in *Invisible Man* that the world does not move "like an arrow, but a boomerang" (5).[21] Thus, all of the images reproduced here are taken from graphic narratives that remediate lynching imagery without replicating their initial purpose or supporting their original message. To contextualize these remediations, I point to places where the original images can be accessed, illuminating the secret origins and continuing prevalence of lynching for contemporary versions of the superhero as well as for continuing notions of Black (super)heroism. I ultimately agree with Wood and Donaldson: "To look at these images is to recognize the objectifying gaze of the perpetrators and to position ourselves in relation to that gaze" (14-15). This twofold process of recognition and self-positioning necessarily entails an ethical dimension that remains vital in our current moment.

Writing in 2008, Wood and Donaldson discerned "a larger effort to activate social memory about lynching, to create a new kind of popular consciousness about America's racist and violent past in the face of what has been a profound mis-remembering of lynching" (6).[22] My analysis here constitutes part of this effort, not only activating social memory about lynching but illuminating the secret origins of the comic book superhero. This analysis engages in "a struggle with mediation itself" (Chaney, "Drawing" 179), developing productive ways of coping with the visual "legacies of lynching" (to use Markovitz's phrase) while acknowledging that the primary access to the material is through the "historical archive of racist visualization" (Chaney, "Is There" 73). "Informed by historical structures of spectacle," Michael A. Chaney writes, "the display of black bodies undergoes a process of media negotiation in graphic novels by black authors and writers" ("Drawing" 176). These narratives propose a process of "visual signifyin'" (198) that moves from replicating harmful images and reinflicting the violence of the past to a practice Henry Louis Gates Jr. has labeled "repetition with a signal difference" (*Signifying* xxiv). In addition, the graphic narratives update the practice by moving beyond Gates's focus on language and Chaney's interest in images to include other constitutive sights and sounds.

LYNCHING SCENES IN JEREMY LOVE AND PATRICK MORGAN'S *BAYOU*

Bayou is an unfinished two-volume meditation on Southern racism that commemorates the life of Emmett Till, who was lynched in 1955. In *Bayou*, Till appears in the guise of Billy Glass, and a young Black girl, Lee Wagstaff, is sent to retrieve his corpse from a nearby bayou. Love and Morgan are forthright about the fact that Billy is modeled on Till: a character sketch at the end of the first volume features a pencil drawing of Billy with the word *Emmet* next to it and the caption, "Notice Billy's original name was not 'Billy.'" The decision to connect the story with Till is crucial for at least two reasons. First, it underscores the idea that lynchings have an afterlife. Till was murdered more than seventy years ago, but race-based lynchings continue (see Yancy; McLaughlin).[23] Second, Till's death and especially his funeral changed public perceptions of lynching. They provided a major impetus for the civil rights movement and affected collective memories of lynching. Photos of the teenager's mutilated face appeared in *Jet* magazine, while *The Chicago Defender* ran a dapper image of Till (cf. Apel and Smith 66), and they "became the turning point for the representation of the black subject in lynching imagery" (Apel and Smith 64; cf. Goldsby 6). By insisting on an open-casket funeral, Till's mother Mamie Till-Mobley confronted the photographic archive of "spectacle lynchings" with a "spectacle funeral" (Apel and Smith 44, 45). Till's appearance contested the logic of white supremacy and wagered the vulnerability of the Black male body against "the creation of sympathy and pity for a grieving mother and of anger for the outrageous violation of sacrosanct motherhood" (Raiford, *Imprisoned* 53). Apel maintains that the photos of Till's funeral "remained outside the network of lynching photos that circulated among white supremacists. The image of the black subject *as a subject* violated the code of lynching photographs by which black bodies were always objects to be acted on by white subjects" (Apel and Smith 64). The image of Till in the casket, footage of his sobbing mother, and coverage of the many mourners publicly grieving over the teenager's death not only countered the prevailing lynching iconography but also enabled Till-Mobley to reclaim "the humiliated black body" and reendow it "with dignity and humanity" (64).[24]

In evoking Till through the figure of Glass—an anachronism (the story is set in 1933) that emphasizes lynching's transhistorical sway and marks another instance of epiphenomenal time that sidesteps the conventional "overreliance on [. . .] linear progress narratives" (Wright, *Physics* 5)—Love and Morgan activate mediated forms of public memory of a moment in US history when one particular lynching provided a powerful impetus for a social movement. The appearance of Till's body in the spotlight was certainly forced in the sense that his killers (who escaped conviction) took control of his body, tortured him, and then murdered him. Yet his postmortem visibility hinged on his mother's decision to display his corpse as a strategic move to dramatize the injustices of racial discrimination, segregation, and anti-Black violence. Undermining traditional lynching iconography, which depicts mutilated victims and triumphant audiences posing for the camera, Till's "spectacle funeral" implemented a visual discourse that invested the Black body with political potential, serving as a cause for outrage as well as activism and affording that body with "agency despite victimization" (Wanzo, *Content* 64). Moreover, by turning Till into a comic book character—a mythical creature whose butterfly wings suggest the possibility of transformation—and responding to the black-and-white photographs of his funeral with the colorful sequential narration of *Bayou*, Love and Morgan suggest that the ghosts of lynching can take on new and inspiring forms, giving "an account of how disruptive intergenerational memory can function as both a reminder of past atrocities and as a cue to readers into their continued *presence*" (Polak 150; on the intergenerational trauma of slavery, see Graff). In doing so, "*Bayou* dares to imagine an afterlife in which the young black victim can find a measure of comfort amid a sacred, loving community," Qiana J. Whitted writes, noting that the brief comfort the narrative offers its characters does not erase the historical trauma: "We need only to call attention to the scars that remain on" Billy's skin "to understand the interdependent relationship that Love imagines between the spirit world and the 'fleshly brothers and sisters' of the South" ("Intertextual" 201–2).[25]

These scars and traumas also haunt the figure of the superhero. After all, *Bayou* was published by DC Comics and features a benevolent green swamp creature (the titular Bayou) that evokes Stan Lee and Jack Kirby's Incredible Hulk as well as Alan Moore, Steve Bissette, and John Totleben's Swamp Thing (Whitted, "Of Slaves"). Unlike these (somewhat monstrous) superheroes, Bayou must endure a severe lashing by one of evil General Bog's hooded henchmen. The henchman's whip cracks open Bayou's back in panels that reference a key trope of antislavery discourse (the whipped victim of enslavement) and conjure up one of the most well known nineteenth-century abolitionist photographs, "The Scourged Back," attributed to McPherson & Oliver and taken in 1863, which shows the scars on an enslaved man, Gordon. But unlike the photograph, which Jackson argues "offers the suffering black male body as an object of white desire" (12), Love and Morgan's sequential narrative takes a fantastically grotesque turn when Bayou rips off his torturer's arm, playing into the conventions of the Southern gothic.[26] Even more significantly, Bayou is afforded an interiority that the photograph cannot grant the man with the scourged back. Bayou's decision to maim the hooded man is triggered by a panel showing two children with chains around their necks who are being yanked away as they scream for Bayou's help (see Stein, "Zu den Potentialen"; Stein "Black"). The identity of these children and how they relate to Bayou can only be deduced from the few clues scattered throughout the narrative when he shares fragments of his traumatic past. They are his lost children, and their memory humanizes the gentle giant (the next panel is a close-up of his face with a tear running down from his left eye). In the first volume, he tells Lee that "Bayou just want Nuh-Nandi to be safe" in a panel that is preceded by an image of a Black girl in African garb who might be his lost daughter, of whom Lee reminds him. After Jubal the Bloodhound threatens Bayou and Lee—"Bayou! You shiftless cur! You and that pickaninny will surely suffer"—Bayou exclaims in agony, voicing one of the main fears of Black parents during slavery, "Bayou never gon' see his chilluns again." And in the second volume, Bayou shares the traumatic loss of his children with Lee: "Buh-Bayou done forgot my chirren's faces long time ago. But Bayou 'member they laughin' and playin' and sometimes Bayou dream about 'em . . . . . . and dat there make Buh-Bayou feel real good inside. Dat's just gon' have to duh-duh-duh do till Bayou's chirrens come back."[27]

Bayou can thus be read as a different kind of superhero and Lee Wagstaff as a different type of sidekick (or vice versa). Lee's first mission is to retrieve Billy's body from the bottom of the bayou; her second assignment is to rescue her father from a lynch mob after he is falsely accused of kidnapping and killing a white girl, Lily. In addition, after the supervillain Bossman sets a trap in which Lee is impaled on pointed wooden pegs hidden in a pit, she comes back from the dead with the help of Bayou's magic potion ("Little o' dis. Little o' dat," as he describes the ingredients), which recalls another superhero trope: butler Alfred mending the wounds Bruce Wayne sustains while fighting as Batman. By also remediating the movie poster for Griffith's *The Birth of a Nation* in the first volume and by including several lynching scenes, Love and Morgan offer persistent commentary on the secret origins of the superhero genre.

Indeed, Love and Morgan make sure that readers recognize the significance of lynching for his story and for the superhero genre. One of the opening splash pages directly follows a depiction of a pastoral Southern scene (a quaint cabin shaded by big trees and surrounded by cotton fields reminiscent of one of the tableaus in the opening credits of Disney's *Song of the South* [1946]) and an image of a pickup truck racing past a sign welcoming people to Charon, Mississippi, with an image of the Confederate flag.[28] The next page features an insert panel of a lynching next to a "colored entrance" sign with a crow on top of it, symbolically linking lynching with the Jim Crow system of racial segregation (fig. 2.1). The lynching image shows two bleeding Black feet next

Fig. 2.1: Empty-faced onlookers, a truncated Black body, and an unusual perspective in *Bayou*.

to the trunk of a big tree, with five white men and a white child looking on.[29] The image includes many elements of a typical lynching photograph, among them the antagonistic juxtaposition of onlookers and victim. Yet it also challenges these photographs, refusing to show (and thus expose) the victim and resigning itself to depicting the bloody feet as a *pars pro toto* for the lynched body. In addition, the point of view differs from the positioning of the camera in more conventional images as well as from the distanced vantage points in the lynching tableaus displayed in Johnson and Pleece's *Incognegro* (7, 106, 108).[30] Located slightly lower than the dangling feet, the point of view in the initial lynching image in *Bayou* hovers over the earth in a position of powerlessness. Anchored near the lynched body and away from the white onlookers, the vantage point raises the question of who is looking at this image and who could historically have been positioned in the spot from which the image is rendered. It is certainly not a distanced position that would allow disassociation from the depiction, and it does not offer easy answers about who the victim might have been, who might have committed the crime, and who might have witnessed it.[31]

The five rather well-dressed and orderly looking men who gaze at the lynched body and thus also in the direction of the reader do not evoke the chaos and mayhem generally associated with acts of mob violence. Yet these men certainly are not innocent bystanders but are either members of the murderous mob or onlookers who relish witnessing the killing and its aftermath. That the faces of these figures are empty—Love and Morgan do not grant them individual facial features—removes the image from any particular historical context and gives it a transcendent, timeless quality. This event could have happened at any of a variety of places and times, the image suggests, yet it is not a random snapshot but rather one installment in an ongoing series. The photographic archive is filled with images of white audiences watching the lynching spectacle, and some photographs show children in attendance, so Love and Morgan's remediation is rooted in recorded history.[32] Nonetheless, the fact that the onlookers lack facial features should not be interpreted as Love and Morgan's unwillingness or inability to assign individual responsibility. Rather, leaving the faces empty but keeping the pencil sketch lines visible indicates that we are seeing a hand-drawn remediation of historical events, not merely a replication of famous lynching images but a repetition with a signal difference. As Hillary L. Chute notes about the "productive divide between what is captured with a lens and what is captured by hand," "a comics text has a different relationship to indexicality than [. . .] a photograph does. Marks made on paper by hand are an index of the body in a way that a photograph, 'taken' through a lens, it not" (20). This indexicality performs significant political work in *Bayou*, as it connects, via the graphic signs on the page, the body of the victim with Love's body as a graphic artist and the bodies of the readers as they hold the smallish, landscape-format comic book.

What is captured by Love's hand and colored by Morgan foregrounds the urge for a different aesthetics of lynching images that acknowledges this form of terror but struggles to find creative ways of defamiliarizing it to wring new meanings from past atrocities. The Black body has been traditionally subjected to what Wanzo calls the "situational grotesque," where it "would not be grotesque in itself without the conditions that either act on the body or provide a jarring contrast to it" (*Content* 147). Resituating it to new contexts—for instance, from black-and-white photography to a colorful graphic narrative—and giving it an alternative visibility, as Love and Morgan do when they reimagine Till as Billy Glass, may ease the burdens of the past without erasing them from the record. Kate Polak describes this as a process of "memory as curation" (150), where the past is understood not as a stable archive holding documents and images to be enlisted in the struggle for "purposeful forgetting" (147) but rather as a "process of narration" that "depends on the situation in which we're telling the story" (145). The point, then, is not so much "to *recall* what happened to the enslaved, the lynched, the marginalized" as "to understand that these memories have a clear and obvious place in the present" (175).

Thus, instead of flies circling the lynched body in search of flesh and blood, Love and Morgan surround the victim's feet with butterflies, which are often associated with beauty and grace as well as with resurrection and immortality (cf. Werness 63–65). By connecting the victims of America's lynching past with these beautiful insects, which serve as a leitmotif throughout the story, Love and Morgan contrast the popular association of Black bodies with the monstrous and the grotesque.[33] While these victims cannot be brought back to life, contemporary artists like Love and Morgan invest the victims' afterlives with dignity and purpose. Like caterpillars transforming into butterflies, the lynched Black bodies in *Bayou* become emblems of beauty and freedom in a complex process that Elihu Bey, the illustrator of Roland Laird and Taneshia Nash Laird's *Still I Rise*, describes as showing "the beauty in things that are not beautiful" (qtd. in Charles Johnson, "Foreword" xvi).[34] Moreover, this process exposes historical images of Black degradation to a new aesthetics that keeps this degradation in the public limelight but also claims graphic authority over it. This amounts to what Kimberly Juanita Brown calls "a totality of vision—the image and the afterimage" (*Repeating* 3) that refuses to yield primacy to the original images, insisting on viewing the original through its critical remediation.

Using the sequential structuring typical of comics, graphic narratives like *Bayou* employ specific mechanisms in portraying the afterlife of lynching photographs. Love and Morgan use the formal means of the medium to subtle but maximum effect. The panel that follows the initial lynching image is located on the next page, and it introduces a change from the static opening splash panels to the multipanel organization of the main storyline. (The use of opening splash pages is a typical element of superhero comics, so *Bayou* references this genre also on a structural level.) This panel shows Lee Wagstaff wading through the murky bayou, a "bad place" where "nuthin' good ever happened."[35] She is about to dive into the water in search of Billy's corpse; to stay connected to the shore, she is grabbing a rope in her right hand, with her father, Calvin, holding the other end for safety. The rope reaches out of the left side of the panel frame and thus points back to the previous page, reminding the reader that what is about to happen is literally and figuratively tied to the lynching logic of the Jim Crow South. When Lee discovers Billy's body, the noose is still wrapped around his neck, signaling his cause of death. As Lee is about to tie the rope around his foot, she sees what she believes is "Billy's soul on his way to glory," visualized as a Black body with butterfly wings.

Only nine pages (twenty-two panels) into the narrative, the reader has already encountered a whole network of lynching references, from the rope in Lee's hands to the noose around Billy's neck and from the hanged man's bloody feet to the young boy's foot around which Lee seeks to tie the rope. Love and Morgan follow the dense symbolism of the opening splash pages—the space reserved in superhero comics for particularly striking poses or overly dramatic fight scenes, superimposed here with such visual codes of the "gallant South" as cabins and cotton fields, the Confederate flag, Jim Crow, and lynching—with an alternative symbolism. This includes the butterflies (hovering around the bloody feet and then accompanying Billy's soul) as well as two

Fig. 2.2: The remediation of lynching photography as a beautified comic book panel in *Bayou*.

silhouette portraits of Lee as she is tying Billy's feet and then being dragged out of the bayou by her father, the white sheriff, and his helpers. Recalling Kara Walker's silhouettes ("Kara"; see also Saal), these portraits register artistic engagements with Black history beyond the comics medium.[36] These engagements, and Love and Morgan's equally critical work, challenge the power of an archive that solidifies the slanted perspective of white supremacy. In *Bayou*, this archive produces a newspaper report about Lee's loving and caring father as a "Negro suspect" accused of kidnapping and rape, and another article in the same paper maligns Calvin as "a big and burly wretch, with long, sinewy, apelike arms and massive hands." Love contrasts and contradicts this "evidence" from the supremacist archive with his African American characters' troubling intergenerational memories.[37]

Bayou contains additional lynching scenes, the most harrowing of which involves Lee as she is running away from Cotton-Eyed Joe, who has just eaten Lily. Hastening through the woods, Lee comes upon the lynched bodies of five men and a woman (fig. 2.2). All of them have been hanged, and the scene mirrors the reader's initial encounter with the lynching victim's bloody feet on the narrative's opening pages. Here, however, instead of a single, fixed image, Love and Morgan present a sequence spanning three pages and four panels. This alone unmoors the visual spectacle of lynching from its static nature, presenting the usually nonvisualized immediate prehistory and immediate aftermath of the lynching photographs. The creators certainly remediate existing photographs in their graphic tableau: one possible inspiration is a photograph of a 1908 mass lynching in Sabine County, Texas, that was printed as a postcard alongside a poem: "Let this a warning to all negroes be, / Or they'll suffer the fate of the DOGWOOD TREE" (qtd. in Whitted, "Intertextual" 200; *Texas*; cf. Hershini Bhana Young 283).[38] But Love and Morgan also offer what Whitted calls a "visual manifestation" of "Toni Morrison's concept of 'rememory'" ("Intertextual" 200), a kind of transcendental recall of all the violence inflicted on Black bodies across time and space. But showing Lee's shocked reaction at her first sighting of the dangling feet (one foot bare, the other still wearing a shoe) and again when she feels the feet closing in on her also counteracts the usually unshocked facial expressions of the white onlookers in many lynching photographs.

In the scene in which Lee encounters the lynched bodies, Love offers multiple layers of visual signification to complicate rather than replicate the visual impact. He once more includes butterflies and other swamp insects, adding a sense of movement (as well as swamp sounds) to the otherwise still tableau, and he creates visual echoes between the missing shoe on the victim's foot and Lily's shoe, to which Lee clings as a memento mori of the white girl. Finally, Love positions readers directly behind Lee, forcing them to share the girl's perspective and acknowledge the murdered bodies without insinuating that they could effectively take her place and experience the scene through her eyes (thereby preventing any simplistic form of sentimental identification with the girl).[39] This is a different kind of compulsory visibility. It compels readers to process the intrusion of lynching imagery into the pages of a DC comic by "visualiz[ing] precarious identification with the mute and illegible objects of traumatic history," as Chaney notes about Lewis, Aydin, and Powell's *March* (*Reading* 147). Curiously, Love gives the scene a celestial shine, which may be sunlight seeping through the foliage but is nonetheless suggestive of a heavenly glow, emphasizing the transcendental beauty of the Black bodies rather than their abjection, while the swamp sounds add a "phonic substance" (Moten 10) to the otherwise still images.[40]

Till's lynching is narrated in *Bayou*'s second volume. Instead of presenting readers with the result of the lynching—the dead Black body, which newspaper and television coverage of the spectacle funeral was forced to do—Love takes poetic license by graphically imagining the events that led to the murder. In doing so, he substantiates Raiford and Heike Raphael-Hernandez's notion of "identities that are at once 'rooted' in the 'real' of specific places, times, and circumstances, yet also 'routed' through fantasy and surreal imagination that unlock from those real temporalities" (Introduction 7). Love shows Billy being beaten and cut in a series of close-ups, extending the lynching over six panels. These panels both detail the acts of the faceless murderers and foreground Billy's (and thus, by implication, Till's) humanity as a defiant boy whose fears are mitigated by the mythical creature Mother Sista, who tells him, "Be brave.

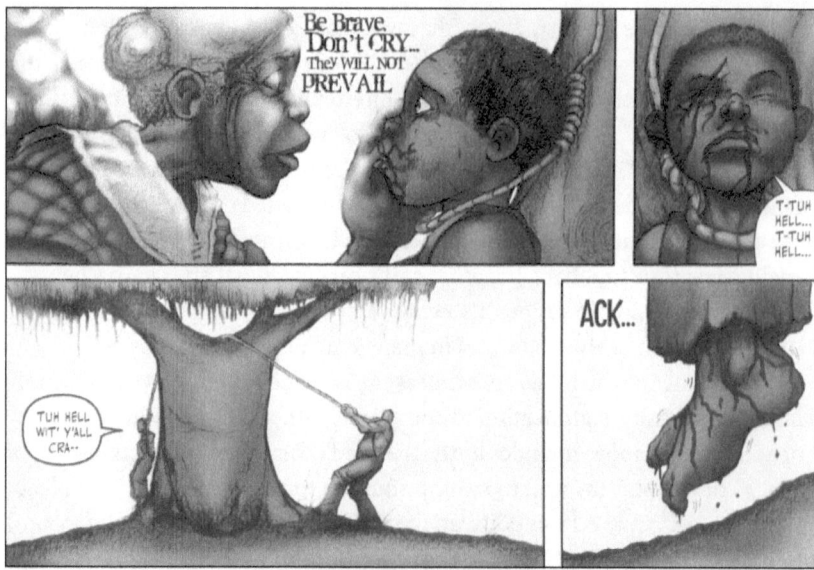

Fig. 2.3: The lynching of Billy Glass in *Bayou*.

Don't cry. They will not prevail" (fig. 2.3). Mother Sista's words may be read as the consoling message of a mythical mother figure or as a figment of Lee's imagination, but they point to Till's spiritual survival—his afterlife as part of US history in the extratextual world and his reappearance as a soulful creature in *Bayou*'s storyworld.

This alternative reading of the boy's death is followed by a yellowed lynching photograph that falsely accuses Billy of being a rapist and capitalizes on this mischaracterization: "Negro LYNCHED for RAPE, Charon, Mississippi, by Newman. $4 Dollars." Whitted suggests that "the postcard joins other intratexts—newspaper clippings on the opposing page as well as other documents from supposedly objective, trusted sources that reinforce the systemic dehumanization of black southerners" ("Intertextual" 201). She argues that "the photo creates a tension that may make viewers feel complicit as spectators at the scene of the crime," reminding readers that the motivation to photographically fix Billy's murder in a commercially available postcard and the comic book commodity that is Love and Morgan's graphic narrative both stem from the same culture—one that puts a price on Black bodies. According to Whitted, "*Bayou* does not allow readers to adopt this objectifying gaze for long. The comic takes us behind the blank faces of the lynching photo and beneath the newspaper account describing how Billy was disposed in the river, to arrive at the moment when Lee comes to retrieve his body and an ancestral figure named Mother Sista comes to reclaim his spirit" ("Intertextual" 201). Yet it is not entirely clear to me that the blank faces on the remediated postcard are those of the white onlookers normally found in lynching photographs. In fact, these men and the child depicted around the lynched body may be Black: they have racially ambiguous facial features, and the clothes and posture of the man in the black hat standing on the left next to the tree echo Love and Morgan's depiction of the mythical badman Stagger Lee elsewhere in the narrative. If they are indeed Black, the image would not be a remediated pro-lynching postcard but rather a more complex tableau of Black Southerners surrounding the murdered boy, whose face Love leaves empty perhaps to protect his dignity and/or to signal that lynch mobs reduced their victims to physical objects, detaching the Black body from the human being in order to torture and kill.[41] These figures stare into the camera and thus directly into the eyes of the reader, maybe to challenge a distanced gaze at the scene and prevent voyeuristic pleasure, demanding an ethical response that would work against what Hortense J. Spillers, Alexander G. Weheliye, and others have criticized as "pornotropic representations that eroticized black suffering" (Wanzo, *Content* 88; see Spillers 67; Weheliye chap. 6).[42] The difference is between a disembodied gaze that would allow the reader to escape a sense of involvement versus a kind of embodied seeing that disallows an easy escape from history (cf. Chaney, "Drawing" 195).

Further foregrounding the discrepancy between the flatness of the racist archive and the depth of feeling that lynching photographs and their graphic remediations may trigger, the page directly following the remediated postcard shows Billy's body being dragged underwater by a massive stone that his murderers have attached to a chain tied around his belly. The somber two-image sequence is contrasted by a short, overlaid newspaper notice that flatly states the facts of Billy's lynching but conveys nothing of its affective heft. Against the archival trace of the lynching, which falsely states that Billy had assaulted a store owner's wife (Till certainly did not assault the woman) and gives no details at all about his killers, thus essentially excluding Billy's story from the official record, the sequence depicts Billy's descent toward the bottom of the swamp, marking at once the cruelty of the crime and the dignity of the victim while positioning the reader in the role of witness to a historical atrocity.

In its uncanny temporality, the image further recalls the moment in Baker's *Nat Turner* when the baby is thrown overboard from the ship by the Africans who want to spare the child the horrors of slavery. While the baby's body is arrested in its fall toward death and thus suspended in an eternal death-bound state, Billy's descent into the swamp slows down narrative time, effectively preventing us from knowing how long it takes for the body to hit the bottom while also zooming out from the scene, only to zoom back in for an extreme close-up on the next page. By graphically accompanying Billy's descent, Love and Morgan heighten the affective powers of comics storytelling, making the most of the medium's spatial arrangement of time. They also highlight its epistemological limits, as the depiction can only insinuate but never instantiate the seamless sinking of the descending body.[43]

My central premise that lynching constitutes the superhero's origins and my assertion of its continuing relevance for the genre could be construed as an overstatement. But Love and Morgan include many instances that visually signify on superhero comics, as becomes apparent in the portrayal of Billy's lynching. Billy's death—the moment when the rope breaks his neck—takes place in a panel that shows only his feet, repeating one of Love and Morgan's most powerful visual tropes. Yet the panel also contains the sound word *ACK*, which signals the end of Billy's life and recalls one of the most significant events in superhero history: the death of Gwen Stacy, whose passing was marked by the sound word *Snap* in *Amazing Spider-Man* 122 (Roy Thomas). Gwen also dies at the end of a suspended rope, as Spider-Man shoots his webbing to break her fall, catching her feet but snapping her neck. Many fans mourned Gwen's death as a tragic event, and Love and Morgan are asking readers to connect Billy's death and thus the history of lynching with one of superhero comics' most tragic moments. In doing so, they juxtapose the death of a fictional character whose function in the comics had been to afford Peter Parker with a sex life (never explicitly shown) with the sexual politics of lynching, which punished any sense of sexual transgression (Till's alleged whistling at a white woman) with torture, dismemberment (including castration), and death. Love and Morgan's depiction of Billy as a child rather than a teenager works further against the fatal myth of a monstrous Black sexuality that can be contained only through lynching and other forms of racialized violence.

Cognizant of the long history of "black suffering and abjection" (Hershini Bhana Young 276), Love and Morgan's transformative treatment of Till's lynching suggests a need to unfix the public commemoration of Black history from narrative stasis.[44] *Bayou* does so by contesting established lynching iconography that tends to confine the Black subject to an eternal state of corporeal negation, displaying the Black body only when it becomes (or has just become) a corpse and archiving only the death and not the life of the victim. Love and Morgan launch this contestation through the fictional reanimation of Till as Billy Glass, affording Till an afterlife in the comic but pairing this historical figure with Lee, who "functions similarly as fugitive/revolutionary body whose resistance to racial subjection remakes the space of the bayou" (Hershini Bhana Young 276). If Lee becomes a superhero, it is certainly of a different kind: she is not equipped with superpowers such as the ability to fly, heal, or transcend the physical limitations of ordinary human beings but is nonetheless a fierce fighter for justice and a resilient figure of great beauty and compassion. As such, she embodies a superhero ideal distinguished from the white—often nationalist, sometimes fascist, and routinely supremacist—mold against which Love and Morgan carve her character.

LYNCHING SCENES IN KYLE BAKER'S *NAT TURNER*

Another fugitive and revolutionary figure appears in Kyle Baker's *Nat Turner*, a graphic adaptation of *The Confessions of Nat Turner* (1831). The historical Turner was the leader of an (in)famous 1831 rebellion in Southampton, Virginia. He was eventually caught and hanged, and Baker's retelling of these events culminates in a depiction of Turner's public execution.[45] Marc Singer has criticized *Nat Turner* for its "fight scenes and huge Frank Miller heroes who battle dozens of guys in silhouette," proposing that it is "not a history but a romantic fiction, a Frank Miller comic in slave-narrative drag" (qtd. in Fisher 260).[46] What Singer sees as a weakness may in fact be one of the narrative's major strengths, especially if it is read in conjunction with Baker's representations of the Middle Passage and of lynching. Wanzo observes that "African American agency is depicted almost entirely through black bodies in action" (*Content* 89), and superhero comics excessively stage the movement of bodies. However, Baker's portrayal of Turner's execution offers a substantially different take on conventional narratives of Black (super)heroism by contrasting his previous actions with the final stillness of his lynched body.

Superhero references beyond the fight scenes that center on the enslaved Will, who maims his white pursuers in Hulkish fashion, include the depiction of an African woman trying to escape her enslavers by leaping off a cliff (Baker, *Nat Turner* 27). Wanzo correctly notes that her leap "mimics images of flying superheroes" (*Content* 88), but the image also revises Flora's melodramatic suicide in Griffith's *The Birth of a Nation* and thus evokes the superhero's lynching origins.[47] Moreover, here too Gwen Stacy's death undergoes a critical reformulation, as the woman's descent is arrested in midair when one of her pursuers catches her right foot with his lasso—without snapping her neck (Baker, *Nat Turner* 28). Instead, the woman is shackled and chained to fellow captives, becoming one of the many nameless bodies caught up in the transatlantic slave trade. There is no escape from this large-scale system of human enslavement, the scene alleges.

Even though Baker's connection of the Middle Passage and slavery with the American superhero may be read as an analogy that threatens to curb historical complexity, it enables Baker's critical commentary on the superhero's secret origins. A disparity certainly exists between the momentous history of American slavery and a popular serial genre like superhero comics, but this history is so formative for modern entertainment and its wake so expansive that genres that do not explicitly deal with this history—and even those that even ignore or deny it—cannot escape its specter. Baker affords Turner an origin story that not only evokes Bruce Wayne's parental loss but also identifies Africa, the Middle Passage, and life in slavery as points of departure and narrative beginning. While young Bruce witnesses his parents' murder in a Gotham alley, slavery deprives little Nat of his parents. And while the traumatic experience inspires Bruce to become Batman and dedicate his life to fighting crime, Turner transforms himself into a religiously driven insurrectionist set on toppling the peculiar institution. While Bruce serves as a defender of the status quo, a masked vigilante who claims to uphold the law by frequently stepping outside its bounds and appealing to a higher moral code (arguably vested in the system of white supremacy), Turner attacks the status quo in his pursuit of freedom and racial justice. That Baker tells this story, including Turner's lynching, in a graphic narrative that stands apart from the superhero genre raises interesting questions about the genre's conceits. As *Nat Turner* suggests, a historically grounded Black superhero can be neither invulnerable nor impervious to killing and is thus at odds with superhero convention. At the end of the narrative, Turner and his posse have murdered fifty-five people, and he is hanged. This ends the dream of revolutionary change in the 1830s while also rejecting the superhero's possibility of endless renewal and serial fluxing.

The climax of the narrative, Turner's lynching, is carefully prepared by Baker's frequent recourse to ropes and chains, which suggests that Turner's demise is not a singular event but only one of the most visible and historically most glaring examples of white supremacist power over Black bodies.[48] The lasso that catches the leaping woman's foot, the shackles that bind the enslaved as an anonymous mass of property, and the whips wielded over enslaved Americans ensure that the final lynching scene appears not as a singular gruesome excess but as the logical culmination of systemic racial subjugation. Will's violence—he initially plays the role of the punisher for his owners but later chops off a white toddler's head in an act of violent retribution—is difficult to stomach but must be read against the stillness of Turner's lynched body.

Baker's treatment of Turner's execution appears in a segment, "Triumph," whose title evokes a sense of martyrdom while acknowledging the enslaved man's afterlife as the subject of *The Confessions of Nat Turner* and later retellings of his story, including Baker's. The page that precedes the segment's title page shows an image of the hanged Turner that foreshadows the events to come (fig. 2.4). It activates the shadow archive of lynching photographs, offering an iconic encapsulation of the scene by mobilizing the popular script. Subsequent pages, however, overcome the typical absence of a before and an after as well as reject the reduction of the Black rebel to the stillness of a corpse by offering a sequential depiction of the events.

Fig. 2.4: A peaceful Nat Turner as a counterimage to the abjection of Black bodies in lynching photography in *Nat Turner*.

Yet even the initial image undermines the iconographic tradition, as Turner's body is bathed in a ray of heavenly light and suggests spiritual absolution for his deeds (recalling the celestial shine of one of Love and Morgan's lynching scenes). Moreover, Turner's body is drawn in a slightly more realistic, less cartoonish, style than those of the surrounding white onlookers.[49] Baker thereby references the photographic archive while placing Turner in a different ontological realm from the spectators, perhaps memorializing the historical figure at the expense of the white mob, whose gleeful demeanor is, however, shown a few pages later.

While Baker anachronistically draws on photographs to reimagine Turner's lynching, Ho Che Anderson's *King* reproduces an actual lynching photograph, breaking out of the constraints of the comics medium to include archival evidence—a technique Baker also uses, but not in his portrayal of Turner's lynching. Anderson reprints Lawrence Beitler's photograph of the lynching of Thomas Shipp and Abram Smith in Marion, Indiana, on 7 August 1930 as well as the photographs of Till (29, 31), indicating a visual history that many African American creators (including Love and Morgan) engage. In "Creating King: Personal and Professional Reflections," Anderson recalls being profoundly disturbed when watching a documentary about King's life and encountering the photographic legacy of lynching: "I'm struck by the image of the burning cross, by the sight of men and women hanging by the neck from a tree. Even in death they are brooked no respect; their bodies are further defiled, spit on, pissed on, beaten, and finally set ablaze in grim echo of that burning icon or worship" (236).[50]

Seeking to overcome this visual record of defilement, Baker does not remediate lynching photography but associates Turner's death with the resurrection of Jesus Christ, an association Turner made when he countered Thomas Gray's question, "Do you not find yourself mistaken now?" with the question, "Was not Christ crucified?" (189). Turner's boldness so shocked Gray that he broke his pen.[51] In Wanzo's interpretation, the ensuing lynching scene depicts Turner "in profile, with a strong silhouette, and at peace." In contrast, "it is the white audience whose faces are contorted and grotesque. [. . .] Confronted with serenity, their smiles are wiped away. Baker's attentiveness to the face is an intervention into traditional slavery representations because the iconography was never about the face. The whipped back, the supplicating body, and other unindividuated representations contribute to a discourse that fails to see black people as individuated subjects" (*Content* 94). Wanzo emphasizes Baker's "attentiveness to the face," his repeated use of close-up portraits of Turner's head and facial features, which exude a sense of calmness that counters the conventional narrative of the Black brute who deserves to be killed for committing monstrous acts. Turner's death is symbolically charged with another ray of light and a falling leaf. The leaf marks the moment when Turner passes from the realm of the living into the realm of historical remembrance, when he becomes if not a superhero then at least a revolutionary figure whose story foregrounds the essential incompatibility of superhero conventions with narratives of Black liberation.[52]

LYNCHING SCENES IN OTHER GRAPHIC NARRATIVES

Baker's portrait of the lynched Turner becomes even more powerful when compared with Mat Johnson and Warren Pleece's *Incognegro*, which also enlists the narrative of superhero transformation, most obviously through its passing narrative, in which the light-skinned Zane Pinchback takes on the guise of the pseudonymous journalist Incognegro, who travels South to cover lynchings for a Northern newspaper. Tim Caron suggests that Zane, who is modeled on light-skinned NAACP activist Walter White and his lynching investigations in the South, is not "a superhero *per se*" but that his ability to become invisible (i.e., blend in with the white spectators) can be understood as a quasi-superhero power (143).[53] The narrative devotes a full page to the transformation from

Zane to Incognegro but ultimately cannot resolve the paradox of the Black superhero: as Chaney observes, "The superhero's unlikely influence makes ideological trouble for Pleece and Johnson" because "the comic book references in *Incognegro* strive for [. . .] recognition in a visual idiom historically reserved for white avengers" (*Reading* 149).⁵⁴

Incognegro also causes ideological trouble for the comic book superhero by showing the figure's inherent limitations. As Chaney notes, the narrative's two lynching scenes feature a "deliberately aerial view that obscures the lynched body," reflecting "the graphic novelists' retreat from the burdens of historical representation into fictive enclosures. [. . .] The distance afforded the viewer to apprehend these parts in their panoptic totality revises privilege, redefining it as a comforting, unifying distance from spectacle" (*Reading* 155, 156).⁵⁵ But the image also insinuates the perspective of a superhero arriving at the scene of the crime, descending from above to save an innocent victim. On the next page, the perspective is situated in the middle of the action, first through a close-up of the Black man's battered face and then in a semi-close-up that shows the victim's castration by a hooded Klan member. Chaney rightly suggests that the accompanying captions, which represent Zane's retrospective bragging about his role as a clandestine reporter, threaten to overwhelm the seriousness of the situation. But in combination with the fact that the gaze retreats further in the third panel, the changing perspectives and the captions suggest that Zane can merely cover the events for the press. He is ultimately powerless, unable to prevent the lynching. In that sense, he is also "de-masculat[ed]" (Mat Johnson and Pleece 8), deprived of the male superhero's strength and therefore forced to wield the power of the pen. This position is certainly one of weakness in the superhero genre if journalism is considered the provenance of Superman's squeamish alter ego, Clark Kent (a writer for the *Daily Planet*) and a mere side job for Spider-Man's alter ego, Peter Parker (who delivers photographs for the *Daily Bugle* and suffers from harassment by editor J. Jonah Jameson).

Zane survives—at a later point, a mob mistakenly assumes that his friend Carl is Incognegro and lynches him, with Zane forced to watch the murder—and transforms his experiences into writing, thereby allowing him to act simultaneously as journalist and witness. One major difference between Baker's depiction of Turner's death and *Incognegro* is Johnson and Pleece's inclusion of a photographer, who is walking into the scene in the opening splash page (something that occurs even more frequently in the *March* trilogy), with one spectator pointing his finger in the direction of the victim. The pointing man remediates a section of Beitler's photograph of Shipp and Smith, where an unidentified man at the center of the image locks eyes with the camera and directs the viewer's gaze toward the corpses hanging from the tree.⁵⁶ By adding the cameraman to the scene, Johnson and Pleece foreground the orchestrated and mediated nature of the event, making visible the apparatus that recorded the lynching photographs but that generally remains invisible to the viewer. In doing so, they indicate the relevance of Ariella Aïsha Azoulay's remarks about "the relation between the photo and photography, between the printed image and the photographic event—that is, the event that took place in front of the camera, constituted by the meeting of photographer and photographed object that leaves traces on a visual support" (*Civil Contract* 166).

The case of Turner's body in Baker's narrative differs somewhat. Apart from the fact that lynchings were relatively uncommon during slavery and were reserved mainly for "those who threatened the slave system itself" (Cone 4), they were also not subject to the widespread mediatization, enabled by technological advances in photography and its reproduction, that propelled postbellum lynchings across the nation.[57] Kenneth Robert Janken emphasizes "modernity and its attendant culture of consumption, which profoundly affected the lynching industry," including innovations in public transportation (trains, increasing car ownership) and communication technology (the "growing telephone network" and the "widespread appearance of inexpensive photographs") (xiv). Speaking of a "popularizing of spectacle violence and its commodification," which turned lynchings into "a shared cultural event," Janken writes that "notice of an impending lynching could be sent out in advance; participants and observers could organize special railroad excursions or car caravans; photographers could appear and quickly develop souvenir photos for those who wanted to send a postcard to family or friends or who were simply not lucky enough to procure a part of the victim's body" (xiv).[58] Turner's body may have been dismembered during the autopsy—perhaps for medical reasons, perhaps to sell off parts as souvenirs—and his life story survives in the truncated form of his confessions, but the event is much less a media spectacle, the process of its public mediation occurring much more slowly than in many later lynchings. Nonetheless, Turner's confessions—as recorded by Gray, bound into a book, and then available for sale—end up in the hands of a female Black servant, who, on the final page of *Nat Turner*, takes them into a dark corner of the doctor's house and starts to read. This may not exactly be an act of superhero fluxing as Fawaz describes it, but it narrates the transubstantiation of Turner's body into a cultural artifact that, like the lynching photographs and press coverage many decades later, will outlast his earthly existence, to be consumed by generations to come and to be transformed into a graphic narrative by Baker.

Nat Turner and *Incognegro* join other graphic lynching narratives in the search for "new frames of reference—new origin stories—that more effectively contextualize acts of African American social and moral distance" ("Blues" 237), as Whitted notes about McCulloch, Hendrix, et al.'s *Stagger Lee*, an exploration of that badman figure of American folklore. This narrative, too, repeatedly turns to lynching, since popular accounts hold that Stagger Lee was lynched. McCulloch, Hendrix, and their cocreators add a more irreverent tone to their depiction, such as when Lee replies to songs about the community's glee over his demise with the words, "Well, I ain't glad" (47). This deadpan response follows the narrator's more serious observation that "Black" and "white" songs (by Mississippi John Hurt and Woody Guthrie, respectively) offer different takes on Lee's execution.[59] "Apparently without exception," when the verse that narrates the lynching "is sung by a white artist, 'we' are all glad to see him die. When sung by an African-American, 'they' are glad" (47). This difference harks back to Susan Sontag's assertion that "no 'we' should be taken for granted when the subject is looking at other people's pain" (7) but also factors in the racialized logic of an America shaped by enduring fantasies of the color line that fail to account for "the complexity of black spectatorship" (Raiford, *Imprisoned* 48).[60]

Further, the images of the lynched Lee join the chorus of works that utilize the trope of the hanging feet as a *pars pro toto*, albeit with a significant twist. The second image on page 47, where Lee says, "I ain't glad," returns the lynched man to the realm of the living, at least in fiction, where he appears not as a remediated historical image but as a visualization of the song lyrics celebrating the Black badman. Lee is speaking back to the mob as well as to the narrator and the reader, breaking the fourth wall to foreground the complicated ethics and aesthetics of lynching. An image on the preceding page directs the reader's gaze into a gaping gutter in the middle of the page, flanked by drawings of Hurt and Guthrie. A little higher up, placed slightly in front of the two panels, are Lee's dangling feet. Centered on the page, overlaying the gutter, these feet reinforce the gap between Black and white versions of history. It is as if this massive gutter reimagines the color line as an abyss filled with Black bodies (or body parts) and this abyss opens directly in front of the reader.[61]

A final image from *Stagger Lee* juxtaposes the man and the myth (27). Whitted interprets this image of Lee Shelton versus Stagger Lee as a graphic enunciation of the figure's "dual identity" ("Blues" 240) that recalls the superhero's double life as a superpowered figure behind the mask and as an inconspicuous private citizen. According to Whitted, the image unmasks "Shelton's hypermasculine physical frame" as "a projection of social fears about black men" (240). Recalling the difference between scientist Bruce Banner and the enraged Hulk, the image nonetheless emphasizes the racialized subtext of the superhero narrative, pitting Lee Shelton's puny and passive-looking body against Stagger Lee's huge and menacing frame (extending toward the reader through the two pistols he is holding in his hands). Instead of a hero, Stagger Lee appears as a Black badman (Whitted, "Blues" 245), suggesting that a more conventional Black superhero might be a contradiction in terms. Of course, this juxtaposition also raises questions of agency, insinuating that the racial stereotype impinges on Black citizens' ability to act as full human beings and masters of their own lives. The fact that Lee Shelton's posture evokes the hanging body of the lynching victim whereas Stagger Lee's posture expresses the potentially deadly swagger of the Black brute narrows the options for inscribing the Black body down to two states of being that cancel out each other rather than enable superheroic transformation: puny victim versus monstrous perpetrator. No middle ground seems possible; the gulf between the races, visualized here as a gutter between Black and white narratives of deviant masculinity, is wide.

BLACK BODIES SWINGING: ILLUMINATING LYNCHING

Three images that are not part of a longer graphic narrative can help us place this lynching imagery in the broader scope of US visual culture: an image by an unknown photographer of the 1930 lynching of George Hughes in Sherman, Texas; *Death* (1934), a metal sculpture by Japanese American artist Isamu Noguchi based on this photograph (cf. Apel and Smith 50–52); and recent iterations of Miles Morales as Spider-Man swinging from rooftop to rooftop in Marvel's version of New York City. As Rushdy (*End* 65) has suggested, we should ask whether such images of "the spectacle of the dead black other" (Shawn Michelle Smith 138) can be "made to signify differently"(Raiford, *Imprisoned* 35).

Reflecting on his conflicted reaction to civil rights photographer Danny Lyon's *The Cotton Pickers, Ferguson Unit, Texas* (1968), which depicts Black prisoners hunching over rows of cotton, Teju Cole writes,

> Images make us think of other images. Photographs remind us of other photographs, and perhaps only the earliest photographs had a chance to evade this fate. But soon after the invention of photography, the world was full of photographs, and newly made photographs could not avoid semantic contamination. Each photograph came to seem like a quotation from the great archive of photographs. Even the earliest photographs are themselves now burdened by this reality, because when we look at them, we do so in the knowledge of everything that came after. All images, regardless of the date of their creation, exist simultaneously and are pressed into service to help us make sense of other images. This suggests a possible approach to photography criticism: a river of interconnected images wordlessly but fluently commenting on one another. ("Photograph")

Cole emphasizes the peculiarities of the photographic archive, whose contents are always already contaminated semantically because each image inevitably evokes other images as new images retroactively change the meanings of older photographs and older photographs shape the perception of new images. If photographs—and graphic narratives, which can evoke other graphic narratives as well as images across media—can "summon" other images and if this process is not restricted to any fixed chronology, a lynching photograph from 1930 and a commemorative sculpture from 1934 can summon twenty-first-century images of Spider-Man and vice versa just as Lyon's photograph "reaches back to images from the 19th century and before, and it stretches forward to the crouched and hooded prisoners of Guantánamo Bay" ("Photograph").

Cole is correct in proposing such a sweeping sense of interpictorial connectedness, but not all images are equal and not all associations between them are equally likely. Viewers are always embedded in a visual culture that favors some types of images over others and makes some connections more plausible than others. As Apel and Smith write about photographs, "Because their meaning is determined by context and circulation and the interests of specific viewers, the evidence in them cannot be fixed. Even though they seem to offer a stable glimpse of the past, their meaning changes over time and according to who is viewing and to what ends. What is seen and not seen in photographs depends on the cultural filters through which they are viewed, and on the repertoire of images that have shaped looking. Viewers always see photographs through other images" (15). Context and circulation, cultural filters, repertoires of images, and the proposition that all images are potentially connected and can summon other images from different media and times are the parameters for reading the three images discussed here. Even though any strict sense of temporal succession is to an extent moot in light of Cole's and Shawn Michelle Smith's notions of the photographic archive, the order in which we encounter images and the question of what other images they summon still matters. The secret origins of the superhero are seldom acknowledged, and explicit connections to the history of racially motivated lynchings are exceedingly rare, as is evidenced by a recent iteration of one of the most iconic of all comic book superheroes, Spider-Man. What other images can Spider-Man swinging from rooftop to rooftop conjure up? What other histories can the figure evoke? How can we see something in Spider-Man that may not ostensibly be there but that nonetheless shapes the figure? How can we make Spider-Man signify differently?

First, Marvel made headlines when the company decided to supplant Peter Parker in its Ultimate Comic line with teenager Miles Morales, who was created by Brian Michael Bendis and Sara Pichelli and is of mixed African American and Puerto Rican descent. Miles is a superhero of color, meaning that he represents the paradox of the Black superhero, and has evocative iconography, including a dark suit with a red web design and textured spider webbing. What seems like an innocent enough ethnic variation on the superhero formula

Fig. 2.5: Isamu Noguchi, *Death (Lynched Figure)*, 1934. Monel metal, wood, and rope on metal armature, 88 3/4 × 31 7/8 × 22 1/8 in. (225.4 × 81 × 56.2 cm). Collection of the Isamu Noguchi Foundation and Garden Museum, New York. The Noguchi Museum Archives, 00028. Photo: Sarah Wells. ©The Isamu Noguchi Foundation and Garden Museum, New York/Artists Rights Society [ARS]

takes on a different hue when it is confronted with the legacy of an altogether different image repertoire: lynching's shadow archive.

Noguchi's *Death* (fig. 2.5), based on a photograph of the lynched George Hughes, bears several uncanny resemblances to a comic book cover depicting Miles Morales as Spider-Man (fig. 2.6). The two bodies have similar shapes, with Spider-Man bearing a few more muscles than the sculptured corpse but still slim enough to appear as the sculpture's alter ego or contemporary encapsulation. The posture of the bodies underscores the resemblance, even though Spider-Man is swinging from one rooftop to another and grabbing his webbing (which looks rather rope-ish), in full control of his movements, whereas the sculptured figure hangs suspended from a rope and has lost all corporeal control.

The second image that completely shatters the cultural filter through which the superhero is conventionally viewed is the photograph of the lynched Hughes, a Black farm hand who had pleaded guilty to raping his employer's wife.[62] Before the photograph was taken, a mob of more than five thousand people gathered around the steps of the county courthouse and then went to the district court vault, where Hughes was being held. Despite resistance

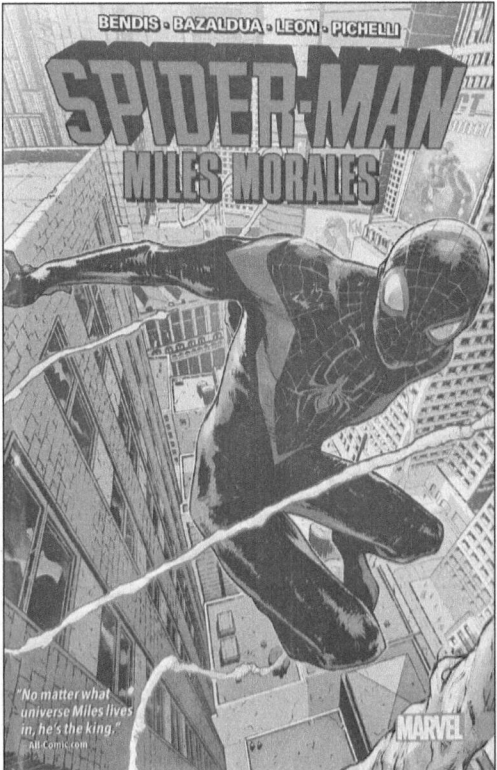

Fig. 2.6: The cover of *Spider-Man: Miles Morales*.

from Texas Rangers, the mob pried open the vault and tied Hughes to a tree. The killers then built a fire, mutilated the body (cutting off his penis), and burned it. Then, "in a display of unmitigated mob violence, they destroyed Black-owned businesses and ran the Black residents out of town, forcing them to take refuge in thickets, bushes, and sewers," Dustin Crawford writes. The anti-Black violence thus went far beyond the extralegal punishment for Hughes's alleged crime and encompassed the Black community as a whole. Moreover, as Wiegman reminds us, lynchings were always more than a form of violence directed at the individual victim, figuring the "victims as the culturally abject—monstrosities of excess whose limp and hanging bodies function as the specular assurance that the racial threat has not simply been averted, but rendered incapable of return" (81). The repeated destruction of Hughes's body—burned, hanged, mutilated—underscores this interpretation of a Southern white community reassuring itself of its ability to control and dominate the local Black population.

Focusing on Hughes's scorched remains, the photograph is a rather typical specimen of its genre in that it centers the dead body, illuminating it with the flash of the camera and placing a selection of more or less well-dressed onlookers in the frame.⁶³ Instead of watching the lynching, which had already occurred, these male spectators look directly into the camera, conveying no sense of shame as they pose for the shot. Indeed, as Apel and Smith note about the composition of lynching photographs, the camera flash exposes only a "partial scene of night, illuminating the aftermath of a grotesque carnival" and offering "only a glimpse of a longer ordeal" (12).

The New York Times described what had happened before the picture was taken, labeling it "Sherman Goes on a Rampage": "When the men who went into the vault shoved the body through the hole and threw it to the ground two stories below, women clapped their hands and a great cheer went up from the mob" ("Troops" 1). The article notes the presence of women at the scene (though none appear in the photograph) and describes the mob's lawless actions. Here, the "chaos of surrounding disorder" (Bukatman, *Matters* 56) that makes the superhero's armored body spring into action fuels the "frenzied rioters" ("Troops" 1), but when the deed is done and white supremacy has been reestablished, these rioters reform themselves into respectable-looking citizens posing for a picture with the corpse (as they do in Love and Morgan's initial lynching scene in *Bayou*). The photograph shows an arranged and staged scene, the reiteration of a lynching tableau with which the men in the photograph and readers who might have encountered it in printed media would have already been familiar (Apel and Smith 5, 7, 11–12).

Yet the photograph is also peculiar because it "stretches forward" (Cole, "Photograph") to images of Miles Morales as Spider-Man, facilitated further through Noguchi's metal sculpture. If we look at Miles Morales after having seen this lynching image and its commemorative sculpture, how could we unsee the connection? This moment of recognition is initiated by the visual resonances among these images of twisted Black bodies, but it is also the result of always already associating Black bodies with death in what Kimberly Juanita Brown calls a state of *mortevivum*, where "the hyperavailablity of images in media that traffic in tropes of impending black death [. . .] cohere around an ocular logic steeped in racial violence" that makes "any tragedy, any crisis, an opportunity for viewers to find pleasure in black peoples' pain" (*Mortevivum* xix).

I am not arguing that Marvel's reincarnation of Spider-Man as Miles Morales is directly expressive of the cultural logic of lynching or that even nonwhite superheroes are racist vigilantes in disguise. Nor do I contend that the makers of Spider-Man are consciously evoking the specter of lynching or that we can immediately see the connection. But visual inscriptions of the Black body are neither static nor endlessly transformative but oscillate between stereotypical fixing (the lynched Black body) and emancipatory fluxing (the agile Black superbody). "The relationship between superhero movies and the photographs from Black Lives Matter is not a matter of photographers trying to make protesters look like superheroes," Cole observes in a related context. However, "when such photographs emerge from the countless thousands taken at rallies and similar events, they are immediately recognized by a crowd already sensitized to their formal qualities" ("Superhero").

After the opening splash of *Spider-Man: Miles Morales*, reprinted in Marvel's first omnibus edition of the character, which shows the new Black Spider-Man as he is swinging across the New York City skyline, his webbing floating through the air, we follow the superhero's gaze as he encounters a scene of devastation and carnage. Destroyed buildings and limp bodies of superheroes strewn across Fifth Avenue evoke not only images of war-torn cities but also, in light of the genre's lynching origins, the chaos caused by a frenzied lynch mob (and maybe even the Greenwood district after its destruction during the Tulsa Race Massacre). The next page, a double splash page showing Spider-Man facing his new nemesis, the demon Blackheart, offers readers their first glimpse of Morales's body. His suit is torn at the shoulder and thigh, and we see his brown skin. This is quite a subtle introduction to the new Spider-Man's racial identity, which is further emphasized when he encounters the white Spider-Man (Peter Parker) shortly thereafter. This superhero does not supplant his white predecessor but is marked as the variation of an otherwise white norm.[64] Yet we can see that this new Spider-Man, while notably Black in his private life, still reaffirms the basic logic of the genre, fighting alongside other superheroes and talking excessively, often to himself during fight scenes, in the kind of jocular, funny patter readers would know from Peter Parker. This, then, offers a stark contrast to the Hughes photograph and Noguchi's sculpture, which exude a sense of stillness, a final muting of the Black body. Moreover, Morales's face is invisible underneath the mask, like Love and Morgan's Billy Glass on the remediated postcard, and the red webbing and spider on Morales's costume, in combination with the rope-like webbing, evoke the hanged and bloody corpse of the lynched person, interpretive possibilities that emerge when this Black Spider-Man is added to the "river of interconnected images" (Cole, "Photograph") that irrigates the shadow archive of lynching.

Along this line of interpretation, the name of the villainous Blackheart conjures up notions of blackness, while his proclaimed purpose—"subjugation"— evokes the specter of slavery and postslavery segregation. A few pages into the first issue, Blackheart tells Spider-Man, "When I take this planet, you will be my slave." To the left of these panels, Spider-Man is wielding his webbing and punching Blackheart, echoing the enslaver's rope breaking the African woman's fall in Baker's *Nat Turner* as well as the lash a hooded henchman wields over the swamp creature's tied body in Love and Morgan's *Bayou*. There is, of course, a signal difference: Spider-Man controls his body. He is the agent of his actions and eventually prevails, and the audience is expected to cheer him on. This does, however, not change the fact that directly after he has defeated the demon, a policeman points a gun in Spider-Man's face and threatens to shoot him in a scene that acknowledges the pervasiveness of police brutality and the efforts of today's activists to battle racial injustice.[65]

In one panel during the fight scene, a woman holds up her cell phone, filming Spider-Man's fight with the villain. Later in issue 2, when Miles is back in his room with his Asian American friend Ganke, they use an iPad to watch a YouTube clip posted by a girl who videoed the fight. The one image she puts up on the screen remediates the panel that shows Spider-Man ensnaring and punching the demon. These representations of recent technology, from cellphones to iPads, are crucial, as they both foreground and modernize the technology that had once recorded the lynchings (the analog camera) and further insinuate a genealogy from lynching to superhero.[66] Moreover, this new technology focuses on the Black body. Studying the footage of the fight, the girl has noticed Spider-Man's torn suit, and when she zooms in, the audience can see that "the new Spider-Man is brown. He's a kid of color. [. . .] Is he African American? Is he Indian? Hispanic? I don't know. But he's def color." This speculation forcefully acknowledges the nation's ethnic and racial diversity; from a historical viewpoint, it can also serve as a reminder that not all lynchings targeted African Americans.[67]

The language of Abel Meeropol's antilynching poem and Billie Holiday's recording "Strange Fruit," along with its visual and sonic evocations continue to resonate with contemporary artists and constitute one of the most powerful and historically intransigent touchstones for assessments of lynching.[68] The phrase raises difficult questions of agency. In the poem, the lynched bodies are "swinging in the Southern breeze," evoking the Black person as an object that has been violently rid of its agency. But when a Black Spider-Man is swinging through the cityscape and accepting great responsibility in his efforts to protect his community, agency is restored. By transforming the ghosts of lynchings past through sequential narrative, such attempts at recuperating lynching's lost agency through the process of graphic remediation remove these images from a state of passive archival storage and place them into the canon of active cultural memory (Assmann, "Canon" 103–4). In Sandy Alexandre's words, "The *emotionally* and *physically* moving image of what Holiday croons as 'black bodies swinging' works not merely as an effective synecdoche for lynching but also as a political signifier of and (indeed) a strange metronome for recording the very unsteady, unstable place of the black body scourged, dangling to and fro, on the American landscape" (27).

The notion of black bodies swinging thus expresses a sense of reverberation and resonance that may indeed be sonic, as in Holiday's performances of the song or in Fred Moten's notion of an image's "phonic substance" (197). As such, an image may unsettle the stillness of the photographic record.[69] Or as Alexandre puts it, "The pendulous positioning of 'black bodies swinging' [...] is quite resonant" (27). But the notion also foregrounds one of the central contradictions of US modernity: the fact that comic book superheroes can be celebrated as powerful beings with agile armored bodies, able to scale the heights of the (post)modern metropolis, swinging from rooftops and from building to building to save the lives of innocent people, while the nation's Black citizens must contend with lynching "as racial 'uplift' in its most perverse, literal, and structural form" (Alexandre 23).[70] When Bukatman speaks of the superhero's corporeal "mapping of the subject into a cultural system" (*Matters* 49), we are compelled to recognize lynching not only as the superhero's secret origin but as a phenomenon central to US modernity: as a publicly staged, photographically captured, mass-mediated, widely archived, and constantly remediated practice rather than an aberration of an otherwise progressive national narrative.

Such photographic but also televisual mediations of anti-Black violence and Black resistance are remediated in graphic narratives dealing with the twentieth-century civil rights movement. Questions of archival retrieval and creative fabulation are crucial in the graphic depictions of the movement and its key figures and events as they appear in works such as Lewis, Aydin, and Powell's mixture of autobiography and biography in the *March* trilogy and Anderson's biographical *King*, which carve out their own positions vis-à-vis the tropes of superhero comics and which are perhaps most remarkable for their didactic potential.

CH. 3

Chapter 3

CIVIL RIGHTS PEDAGOGY

Michael A. Chaney opens his analysis of the first book of John Lewis, Andrew Aydin, and Nate Powell's bestselling three-part graphic memoir *March* (2013, 2015, 2016) with reflections on his students' reaction to its depiction of the US civil rights movement: "Monumental though Lewis and his text may have been, [...] neither he nor his memoir could satisfactorily rebuke the injustices associated with what seemed" to be "a daily report of chilling police shootings. Many demoralized students wanted a graphic text with more bite." He continues, "They wanted a text in aggressive proportion to the fatal onslaught of state-sanctioned brutalities perpetrated against innocent, often poor black subjects. Contrary to the unsteady consensus of the moment, *March* was perceived to be eking out a message of ultimate trust in the state and state processes." Some students even "found *March*'s narrative framing of political optimism staggeringly inappropriate to the Uzi spray of racism from media outlets. Beyond harboring an agenda of black political conformity, *March* smacked of chauvinisms both political and otherwise, tying the graphic memoir to a type of black resistance widely thought to be ineffectual in our contemporary moment" ("Misreading" 25). Gauging the students' reaction as dissatisfaction with "the text's political failings and historical fetishes" (25), Chaney recognized a yearning for more confrontational narratives and more aggressive political options than Lewis's philosophy of "good trouble," exemplified by the dignified forms of nonviolent protest that defined significant parts of the civil rights movement. At a time when police killings of Black Americans dominated the news and the Black Lives Matter movement was gaining traction, *March* celebrated nonviolent forms of resistance, expressing a continuing belief in the American political system and turning to the lessons of the past instead of addressing the problems of the present.[1]

When the first book of the trilogy appeared in 2013, however, Barack Obama was still president and Oscar Grant, Michael Brown, Miriam Carey, Eric Garner, Mya Hall, John Crawford, Tamir Rice, Freddie Gray, Sandra Bland, Lajuana Phillips, Ahmaud Arbery, Breonna Taylor, George Floyd, Ma'Khia Bryant, and many other victims of anti-Black violence were still alive (see Rankine, *Citizen*). Of course, a racially motivated backlash against Obama had existed from the very beginning of his presidency, and racially motivated killings of African Americans certainly predated the 2010s.[2] Nonetheless, Black civil rights legend and US congressman John Lewis, his aide Andrew Aydin, and graphic artist Nate Powell found sufficient inspiration in Obama's election to present Lewis's lifelong struggle against racism and discrimination as the prehistory to and precondition for the nation's first Black president by suffusing the narrative with images of Obama's first inauguration.[3] Lewis and his collaborators celebrate what the books pitch as the long-term impact of the civil rights movement, especially of the Selma, Alabama, campaign, in which Lewis was involved as a member of the Student Nonviolent Coordinating Committee (SNCC). In *Selma's Bloody Sunday: Protest, Voting Rights, and the Struggle for Racial Equality* (2017), Robert A. Pratt affirms that "the election of the first African-American president in 2008 perhaps reflected the apex of black political power" (3–4), which supports *March*'s presentation of the civil rights movement as an eventual success story. Yet Pratt also sees a paradox according to which Obama's election revealed "a rapidly changing political landscape [that] prompted white conservatives to resort to a new campaign of voter restrictions" (4). Pratt's conclusion "that the lessons of Selma have yet to be learned" (4) complicates the historical trajectory proposed by the *March* books. This chapter investigates the political power as well as the potential shortcomings of the books' vision of civil rights history not only as it emerges from the narrative itself but also in contradistinction to other graphic accounts of the movement, particularly Ho Che Anderson's biographical *King* (1993–2002; 2010).[4] *March* and *King* differ substantially in terms of their intended teachability, with *March* addressed to a young reading audience and marketed as a resource for teaching and *King* positioned more as an artistic engagement with King's life and legacy and less as a didactic text.

Writing more than a decade before Pratt and around the same time Obama prepared his bid for the presidency as a speaker at the 2004 Democratic National Convention, Jacquelyn Dowd Hall maintained that rather than unfolding along a straight line, the civil rights movement developed from a "dialectic between the movement and the so-called backlash against it." This backlash "arose in tandem with the civil rights offensive in the aftermath of World War II" and did not end in the 1970s, as common movement history alleges, but "culminated under the aegis of the New Right" ("Long" 1235). Among the

March books' most prominent political failings may thus be their underestimation of the backlash against the long-term advancements of the movement, a backlash that gathered steam during Obama's "eight years in power" (Ta-Nehisi Coates's phrase), broke out into the open with the election and reelection of Donald J. Trump, and undermines the optimism of the trilogy.[5] *King* is much more reserved about claiming the movement's lasting impact, ending the historical storyline with King's assassination in 1968 and spending a significant amount of space detailing the leader's self-doubts, the mixed outcome of the activism by the Southern Christian Leadership Conference in Chicago, as well as the mounting pressure on King and his associates from a more radical new generation of activists embracing Black Power (see Peterson).

Scholarship on *March* has only begun to account for the trilogy's political thrust, and work on *King* is even more scarce. Those who have engaged with the *March* books have noted their entrenchment in what Jacquelyn Dowd Hall defines as the "dominant" or "master" narrative of the movement, the "confining of the civil rights struggle to the South, to bowdlerized heroes, to a single halcyon decade, and to limited, noneconomic objectives" ("Long" 1234).[6] Yet Katharine Capshaw, Michael A. Chaney, Joanna C. Davis-McElligatt, Susanna Hoeness-Krupsaw, Markus Oppolzer, Jorge Santos, Johannes C. P. Schmid, Leah Milne, and other scholars have also shown that we should not discard the powerful lessons the *March* books may teach us about this pivotal period in US history and its contested memorialization. The trilogy may sit uneasily with some observers because of its preoccupation with the past and its advocacy of nonviolent resistance. Advertising it as a "roadmap for another generation" (as Lewis did on *The Late Show with Stephen Colbert*) and dedicating it "to the past and future children of the movement" (as the dedication of each of the three books reads) may strike others as overly didactic—which *King* is explicitly not, even though it still teaches lessons about civil rights. *March*'s focus on the "classical" phase of the movement—bracketed by the US Supreme Court's 1954 *Brown v. Board of Education of Topeka* decision and the civil rights legislation of the mid-1960s—and its relative neglect of "the interweavings of gender, class, and race" (Jacquelyn Dowd Hall, "Long" 1235) certainly indicate its historical conservatism.[7]

Despite these caveats, the *March* books deserve critical scrutiny as they join other graphic memoirs of the movement, such as Mark Long, Jim Demonakos, and Nate Powell's *The Silence of Our Friends* (2012) and Lila Quintero Weaver's *Darkroom* (2012), in transposing movement history into graphic form (see Santos, *Graphic*). Lewis's works reiterate but also complicate the master narrative not so much by extending what Waldo E. Martin Jr. and Patricia A. Sullivan criticize as "a limited, all-too-familiar repertoire of events, places, and people" (xiv) but by negotiating the many layers of mediation and remediation that constitute what has come to be popularly understood as the civil rights movement—that is, by remediating what Leigh Raiford in her work on civil rights photography calls the "media-mediated events" ("Come" 1150) that shape the mainstream sense of the movement.⁸ Using the tools of graphic storytelling, the *March* books and *King* to an even greater extent alert readers to the highly mediated "process by which history is told and retold, produced and reproduced, and narrativized and renarrativized before becoming enshrined in our memories and disseminated for sociopolitical purposes" (Santos, *Graphic* 3). These works profess "a metacritical awareness of history as an editorial and curative process" (3) by constructing vastly different accounts of the movement that also serve as a critical engagement with its initial mediation, particularly through photographs and television footage, and as a retroactive memorialization through graphic remediation.⁹ Moreover, while the *March* books elicit a fairly straightforward "metacritical pedagogy" (Santos, *Graphic* 8) that empowers them as didactic tools for investigating popular representations of US history, the workings of social protest movements, and the moral questions that continue to haunt the present, *King* represents a murkier, less easily teachable, case.¹⁰

In that sense, graphic memoirs of the civil rights movement are usefully contrasted with biographical accounts of this period in US history, whose claims to historical relevance cannot be as easily legitimated through the narrator-protagonist's personal knowledge and recollection of the events and which therefore tend to foreground the difficulties of historiographic reconstruction more proactively than first-person accounts. Juxtaposing the *March* trilogy (itself a mixture of Lewis's autobiography and Aydin's and Powell's bio/graphical investment) with Anderson's more expressly biographical *King*, which casts a less affirmative and more ambivalent glance at its titular figure, illuminates not only different facets of civil rights memory but also different techniques of (re)constructing history through the means of graphic narrative. Recalling his initial approach to his subject, including its convoluted production and publication history (three parts over the course of a decade), the London-born, Canada-based Anderson writes, "In a way I'm ambivalent about the subject matter. King, while a figure I respect, isn't someone I've spent much time thinking about. Part of me feels like this should be done by someone with a lifelong passion for the man and the movement. That person is not me. Another part of me thinks perhaps that kind of objectivity is exactly what this endeavor needs. Being an outsider may afford me a slightly different perspective on America" ("Creating" 236). While he admits to eventually becoming more "immersed in the material" (236) and notes the difficulty of not being "in awe of my subject" (237), Anderson is also explicit about his attempts to find the right emplotment (Hayden White's term) for King's life story: "I'm still figuring out how exactly one goes about chronicling another man's life, using his existence as the raw material for some orchestrated drama" (235). Anderson moves from the notion of chronicling a life, evoking its traditional affiliation with unstoried chronology and lists of important events and people (as also theorized in White's *Metahistory*), to the idea of an orchestrated drama, with its fully self-conscious rearrangement of historical information for the benefit of telling a particular story. But Anderson goes one step further: "I decide I want it to be epic. Because the parameters of King's life demand the story be epic. And it's easy to be epic in comic books. A cast of thousands costs no more than a sore drawing hand" (235). The end result may be epic mostly in its density and complexity and not so much in its treatment of King as a heroic figure: in *King*, that figure vies against other decidedly nonheroic images.

Taking these metahistorical reflections as a starting point, this chapter investigates the representation of civil rights history in *March* and *King* by heuristically distinguishing between the didactic impulses of these books and their usefulness as didactic resources in and beyond current pedagogical settings. I agree with Jessica Boykin's assertion that "comics are radically invitational in their explicitly incomplete construction" and generally support her claim that "conventional memorials typically function pedagogically, while comics situate the reader as a collaborator" (69) but move beyond the implied antithesis in civil rights memorialization (pedagogy versus collaboration) by pinpointing these works' collaborative pedagogical implications. How do they invite and enlist their readers in acts of historical reconstruction through graphic storytelling, using what Chaney calls the "inherently pedagogical comics form," premised on a focus on "the method rather than the content of the comics" (*Reading* 7), to propose their politics? As the title of Hasan Kwame Jeffries's *Understanding and Teaching the Civil Rights Movement* (2019) suggests, recognizing how these works excite, engage, educate, encourage, enable, empower, enlist, and therefore make their readers understand civil rights history is crucial to thinking more specifically about implementing their lessons in the classroom and in the wider public sphere.[11]

DIDACTIC IMPULSES IN *MARCH*

The *March* books tell the life story of US congressman John Lewis from his birth into a poor family in rural Alabama to his seminal role in the Black freedom struggle of the 1950s and 1960s. As a former president of SNCC and the only member of the Big Six who was still living when the graphic memoir was published, Lewis was at once an eyewitness to some of the movement's most important moments and a historical figure whose legacy the *March* books celebrate.[12] We can identify his triple role as participant, politician, and autobiographer as a prerequisite for the narrative since Lewis's life is inextricably connected with the national past and because the retelling of this past is both a personal and a political project. *March: Book One* visualizes this connection in an image of the present-day Lewis spending time with a visitor and her children in his office in Washington, DC. He is gesturing toward a wall filled with photographs as he is about to tell a story from his childhood. Lewis is used to narrating such stories, it seems, and has already assembled a comic-book-like version of his life—a sequence of framed images—on that wall. Instead of pretending to offer a strictly factual account of the movement, the scene introduces a moment of self-awareness about its status as a graphic narrative that remediates an already mediated biography. This narrative self-consciously emerges from the congressman's personal experiences and convictions but pursues a broader agenda, offering lessons about the civil rights struggle especially for the younger generation.

The scene also teaches us a lesson about genre. As a graphic memoir, *March* belongs to the realm of creative nonfiction and differs from scholarly studies of the civil rights movement in terms of how the story is narrated and of the evidence enlisted. This generic middle ground—personal recollection, historical account—opens up a productive line of inquiry into the nature of creating autobiographically inflected history in graphic narrative. This is crucial because scholarly accounts and graphic nonfiction rely on the same archive of images, especially photographs and television footage that "have shaped and informed the ways scholars, politicians, artists, and everyday people recount, remember, and memorialize the 1960s freedom struggle" (Raiford, "Come" 1130). That we are perusing a collaborative work by Lewis, Aydin, and Powell further complicates notions of autobiographical authenticity and access to personal memory. Powell's visuals set the tone of the narrative, though the artist was born after the movement's heyday and, like Aydin, cannot draw on his own memories to craft the story.

A scene in *March: Book Two* addresses this complex mixture of recounting, remembering, and memorializing the movement. The year is 1962, and Lewis, as SNCC's field secretary, is leading a protest against a racially segregated public pool in Cairo, Illinois. Presenting a subjective account of this event would have afforded Lewis special narrative authority and political credibility as an eyewitness, but the depiction foregrounds the fact that readers' access to the event depends on multiple layers of mediation and remediation. A small insert panel on the left shows photographer Danny Lyon, a white Jewish New Yorker who covered the protest for SNCC's Photo Agency, which was founded to retain maximum control over the documentation and presentation of the group's activities and deliver raw material for media campaigns (Raiford, "Come" 1139). Lyon took the photograph that became "probably the most popular poster of the movement" (*Book Two* 120, quoting Lewis with D'Orso [1998] 192), and Powell remediates the image on the same page.¹³

In 1963, SNCC used a cropped version of Lyon's photograph for the poster, adding the slogan "Come Let Us Build a New World Together" and selling ten thousand copies (Raiford, "Come" 1133). The visual depiction of the scene in *March* differs from the rest of the page, indicating a chain of mediations and remediations from photographic image to poster to graphic memoir. This chain precludes any clear distinction between the historical event, its initial photographic mediation, and its later narrativization for various political purposes. The sequential presentation of the event motivates a look into the many media representations of the movement, turning readers into active sense-makers by prodding them to grasp the nature and scope of the movement's visual archive. This includes SNCC's practice of hiring Lyon and other "field workers with cameras" (Raiford, "Come" 1139) whose photographic records were not only widely circulated but also repeatedly framed by different institutions, from SNCC's "propaganda machine" (1141) to *The New York Times*, *The Washington Post*, and other newspapers.¹⁴

As active sense-makers, attentive readers will discern a discrepancy between the original photograph and the poster, both of which *March* evokes. Whereas the poster centers three kneeling figures (a girl flanked by John Lewis on the viewer's left and another young man to the right), the photograph shows another girl to Lewis's right, though half of her face and body are outside the frame.¹⁵ Transforming Lyon's photograph into the poster, SNCC cropped the image and erased this other thirteen-year-old girl (cf. Lyon 26) from the visual narrative, literally placing her outside the political frame. But *March* rehabilitates her as a central figure of the protest by providing a longer sequence of events already recalled in Lewis's autobiography, *Walking with the Wind: Memoir of the Movement*, visualizing "what happened just after that photo was taken" (*Book Two* 120). In the extended scene in *March*, a pickup truck is racing toward the girl, who is standing in the street, transfixed by the approaching vehicle. The truck suddenly stops before speeding away, leaving the shocked girl behind.

This sequence represents a complex co-presence of personal memory, recorded history, and creative memorialization. Recorded by Lyon's camera in 1962, remediated in the following year through the SNCC poster, recalled in prose memoirs by Lewis and Lyon (who includes the poster but not the original photograph; see 26) in the late 1980s and early 1990s, and then re-remediated through Powell's drawings, the Cairo protest has been widely visualized and narrativized. But as the scene in *March* demonstrates, the photograph and the poster provide only glimpses of the event; they are snapshots whose iconic power stems precisely from their status as single images that absent more than they present (Lyon took other, lesser-known photographs that day). Moreover, it is impossible to gauge to what extent Powell's representation is based on the photograph, the poster, and/or Lyon's and Lewis's memories of the moment, which also complicates Lewis's status as an autobiographer since memories of the past intersect with multiple media images. While *March* may be complicit in the master narrative of the movement, it reveals a reliance on different forms of mediation and remediation, venturing beyond dominant images and including protest outside the South.[16]

March, then, is "a memoir that also serves as a recruitment tool for political activism" (Oppolzer 235) rather than merely as a graphic documentation of US history. We must therefore situate the trilogy vis-à-vis a vast archive of verbal, visual, and audiovisual treatments of the movement, where emancipatory narratives continually struggle against hegemonic stereotypes of blackness and against a long history of racist caricature to challenge the "historical archive of racist visualization" (Chaney, "Is There" 73).[17] In this context, the photograph at the end of each of the *March* books that shows Lewis with his arms around the white Aydin and Powell as they stand on Selma's Edmund Pettus Bridge, the scene of the pivotal showdown between the Black protesters and the state troopers in 1965, is reconciliatory. By presenting the long-term effect of this showdown as a friendship that "is not only interracial but also cross-generational" (Schmid, "Graphic" 7), the photograph strikes a note of reconciliation and dreams of a racially inclusive America, dismissing opposing notions of divisiveness and racialized hatred. It superimposes an image of harmonious collaboration over the violence and suffering that are so vividly stored in the civil rights archive.

These tensions also shape the graphic memoir's didactic impulses. Aydin named "inspiring young people to get involved and also teaching them the tactics" as the books' central aim (Sarah Jaffe). In another interview, he claimed, "Our goal was to use this to teach and inspire another generation" (Hudson). The cross-generational framing of the narrative and the yearning to teach the lessons of the past—especially nonviolent resistance to state-sanctioned discrimination—suffuse the paratextual packaging of the three volumes, bringing readers closer to the narrative without immersing them in it. Gérard Genette defines paratext (and especially its more narrow variant, peritext) as everything that is materially adjacent to but not directly part of the narrative proper—book titles, cover illustrations, epigraphs, introductions and afterwords, footnotes—and understands it as "a zone not only of transition but also of *transaction*" (2) between the text and the outside world, between author and reader. The *March* books invite us into this zone with a profusion of paratexts—for instance, by choosing a title that wavers between historical event, movement tactic, and moral imperative. The word evokes forms of mass protest like the March on Washington for Jobs and Freedom (1963), where King delivered his "I Have a Dream" speech and where Lewis voiced his indictment of American racism, as well as the march from Selma to Montgomery, which serves as the climax of the trilogy. The word also captures the ethos of nonviolent resistance: marching through segregated areas without fighting back against white aggressors, meeting racist hatred with Christian love. As an imperative, it calls on young Americans to embrace marching as an appropriate means of voicing dissent, urging them to battle injustice through peaceful activism. Finally, the Bloody Sunday confrontation between the protesters and Alabama state troopers took place in March, adding a temporal dimension to the title's associative web of meanings.[18]

The trilogy paratextually presents Lewis's life story as a paean to an exceptionally US type of heroism that rewards a nonviolent marcher with a political career and ultimately produces a Black president. To justify this trajectory, *March* evokes the rags-to-riches story and its African American variant, the story of racial uplift in the tradition of Booker T. Washington. The inside flap of *Book One* features a photograph of Lewis and a biographical sketch that identifies him as an "American icon." His "commitment to justice and nonviolence has taken him from an Alabama sharecropper's farm to the halls of Congress, from a segregated schoolroom to the 1963 March on Washington, and from receiving beatings from state troopers to receiving the Medal of Freedom from the first African-American president." Lewis may have started small by honing his preaching before the chickens on the family farm (*Book One* 27–28), but he becomes a civil rights leader whose speech at the March on Washington receives extensive narrative space in *Book Two* (166–71). President Lyndon B. Johnson invites Lewis to witness the signing of the Voting Rights Act of 1965 (*Book Three* 240–43), and Lewis embraces Obama at the beginning of his inauguration ceremony (*Book Two* 51).[19] The signing of the Civil Rights Act first appears on page 85 of *Book Three*, which shows Johnson at his desk in the Oval Office signing the document with politicians and King and other civil rights leaders standing directly behind the president. The page combines a summary of the act with Lewis's personal commentary (he stayed in the South because he felt he was "in the middle of a war"). This image as well as the later depiction of the signing remediate popular photographs of the event, signaling once more the graphic narrative's historical and pedagogical objectives.

This uplift narrative locates Lewis's "personal, political, and moral success [. . .] within the democratic institutions of the United States" (Schmid, "Graphic" 5). Calling Lewis's resistance "revolutionary nonviolence" and suggesting that the "principles and tactics" developed by the movement "remain vitally relevant in the modern age," the sketch characterizes Lewis as both a revolutionary activist and a member of the political establishment. Yet what can, with some legitimacy, be criticized as an overly optimistic narrative that downplays the problems and demands of the present (voiced quite prominently by the Movement for Black Lives) and silences more aggressive efforts to fight for justice (such as the Black Panther Party) can also be read as an act of resistance against a master narrative that claims the demise of the movement in the late 1960s by embracing a problematic "rhetoric of color blindness" (Jacquelyn Dowd Hall, "Long" 1238).

The cover images of the three books highlight the tension between the uplift narrative and SNCC's "radical pedagogy" (Jacquelyn Dowd Hall, "Long" 1253) by conjuring up key methods of the movement: sit-ins, demonstrations, freedom rides, and political speeches.[20] These methods were widely documented at the time, but instead of merely translating archival material into graphic form, the *March* books interrogate the process of historical documentation. Lewis appears in all three cover images, first in the center of the boycotters at the lunch counter, then as a speaker at the March on Washington, and finally as one of the protest leaders on Bloody Sunday. While he is clearly presented as the key figure, his graphic avatar seldom dominates the image. He is usually depicted as part of the movement, appearing as a leader whose effectiveness depends on fellow activists' willingness to risk their lives by joining the boycotts, signing up for the rides, attending speeches, and marching. The covers thus support Santos's conclusion that *March* is "more than the memoir of one great man—it is the biography of a movement" (*Graphic* 51). They mobilize the same tension between personal success story and political history that informs the subtitle of Lewis's *Walking with the Wind: A Memoir of the Movement*. In fact, while the cover of the 1998 edition of *Walking with the Wind* focuses singularly on Lewis, playing into the "great man" approach to history, the 1999 edition combines Lewis's portrait with a photograph of the standoff on the Edmund Pettus Bridge, prefiguring the top-to-bottom structure of the first two *March* covers. The covers of the prose autobiography and the *March* trilogy therefore mobilize the dominant narrative of the movement—the focus on "charismatic personalities (who were usually men) and telegenic confrontations [. . .] in which white villains rained down terror on nonviolent demonstrators dressed in their Sunday best" (Jacquelyn Dowd Hall, "Long" 1236)—while suggesting that there is more to this narrative than meets the eye.

Equally noticeable is the trifurcated *mise-en-page* that shapes all three covers even as their architecture shifts from the first two books to the third. The cover of *Book One* shows the protesters at a lunch counter at the bottom (fig. 3.1). The title and the names of the authors divide the lower third of the cover from its upper third, which shows marchers with their heads and upper torsos truncated. The image in the upper third of the cover evokes a photograph by Charles Moore that shows some of the 1965 marchers from the waist down (Durham 155). This is not the first time we encounter marching feet and legs in graphic narratives of the movement. Long, Demonakos, and Powell chose this motif in *The Silence of Our Friends* (126), and Weaver uses a similar depiction in *Darkroom* (140), suggesting that these narratives share a common iconography.[21]

Fig. 3.1: The cover of *March: Book One*.

Chaney holds that the "arrangement of images and texts" on the cover puts the "tension between past and present, words and pictures, doing and looking on prominent display" ("Misreading" 28). The only way to come to terms with this tension is to perform repeated acts of closure, which Scott McCloud defines as "observing the parts but perceiving the whole" and as "mentally completing that which is incomplete based on past experience" (63). Acts of mental completion induced by the cover of *Book One* include the need to attach full bodies to the marchers' feet and connect these bodies with the civil rights demonstrations. These acts entail processing the possible disjuncture between the reductive assumption that all protesters were African American and the presence of a white boycotter in front of the lunch counter. Enticing an active reception by figuratively reopening the closed lunch counter through a call for closure, the cover challenges readers to consider their own implication in the nation's history of racial segregation. It places viewers behind the counter, on the "white" side of history, while setting them in opposition to the two white servers, whose bisected faces stare from the left and right edges of the image and yearn to be made whole.

Fig. 3.2: The cover of *March: Book Two*.

The cover of *Book Two* retains the structural setup of the first cover, portraying Lewis in midspeech at the bottom as he faces the Washington Monument and addresses the crowd gathered around the Lincoln Memorial Reflecting Pool on 28 August 1963 as part of the March on Washington (fig. 3.2). The upper third of the image remediates a photograph of a burning Greyhound bus transporting freedom riders to Alabama, taken near the city of Anniston on Mother's Day, 14 May 1961 (see Arsenault). In conjunction with the lower third, the cover signals the movement's multipronged tactics, which included political speeches and grassroots voter registration, and announces the situation's increasing intensity, including a violent backlash, as things are literally heating up. The rising tension in the overall narrative is indicated by the middle section of the cover, which includes the title and authors' names tilted slightly up toward the right. Chaney maintains that "the dual cover imagery of the first two books champions a recovery project that refuses to differentiate between causes and effects," since it is impossible to determine whether the incineration of the bus caused Lewis's appearance in Washington or vice versa ("Misreading" 33). Without a certain telos, different temporalities collapse "into the paradoxes

Fig. 3.3: The cover of *March: Book Three*.

of revolutionary time," embodying a "chronotopos of black revolution" (35) that is steeped in the popular iconography of the movement but refuses to be limited by it. Juxtaposed with more recent media images of burning vehicles, such as those of the Ferguson unrest after the killing of Michael Brown on 9 August 2014, these images might indeed evoke Amiri Baraka's notion of "nation time," the "sense that African Americans are no longer outside of history but at its center" (Raiford, *Imprisoned* 126; cf. Chaney, "Misreading" 35).

The cover of *Book Three* almost abandons the established structure by positioning the Black protesters even more clearly at the epicenter of American history (fig. 3.3). It presents only a single image of the marchers heading toward heavily armed state troopers, and the title/author section is almost vertical. Rather than establish a contrast to the first two covers, the image offers a compressed visualization of a critical moment in US history that retains a sense of division even as it seeks to transcend it, suggesting the possibility of progress confronting resistance. In fact, the cover literalizes Genette's definition of the paratext as a zone of transition and transaction by depicting the confrontation between troopers and protesters as a shift in US race relations (transition) while creating an image that admonishes us to turn the recognition of racial injustice into an inspired form political protest (transaction). Placing television cameras and press photographers at the sides of the road, the cover introduces into the equation a third party that does not appear on the covers of the first two books but that played a significant role in changing public sentiment toward the movement. In this historical moment, race-based segregation—evoked through the trifurcated structure of the covers, with the book title serving as a metaphorical color line—is about to give way to a more inclusive sense of national cohesion. As the marchers approach the state troopers, who have already drawn their weapons, this is a hopeful scene only if we understand its significance as a memory of the movement's *longue durée*. We already know that the marchers will be beaten and that more action and resolve will be required to gain at least some measure of legal equality through federal legislation, let alone full social and economic justice.

Ironically, the image does not bring readers closer to the action but chooses a cinematic high-angle viewpoint that takes them away from the confrontation. This perspective transports them from the sense of immediate implication created by cover of *Book One* and the broadened scope of *Book Two* to an "ennobled perspective of the voyeur," foregrounding a "voyeuristic tension that has been anticipated by the presence of the media" (Chaney, "Misreading" 39).[22] It changes the focus from the movement to its mediation and memorialization and casts readers either as voyeurs, as Chaney suggests, or as metacritical observers becoming aware not only of the movement but also of its initial mediation and ongoing remediation. As voyeurs, readers might appreciate Powell's beautiful graphic rendition or find solace in the movement's successes. As metacritical observers, however, audience members must account for the narrative framing and material packaging of this account. The covers nudge readers in this direction by including simulated remnants of tape on the books' spines and what looks like the brittle binding of a library edition or a textbook. These books are meant to be used like the Fellowship of Reconciliation's *Martin Luther King and the Montgomery Story* (1957), a comic book that served as a political primer and tactical handbook.[23]

Moving from paratext to the text proper, *March* establishes a network of references that contextualize the narrative and communicate historical awareness. The books facilitate further research by including a list of dos and don'ts Lewis composed as protest guidelines for members of SNCC (*Book One* 97), by reprinting the Reverend Jim Lawson's statement of purpose for SNCC (*Book Two* 118), and by devoting a whole page to a visually striking portrait of King in a cell above which hovers a central sentiment from his "Letter from Birmingham Jail" (1963), published by news outlets such as the *New York Post*, *Liberation*, *The New Leader*, *The Christian Century*, and *The Atlantic*: "I submit that an individual who breaks a law that conscience tells him is unjust, and who willingly accepts the penalty of imprisonment in order to arouse the conscience of the community over its injustice, is in reality expressing the highest respect for law" ("Negro" 77). The page design showing the guidelines reinforces the sense of readerly identification with Lewis's perspective on the events, as the white space reaches outside of the unframed book page and thus toward readers, who, following the logic of the visual arrangement, are holding the page in their hands (a thumb is pressing on the page's upper left corner). *March* also incorporates declarations by segregationists like Birmingham chief of police Eugene "Bull" Connor and Alabama governor George Wallace (*Book Two* 48, 124–25) as well as passages from political speeches by Lewis, King, and their fellow civil rights advocates (*Book Two* 166–73). *Book Three* devotes seven pages (107–13) to Fannie Lou Hamer's televised testimony at the Democratic National Convention in 1964, which follows speeches by New York governor Nelson Rockefeller and Arizona senator Barry Goldwater at the Republican Convention (102–3). Frequent radio announcements, television broadcasts, and newspaper headlines underscore the trilogy's claim to historical accuracy and suggest an archive of audiovisual and printed materials waiting to be accessed for a better understanding of the movement.

March reinforces its status as a didactically powerful graphic narrative through its evocation of the sounds of the movement, which fosters a multimodal and multimedia approach that can be useful in the classroom and can reinforce the idea that efforts toward historical reconstruction and recuperation must grapple with the sights and the (at times less reliably documented and archived) sounds of history as well as open up different pathways for students to engage with the material. In *Book One* (103) and *Book Three* (120, 214), protesters sing "We Shall Overcome," the movement's unofficial anthem, whose lyrics express the pining for a life of peace and a belief in eventual triumph over racism. Powell's depiction of the song includes snippets of the lyrics that visualize the singers' dedication to a common cause and their affirmation of community, captured by the promise to walk hand in hand. Powell uses "singing balloons," stylized like wafting bands that meander across the page and connect people via visualized sound. These bands function as a leitmotif, a stylistic device that Powell introduced in *The Silence of Our Friends* (and that Anderson had already used in *King*), but they also retell a familiar story. They remind us that any account of the movement should include the music that sounded protesters' fears and hopes and infused the fortitude to withstand physical and mental abuse.[24] The final stanza of "We Shall Overcome" clarifies the connection between future and present, aspiration and action. The lyrics state that the singers are not afraid *today*, marking the moment when the hymns' spiritually grounded hope for a better time in heaven transitions into an expression of earthly resolve.

From a present-day perspective, such references to the movement's music may seem overly optimistic, especially since they support a teleology that ends with Obama's presidential inauguration. The message seems to be that the election of a Black man to the nation's highest office means that the protesters have finally overcome the racial restrictions of the past. *Book One*, Chaney notes, "closes on a note of optimism, of narrative and affective simplicity. The problem at the beginning, of there being no voice loud or legible enough, is solved by the end. Whose American voice speaks louder than that of our black president? History is progressive in this formulation, [. . .] and it is also optimistic in a conservative way, perhaps even a radically conservative way. Social problems are to be solved by the official political system" ("On the Nature" 54). Yet as Chaney also acknowledges, history in *March* is not always linear, and closure may only be temporary. The musical references underscore this sense of nonlinearity. Having been sent to the notorious Mississippi State Penitentiary, better known as Parchman Farm, on charges of disturbing the peace, the protesters sing to preserve their dignity and irritate the guards. Singing becomes audible as a nonviolent form of resisting dehumanization, creating solidarity among the inmates (*Book Two* 103–7). It transforms linear prison time, meant to force them into submission and accepting racial segregation by arresting their ability to act on their beliefs, into nonlinear protest time, subjectively shortening the jail experience by investing it with a transcendent purpose.

The most politically resonant musical reference occurs in *Book Two*, when soul singer Aretha Franklin performs "My Country 'Tis of Thee" at Obama's inauguration (79–82). Not only does the phrase "let freedom ring" echo King's "I Have a Dream" speech, but while the patriotic lyrics are flowing from the top left of page 80 to the lower right of page 81, the narrative of American greatness is undermined by six rectangular insert panels. These panels document activists' historical sacrifices and segregationists' violations of the nation's foundational creeds. On the page that precedes Franklin's depiction on the steps of the US Capitol, the song's titular opening line appears across the carnage at a Greyhound station in Montgomery after a white mob attacked a group of protesters there in 1961. Powell uses the same technique on the next page, where the line "Oh let freedom ring!" carries us from the image of the singing Franklin in the narrative present to the throwing of a Molotov cocktail in the past. According to the sequential logic of comics, Franklin is pointing back to the past, signaling a need to remember history, whereas the white hand that throws the bomb gestures into the future and thus reminds readers that believing that American racism has been overcome would be foolish. Musical representation therefore complicates the notion of linear time and the hope for a progressive movement toward a better America.[25] History is linear as well as circular: "Rather than creating paradox," Chaney suggests, "that seeming contradiction reveals how our conception of past experience depends upon circularity, recursivity, even simultaneity" ("On the Nature" 55).

DIDACTIC IMPULSES IN *KING*

Identifying the didactic impulses of Anderson's *King* is a tricky task. Anderson aims his narrative at an older, politically more mature readership than do Lewis, Aydin, and Powell, whose narrative is explicitly geared at a young adult audience. Thus, Anderson's civil rights activists speak a language that is much closer to the colloquial and vernacular expressions of strategy sessions behind closed doors, where jocular banter and a liberal amount of cursing (including use of the N-word by movement activists and in other contexts by white supremacists) takes place. In addition, while the *March* trilogy was specifically created to encourage young readers to become politically active, *King* began as a biographical assignment and ended up as a treatise on the history and historiography of the civil rights movement. According to Anderson's "Creating King: Personal and Professional Reflections," he knew that Gary Groth of Fantagraphics wanted "a bio," but Anderson's goal was "to tell a broader tale, one that discusses violence versus nonviolence, one that puts into stark opposition civil disobedience and a more militant stance that embraces arms" (235–36). But as Anderson explains, this broader tale (which contains little information about King's childhood and thus departs from the standards of conventional biography) is based on historical sources that include biographies of and scholarship on King as well as on the two-part television documentary *Eyes on the Prize* (1987, 1990). After the bibliography at the end of Anderson's essay, he acknowledges, "All that reading and I still messed some shit up" ("Creating" 242). Anderson is interested in doing justice to what Boykin describes as "not only King's complexity but also the complexity of the movement" (74) but recognizes that historical accounts, however well intentioned and thoroughly researched, will inevitably get some things wrong.[26]

Perhaps the two most curious and epistemologically fundamental didactic impulses in *King* follow from Anderson's decision to tamper with the archive of photographic and televisual images and his choice to amend this appropriation with the recurring talking heads of "witnesses," who relate their own, often divergent, memories of the civil rights leader's personal and political impact. These witnesses first appear on a double page at the beginning of the narrative (directly after the prologue, which shows King as a boy serving his father, and the title page), and they are clustered into a rigid three-by-three-panel grid that affords them equal status and significance. This structure implies that all of these perspectives are valid or at least deserve to be heard.

Fig. 3.4: The witnesses in *King*. Page one of two.

Seven of the nine speakers are male, in keeping with the overall dominance of male figures and perspectives in civil rights historiography (fig. 3.4). At least some of them are modeled on existing photographs, though not necessarily of actual witnesses of the movement.[27] Moreover, Anderson's use of a "noir style of chiaroscuro and high contrast lighting" (Chaney, "Drawing" 181),

Fig. 3.4: The witnesses in *King*. Page two of two.

with its references to Harlem Renaissance artist Aaron Douglas, can make it difficult to identify a witness's racial affiliation.[28] In some cases, overtly racist and white supremacist commentary gives the speaker's identity away, while linguistic markers such as "the brother" (8) and some facial features suggest an African American speaker.

Observing that these "witnesses function like a Greek chorus in how they narrate events in King's life" and "provide a diverse array of perspectives that draw attention to the ways King's contemporary audience perceived and interpreted his actions" (74), Boykin acknowledges both the dramatic orchestration of Anderson's work and the creator's interest in multiplying the interpretive possibilities for King's life and his historical impact rather than promoting a single message. The effect of this lesson is heightened in light of Anderson's other formal choices. First, by containing these witnesses within the panels of his rigid grid and showing their talking heads as close-ups, Anderson simultaneously evokes the kind of footage readers would know from the conventions of documentary film and produces a prison-like atmosphere that at least figuratively puts these witnesses behind bars, encasing them within their individual political cosmologies and personal views of the world. Boykin associates these recurring tableaus with the "voiceover in a documentary" and suggests that the witnesses appear "frozen in time" in a static state (however often a witness speaks, the same image always appears in the panel) that disrupts "the narrative to create breaks in the text" (75, 77).[29] Boykin's conclusion that "Anderson has created a sense of recorded testimony as opposed to witnesses directly speaking to the reader" (75) offers another important lesson: finding meaning in US history and in the lives of figures like King requires more than contentment with already established views; we must actively work to determine our standpoint in an ongoing critical dialogue with the complex and potentially confusing array of archival materials and personal memories. The fact that some witnesses express uncertainty about their firsthand recollections—"but I probably remember wrong" (49); "if memory serves" (57)—indicates the need to consider an array of sources rather than a single speaker or authority.

Apart from adding this chorus of witnesses to the narrative, Anderson devotes quite some space to the philosophy of the movement. One effective way of outlining King's nonviolent philosophy are excerpts and paraphrases from some of his famous speeches and essays: in the context of the activists' push to elicit violence from Connor's men in uniform, Anderson's King declares, "We will meet your physical force with soul force. We will not hate you, and yet we cannot in good conscience obey your evil laws" (127), the wording of which is taken (though not verbatim) from King's sermon "Loving Your Enemies." King's sentiments, which include references in the comic to "bomb[ing] our homes" but promise that "we will not only win our freedom" but "will win you in the process" (127), appear as boxed captions over grainy reproductions of photographs of police violence.[30]

The pages that feature King's declaration show a close-up photograph of Bull Connor ordering his forces to "let 'em have it" (124) and then a series of some of the most iconic historical images of protesters being sprayed by water hoses and attacked by police dogs. In addition to his depiction of one of the movement's most prominent events, Anderson here and elsewhere includes elements of verbal violence that works like *March*, with its target audience, must exclude. "Motherfucker, what the hell you think this is?" a furious Connor yells at King at the outset of the confrontation. "N*****, you ain't no Israelite, and this ain't no Jericho" (124), the police chief spews before ordering his men to attack the protesters.

While Anderson includes such moments of aggressive action and hateful verbiage, his narrative is not really action-driven. He believes that comics "really allow for exploring the minutiae of character because they don't always require a jolt a minute as some other popular media do, they're much more forgiving if a scene is slow in building to its resolution" (Dale Jacobs 372). Moreover, we know from the beginning that the story will end with King's assassination, and even the main events of the movement—the Montgomery Bus Boycott, the freedom rides, the March on Washington, John F. Kennedy's assassination, Johnson's signing of the Civil Rights Act and Voting Rights Act—are expected elements of any King biography. Anderson acknowledges this by emphasizing his role in reshaping King's story: "The life of Martin Luther King was the script. I had to be the director," he notes, insisting on his own aesthetic impact by continuing the cinematic analogy: "These are my camera angles, my close-ups, my decisions of when it's going to be black and white or in color or whatever" (Dale Jacobs 381).

That *King* remains beholden to the master narrative of the movement at least to some degree is underscored not only by the fact that King's death marks the end of the narrative but also by the relatively long buildup to the assassination (whose depiction borrows from cinema the look through the rifle scope, the red dot over King's neck, and the following subjective point-of-view images that dramatize King's fading out of consciousness). This includes a three-page segment with extensive references to King's final speech before his death, which is riddled with premonitions of his premature demise (213–15). However, some of the material Anderson includes might be new to readers, and the narrative also pushes against the boundaries of the master narrative by devoting much space to King's discussion with more radical leaders such as the national director of the Congress of Racial Equality (CORE), Floyd McKissick, and SNCC chair Kwame Ture (Stokely Carmichael) (176–79), who challenge King's nonviolent ethics and trigger his dismissal of the Black Power slogan (176–81).

What takes on more weight than the scattered action scenes is the repeated and extensive depiction of strategy talks, either when King and the man he seems to trust the most, Ralph Abernathy, discuss policy or when a larger group of activists plots the Southern Christian Leadership Conference's campaigns and debates the details of every next move. During these extensive and complex talks, Anderson's *King* offers readers much food for thought. "I think sometimes we orchestrate these things as though they were no more than elements in a story ... It's easy to forget that these events will have real meaning in peoples [*sic*] lives" (104), King muses as he and his team are planning the Birmingham protest. Coupled with his public speeches, which Anderson covers at length and which position King as a reformer rather than as a revolutionary in the strict sense of the term—to gain support for the Montgomery Bus Boycott, he tells his church audience, "Our protest is a revolt with the system, not against it. We are out to reform, not tear down" (44)—these strategy debates illuminate a much more conflicted and much more ambivalent King than the one most readers would know from more mainstream accounts of his life.

Another significant didactic impulse in *King* is Anderson's treatment of this comics biography as an opportunity to reflect on the person and the movement's historical and contemporary mediation. As such, *King* prefigures the engagement with the movement's media strategies and the intersecting and sometimes oppositional strategies of the press (especially newspapers and television) in the *March* books. *King* goes one step further by offering the reader what Chaney calls a form of "negotiated vision" that "conjoin[s] the seen and the unseen" ("Drawing" 180) and favors a collage-like and at times quasi-cubist and altogether heterogeneous stylistic approach to visualizing the personal and professional contradictions that made King's life so remarkable.[31] For one, *King* is filled with media images—from better- and lesser-known photographs of central figures and events, including King's family life, to graphic remediations of television footage—that Anderson treats as archival raw material for his revisionist historiography. Moreover, the narrative includes many instances in which we see and hear King giving interviews to reporters, formulating the Southern Christian Leadership Conference's strategic goals and seeking to frame these goals in a manner conducive to their attainment.[32]

Chaney thus has a point when he speaks of the narrative's "citational and expressionistic design," a design that produces a sense of provisionality and contradicts the professed certainty of more conventional accounts of civil rights history (e.g., in museums, high school curricula, college textbooks). Chaney discerns in *King* "an alternative methodology that posits value based on a fundamental codependence between the archival images comprising King's life and the graphic novel's mechanics for re-circulating, re-framing, and re-animating them" ("Drawing" 180). If rather than reproducing factual information from King's biography, Anderson's work "lays bare the processes of public memory and hagiographic memorialization that constitute these images as facts at all" (180), *King* becomes a metacritical investigation of national history-making that calls on readers to acknowledge how history is made after the fact and how different forms of mediation shape this endeavor.

Television screens appear repeatedly in the graphic novel. The four pages covering King's interview with Murray Myron (59–62) switch back and forth between a point of view provided by the television cameras and a perspective somewhere in the studio that focuses on the camera equipment. In the middle of this sequence, the perspective shifts into the control room, where King's and Myron's heads, captured by the cameras, appear on the engineer's monitors and where the two men can also be seen through the engineer's window as they sit in the studio talking to each other. The remediated footage further includes extreme close-ups of King's mouth and his hand as he puts out a cigarette, both of which seem atypical for a television interview. These images, along with a large panel that shows, in stark colors, the bombing of King's house (whether in King's imagination or an image on the TV screen), paradigmatically represent the "negotiated vision" this graphic narrative affords as an enticement for readers to think about the "re-circulating, re-framing, and re-animating" of historical images.

DIDACTIC IMPLEMENTATIONS: FROM *MARCH* TO *KING*

Asked about "how to use *March*—whether to teach it as a primary and secondary source, or something in between," Andrew Aydin downplayed the metacritical challenge: "We worked really hard to make sure that every detail was as accurate as possible. We've been in contact with at least a dozen of the photographers from the movement. You know, folks who were there during the March on Washington, who were there during the early days and the later days. We used an incredible amount of reference photos to make the visuals as accurate as possible" (Heaney). Aydin's touting of historical veracity is certainly apt, but it also rubs against the trilogy's more complex negotiation of media images, personal memory, and collective testimony. If the movement is "the most documented, photographed, and televised political phenomenon in US history" (Santos, *Graphic* 2), achieving historical accuracy must be more complicated than Aydin suggests because the polyphony and polysemy of available images and their incessant remediation make it impossible to reconstruct any singularly authentic narrative. And if we approach the trilogy from a metacritical perspective that recognizes its repeated remediation of already mediated images, we must develop a metacritical pedagogy that is aware of its active role in (re)shaping public memories of the movement.

Any engagement with civil rights memory participates in "a process of negotiation [. . .] in which meaning of the movement is constantly remade," Romano and Raiford note (1). The discrepancy between Lewis's promotion of the narrative as an entertaining, quasi-superheroic work—"It's dramatic.

It's alive, it's movement, it's action" (Joseph Hughes), he suggested, evoking the line "It's a bird, it's a plane, it's Superman"—and Aydin's insistence on its documentary ethos point to larger questions about "memorializing the movement" that prove especially vexing "in the arena of popular culture" (Romano and Raiford xiii, xii; see also Hoeness-Krupsaw).[33] But these questions are no less vexing in the realm of education, where instructors must make difficult and politically volatile decisions about how to frame their lessons and how to access movement historiography with their students.[34] According to Lewis, the books specifically appeal to educators—"It's a lot of fun to get out and talk about this book, and to see the reaction of people, especially teachers, librarians and children" (Joseph Hughes)—who might embrace them as an opportunity to teach new lessons about US history, a decision that brings a specific set of questions to bear on this particular text: Is it factually accurate? Is it accessible and thus productive for teaching? Is it pedagogically valuable? Is it suited to the expectations and sensibilities of the intended audience?[35]

Judging from the wealth of available teaching guides, *March* is present in US high schools and colleges and universities, which is not surprising considering the popularity of graphic novels and the pedagogical prominence of civil rights history as well as the fact that *March* is a prizewinning publication (a National Book Award and two Eisner Awards).[36] Its publisher, Top Shelf Productions, produced a teachers guide aimed at "Grades 6–12" and "extensible to higher education" (Gutierrez) that didacticizes *March* in a way that is compatible with state and national curricular standards. The guide includes before-reading, during-reading, and after-reading activities as well as worksheets, discussion questions, and links to online sources.

The books already come with their own didactic devices, as events, places, and people are explicitly named to encourage further research. *Book One* includes what appears to be a portrait of the Reverend Jim Lawson in profile in front of a black background as Lewis contemplates the power of Lawson's vision. Three short sentences—"His words liberated me. I thought, this is it ... This is the way out" (78)—hover above Lawson's head, and the page design could be taken as an inspiration for student-created single-image portraits of civil rights figures and sentiments associated with them. *Book Two* contains biography pages of A. Philip Randolph (146) and Malcolm X (149) that can be used as models for assignments to produce similar pages for other members of the movement, whereas the FBI's flyer announcing that CORE field workers Michael Schwerner, Andrew Goodman, and James Chaney were missing in Mississippi and short biographies of the activists in *Book Three* (70) introduce more unlikely heroes of the movement and, through the overall page design, deliver memento mori for these slain activists in graphic form. (The full story of their disappearance and murder is recounted a few pages later.) *Book Two* also reprints the original draft of Lewis's speech at the March on Washington, which students could contrast with the less confrontational speech he delivered.[37]

While King is certainly a looming presence in the trilogy, his "I Have a Dream" speech gets relatively short thrift in *Book Two*. Of the sixteen pages devoted to the March on Washington, only the final double splash page (172–73) shows King speaking: a white light encircles his frame and suggests a sense of spiritual intensity (bringing light into a dark world). But King's words are not part of the depiction; instead of unfolding his vision, the narrative presents Lewis's recollections of the speech, expressing the sentiments of the movement ("Dr. King made plain all of our hopes, our aspirations [. . .] everything we dared to imagine about a new America, a better America") as they are channeled through King's charismatic persona but voiced by the narrator in control of the narrative. In addition, King's conciliatory dream, with its hope "that one day on the red hills of Georgia, the sons of former slaves and the sons of former slave owners will be able to sit down together at the table of brotherhood," is announced by a speech balloon reaching into the image ("Tell 'em about the dream, Martin") but is preceded by six full pages of Lewis's speech. Marking the difference between Lewis and King, Lewis's oratory ends with an imperative: "We must say: 'Wake Up, America! Wake Up!!'" (171), advocating being awake rather than dreaming. The inclusion of the draft of Lewis's speech, by contrast, points to the larger project of the trilogy, which is to reiterate in a popular medium the "consensus memory" (Romano and Raiford xv) of the period while at least partially depicting "what is missing from the master narrative" (Santos, *Graphic* 3). As such, the *March* books are particularly valuable teaching tools that can build on students' familiarity with "the deeply flawed version of the movement" (Jeffries 4) that is frequently taught in high school and even college as a starting point for a critical engagement with the historical material and its many mediations and remediations.

Such critical engagement could include discussion of lesser-known members of the movement such as voter registration organizer Bob Moses, one of the key figures behind the March on Washington; the gay Bayard Rustin; and women activists Ella Baker, Diane Nash, and Fannie Lou Hamer (cf. Santos, *Graphic* 55), all of whom *March* depicts.[38] Asking whether the trilogy goes far enough in addressing the "hidden meanings [and] omissions" of the master narrative and in supplanting its male hero specter with "a multiplicity of participants across time, gender, socioeconomic backgrounds, and races" (Alridge 9, 4) could lead to productive class debate. At one point, *Book Three* directly addresses the gender imbalances of the movement but does not clearly take a stance. Citing from Mary King and Casey Hayden's internal SNCC paper "The Position of Women in the Movement" and noting that "as more and more women joined the movement, the question of gender equality took hold as powerfully as any challenge within SNCC," the page concludes with Ture's notoriously sexist quip, "The position of women in SNCC is prone" (140). This comment invites discussion about sexism and misogyny within and outside of the movement, perhaps by way of reading bell hooks's *We Real Cool: Black Men and Masculinity* (2004).[39]

A particularly fruitful way to approach the *March* books would be to follow the archival pathways created by their intertextual and intermedial references. Of course, readers must be at least aware of this archive before they can "locate the many pasts of Lewis's trilogy, its multiple presents, and complicated racial futures" (Chaney, "Misreading" 26), but the books themselves are explicit about which lines of inquiry to pursue. The story of the freedom rides told in *Book Two* could, for instance, launch an investigation into the particulars of these efforts as well as into how they contribute to the movement's iconography. The fact that the memorialization of the rides includes concrete objects—especially buses as signifiers of racial segregation on public transportation—offers opportunities to explore the material legacy and continuing visualization of this historical period.

Other examples include the popular photograph of Rosa Parks taken in December 1956 as an emblem of the successful Montgomery Bus Boycott and the photograph of the blazing Greyhound bus near Anniston, Alabama, that is remediated on the cover of *Book Two*. *King* also covers Parks's arrest and includes photographic elements to show the boycott's consequences. However, Anderson (40) uses a different 1956 photograph taken by Dan Weiner: a white woman alone on a bus. In addition, Anderson exposes the language spoken by the police (one of them yells the N-word on the bus) and by the other Black people present at the scene ("Fucking cops"; "Tired of this shit" [36]), indicating an expressive dimension of the protest that might be closer to the historical moment than the more sanitized depiction in *March*.

Nonetheless, books aimed at young readers like David Aretha's *The Story of Rosa Parks and the Montgomery Bus Boycott in Photographs* (2014) and Faith Ringgold's children's book *If a Bus Could Talk: The Story of Rosa Parks* (1999) offer material for discussion and creative engagement with *March*, while connecting *King* with videos of more recent police arrests, which frequently include rough language, might be a way of bringing this part of US history into college classrooms. Another option would be to turn to autobiographical narratives that shed light on areas of the movement that are not commonly included in historical accounts. Sarah E. Gardner suggests Anne Moody's *Coming of Age in Mississippi* (1968) and Deborah McDowell's *Leaving Pipe Shop: Memoirs of Kin* (1996) as works that grant insights into the lives of people who were not directly active in the movement. "Not everybody participated in sit-ins, went to jail, or was sprayed by fire hoses and attacked by dogs," Gardner writes, emphasizing "aspects of black life that have been relegated to the margins" (105).

In addition to these prose autobiographies, other graphic memoirs can support as well as challenge *March*. Lila Quintero Weaver's *Darkroom: A Memoir in Black and White* offers a Latinx perspective on the struggle for racial integration in Alabama, including the shooting and subsequent death of Jimmie Lee Jackson, which intensified activists' determination to march from Selma to Montgomery. An Argentinian immigrant whose parents moved to Marion, Alabama, when she was five, Weaver offers an account that troubles the neat divide "between black and white" found in conventional movement historiography, introducing "a sliver of gray into the demographic pie" (19).[40]

Mark Long, Jim Demonakos, and Nate Powell's *The Silence of Our Friends* (2012), a semiautobiographical account about a Black family and a white family in Texas in 1968, offers multiple opportunities to further contextualize the *March* books.[41] This graphic narrative tells the story of a friendship between white television reporter John Long and college instructor and Black activist Larry Thompson and their families. Told primarily from the perspective of the white reporter, the book raises interesting questions about interracial solidarity and moves the action into a region not always at the center of civil rights memory. Moreover, since it is drawn in a graphic style that is congruent with *March* and introduces a visual vocabulary that also shapes the trilogy, *The Silence of Our Friends* reminds us that graphic renditions of the movement are aesthetic and narrative constructs that create the movement even as they document it.

Darkroom and *The Silence of Our Friends* retell the story of the movement as a story of its mediation, with Weaver taking her father's passion for photography and film and the resulting visual archive as a starting point for thinking about the ways in which these technologies have impacted the documentary record and shaped the narratives afforded by this archive. The book includes scenes in her father's darkroom, where we witness the process of developing photographs, recollections of rewinding film footage, and an attempt to retell the events of the night when Jimmie Lee Jackson was killed and "nobody at all got a shot of what happened just one block from our house on February 18, 1965" (25). Like *Darkroom*, *The Silence of Our Friends* repeatedly shows camera equipment, and it also remediates television footage of the protests, encapsulating the images in panel frames shaped like television screens (131–38, 162–64) and showcasing events that remained unrecorded. When a ricocheting bullet kills a policeman during a protest, five Black students are put on trial for murder. The case is decided not on the basis of John's camera footage, which did not capture the moment, but on the grounds of his eyewitness testimony. Both graphic narratives emphasize the need to fill in gaps in the documentary record with creative nonfiction that draws on other forms of evidence and is willing to imagine and graphically represent what may be missing from the official story.

In a college or university setting, frame theory could further inform the analysis. Robert M. Entman defines framing as involving "*selection* and *salience*. To frame is to *select some aspects of a perceived reality and make them more salient in a communicating text, in such a way as to promote a particular problem definition, causal interpretation, moral evaluation, and/or treatment recommendation* for the item described" (52). Referencing Entman, Johannes C. P. Schmid suggests that frames "'diagnose, evaluate, and prescribe' an event or situation and thus assign causalities, roles, and relations to the actors and objects involved" ("Graphic" 3).[42] In the *March* books, framing includes the heroic scope of the narrative, its religious iconography, and its political agenda of celebrating nonviolent resistance.[43] It occurs forcefully in the celebration of "good trouble" as the most effective form of protest in opposition to more aggressive forms as advocated by Malcolm X, Ture, and Angela Davis, who proposed more devastating views of the United States and its state institutions. Confronting the text with less heroic, less religiously invested, and less-male-centered perspectives, both from the civil rights movement and from the current moment, could facilitate a critical approach to the trilogy without necessarily undermining its historiographic achievements.[44]

Focusing specifically on the contributions of women, which M. Bahati Kuumba advocates as a way of "looking between the cracks" of the master narrative, could reveal additional forms of "submerged activism" hidden by the male-centric gender politics of civil rights historiography (182).[45] One outcome could be that students learn to recognize structural similarities between the debates within the older civil rights movement over the right course of action and past and current doubts about the effectiveness of peaceful protest as well as about what Jacquelyn Dowd Hall calls "the triple oppression of black women—by virtue of their race, class, and gender" ("Long" 1247)—in and beyond the movement.[46]

King does not account for this triple oppression in detail, but the section on the Chicago Freedom Movement is explicit about the conjunction of race and class, while the issue of gender oppression becomes most glaring in the coverage of King's philandering, which includes sexist and misogynist comments; fights with his wife, Coretta Scott King, about his responsibilities as a husband and father; and his conservative stance toward women's liberation, voiced to Coretta before they marry: "I believe the woman's place is in the home" (21). Apparently aware of the danger of reinforcing the male machismo and bravado of King and his associates, Anderson places an invented female character, Caroline Longstreet, in their midst. She does not support King's views on women, but the men appreciate her wits. Anderson describes her as "one concession to the need to insert fiction into comic-book reality" to provide "a counterbalance to the King/Abernathy/Young boys club that formed the core of this story" (289).

However, a media-specific aspect must be considered when thinking about teaching *March* or *King*. In comics, framing takes a particular form, as Hillary Chute maintains: "While all media do the work of framing, comics manifests material frames—and the absences between them" (17). Entman's processes of "selection and salience" indeed constitute the basic narrative grammar of comics: the panel border as a frame that has a particular effect on the reader, the page or double page as a materially framed narrative unit, or shifting points of view as conveyors of meaning. What to include and exclude in a panel are fundamental decisions routinely made in the sequential structuring of the narrative and repeated acts of closure. As Hall observes, "Remembrance is always a form of forgetting, and the dominant narrative of the civil rights movement—distilled from history and memory, twisted by ideology and political contestation, and embedded in heritage tours, museums, public rituals, textbooks, and various artifacts of mass culture—distorts and suppresses as much as it reveals" ("Long" 1233). Graphic narrative is predisposed to visualize the tension between historical suppression (the gutter) and revelation (the panel).

The Bloody Sunday confrontation between the protesters and the Alabama state troopers in *Book Three* uses extensive framing to deliver *March*'s message. It presents an ideal occasion for investigating and teaching not only the contents of the narrative but also the mechanisms through which *March* memorializes the movement and the political implications that follow from this memorialization. *Book Three* features a particular shift from the earlier depiction of movement photography, exemplified by Lyon's Cairo photographs and SNCC's poster as cases of self-controlled image-based agitation, to the "seductive new medium of television" and its less regionally grounded and less grassroots-oriented production of moving images. Bloody Sunday was covered by the major news networks and reached a national viewership when the reporting aired on prime time (cf. Bodroghkozy 116). If the civil rights movement was the networks' "first major ongoing domestic story" (2), Bloody Sunday was a "point of maximum visibility for the [Selma] campaign as a national news event" (116). Rather than embrace the television images naively as innocent raw material against which to assess the depiction in *March*, students should achieve a critical consciousness about these images. They can improve their media literacy by recognizing that the television reportage was part of an ongoing interaction among networks, movement activists, and Southern segregationists that played out in front of a national audience. For movement leaders like Lewis and King, television was a powerful platform for presenting their case to the American people despite the lack of control over which images were broadcast and how they were framed.

Eleven days after Bloody Sunday and in the wake of television images that showed policemen in Montgomery attacking a biracial group of student protesters on 17 March 1965, King told reporters, "We are here to say to the white men that we no longer will let them use clubs on us in the dark corners. We're going to make them do it in the glaring light of television" (qtd. in Bodroghkozy 2). The news networks had a vested interest in broadcasting these images to the nation as the media shared an "urgent desire to forge a new, and newly *national*, consensus on the meanings and functions of racial difference" (Torres 6) and framed the conflict in a double sense. They added the media-specific frame of the television camera but also presented the events through the lens of a particular political narrative, both of which shaped the "selection and salience" and "moral evaluation" of the images (Entman 52). The *March* books acknowledge these processes by framing well-known footage with the apparatus of the television set.

Before analyzing the depiction of the events in *Book Three*, students should learn about this crucial backstory through preparatory readings that could include Sasha Torres's *Black, White, and in Color: Television and Black Civil Rights* (2003); Aniko Bodroghkozy's *Equal Time: Television and the Civil Rights Movement* (2012); or Danielle Smith-Llera's *TV Exposes Brutality on the Selma March: An Augmented Reading Experience* (2019), which includes original television footage. Selma Online, an interactive website created by the Hutchins Center for African and African American Research at Harvard University, provides intriguing digital inroads into civil rights history. In addition, students should familiarize themselves with comics narratology so that they can identify the intricacies of sequential storytelling and be aware of the mental processes of closure. Teachers can introduce key terminology and practice its application before turning to *March* and can use central scenes from the graphic memoir to train their students in basic comics literacy.

How does *Book Three* "diagnose, evaluate, and prescribe" (Entman 52) Bloody Sunday as a historical moment of maximum visibility from the vantage point of the present? How does it use this moment to memorialize the movement? The depiction begins by segmenting the account into a sequence of double pages that capture the magnitude of the event and the individual perceptions of the marchers and onlookers through specific panel arrangements and shifting points of view. The first of these double pages (196–97) presents the symbolically charged appearance of the bulging Edmund Pettus Bridge. The bridge is shown on the upper third of page 196 from a somewhat removed perspective, as we witness the marchers making their way to the top. On the upper half of page 197, we are already on the bridge, placed in a slightly elevated over-the-shoulder position that moves us closer to the marchers, who are looking down the bridge at the troopers blocking passage. These ascending and descending views of the bridge can be decoded as a metareference to drama's rising and falling action: they indicate that the narrative is about to reach its climax and signal that we are entering a particular framing of the depicted events. More significantly, the first image of the bridge foregrounds a press photographer covering the confrontation, which is also why we can interpret (via closure) the second image as a representation of this photographer's point of view or a view close to it. Yet the other panels on the page do not endorse any single perspective; they zoom in and out of the action, combining alternating close-ups of the marchers' faces and the conversation between Hosea Williams and John Lewis with panorama shots of the scene and moving from the protesters' position to that of the state troopers.

These perspectival shifts suggest a variously photographic, televisual, and cinematic approach by remediating existing photographs and television footage to convey a sense of historical verisimilitude. The top panel on page 195, for instance, which shows the protesters advancing, is an almost exact remediation of one of Charles Moore's civil rights photographs (Durham 155). The only differences apart from the change in medium are the absent background, which invests the image with a sense of temporal transcendence, and the fact that the long line of marchers begins at the bottom of the preceding page, thereby underscoring the mass of people as well as the page-crossing and politically transgressive action. Yet the sequential arrangement of these scenes also suggests a filmic sensibility, an effective editing of images from different cameras that ventures beyond documenting the scene and into the realm of cinematic dramatization. Ava DuVernay's *Selma* (2014), released two years before *Book Three*, could serve as the basis for a comparison of Powell's *mise-en-page* and the filmic depiction of the encounter on the bridge. Such a comparison could draw attention to differences in media-specific techniques both historically (in terms of movement photography and the televisual depiction of the struggle) and presently (in terms of how film and graphic nonfiction memorialize the events).

Pages 198 and 199 bring us even closer to the action, placing us between the protesters and the troopers. The first image shows the troopers putting on their gas masks and ordering the marchers to disperse. Oversized lettering and scraggly balloons indicate the harshness of the orders. The double page contrasts the troopers' aggressive demeanor with the peaceful and dignified conduct of the protesters, who react to the commanding officer's denial of their request to speak with the major—"There is no word to be had"—by kneeling down and praying. The penultimate panel conveys a sense of quiet resolve in the pivotal moment by evacuating everything except the marchers from the image. All the surroundings, including the panel frame, have disappeared: what counts is the spiritual preparation for what is to come. In McCloud's terms, this missing panel frame is a bleed, a visual marker that signifies meaning through conspicuous absence. Bleeds occur "when a panel runs off the edge of the page" and "time is no longer contained by the familiar icon of the closed panel, but instead hemorrhages and escapes into timeless space" (103). The *March* books use panel bleeds to suggest the timelessness of the civil rights movement as a struggle for social and racial equality that cannot be confined to a limited period of US history (and the ensuing events will include bloodshed).[47]

The final panel on page 199 affords a measure of rest to the protesters and readers, a moment of calm before the storm that begins when the page is turned. The image is devoid of sound and movement and gives no indication of its supposed duration. It visually encapsulates the fact that the "movement's most consistent and effective gesture against segregation was to contrast the racial terrorism of the South with national ideals and democratic discourses" (Torres 6). In terms of framing the struggle, the image not only pits the praying protesters against the armed and masked state troopers but inserts between them three cameramen/news reporters, the third time on this double page that these media representatives appear. They accompany every step in this unfolding drama and raise a number of questions about the instantaneous, real-time memorialization of the movement, including the fact that a photographer such as Moore was sometimes close enough to the demonstrators "that he wound up in the frames that other photographers were taking from farther away" (Gene Roberts and Klibanoff 317; Raiford, *Imprisoned* 81–82). Most significantly, the journalists complicate the "ontological status" (Oppolzer 228) of the graphic presentation. Are we reading a comic based on Lewis's memories or on the photographic and televisual images recorded in 1965 that Powell remediates to establish an authoritative depiction? Can unmediated memories of these moments even exist? What are the connections among the graphic narrative, the historical images on which it draws, and Lewis's recollection of the events as presented in *Walking with the Wind* and recounted many times since the mid-1960s? What other eyewitness accounts contributed to the scene's construction, and what did the photographers Aydin consulted add to the story? These questions are useful prompts for classroom activities, from a comparative close reading of *Walking with the Wind* and *March* to cross-media analysis of movement photography, moving images, and graphic narrative.

Pages 200 and 201 zoom in even closer to the action. The first page depicts the transition from prayer to physical violence; the second shows the initial attack, focusing on Lewis as he is beaten and falls down, his backpack flying through the air. The troopers emerge as the aggressors here, as their leader orders the attack ("Troopers—advance!!") and as they use batons and tear gas against the unarmed protesters. In terms of layout, the relatively ordered structure of the preceding pages gives way to a more crowded, hectic panel

Fig. 3.5: Levels of consciousness: John Lewis on the Edmund Pettus Bridge in *March: Book Three*. Page one of two.

arrangement. These panels' increasingly irregular shapes evoke a sense of brokenness, like shards of glass splintering from a smashed window. It is as if the images are bursting out of a shattered television screen that can no longer contain the horrific events. Viewpoints oscillate between extreme close-ups of Lewis's face, medium shots juxtaposing legless troopers with the marchers' metonymic feet, and long shots simulating the confusion of the moment while

Fig. 3.5: Levels of consciousness: John Lewis on the Edmund Pettus Bridge in *March: Book Three*. Page two of two.

affording a more distanced view of the carnage. While the storytelling is effective in its attempt to immerse the reader in the depicted action, its cinematic qualities as well as the manga-style sound words ("KRAK," "SPLATT") mark its indebtedness to the conventions of popular storytelling.

Pages 202–3 are even more explicit in their remediation of cinematic strategies (fig. 3.5). Switching from close-ups of Lewis's battered face and head as he is losing consciousness to an unframed subjective shot that shows complete darkness except for the words "I thought I was going to die" in white letters, the narration offers a moment of internal focalization where we become privy to Lewis's (recollected) thoughts. The opposite page zooms out again, supplanting the blackout scene with a high-angle shot of Lewis slowly coming to his senses and then zooming back in. "Get up. Keep moving," the words accompanying these visuals read, changing the narrative situation from the first-person narrator's retrospective view represented in block letters to character discourse in cursive.[48] These details matter, since they shape our interpretation of the history constructed by the narrative as well as its emotional impact. Employing more or less subtle means of telling the story of the civil rights movement and of (re)memorializing already heavily mediatized events for new audiences in a new medium, the *March* books request and reward a closer look.

Like the *March* books, Anderson's *King* is an award-winning publication, having received the Harvey Awards for Best New Talent (1991) and Best Graphic Album (1993) as well as a Parents' Choice Award (1995). However, few teaching guides for this comics biography exist (Meryl Jaffe), which is not surprising considering the density of the narrative, its stylistic promiscuity, and its resistance to reducing King's life to a single message. Yet from a teaching perspective, it would be unfair to tout *King*'s ambiguities and artistic aspirations and take *March* to court for its stronger didacticism and less confrontational verbal and visual rhetoric since the works come with different premises and pursue different goals. While *King* defamiliarizes its biographical subject to make readers consider the hero of the story from a new and not necessarily heroic perspective, the *March* books launch their narratives of heroism and political achievement to motivate young readers to engage politically. Both approaches are valid, but the pedagogical implications and didactic possibilities shift depending on which text is taught.[49]

How can *King* be taught in close conjunction with as well as in contradistinction to the *March* books? To answer this question, I conduct a comparative analysis of two key events that are depicted in both works: the freedom rides and the March on Washington.[50]

The major difference in the depiction of the freedom rides is the choice of narrative perspective. Because the *March* books are narrated in Lewis's first-person singular voice, the narrative has a sense of autobiographical credibility even though the images were drawn by Powell and the narrative itself was adapted and collated by Aydin. *King*, in contrast, does not use a narrative voice and instead reverts either to character speech (presented through traditional speech balloons or square narrative boxes that tend to feature spoken words in images that do not show a speaker) or to witnesses (who appear from time to time to comment on the events and offer subjective interpretations).

King's words in the third part of the narrative are represented in blue balloons, whereas all other speech is represented in red (Abernathy) or in conventionally white (other speakers) balloons.[51]

Anderson begins the segment on the freedom rides with testimony from a former CORE member whose account of the events is largely positive ("I give [King] a lot of credit"; "he played a supportive role" [90]) but whose repeated use of "I think" indicates that he is drawing on personal memory rather than verified history. Moreover, while Lewis, Aydin, and Powell dramatize the violence of the freedom rides by remediating the photograph of the burning bus and the peaceful protesters as they run away from a mob of white supremacists, Anderson starts the sequence with a remote image of two buses from which emanate the sounds of the riders' happy singing. The initially boisterous atmosphere, shown also on the first panel of page 91, turns to grave concern as the buses are stopped by white citizens armed with canes and sticks. But Anderson refrains from displaying the ensuing violence and instead creates a complex mélange of panels and speech acts over the following two pages. These panels include an image of a bus being shattered; a close-up of stick-carrying fists raised in the air; a view of the King family's living room with Martin and Coretta watching a news report of the event and their daughter asking them to stop her brother from bugging her; an extreme close-up of half of King's face overlaid by his daughter's demand, "Daddy—do something!"; a small headshot of a television reporter expressing his shock that the police seem to be granting the Klan members a "grace period" to attack the bus and the protesters; a three-panel sequence that zooms in from an extreme bird's-eye view to King sitting in a car, wondering "what the fuck is going on in this country" and telling the driver that he has informed the attorney general that he is standing by the riders; a cropped grainy copy of a historical photograph of the burning bus and the fleeing freedom riders; and a panel featuring the head of the single witness on this page, who laments the fact that God allowed the attack on the peaceful activists.

This is indeed a lot to process, and it combines several layers of representation that students must unpack to make sense of the narrative. In this process, the static nature of the medium, its habitual arresting of action into sequences of unmoving images that can be lingered over and pondered at will, is helpful. But this still leaves open the question about what is being represented by whom and with what consequences. The television coverage draws on archival material and showcases the role of reporters and the medium writ large in framing the events. "I'm sorry, ladies and gentlemen," the reporter confesses, with the mediatization of his speech marked by its representation in rectangular boxes with white letters over a black background. "Anyone who hasn't known or hasn't *wanted* to know what's happening in the American South today, please, *please,*

Fig. 3.6: Martin Luther King's "I Have a Dream" speech in *King*. Page one of two.

don't turn off your television sets," the reporter pleads, marking the active role of television in the nationwide framing of the conflict and connecting the newsworthiness of the report with the appeal to viewers to spend more time in front of their TVs. Then there is the photograph of the bus, not only reminding us of photography's power to mold public sentiment but also warning us that

Fig. 3.6: Martin Luther King's "I Have a Dream" speech in *King*. Page two of two.

the photographic archive must vie with other forms of remembrance to create a fuller picture of this historical moment. The unidentified witness further complicates the convoluted messages of the two pages by adding a third layer of representation—personal memories—to the televisual and photographic documentation. Finally, there is the comic book layout, design, and rendering of the whole page, including its subdivision into panels separated by gutters, speech balloons, and Anderson's abstract drawing style. Unfolding its narrative on so many layers, *King* challenges linear and one-dimensional views of the movement and can help students become versed in acts of meaning-making that will transform them into collaborators in the search for historical truth (without necessarily suggesting that a single truth may be found).

Not surprisingly, *March: Book Two* focuses on Lewis's speech at the March on Washington, whereas *King* concentrates on King's. Powell chooses a conventional arrangement to visualize Lewis's words, varying panel sizes, avoiding a strict sense of a grid structure, zooming in to show the intensity of Lewis's sentiments and out to display the size of the crowd and overall scenery, and using a moderate number of iconographic techniques (motion lines to indicate passion, scraggly balloons to indicate a loud voice) to animate Lewis's words. Anderson takes a much more radical approach to depicting King's less radical speech. More than half of the six pages devoted to the speech are made up of graphically altered photographic images. Some feature the actual event, while others are taken from the image bank of US racism (e.g., a white supremacist poster; an image of two lynched women and a sign noting the "83 women lynched since 1889" (144); images of the sit-ins at the Woolworth lunch counter, of the Ku Klux Klan, of John and Robert Kennedy, and of King and Malcolm X) (fig. 3.6). Powell uses a comparable assemblage of images from the American past when he depicts Aretha Franklin singing at Obama's inauguration, but Anderson's use of photographs creates a stronger sense of an ugly history beyond the comic book page. Anderson also places scraggly tailed speech balloons next to photographs of what seem to be people listening to the speech on the radio, foregrounding once more the media war over the issue of civil rights. He ends the multipage sequence with an image of King raising his right hand to a superimposed American flag. While the Hitlerian echo of this image might have been accidental rather than intentional, it nonetheless foregrounds the discrepancy between King's nonviolent dreams for a better America and the nation's centuries-long devotion to white supremacy.[52]

POLITICAL FAILINGS AND HISTORICAL FETISHES

Advocating attention to *March*'s mediation and remediation of history, identifying the framing mechanisms used, and confronting the graphic narrative with the more radical visions of *King* does not absolve these graphic narratives of their "political failings and historical fetishes" (Chaney, "Misreading" 25). In fact, these failings and fetishes are instructive in their own right and can serve as teachable moments. Several selected splash pages in *Book*

Two further trouble exclusively enthusiastic readings of the work. Page 99 shows a bus carrying a group of Black prisoners to the Mississippi State Penitentiary, known as Parchman Farm, and describes it as "21,000 acres of bullwhip-wielding guards and human bondage." The accompanying image recalls photographs of Nazi death camps, suggesting at least a tenuous connection between the Holocaust and the suffering of African Americans in the Deep South as represented by guards with rifles drawn who greet the freedom riders from a watchtower, a massive fence topped by barbed wire, and a sign over the entrance gate stating "Mississippi State Penitentiary" (evoking Auschwitz's "Arbeit macht frei").[53] To the left on page 98, the prisoners' clothes, called ring-arounds (Oshinsky 137) and documented in historical photographs, also recall the uniforms of concentration camp inmates. Taken together, these visual allusions to the Holocaust and the depiction of the freedom riders' initiation into the prison—they are ordered to undress, forced to shave, and compelled to put on prison clothes in a process that is "dehumanizing" and "part of an effort to strip away our dignity" (*Book Two* 102)—establish a simultaneously powerful and potentially fraught analogy between the centuries-long oppression of the African American population (including shaving and branding as newly enslaved Africans were loaded onto ships) and the genocide of the European Jews, an analogy that also briefly surfaces in Anderson's *King*. Talking about North Carolina students' lunch counter boycotts and demonstrations and the 1960 police invasion of the Alabama State College campus, one of the biography's recurring witnesses recalls, "When Dr. King telegraphed Eisenhower about the 'gestapo-like' actions of the Montgomery police, he was ignored" (70).[54]

The analogy is powerful because it embeds the civil rights movement's depiction in a longer history of systemic unfreedom, from the bondage of the enslaved to Parchman's status as "the quintessential penal farm, the closest thing to slavery that survived the Civil War," and an embodiment of a "powerful link to the past—a place of racial discipline where blacks in striped clothing worked the cotton fields for the enrichment of others" (Oshinsky 2, 155). In addition, by stating that "Parchman was the stuff of legends—dark legends" (*Book Two* 99), Lewis and his collaborators conjure up the prison's symbolic significance as a testament to what the subtitle of David M. Oshinsky's study describes as "the ordeal of Jim Crow justice." In terms of teaching methodology, the visual evocation of the Holocaust could be used as a prompt to discuss the *March* books alongside Art Spiegelman's seminal *Maus* (1986/1991), the first volume of which is titled *My Father Bleeds History* and thus evokes Powell's use of bleeds as a central stylistic device. The imprisoned freedom riders' singing could prepare the ground for an exploration of Parchman's appearance in classic blues songs by Son House and Bukka White.

Yet the analogy between Jim Crow and the Holocaust, Parchman and Auschwitz, as subtle as it may be, is also fraught because it threatens to obscure the historical specificities of both events and might manipulate readers' emotional responses by tapping into a transhistorical and transnational visual archive—watchtowers, armed guards, fences and barbed wire, prison gates, dehumanized inmates. But then again, as James Q. Whitman has shown, the Jim Crow system inspired Hitler's policies, particularly Nazi race law. And even after World War II, thirty-one prisoners, twenty-three of them Black, were sent to Parchman's gas chamber between 1954, the year of *Brown vs. Board of Education of Topeka*, and 1964, when the nationwide moratorium on capital punishment began (Oshinsky 229). The analogy between the Jim Crow prison and Nazi death camps may be less far-fetched than it seems at first glance, reminding readers, as Ta-Nehisi Coates once claimed for African Americans, that "you cannot disconnect our emancipation [...] from Jim Crow from the genocides of the Second World War" (*Between* 96–97). Nonetheless, this scene and the many other jail scenes that place movement activists behind bars are never explicitly connected to the sprawling prison-industrial complex and the mass incarceration of African Americans, thereby creating a certain disconnect from present concerns.[55] Delving into these difficult issues could encourage students to think not just beyond the Southern focus of civil rights memorialization but also beyond an overly US-centric historiography.

If the Parchman prison scenes evoke the terrors of the Jim Crow South as well as the atrocities of Nazi Germany, another splash page in *March: Book Two* offers a sense of sentimental relief. A white police officer kneels down to interact with a Black girl holding a sign saying "Can a Man Love God and Hate His Brother" (135). The girl, according to the preceding page, was one of "nearly a thousand of Birmingham's black children" arrested on that day for protesting racial injustice (134). While the caption calls the arrest of the children "an embarrassment to the city" and while we see a white officer escorting a line of Black children into a police van, another officer affirms the girl's humanity when he looks at her and asks, "What do you want?" (135). The answer—a toothy "F'eedom"—shows the depth of the yearning for racial equality even among the city's youngest. This gesture of racial reconciliation is one of several in the narrative, which begins with a close-up of Lewis's Black hand shaking President Kennedy's white hand. *March* is invested in a sentimental tradition of Black-and-white reconciliation—think of Harriet Beecher Stowe's novel *Uncle Tom's Cabin* (1851–52) and Stanley Kramer's film *The Defiant Ones* (1958)—but threatens to downplay the *longue durée* of racial antagonisms in US history.[56]

The narrative becomes overly sentimental and didactic at a few other moments as well. At one point, a white segregationist throws a stone through a stained-glass window at Montgomery's Sixteenth Street Baptist Church, leaving a hole that obliterates Jesus Christ's head and thus symbolically frames the segregationist mob as un-Christian and the Black activists as good Christians (*Book Two* 87). The scene is based on historical fact—the 1963 bombing of the church by local members of the Ku Klux Klan that not only killed Addie Mae Collins, Cynthia Wesley, Carole Robertson, and Denise McNair and injured others but also damaged one of the building's stained-glass windows in precisely this way (see *Sixteenth Street*). This somewhat heavy-handed symbolism takes on a more suggestive dimension in *Book Two*'s final scene, which depicts the bombing in a rather cryptic fashion that presupposes readers' familiarity with the incident.[57] The sequence on pages 176–79 moves from Obama's inauguration speech to a man in a phone booth (connected by the notion of "sacrifices borne by our ancestors" in the speech balloon that crosses the pages) to the bombing and its aftermath. Jesus's missing face occurs again here, but this time, the blast has crushed his heart. The message is certainly sentimental, but it is also powerful because the not-so-subtle symbolism of the stained-glass window is accompanied by the smoke from the explosion, the sirens of police cars and ambulances, and two words in a brittle speech balloon: "Denise? Addie?" Completing the act of closure, we are forced to come to terms with the fact that there can be no satisfying response to these words and that all we can do is develop our own response and formulate our own answers to this call for compassion.

While the works examined in this chapter mobilize the comic medium's didactic potential to make the historiography of the civil rights movement relevant for today's readers, the *Black Panther* comics analyzed in the next chapter change the focus from US history to an African context and move from the auto/biographical scope of *March* and *King* to science fiction and Afrofuturist sensibilities that pitch the project of recuperating and remediating Black history more squarely from the position of a popular serial franchise.

CH. 4

Chapter 4

AFRODIASPORIC ARCHIVES

When it was announced in 2015 that Black Panther, Marvel's first mainstream Black superhero, created by Stan Lee and Jack Kirby in the July 1966 issue of *Fantastic Four*, would be scripted by Ta-Nehisi Coates, a celebrated African American author and a national correspondent for *The Atlantic*, superhero fans were not alone in taking note. Major news outlets like *The New York Times* (Gustines) and NBC (Mannion) hyped Coates's spectacular foray into comic book writing and set high expectations for the initial twelve-issue run of the series, titled *A Nation Under Our Feet* and drawn by the acclaimed Brian Stelfreeze, among others. Much of the discourse centered on whether Coates would be able to infuse the comics with the depth and scope of his earlier nonfiction writing, such as the autobiographical *The Beautiful Struggle* (2008) and *Between the World and Me* (2015), which Toni Morrison had deemed "required reading" in a cover blurb. *Rolling Stone* had even called Coates "the most important essayist in a generation and a writer who changed the national political conversation about race" (Fear). Many critics wondered how Coates's views on racism in the United States and beyond would impact his treatment of the iconic Black Panther.[1]

In a piece in *The Atlantic* that contextualized his gravitation to comics, Coates labeled his work "The Return of the Black Panther" even though the character had appeared in a fairly recent run by writer Reginald Hudlin and artist John Romita Jr. (2005–8; 2009–10). Hudlin and Romita had introduced Black Panther T'Challa's sister, Shuri, in 2005, and the 2009 storyline *Deadliest of the Species* (with Ken Lashley; in Hudlin et al. vol. 3) extended her role in an effort to strengthen the depiction of women in the series, building on writer Christopher Priest (the first African American assigned to script the character) and artist Mark Texeira's invention of the Dora Milaje (Adored

Ones), T'Challa's extensively trained, no-nonsense female bodyguards, in a 1998 storyline.[2] In addition to creating a strong female protagonist, Hudlin had also associated the Black Panther with one of Marvel's most significant acts of historical revisioning: Robert Morales, Kyle Baker, et al.'s retconning of the Captain America mythos in the seven-issue miniseries *Captain America: Truth* (2003), announcing a historicist orientation that also informs Coates's treatment of the character.[3]

More important than the notion of the Black Panther's return, however, is the connection Coates established between his superhero storytelling and his journalism, which provides the foundation for the popular archive of global diasporic blackness constituted in and through his *Black Panther*:

> Despite the difference in style and practice of storytelling, my approach to comic books ultimately differs little from my approach to journalism. In both forms, I am trying to answer a question. In my work for *The Atlantic* I have, for some time, been asking a particular question: Can a society part with, and triumph over, the very plunder that made it possible? In *Black Panther* there is a simpler question: Can a good man be a king, and would an advanced society tolerate a monarch? Research is crucial in both cases. The Black Panther I offer pulls from the archives of Marvel and the character's own long history. But it also pulls from the very real history of society—from the pre-colonial era of Africa, the peasant rebellions that wracked Europe toward the end of the Middle Ages, the American Civil War, the Arab Spring, and the rise of ISIS. ("Return")

With this statement, Coates introduces four ideas that anchor my analysis of his *Black Panther* run, which encompasses more than three dozen issues (gathered into eight trade paperback collections) as well as two spin-offs co-scripted by Coates, *World of Wakanda* (with Roxane Gay, 2017) and *Black Panther & the Crew* (with Yona Harvey, 2017), as well as the spin-off series *Shuri* (2018–19), scripted mainly by the Nigerian American writer Nnedi Okorafor.[4] First is the claim that his writing for the comic book series is driven by a journalistic ethos that requires extensive research about the relationship between contemporary society and the past.[5] *Black Panther* comes off as fiction rooted in history, as a serial treatment of the character cognizant of the political baggage that any serious engagement with Western colonialism and imperialist expansions into Africa must consider. This engagement—in the form of a US superhero comic, a genre that has often been associated with a nationalist ethos (see Dittmer)—raises difficult questions, including regarding cultural appropriation, the dangers of exoticization, and the glorification of geopolitical power imbalances. In issue 5 of Okorafor et al.'s spin-off series *Shuri*, the princess solicits Iron Man's help in fighting Moses Magnum, an African "terrorist with seismic powers," prompting the villain to exclaim sarcastically, "Iron Man in Mali? Ugh, another Westerner meddling in African affairs." This comment points beyond the diegetic world of the comic, as it casts a critical eye at US geopolitical activities and neoimperial policies on the African continent (see Dittmer and Bos). Moreover, it suggests that US-driven superhero fantasies about Africa may tell us more about popular constructions of the continent than about African culture and politics per se, about what Achille Mbembe critiques as "the paradigm of 'the one'" (which includes the attempted erasure, political and discursive, of African multiplicities), and places comic book African nations to some extent "under the sign of the multiple" (Blaser). "Africa is a false creation that over time grew a soul," one of the members of the Pan-African alliance Egungun tells Shuri in the Okorafor-scripted story, while the miniseries *Black Panther & the Crew*, written by Coates and Harvey, traces the presence of superheroes in Harlem to the 1955 Bandung Conference, which brought together leaders of twenty-nine Asian and African countries to discuss economic and cultural development beyond the West's colonial powers. In the comic, one speaker declares that "the curse of colonialism lives . . . so long as any corner of Asia and Africa remains in chains" (issue 2).[6] Coates, Okorafor, and others integrate notions of African American and especially (Pan-)African history into the corporate cosmos of the comic book superhero.

Second, by juxtaposing journalistic inquiry ("Can a society part with, and triumph over, the very plunder that made it possible?") with the basic precept of the comic ("Can a good man be a king, and would an advanced society tolerate a monarch?"), Coates intimates that although past injustices are relevant for *Black Panther*, we must also consider the comics' genre- and medium-specific requirements. Indeed, the series often depicts superhero bodies in spectacular action and features page-turning battle scenes that reproduce genre conventions and play into mainstream expectations. But Coates connects these elements with a storyline that centers on the struggles of Wakanda, the fictional African country and ostensible Afrofuturist utopia (see Chambliss, "Different"; White and Ritzenhoff) ruled by King T'Challa, the current Black Panther, which faces internal unrest while slowly transitioning from a monarchy to a democratic republic. Eli Boonin-Vail notes the contrast between the narrative captions (white letters over a black background) used to represent T'Challa's thought processes—his many "regrets, anxieties, and political considerations"—and the frequently intense physical action and splashy artwork (141), indicating Coates's attempts to combine superhero spectacle with his journalist research and political commentary.

Third, while Coates acknowledges the strictures associated with scripting superhero comics when he mentions "the character's own long history," he ultimately advocates a look beyond the fantastic conceits of the genre at the "very real history of society," which includes a transnational interest in Africa, Europe, the United States, and the Arab world.[7] Yet if "popular fantasy describes the variety of ways that the tropes and figures of literary fantasy (magic, superhuman ability, time travel, alternate universes, among others) come to organize real-world social and political relations," as Ramzi Fawaz suggests (27), the connection between superhero fantasy and history can be integrative rather than oppositional and can serve as a venue for "fantasizing against antiblackness" (Darieck Scott, *Keeping* 8).

Fourth, Coates speaks not only of the history of the character but of "the archives of Marvel" from which his reimagination of the character springs. This last point raises questions about historical access, the ability to pull materials from the archives, and the wielding of discursive authority, which have informed much theorizing in the wake of the archival turn in the humanities. It also speaks to recent investigations of comics and archives and work on the precarity of diasporic archives.[8] As a comic book superhero and a "diasporic icon" (Boonin-Vail 138), Coates's Black Panther brings these issues to the attention of a mainstream readership that may not otherwise be interested in the histories of marginalized people, "untaming comics memory" (Ahmed and Crucifix 1) by connecting the content of the Marvel universe with global political histories.

Coates's take on the Black Panther is invested in the idea of a global Black diaspora whose historical genesis and present condition are closely connected to the notion of the archive, which has come to figure as "a highly suggestive trope" (Assmann, "Canon" 102) in contemporary cultural theory.[9] Coates utilizes the suggestiveness of the archive as a critical lens through which his superhero narrative can reflect on past and present implications in the propagation of imperial fantasies and myths of national exceptionalism. Moreover, his version of the character and the evolving storyworld constitute a significant contribution to what Teju Cole calls "global diasporic blackness," defined as a "colonial hangover" that in conjunction with "American experiences of slavery, slave rebellion, Jim Crow, and contemporary racism [binds] the Black Atlantic into a single territory of pain" ("On the Blackness").

Aided by various visual artists and editors, Coates uses the fictional storyworld of the *Black Panther* comic to interrogate postcolonial territories of pain encapsulated in and beyond different forms of archives. He does so on the level of the ongoing narrative, but he also launches the comic itself as a critical intervention into the history of the superhero genre, creating a pop-culturally inflected "critical fabulation" and a "critical reading of the archive that mimes the figurative dimensions of history" (Hartman, "Venus" 11).[10] Advancing what Boonin-Vail calls a "popular intellectual critique" and "juggling the complex and potentially conflicting obligations of public intellectual, prominent Black journalist, political and phenomenological philosopher, and avid comics fan" (135, 137), Coates's *Black Panther* is a significant though not completely unproblematic addition to the digitally enhanced "diasporic public sphere" that Arjun Appadurai understands as "a deliberate site for the production of anticipated memories by intentional communities" (22, 17) but that seems increasingly dominated by global franchises acting as memory-making institutions.[11]

DIASPORIC ARCHIVES

As Diana Taylor notes, we are living in the "era of the archive," in a digitized world "obsessed with archives—as metaphor, as place, as system, and as logic of knowledge production, transmission, and preservation" ("Save As" 2, 4). Coates's *Black Panther* represents and shares this obsession, and it does so largely within the parameters of the superhero genre, which means balancing genre conventions with an inquiry into the functions of archives for the global Black diasporic imaginary.[12] In fact, *Black Panther* imagines two kinds of archives and foregrounds their impact on life in fictional Wakanda: an older, orally inflected and personally communicated archive of stories akin to what Taylor calls an "embodied repertoire" (*Archive* 178), which the comic describes as "the histories before there was history" because they are transforming into a past that "no longer simply harasses us, but now seeks to colonize our country" (book 5); and a new, digitally enhanced, ever-expanding archive that cements the power of an intergalactic empire (another Wakanda that split off from the mother country many years earlier) by robbing people of their memories. While the first type of archive warns against nationalist tendencies and instead advocates a turn to Western-style democracies that remain rooted in African forms of knowledge and cultural tradition, the second type reads like a cautionary tale about archival dispossession and disenfranchisement in a world of digital communication and data storage.[13]

Taylor further reminds us that the "archive is simultaneously an authorized place (the physical or digital site housing collections), a thing/object (or collection of things—the historical records and unique or representative objects marked for inclusion), and a practice (the logic of selection, organization, access, and preservation over time that deems certain objects 'archivable')" ("Save As" 4). *Black Panther* complicates these purposes, undermining the notion of the archive as an authorized place by inventing the mythical space of the Djalia, which holds all of Wakandan history, including what has not been officially recorded. Later in the narrative, the archive becomes a concrete location, a storage facility where the intergalactic empire saves and data-mines the memories it has swiped from the subjugated population. This second archive is an actual place that the enslaved rebels, self-declared maroons, must find to break the power of the empire and restore the stolen memories.[14] In both cases, we encounter not so much archival objects or artifacts as displaced memories, both individual and collective. This indicates Coates's concern with contested forms of cultural memory and suggests an attempt to account for Black diasporic history by positing and imagining "pasts that exceed material documentation" and "setting in motion the possibility behind the archive's limits" (Walters 4, 5).

Connected to the idea of the archive is the function of the library as the place where the canon circulates and where book-bound knowledge can reach new generations of readers. To express this idea, Coates creates Zawavari, a sorcerer who acts as a physical and spiritual embodiment of the library. In book 4, Zawavari states, "I do not fear death. [. . .] I fear the death of the library within me." Moreover, in Okorafor et al.'s *Black Panther: Long Live the King* (2018), T'Challa is introduced as a reader of Wole Soyinka's autobiographical *You Must Set Forth at Dawn* (2006), which not only invests this superhero and the story writ large with a literary sensibility but also establishes a parallel between Soyinka's multiyear exile during General Sani Abacha's reign in Nigeria and T'Challa's temporary time away from Wakanda before the start of Coates's narrative.[15]

Aleida Assmann proposes another distinction: between archival messages, understood as "texts and monuments [. . .] addressed to posterity," and archival traces, which bear "no similar address" ("Canon" 98–99). As scholars like Saidiya Hartman have demonstrated, the archival records of the African diaspora are more likely to contain scattered traces of the enslaved or colonized than consciously implemented messages ("Venus" 2). In the words of Gabriella Giannachi, "Diasporic archives, like colonial archives, constitute records of uncertainty and loss. They are ontologically and epistemologically fragile." "What remains of an archive," she continues, "in particular a diasporic archive, is often the result of destruction or plundering caused by conflict" (100, 98). The resulting gap between the traces of the enslaved and the messages of the enslavers has motivated diasporic writers and artists like Coates to conjure up a more inclusive historical world, confronting archival gaps through feats of the imagination.[16] "What's missing from the archives, the slave's face, the girl's story, her subjectivity, [. . .] also provokes: by exceeding historical awareness and intelligibility, it forces us to acknowledge the archive's limits," Marianne Hirsch and Diana Taylor conclude. Yet as Ann Laura Stoler has shown, even the messages of the colonizers contain "records of uncertainty and doubt in how people imagined they could and might make the rubrics of rule correspond to a changing imperial world" (4). These "epistemic uncertainties repeatedly unsettled the imperial conceit that all was in order" (1). In Coates's *Black Panther*, they provide the impetus for the rebellion of the enslaved people in books 6–8, and on a larger scale, they trouble the continuing US-centrism of the superhero genre despite its increasing interest in transnational themes (see Denson, Meyer, and Stein; *Transnational Graphic Narratives*).

In terms of epistemic uncertainties, we may also think of Michel Foucault's much-cited proposition in *The Archaeology of Knowledge* that the archive is "the law of what can be said, the system that governs the appearance of statements as unique events" (129), which Assmann rephrases: "The archive is the basis of what can be said in the future about the present when it will have become the past." Consequently, "archives of data provide important tools for political power" ("Canon" 102). Coates's *Black Panther* shares this understanding of the archive as the foundation of knowledge and the key to political power, suggesting that control of the archive enables imperial rule and alleging that archival documents are "active, generative substances with histories, as documents with itineraries of their own," as Stoler notes (1). "What was 'left' [in colonial archives] was not 'left behind' or obsolete," she adds. "Colonial archives were an arsenal of sorts that were reactivated to suit new governing strategies" (3).

Stoler's observations point to the distinction between archive and canon proposed by Assmann, who differentiates between "the actively circulated memory that keeps the past present as the canon and the passively stored memory that preserves the past past as the archive" ("Canon" 98). To enable active circulation, archival knowledge is transformed into literature or research and becomes available to the broader public once it is published and presented in libraries, where it can become part of the arsenal in the fight against racism. This is the case not only in Coates's *Black Panther* but also in issue 2 of David F. Walker, Chuck Brown, and Sanford Greene's *Bitter Root*, in a flashback scene set in Harlem in 1904. As a young boy, one of the strongest members of the monster-fighting Sangerye family, Berg, learns from his father about "the Sangerye family arsenal. The real one." "Learning to wield an axe is important," the father explains, "but this is much more essential to your training" (163). The next page is a splash panel of a giant library filled with books waiting to be perused and then used as a weapon—a fount of knowledge—by young Berg and his crew.

Walker, Brown, and Greene thus follow in the footsteps of Tom Feelings's *Tommy Traveler in the World of Black History* comic strip from the late 1950s. Feelings begins the series with Tommy going to the library and learning that he has already read all the books it holds on Black history. The librarian sends Tommy to on old Black man, Dr. Gray, who lives on Vine Street and owns a massive collection of books on "Egyptian history, life of the Asiatic Blacks and Negroes in early American History!!" Here, too, the library takes on the function of an archive, storing information and providing a world of knowledge to the young reader and thus becoming a source of dissident wisdom that will shape Tommy's (and the reader's) outlook on life. It thus functions as a kind of "'grape-vine' telegraph" (to use Booker T. Washington's phrase in *Up from Slavery* [14]), passing illicit or hidden knowledge, a connection to which Feelings alludes with the character's name and residence.[17]

Beyond thinking of archives (or libraries) as stable repositories or as stationary arsenals ready for government deployment, Hirsch and Taylor compel us to conceive of them "as engines of circulation, as archival acts or practices that both mobilize different media and are mobilized by them. Instead of valuing notions of fixity, authenticity, and legitimacy," the authors maintain, we must "look at the archive," including *Black Panther* and other comics, "as the site of potentiality, provisionality, and contingency," as "a haunting provocation" and a "fertile ground for artists and performers who use and at the same time critique its construction."[18] Thus, when writers in the African diaspora turn to history, they often "posit alternate narratives of agency, humanity, and empowerment, as a supplement to the meager traces recorded in the archives of the slave trader, colonizer, or court room" (Walters 1). In fact, Wendy Walters explains, these writers tend to veer back and forth "between the data of the archive [. . .] and the aspirational imaginings of black historical literature," tapping into an "aspirational register" that considers "not just 'what happened' or 'what was said to have happened,' but rather 'what may have happened'" (1). In doing so, creators unmoor "the concept of archive from its stubborn attachment to national narratives" and indicate "the instability of the archive's truth claim to show how it is culturally constructed and open to hermeneutics" (3, 4). This unsettling move from the national to the transnational plays out in Coates's *Black Panther*, which portrays Wakanda's struggle with the transition from monarchy to democracy in the first five books and where the intergalactic empire of an alternative Wakanda in books 6–8 uses the archive to control the enslaved population as a means of both fortifying and extending the empire's sphere of influence.

Finally, we must not only adjust our conception of the archive to a transnational and indeed global or even galactic scope but also make room for the peculiarities of popular archives and popular archiving practices, both of which are vital for the Black Panther universe (see Altınay and Jokić). Rather than following Appadurai's otherwise useful notion of popular archives as records of "everyday life outside the purview of the state" (16), we can approach the *Black Panther* comics more profitably through the lens of Abigail De Kosnik's concept of rogue archives, according to which media users in the digital era "have seized hold of all of mass culture *as an archive*, an enormous repository of narratives, characters, worlds, images, graphics, and sounds from which they can extract the raw matter they need for their own creations, their alternatives to or customizations of the sources" (4). "Engagement with cultural memory" now includes "not only what comes after the making and distribution of cultural texts" but also what "often precedes that making, or occurs at every step throughout the process of making" (4). Coates's *Black Panther* is no exception, as indicated by the more than sixty cover variants reprinted in the trade paperbacks, representing a large range of styles and sanctioning further visual experimentation through fan art. If, as De Kosnik suggests, "each media commodity becomes [. . .] an archive to be plundered, an original to be memorized, copied, and manipulated—a starting point or springboard for receivers' creativity" (4), we may not only note the semantic compatibility of this statement with one of Coates's main political concepts (plunder) but also recognize *Black Panther* as an engine of circulation in this reconfigured production cycle as well as a sort of metanarrative: a story about archival plunder that plunders the archives of popular culture (Marvel comics, most obviously).[19]

A heuristic distinction exists between the depiction of archives in the storyworld (which I call archives in *Black Panther*) and a reading of the comics as an intervention into comic book history as well as into the colonial past that created the African diaspora (which I label *Black Panther* as archival agent).[20] Focusing on archives in *Black Panther* or archives in comics (i.e., archives as a subject matter and element of the storyworld) adds a third component to my ongoing attempt to come to grips with the many relations between archives and popular (Black) agency and aesthetics.[21]

ARCHIVES IN *BLACK PANTHER*

A basic distinction between historical and political archives (Assmann, "Canon" 103) is useful here, even though it ultimately fails to account for the archival complexities the *Black Panther* series envisions. Particularly striking is the shift between books 1–5 and books 6–8 in the presentation of the archive in the evolving storyworld. In the beginning, King T'Challa returns to Wakanda from abroad to find his sister, Shuri, murdered and his country in disarray. Since its inception in the mid-1960s, the fictional Wakanda had been a metaphorical Black mecca whose monopoly on the magical metal vibranium made it "the most technologically advanced society on the globe" (book 1).[22] But in Coates's run, this utopia is on the brink of disaster. T'Challa and his supporters face threats from within through a rebel group named The People, led by Tetu and Zenzi, and from without through various villains and villainous creatures (among them Ulysses Klaue, aka Klaw, killer of T'Challa's father and royal predecessor, T'Chaka) who are seeking to exploit the vibranium.[23] In this situation, T'Challa clings to the dream of Wakanda as a monarchy headed by a virtuous leader who rules over a people united by an allegiance to king and country. Early on, he is told that "power lies not in what a king does, but in what his subjects believe he might do," and he concedes that "what the people know not is the true power of kings" (book 1). Searching the archive for knowledge that would help him quell the rebellion, T'Challa looks to the past and seeks counsel from his ancestors in the spirit world, especially from the assembly of previous Black Panthers, who mock and taunt him. The advice of these male progenitors is not always helpful, as they pressure him to act mercilessly against the Wakandan people as a means of reinforcing his rule. "I feel blinded by the past," "I keep seeing ancestors," T'Challa complains. He prefers the advice of Shuri, who exists in limbo, "a petrified state known as The Living Death" (book 3), and whose "spirit was driven to The Djalia, the plane of Wakandan memory," where she "learned of Wakanda's past, present, and future from a Griot wearing the aspect of her mother, Ramonda" (book 3), and prepared to return among the living.

The Djalia is indeed the plane of Wakandan memory, rendered in a pastel color palette visually distinguished from the rest of the narrative. It functions as a somewhat sentimentalized matrilineal and "metaphysical oasis where Wakandan spirits comingle in a radically disembodied and deterritorialized space that is part afterlife and part archive" (Boonin-Vail 143).[24] In this space, T'Challa, through Shuri, seeks to reconstruct the country's history beyond the written records: "All of it is here. All of the triumph and tragedy of your people," the griot, who describes herself as "a caretaker of all our histories, now lost to the acolytes of machine, and the prophets of this metal age" (book 1), promises Shuri.[25] The Djalia is a historian's dream, a reservoir of memories beyond the officially sanctioned archive, allowing "an Africanist or black world perspective" and promising to overcome what Simon Gikandi, with a view to early American history, has called "this archive without African voices, without African documents, without an African historical a priori" (86).[26]

Shuri must access "the power of memory" (book 1) to recuperate the forgotten histories of Wakanda's peoples and establish national unity. Over the course of book 2, the griot narrates the histories of Wakanda, speaking of "place[s] now lost to your written histories, though not lost to the griot." Challenged by Shuri's question "What is the point of this babble?" the griot responds, "The point is power, girl. [. . .] Either you are a nation, or you are nothing." Here, the archive is tied to the idea of the nation not as colonial venture but as an unstable monarchy struggling to reconcile the mounting democratic pressures ("No one man," the rebels proclaim by the second issue) and violent rebellion with its self-mythologization as a powerful force for good. Wakanda's problem is not colonization: the country's wealth and technological advancement mean that it has never been colonized. Rather, the problem is its false belief in its own grandeur. "We believed our own myths," Shuri, back among the living and strong-minded as ever, tells T'Challa in book 3. "This was our first mistake. If you can't see a world clearly, then you have no hope for mastering it."

A scene early in book 4 illustrates the need to search beyond the national archive, to question the myths of Wakanda as an exceptional nation, as several characters, including T'Challa, refer to it: T'Challa refutes the underlying critique in philosopher Changamire's assertion "But we were supposed to be exceptional" by insisting, "Wakanda *is* exceptional" (book 3).[27] And in book 4, Shuri meets Eden Fesi, an Indigenous Australian, a former member of the Avengers, and a supporter of the Black Panther. He is at the Wakandan Royal Library, combing through history books to learn more about the mysterious snake-men attacking the country. When he tells Shuri that these "snake-men resemble creatures from an obscure translation" of an old saga, she already knows what he is about to tell her. "Old stories have, of late, become a hobby of mine," she confesses. "There is the history of this country—the one you find in books like these—and then there is something older. The story of the land and its peoples long before they took the name 'Wakanda.'" Shuri imagines herself as "Aja-Adanna, the ancient future, bearer of a past so deep it's not even the past. The 'deep past' is all around us, guiding events that we believe to be manifestations of our will."[28] If the commonly known history of Wakanda is the canon in Assmann's nomenclature, Shuri views the past as an archive, although it does not merely contain remnants of the past that have fallen out of use but continually exerts agency over the present and future. In book 5, the Dalija is described as "memory incarnate," and while it contains "the histories before there was history" and offers Shuri knowledge about "Wakanda before its name," it teaches her and T'Challa a powerful lesson: "Did you truly believe that a great nation could be built without another underfoot? [. . .] Every man is the hero of his own story, the champion of his own chosen myth."

Devising the Djalia and proposing the notion of the deep past, both of which cannot save Wakanda from intrusion and fail to cement the king's power, Coates critiques what Assmann conceptualizes as the historical archive in contrast to the political archive. Shuri fails to preserve Wakanda's unity despite her status as a griot: Shuri "had her griot power—the entire history of Wakanda—at her disposal. It was not enough." Alluding to William Butler Yeats's sense, expressed in his poem "The Second Coming" (1920), that the center cannot hold as well as to Chinua Achebe's novel *Things Fall Apart* (1958), Shuri exclaims in book 3 that Wakanda's capital, the "golden city," "must not fall"; soon thereafter, the Black Panther speaks of "the diaspora of the golden city." Achebe had cited Yeats's poem to comment on the crumbling of British colonial rule in Nigeria and the rise of intertribal tensions, and Coates's intertextual reference acknowledges African nations' attempts to achieve independence and political stability and the efforts of the continent's literati to support these developments: "Turning and turning in the widening gyre / The falcon cannot hear the falconer; / Things fall apart; the centre cannot hold; / Mere anarchy is loosed upon the world."[29]

According to Assmann, where "political archives function as an important tool for power, historical archives store information which is no longer of immediate use"; historical archives, therefore, are "part of the passive dimension of cultural memory" ("Canon" 103). She continues, "The knowledge that is stored in the archive is inert. It is stored and potentially available, but it is not interpreted. [...] The archive, therefore, can be described as a space that is located on the border between forgetting and remembering; its materials are preserved in a state of latency, in a space of intermediary storage. [...] It stores materials in the intermediary stage of 'no longer' and 'not yet,' deprived of their old existence and waiting for a new one" (103). Yet Wakanda's historical archive is neither a physical storage space nor an actual place where the past remains passive. Instead, the comic devises an imaginary archival space that claims to differ from as well as contradict the written histories of the African continent and even Wakanda's official—mythologized—version of history. Capitalizing on Coates's journalistic aims and his interest in Black history, the comic supplies charismatically visualized histories of various African peoples that revise many of the more stereotypical depictions of the continent in Marvel comics of the 1960s and 1970s but still exoticize Africa as the West's mythical Other (orishas, griots, gods, tribal customs, colorful clothing, and the like) at least to some degree, as does the tableau of the "Gods of Wakanda" in issue 13 (collected in book 4; fig. 4.1). "From time immemorial, the Gods of Wakanda—our orisha—have safeguarded us," T'Challa tells his wife, the mutant superhero Ororo Munroe, while they reside in New York City, tracing his Black Panther title back to the Panther goddess Bast and then detailing the powers and functions of all the other Wakandan gods (Kokou, Mujaji, Thoth, Ptah the Shaper), whose stylized likenesses accompany the descriptions.

As these examples indicate, the historical archive is always already a political archive in Coates's version of *Black Panther*. Political archives, Assmann writes, serve "the ruling class with the necessary information to build up provisions for the future through stockpiling" as well as offer "tools for the symbolic legitimation of power and to discipline the population" ("Canon" 102). Ironically, in Coates's *Black Panther*, it is Wakanda, the proud African nation, whose royal ruling class seeks to legitimize its power and discipline its population through knowledge of the deep past provided by the Djalia, which is at once historical and political. That historical and political archives are integrally connected becomes obvious in light of the double meaning of the Greek term *arkhé*, the root of the word *archive*, as "beginning" and "government" (Assmann, *Cultural* 327) or "commencement" and "commandment" (Derrida 9). If the archive is

Fig. 4.1: The safeguarding gods of Wakanda in *Black Panther: Avengers of the New World*, Part 1.

understood as "a place where things begin, where power originates," as Carolyn Steedman suggests (1), then the Djalia functions as Coates's popular version of the *arkhé*, his critically fabulated answer to Gikandi's question "How does one commence or command without agency or power?" (86).[30] The Djalia further serves as the main source of legitimization for Coates's revisioning of *Black Panther* as "a post-colonial, post-modern, deconstructionist look at militarism, imperialism and heteronormativity" (qtd. in Boonin-Vail 136), but it is also Wakanda's Achilles heel, as narratives of the nation-state are bound to encounter dissent from the margins even in superhero comics. The Djalia thus functions as an alternative archival space that, unlike the "archive of slavery," does not rest on "a founding violence [that] determines, regulates and organizes the kinds of statements that can be made about slavery" and "creates subjects and objects of power" (Hartman, "Venus" 10) but that can nonetheless be abused for the purpose of totalitarian rule.

An even more obviously political archive appears in *Black Panther: The Intergalactic Empire of Wakanda* (books 6–8). This story arc moves the series into a science fiction universe ruled by a five-galaxy-spanning empire whose origins lie in a space colony founded by a small contingent of Wakandans who left earth two thousand years prior to the narrative present and then turned from self-defense to conquest and enslavement.[31] This story begins with an act of rebellion by one of the enslaved (later revealed to be T'Challa, bereft of most of his memories but nonetheless yearning to go home and revive his old life), who rises up against an overseer of the empire in a fight reminiscent of Frederick Douglass's confrontation with Edward Covey in *The Narrative of the Life of Frederick Douglass* (50). What starts as an individual act of resistance becomes a sci-fi version of an insurrection that pits a group of self-declared maroons against the empire in an extended Nat Turner–meets–George Lucas scenario. Recalling the cultural uprooting during and after the Middle Passage, the enslaved on planet Gorée (named after Gorée Island off the coast of Dakar, the location of the museum and memorial Maison des Esclaves and the Door of No Return) face a devastating future, as they are forced to dig up the vibranium from the mines to supply the Wakandan empire with raw material (a reference also to the ongoing extraction of African mineral resources): "They have stolen your name, your culture, your God. Do not let them steal your mind," another enslaved man tells the rebel as he is haunted by fading visions of his past (book 6). In *Between the World and Me*, Coates had already expressed such sentiment when he noted that the enslaved were "people turned to fuel for the American machine" (70), and Coates's *Black Panther* dramatizes this reduction of the captured Africans first to cargo (as in Feelings's *Middle Passage*) and then to constantly dehumanized "piece[s] of merchandise" (Harriet Jacobs 751).[32]

When Captain N'Yami, the leader of the maroons, presses the rebel about his reasons for joining the rebellion, he expresses a diasporic desire for a homeland—"I fight to get back home" (book 6)—even though he can barely remember this home and does not even know his own name. N'Yami responds by describing their intergalactic diasporic existence: "We are the nameless, my son. Orphans of the cosmos. Flotsam of the Empire. But now is the hour of our restoration. Our handles are taken from the legends of our past. So that we, marooned in the Empire, are nameless no more. And to you I give the name of a man who was born a king and died a hero. Arise T'Challa." From the traces of the past or from the scraps in the archive, N'Yami and her followers develop a revolutionary message aimed to contest the dominance of the empire. Soon thereafter, the new T'Challa learns more about the empire's archives from fellow maroon fighter Nakia (another strong woman in a series that features many remarkable women) (fig. 4.2). The Askari are described in the paratextual explanations as "both the police force of the Empire and the arm of the Wakandan slave trade," stealing memories and storing "them in the imperial archive." Then, "every bit of that archive is [. . .] mined and researched" for anything unknown to the Askari: "Anything. Thoughts, ideas, emotions, stories, methods, half-formed notions. All of it is appropriated for their interests." Nakia continues, "Your memories are knowledge. And the Empire doesn't destroy knowledge . . . . . . they plunder it," a phenomenon she finds "sickening. The Empire speaks of the grandeur of its civilization. And it is grand. But it is also stolen" (book 6). Such passages do more than feed our understanding of the political conflicts shaping the storyworld: they are thinly veiled statements about the world beyond the comic book, serving as a vehicle for Coates's critical assessment of US history and the current threats of big data, especially the systematic mistreatment and disenfranchisement of its enslaved and marginalized populations, and of colonialism as large-scale theft rationalized as the benevolent extension of civilization to the allegedly uncivilized. In book 7, M'Baku, another one of T'Challa's allies and a fellow maroon, specifies the empire's reliance on the archive in a passage that reads like a preview of the second Trump administration:

> Like all Empires, the Empire of Wakanda is counterfeit. It is a Confederacy of villains who've elevated criminality to galactic law. The Empire creates nothing. It enlightens no one. Because, as the great Changamire taught, "Empires do not enlighten, they plunder." [. . .] The font of the Empire's great power is the archive—its vast collection of knowledge. All of it plundered from the memories of the millions they've enslaved. [. . .] It is the archive that gave the Empire its culture and technology. From the Rigellians, the Empire acquired its vast knowledge of the stars. From

Fig. 4.2: Resistance fighter Nakia enlightens T'Challa about the workings of the empire in *Black Panther: The Intergalactic Empire of Wakanda*, Part 1.

the Teku-Maza, they pilfered literature and song. From the Kronan, they learned the true power of Vibranium—life-blood of the Empire. From the Shadow People, they stole knowledge of governance and hierarchy.

This passage characterizes the Enlightenment as a system of mass enslavement and plundering and thus gives another answer to Coates's journalistic question. Filtered through the story logic of the comic, Western "civilization" and especially the United States (this passage implicitly refers to the Southern Confederacy, and the powers of vibranium recall the King Cotton economy) is unmasked as a gigantic fraud, a false claim to cultural and technological superiority derived from knowledge belonging to the colonized that is stolen, stored, and employed against the disempowered, disenfranchised, and disinherited. "Do you know what it is to be haunted?" T'Challa asks in book 6 before connecting the filling of the imperial archive with the stolen memories of the enslaved and the plundered knowledge of their people with the erasure of a Black future: "The Empire doesn't just steal our past, they steal our futures. How can we move forward when we do not know our names? Who we are? Who we love? Even as I have escaped, I am captured, held fast by these questions. Who am I? What promises have I made? And to whom? How can I move forward, knowing not what I am leaving behind?" If the enslaved are robbed of their memories and thus of their past, present, and future, they are assigned a fixed role by the empire.[33] "Empire not only manages a territory and a population but also creates the very world it inhabits," Michael Hardt and Antonio Negri maintain (xv), and this world relegates some to the status of memoryless slaves. But the enslaved refuse to be thus confined. As a rebel commander tells the rebels in book 7, "You've lived three lives—the conquered, the slave, and now the maroon. And all of those lives have existed outside the largesse of the Empire."

This viewpoint resonates with Walters's work on the archives of the Black Atlantic as well as with Hartman's resuscitative project of critical fabulation. "Where the archive records people as slave, coolie, and arsonist," Walters holds, writers of the African diaspora "set these languages mobile, aspirational, and open to the subjunctive, asking: 'what if they were rebel, lover, leader?'" (5). These issues also play out in Rebecca Hall, Hugo Martínez, and Sarula Bao's *Wake* and its tribute to the strength and courage of women who did not resign themselves to their fate as enslaved people and instead became rebels. Coates uses the affordances of popular serial storytelling to "posit stowaways, underground resistance leaders, and literate rebels who would not likely appear in the records of the plantation owner, slave ship captain, and court reporter" (Walters 6). For the rebels in the storyworld, however, such archival interventions are hardly possible. As M'Baku exclaims in book 7, they can aim only "to neutralize the archive. The Empire evolves too fast for us to fight, because the archive is alive. It does not just hold knowledge. It analyzes and dissects it. Searching for patterns. For new ways to conquer. New ways to enslave." While this new type of archive evokes a technodystopian state in which powerful institutions utilize digital tools and artificial intelligence to monitor, control, and exploit the population, M'Baku still has hope: "We are going to avenge its victims, and make them whole. Because the Empire didn't simply steal our technologies and culture—they stole our lives."[34]

Graphically rendered and narratively set up as a scenario of the future, this *Black Panther* story arc speaks forcefully to the demands of the present as well as the significance of the past. As Simone Browne has shown, technodystopias usually build on a longer history of technological development, and technologies of surveillance have for centuries been tied to skin color and racial affiliation. Browne speaks of "racializing surveillance" in cases "when enactments of surveillance reify boundaries along racial lines, thereby reifying race, and where the outcome of this is often discriminatory and violent treatment" (8). Focusing specifically on "the role of surveillance in the archive of slavery and the transatlantic slave trade in particular," she discerns an "enduring archive of transatlantic slavery and its afterlife, in this way making visible the many ways that race continues to structure surveillance practices" (8, 11). In Coates's *Black Panther*, the race-based categorization of the Black population as enslaved merchandise reifies their subjugated status and sanctions the empire's efforts to steal, store, and mine their memories to solidify its political and economic power. While the empire exemplifies "how and why populations are tracked, profiled, policed, and governed," the maroons around N'Yami, M'Baku, and T'Challa represent "the ways that those who are [. . .] subject to surveillance subvert, adopt, endorse, resist, innovate, limit, comply with, and monitor that very surveillance" (Browne 13). By destroying the empire's mechanisms of control and retrieving the stolen memories from the archive, they break out of the cycle of racial subjugation that for centuries has haunted the Black diaspora.

BLACK PANTHER AS ARCHIVAL AGENT

This section builds on Hirsch and Taylor's understanding of archives as "engines of circulation" and sites "of potentiality, provisionality, and contingency" as well as De Kosnik's work on the rogue archives of the digital era by offering a reading of *Black Panther* that moves away from storyworld depictions of archives to focus on the comic's role as an actor or archival agent in the field of superhero comics.

As a current (re)iteration of an older Marvel property, Coates's *Black Panther* represents what Stoler in her analysis of colonial archives calls an arsenal "reactivated to suit new governing strategies" (3). These strategies include Marvel's efforts at "memory management"—cultivating a particular "corporate narrative memory" and using the character's continuity as "a creative and commercial resource," as Jean-Matthieu Méon writes (190, 194). The trade paperback collections of Coates's *Black Panther* foreground the fact that they reactivate as well as revise the original Black Panther comics. The appendixes of books 1 and 2 reprint the earliest Black Panther stories from the 1960s, thereby foregrounding the continuities and dissonances between Lee and Kirby's Black Panther and Coates and Stelfreeze's updated version, which is less beholden to (but also not entirely free from) stereotypes of Africa and which addresses the genre's troubled history of gender representation by affording major roles to a number of female characters (Shuri, Ramonda, Ororo Munroe/Storm, the Dora Milaje [including a queer romance between the renegades Ayo and Aneka explored at length in the *World of Wakanda* spin-off]).[35] In the first appearance of Lee and Kirby's Black Panther, The Thing (Ben Grimm) describes the Black superhero as "some refugee from a *Tarzan* movie," recognizing the comic's indebtedness to popular representations of African Otherness—"the pop culture of plunderers," as Coates writes in *We Were Eight Years in Power* (112)—but also registering the new character's difference from the popular mold: he is revealed to be a master scientist and superior fighter who gives the Fantastic Four a run for their money.[36]

If the backlog of these and other superhero stories is conceptualized as an archive, *Black Panther* intervenes in the messages this archive stores for posterity by retroactively reshaping it, including Marvel's decision to make its first Black superhero hail from Africa as a way of sidestepping racial tensions in mid-1960s America. This choice indicated the publisher's tendency to feature Black superheroes in secondary roles, a phenomenon Coates mocks with the character of Dr. Eliot Augustus Franklin/Thunderball, who complains about having initially been conceived as "the black Bruce Banner" (book 4).[37] The chronology at the end of book 1 maps the history of the Black Panther's comic book appearances and serves as a finding aid for readers interested in digging into the archive of the character, turning the colonial practice of mapping (narrative) territory into a call to critically investigate—or creatively remap—superhero history.[38] Book 5 further revives one of Marvel's archival mechanisms from the 1960s, the editorial footnote, which had introduced a referential system through which readers could navigate their way to earlier stories deemed relevant for the current narrative present. The comic book issues of *Black Panther* even featured letter columns with reader feedback and editorial comments as a throwback to the predigital era, where such columns had been a central element of the genre's evolution (see Stein, *Authorizing* chap. 2).

Moreover, underscoring De Kosnik's assertion that cultural memory is produced "at every step throughout the process of making" (4), *Black Panther* draws on literary and visual archives that are not limited to comic books. This includes references to Douglass; Henri Dumas (an excerpt from the poem "Rootsong" that frames issue 3; see Coates, "Wakanda"); W. E. B. Du Bois (book 2: "Two men are forever warring within me," a reference to double consciousness in *The Souls of Black Folk*); Audre Lorde (the women's leader M'bali paraphrases Lorde's essay "The Master's Tools Will Never Dismantle the Master's House" and presents it as a Zami parable in issue 9, reprinted in book 3)[39]; Ralph Ellison (a rebel leader, Ras the Exhorter, whose name evokes a character in *Invisible Man*); and Edmund S. Morgan, whose argument in *American Slavery, American Freedom: The Ordeal of Colonial Virginia* Changamire summarizes from an Afrodiasporic perspective: "That book chronicles the attempt to raise an entire race of kings. And every year thousands of them were born and charged with keeping thousands more underfoot" (book 3).

In addition, in book 5, the imprisoned rebel leader Tutu discusses the problem of dualities and binaries with the philosopher Changamire, while surrounded by books. Four titles are discernible and not only reveal the character's political thinking but contribute additional works to the canon of literature Coates's *Black Panther* summons: French anthropologist Marcel Griaule's *Conversations with Ogotemmêli: An Introduction to Dogon Religious Ideas* (1948), Ghanaian writer Ayi Kwei Armah's historical novel *Two Thousand Seasons* (1973), Nigerian activist Ken Saro-Wiwa's *A Month and a Day: A Detention Diary* (1995), and Ghanaian American novelist Yaa Gyasi's *Homecoming* (2016). Moreover, Okorafor et al.'s *Shuri* series (collected in 2019 as *Shuri: The Search for Black Panther* and *Shuri: 24/7 Vibranium*) adds musical references to the mix: the space-lubber (a giant grasshopper) grotesquely sings Aretha Franklin's "Respect" (1967) in issue 3, and Shuri quotes Sun Ra's Afrofuturist film *Space Is the Place* (1974) in issue 4. These intertextual and intermedial references can be seen as archival finding aids placed throughout the story or as an intellectual framework—a customization of the comic book sources that sanctions the creative practices of De Kosnik's rogue archivists, who are encouraged to look up these sources and enticed to read or at least acknowledge them—within which the comic situates itself and which it asks readers to enter to grasp the narrative's historical, political, and literary implications.

In addition, a wide range of interpictorial allusions mark the comics' awareness of the larger archive of political images, banking on readers' ability to connect the dots. A splash page in the second installment of Coates's *Black Panther* evokes images of US soldiers tearing down a Saddam Hussein statue during the invasion of Iraq and thus conjures up the post-9/11 failed nation-building projects propagated by American neocons. A first cover variant strategically placed immediately before the beginning of the narrative in book

1 contains Alex Ross's depiction of a grim Black Panther in midair surrounded by policemen aiming their guns at his body. This reference to the Black Lives Matter movement and the nationwide protests against anti-Black violence and police brutality in the wake of the shooting of Michael Brown and the subsequent Ferguson riots sets the tone for the ensuing story. (Coates et al.'s *Black Panther & the Crew* evokes the same historical context and brings up Black revolutionary Black Panther figures from the 1960s like Huey Newton.)[40] These references are further historicized in book 3 when the depiction of Wakandan women protesting T'Challa's power as king recalls photographic and televisual images of civil rights protesters in the 1950s and 1960s as well as of women marching for the right to vote. Some of these visuals do not produce such strong political associations, even though Coates and his illustrators' type of Afrofuturism is hardly an apolitical narrative and aesthetic choice. The comic incorporates creative applications and adaptations of its central imagery to ongoing political conflicts instead of outsourcing this practice to readers and fan creators.[41]

Finally, the trade paperback collections include paratextual "archive stories" (Antoinette Burton's term) that inform readers about the making of the series. These include a "Behind the Scenes" feature with Stelfreeze; character sketches, page layouts, and segments of scripts in a "Process and Development" section; an interview with Coates and Ryan Coogler, "Down with the King"; and a "How to Draw Black Panther in Six Easy Steps" exercise that entices readers to become comics artists. If contemporary media users treat popular culture "*as an archive*, an enormous repository of narratives, characters, worlds, images, graphics, and sounds from which they can extract the raw matter they need for their own creations" (De Kosnik 4), *Black Panther* offers this audience a helping hand. All eight paperbacks include variant cover galleries that disperse the iconography of the Black Panther across an array of graphic styles, propagating a kind of aesthetic multiplicity that no longer insists on an original or authentic urtext and encourages adaptation and revision as integral elements of genre evolution—without, however, abandoning corporate control and the commercial possibilities of superhero franchising.

With regard to franchising, issues 6 and 7 of Okorafor et al.'s *Shuri* spin-off bring the titular character to Brooklyn, where she teams up with Spider-Man and Ms. Marvel to prevent Augustin Torres, a misguided high schooler and ambitious science buff, from messing up his life. Torres is coded as Latinx, further diversifying the main cast of a comic book that includes Afro–Puerto Rican Miles Morales (Spider-Man), Pakistani American Kamala Khan (Ms. Marvel), and the African Shuri. The two issues, written not by Okorafor but by Vita Ayala, do not dwell much on this diversity, but they pull the young

Shuri into the orbit of some of Marvel's more mainline superhero characters and thereby create an archival message in the present that might have lasting consequences when looking back on the time Coates's "return" of the Black Panther, Coogler's two successful movies (*Black Panther* and *Wakanda Forever*), and spin-off series like *Shuri* made substantial inroads into a historically predominantly white genre.[42] An iconic moment in issue 6 that follows on the heels of a longer humorous scene in which both Miles and Shuri talk to their mothers via digital devices shows the two teenagers bonding over "living in an elder brother's shadow" (Miles in Peter Parker's, Shuri in T'Challa's). A medium close-up shot shows them facing each other and fist-bumping as Miles remarks, "Good thing we're both our own butt-kicking people then, huh?" and Shuri replies, "Ha, right!" Part of the pleasure of seeing these two superheroes connect stems from their relationship to and difference from the superhero foil, including older depictions of Marvel superheroes such as the white male Spider-Man and Black male Black Panther. Moreover, Shuri outs herself at the end of the miniseries as "a *Lord of the Rings* nerd" who named one of her inventions "little Sauron" because like Shuri's new gadget, Sauron "wasn't just watching, he was also smelling, hearing, tasting . . . using all the senses" (issue 10). In so doing, Shuri inscribes the character and the series into the larger world of fantasy fiction.

The urge to go rogue with the Black Panther cosmos and make it meaningful beyond the realm of the Marvel-controlled franchise is evident in countless examples of fan art and fan fiction as well as in online discussions of its politics and aesthetics. Individual professional illustrators have created images celebrating the late Chadwick Boseman (Andrade; Santiago); fans have uploaded more than sixty-eight thousand images of characters and scenes based on the comics and films to deviantart.com; the Archive of Our Own website has nearly ten thousand fan fiction stories involving Shuri ("Shuri [Marvel]"); and Joel Osminski's Pinterest page devoted to the franchise (one of many such pages) has 614 pinned images of Black Panther. These examples, along with the many posts and comments on social media and in online forums such as Reddit, show that this phenomenon amounts to more than what Tina M. Campt calls a "burgeoning archive of amateur digital imagery" that would constitute an "everyday archive of Black precarity" (*Black* 5). This is a complex and arguably convoluted mixture of personal postings and commercial endeavors that are significant not so much because they "capture the vicissitudes of Black life" (4–5) but because they claim a stake in a commercial franchise that centers Black characters and a Black universe while remaining subject to the capitalist logic, social relations, and political structures that condition race-based inequality and injustice.

REBELLIOUS WOMEN

When the news that Coates would script the *Black Panther* series broke, George Gene Gustines wrote in *The New York Times*, "Ta-Nehisi Coates can be identified in many ways: as a national correspondent for The Atlantic, as an author and [as a] nominee for the National Book Award's nonfiction prize. But Mr. Coates also has a not-so-secret identity, as evidenced by some of his Atlantic blog posts and his Twitter feed: Marvel Comics superfan." That superfans write superhero comics is not a new phenomenon: generations of writers and artists have self-identified as fans to bolster the credibility of their versions of particular characters or series.[43] But Gustines's remarks highlight a tension that shapes Coates's *Black Panther*. Boonin-Vail's asserts that Coates uses the *Black Panther* series as a vehicle to diversify his author profile and amplify his "popular intellectual critique" (135, 137), and as Julian C. Chambliss asserts, "Coates' approach is informed by ideological frameworks growing from" critical race theory and Black feminist theory ("Different" 210).[44]

Yet as Hollie FitzMaurice has noted, the representation of women in the *Black Panther* comics is conflicted at best. FitzMaurice's assessment is based mostly on a critical reading of Hudlin's *Deadliest of the Species* arc and applies to a lesser degree to Coates's run. Coates certainly presents a wide range of strong female figures both heroic and more villainous. Moreover, some of the resistance against Wakanda's "totalitarian monarchism" (Bibi Burger and Engels 16) is formulated as an explicitly gendered critique of patriarchal structures. "No man should have that much power," Ayo maintains, touting the rebellious actions of the Midnight Angels, while Aneka makes the case for women's liberation in book 2: "Once we were bred by men solely to give our bodies to other men. We have seen how the woman becomes the enslaved. Let us now show them how the enslaved becomes a legend."[45] Yet in Coates's Wakanda, Shuri is initially a spirit, roaming the Djalia in search of memories and thus denied a physical existence, and she later becomes a hard-hitting superheroine whose corporeal depiction, like that of other female characters (especially Storm), does not completely abandon the generic preset, even though her ability to turn her skin to stone and become unbreakable (first shown in book 2 and tied to the heroic story of Queen Mother Sologon) serves as an apt metaphor for the need to shield the female body in the public sphere. Aneka, the rebellious member of the Dora Milaje, appears in the first issue as a conventional, scantily clad warrior figure in an unconventional pose—as a chained perpetrator in the posture reminiscent of a kneeling slave. Moreover, the depiction of same-sex intimacy between Aneka and Ayo (most prominently in *World of Wakanda*) is not entirely beyond the purview of the genre's formative voyeurism, while rebel leader Zenzi is occasionally eroticized, such as when her green cloak exposes her midriff and the lower parts of her breasts in the sixth installment of the series (book 2).⁴⁶ Coates's "popular black feminist project" (Boonin-Vail 146) is in that sense hampered by the weight not only of comic book tradition, with its oppressive tendency to subject female figures to a (white) male gaze, but also by his indebtedness to a line of Black intellectualism that also favors male over female heroes.

In an interview conducted before the release of *World of Wakanda*, Gay confronted Coates with the male-centric worldview of *Between the World and Me* ("Charge"). Coates largely agreed with this critique but also emphasized his homages to authors Isabel Wilkerson, Toni Morrison, Thavolia Glymph, Kidada Williams, Paula Giddings, and Natasha Tretheway. In *Between the World and Me*, he had already acknowledged "that all are not equally robbed of their bodies, that the bodies of women are set out for pillage in ways I could never truly know" (65). Moreover, the comics repeatedly address the subjection of women to rape and concubinage, such as when one of the elder women leaders of the Midnight Angels confronts Tetu with his soldiers' brutal acts: "A revolution in Wakanda that overlooks half the country is no revolution at all" (book 3).⁴⁷ In addition, in *The World of Wakanda*, Aneka kills a prominent village leader known for raping young female sex slaves, justifying her act in court: "I did what had to be done. I am justice" (issue 4). When admonished by the judge that "justice is the responsibility of those who have been appointed to administer it," she cites the superhero's antinomian principle: "You do not dictate my responsibilities. I adhere to a higher code."

This, then, is exactly where Coates's version of the *Black Panther* can do significant cultural work. By claiming a heightened degree of intellectual sophistication through its main author's critical acclaim and the many intertextual references to his nonfiction work and beyond and by associating itself with the journalistic search for historical truths, the comic opens itself up to the kinds of gendered critique offered by Gay and others. Part of its cultural work, then, is the inclusion of female authors and perspectives not only in spin-off series like *World of Wakanda* and *Black Panther & the Crew* but also in works like Okorafor et al.'s *Black Panther: Long Live the King* and the *Shuri* series.

In Okorafor's story arcs "Blackout," "The Sacrifice," and "Obinna's Folly" (collected in Okorafor et al., *Black Panther: Long Live the King*), T'Challa is drawn to the Mute Zone, a section of Wakanda whose inhabitants have disconnected themselves from all of the country's technological advances to practice democracy within the Wakandan monarchy. Their chief is a woman, Ìkoko, a researcher working on a dissertation on quantum computing who seeks to recover the lost work of the scientist Obinna, who had been developing a form of "sentient vibranium." Even though T'Challa ultimately averts the threat, Ìkoko provides him with the necessary information and insights. "It

Fig. 4.3: Shuri's and Wakanda's ancestors as floating figures in *Shuri: 24/7 Vibranium*.

was a brilliant idea, but not a good one," she states at one point, serving as a sensible adviser to the king. Recalling the initial agreement between Obinna and T'Challa's father, who instructed her "to build a weapon he believed would ensure Wakanda's safety forever," Ìkoko's head is surrounded by a flowery kind of ornament that visualizes her intimate ties to her memories—a form of personally stored national memory.

A related memory device appears in Okorafor et al.'s *Shuri: The Search for Black Panther* and *Shuri: 24/7 Vibranium*, where three of Shuri's and Wakanda's ancestors, visualized as tribal masks and totems, appear as floating heads and bodies circling her head as she considers the fate of her brother and their friend Eden, whom she presumes lost in space (fig. 4.3). These nearly translucent ancestral figures, whom only Shuri can see and hear, address her as "Ancient Future" and thus acknowledge her role as Wakanda's present-day leader in charge of T'Challa's fate (she designed the spaceship for the mission). But these figures insist the voices of the past have a bearing on the nation's present and future ("You're never alone," one of them tells Shuri after she has requested "to be alone right now" in issue 1 of *Shuri: The Search for Black Panther*). They come across as an Africanized version of Spider-Man's famous spider-sense, but rather than merely warning Shuri of imminent danger, they regularly talk to and advise her.

Over the course of Okorafor's run, these floating ancestral figures appear frequently to serve as Shuri's conscience, reminding her of her duties ("Princess, shouldn't you be preparing for tonight?" [issue 8]) but also promising their support ("Help me handle it," Shuri pleads, and the ancestors respond in unison, "Always" [issue 9]). In issue 5, they accompany Shuri to a meeting with the Egungun, a pan-African alliance that takes its name from "the Yoruba collective ancestral spirits" (issue 4). T'Challa had launched the Egungun to overcome Wakanda's isolationism and build alliances across the continent, and as Shuri, in issue 5, is walking through the library in which the group is to meet, the ancestors tell her about the destruction of old knowledge: "You know, Shuri, Timbuktu was once the academic hub of the world. Even the Wakandans came here searching for knowledge"; "Astronomy, mathematics, law, medicine . . . so much exchange from so many places." Shuri is aware of the need for the institutional preservation of knowledge from those who seek to destroy it to maximize their power over the people, noting that "militants burned many of the ancient manuscripts only a few years ago. Thank goodness for the book-saving libraries." Rather than privileging scientific over spiritual knowledge, Shuri uses cowrie shells, which one of the ancestors describes as "old African technology" that allows her "to take on aliens." As she accepts the Black Panther's mantle, she states, "Sometimes old African tech is still the best tech."[48]

Shuri's sentiment recalls the first issue of Hudlin's *Black Panther*, which showcases two attempts by outside forces to invade Wakanda. The first attempt, set in the fifth century A.D., depicts a rival tribe trying to sneak into Wakandan territory but being decimated by contraptions that impale them; those who evade these traps are then killed by a hail of arrows fired from giant crossbows. The second attempt takes place in the nineteenth century when supervillain

Ulysses Klaue's great-great-great-grandfather leads a military effort to colonize the country in which he exclaims, "We will not lose our grip on civilization because of those monkeys. We will not be dragged down to their level." But he is killed when the company's Gatling gun, a symbol of Western military advancement, implodes because of the Black Panther's ultramodern technology (the robot-like device standing behind the Black Panther looks much more modern than does the Gatling gun, and the leader's dismissive reference to the tribe's "juju" does not even begin to grasp the science behind the machine). In issue 4, when Klaue is about to attack present-day Wakanda, his colonialist and white supremacist rallying cry is undermined by one of his French mercenaries. "Centuries ago, we brought civilization, commerce, and God to Africa. We dragged them into the 20th century," Klaue declares, prompting the mercenary to respond snidely, "in chains," evoking the history of oppression that marks the Western presence on the African continent.[49]

If Hudlin foregrounds Wakanda's efforts to repel Western forms of colonization and military domination, Okorafor's Shuri at least initially (issue 1) decides to act of her own accord, ignoring the ancestors' warning until she is summoned by Ramonda to a meeting of the country's most powerful women under an ancient baobab tree (later Grootboom the Second). Shuri's mother has revived a council, formerly called the Elephant's Trunk, because of T'Challa's uncertain situation, and its members include "a fairly wide representation of Wakandan women": Okoye, a member of the Dora Milaje; Zuwena, the director of the Extraction Academy; Mansa, a young woman who has just graduated from high school; Tiwa, a mother and professor of physics at Wakanda University; and Bube, who identifies herself as "single mother of two, dressmaker of many." This heterogeneous group of women—selected for their "diversity of thought," as Mansa remarks in issue 2—takes charge of the country's affairs in T'Challa's absence. They profess different opinions about what should be done, from Okoye's reminder "that Wakanda is a constitutional monarchy now" and that "the Black Panther is no longer the ruler of Wakanda, except in spirit" to Bube's rejoinder, "But what's a nation without a spirit?" They ultimately ask Shuri to again take on the mantle of the Black Panther. Shuri declines, citing her previous death and then launching into a political plea: "Let this tradition end and begin a new one. One where Wakanda stands on its own, without needing a symbol or protector. Let's show the world who we really are." The women's varied reactions—"Oh, come on," Mansa replies; "Mscheeeew," Bube exclaims; "Modern African democracy is our best future," Tiwa holds—not only recall ongoing debates about African politics but also model potential reader discussions of Wakanda's political future. Shuri's mother ends the first meeting by conceding, "Clearly we made a mistake asking you, daughter. No, you are not your brother." In so doing, she brings the openness of the deliberation back into the realm of the superhero narrative, where questions of leadership, duty, and

Fig. 4.4: The women's council underneath the baobab tree in *Shuri: 24/7 Vibranium*. Page one of two.

heroism traditionally focus on the thoughts and actions of exceptional—and usually male—individuals.⁵⁰

Yet in the face of T'Challa's continuing absence (after his brief appearance at the beginning of issue 1, he remains lost in space throughout all ten issues),

Fig. 4.4: The women's council underneath the baobab tree in *Shuri: 24/7 Vibranium*. Page two of two.

Shuri accepts her role as Black Panther and learns to value the advice of this women's council, tapping into its collective embodied repertoire of female knowledge even though she does not always agree with the concerns the women raise (fig. 4.4). In issue 8, for instance, Bube restates her conviction that "Wakanda is better off without a Black Panther. We have ancestors to protect us—and our own strength and intelligence," a position that questions the nation's political system, its relationship to the past, and the superhero logic at the center of the Black Panther mythos. Shuri, who is wearing her version of the Black Panther suit (including the cowrie shell necklace), disagrees with the challenge but concedes, "I may need your wisdom in the future."

However, Shuri's acceptance of the Black Panther role makes her own limitations more problematic. She has lost some of her superhero abilities, among them shape-shifting and turning herself into stone. Accompanied by the three ancestral figures who have been with her throughout the narrative and who transform from their iconic form as aestheticized floating heads into full-bodied and realistically rendered tribal Africans, Shuri eventually enters the Djalia and discovers that the space-lubber has been eating some of the ancestral memories responsible for her powers. The young Mansa, who was accidentally projected into space with Shuri and taken by the space-lubber, suggested in issue 4 that "it was like it was . . . mining my memories or something," but only now does Shuri fully understand what is happening. "I learned how to make my skin impenetrable from the memory of Sologon and her power to turn to stone," Shuri observes after having noted the disappearance of the "super-important memory" of Sologon's village and spirit. Although she "can't call back the actual memory," she continues, nothing stored in the Djalia can be completely lost, and her ability can therefore be restored: "Once a story is written," Shuri concludes, "it can never be unwritten. Those memories are somewhere." While Shuri speaks these words within the storyworld of the comic, they can also be interpreted as a metacomment on the serial structure of the Black Panther universe, where attentive readers can decode the remarks about queen mother Sologon in *Shuri* as a reference to a four-page history told by Queen Ramonda as she and Shuri are roaming the Djalia in issue 8 of Coates's run. We learn that Sologon was a fierce warrior who shamed the wise men of her tribe by leading male warriors into battle against an invading army. Sologon's "spirit of iron," the legend goes, made these fighters "unbreakable": they were able to turn their skin into stone.

In the final issue of Okorafor's run, "Living Memory," which also takes place in the Djalia, the ancestors enable Shuri to defeat the space-lubber by instructing her to weaponize Wakanda's memories. "Remember where we are," they tell her; "There are finer weapons here than that ball of chemicals in your hands. We have memories." Mgwazeni, a legendary Wakandan warrior, implores, "You know the stories, Ancient Future. Remember me." Shuri gains the power to save Wakanda from the space-lubber by remembering the stories from Wakanda's past not through any conventionally institutionalized government or historical archive but from the embodied repertoire of ancestral wisdom, coupled with the latest technology and African spirit work (cowrie shells).

This, then, may be a concerted effort to pinpoint what Samantha Pinto describes as "the feminist locations of the African diaspora" (18) in a popular serial genre of graphic storytelling that includes Coates's (to a lesser degree) and Okorafor's runs. This effort recalls fan fiction practices such as retelling a popular narrative from the perspective of a side character or creating more gender-conscious stories by refocusing or even recentering the storyworld to express a feminist consciousness in which male leadership figures tend to be scarce and where the female characters receive extensive attention and depth. When Okorafor's Shuri saves Wakanda from the space-lubber, for instance, one of her female ancestors and predecessors as Black Panther, Turkana, remarks, "You are again Ancient Future, the Griot, Princess Shuri, Head Engineer and the Black Panther. Those are a lot of titles to carry," to which Shuri responds with a grin, "I have strong shoulders" (issue 10). That Turkana's body type does not conform to the stylized bodies of conventional superheroines (including Shuri) adds a significant facet to the continuum of gender representations offered in this narrative, as does Shuri's braided hairstyle, which is prominent in this scene as well as throughout the miniseries and which, in conjunction with a number of other nontraditionally Western hairstyles, invests these characters with a sense of cultural difference that does not racially Other them.

Gay et al.'s *World of Wakanda*, in turn, centers almost exclusively on the story of Aneka and Ayo, two members of the Dora Milaje who reject the rule that the women in this royal guard have to be willing to marry the king should he so desire and who remain loyal to Wakanda rather than to the Black Panther when the nation is in danger. When Aneka scolds Ayo, "We are here to serve"; "We are women T'Challa could marry. We do not question his decisions," Ayo responds: "I will serve, Captain, but I will never marry the king" (issue 2). Aneka later changes her mind, telling T'Challa, "You have lost your soul. You have forgotten what it is to be a son of Wakanda. I am loyal to Wakanda, T'Challa. I have trusted you, but I too see that we can trust you no longer." This daring position makes room for Ayo and Aneka's relationship as lesbian lovers, which drives most of the plot of the miniseries. Coates and Gay offer readers repeated moments of intimate love and a few postsex scenes, albeit rather chaste ones: Ayo covers her breasts with a blanket while speaking with Aneka (issue 2). Their relationship adds complexity to the Black Panther storyworld by affording the female figures narrative space and character depth, but the comic also gives room to the exposure of near-naked female bodies in both fight and love scenes, offering them up to an objectifying gaze that complicates feminist readings of the series.[51]

Another significant element beyond the revisioning of gender relations in Coates and Gay's as well as in Okorafor's writing is the extension of the scope of Afrodiasporic theory and criticism, which has by and large not taken sufficient note of graphic narratives and their contribution to popular discourses about the (new) Black Atlantic.[52] This extension may not be entirely free of the kinds of superhero revenge fantasies that offer a sense of poetic justice where the historical archive prevents closure. For example, in book 7, Coates's Black Panther infiltrates the imperial freighter Taharqua on a solitary mission to upload a jamming virus into the spaceship's computer system and rescue the raw vibranium it carries. He ends up saving another kind of cargo: a young boy who is among the hundreds of newly enslaved captives whose memories the empire is about to steal. Here, the Black Panther is "putt[ing] the knife where it belongs"—doing the right thing—but his righteous act marks a significant departure from the narrative's historical subtext, the Middle Passage, where no superhero ever invaded a ship's hold to rescue the human cargo (but where the enslaved women in *Wake* free themselves by jumping off the ship and rise again at the end of the narrative).[53]

By showcasing that archives are continually constructed and contested and may even go rogue, becoming unhinged from what used to be viewed as the colonizing efforts of the culture industry to maintain control over their properties and reign over the histories and backstories of these properties, Coates, Gay, and Harvey's *Black Panther* and Okorafor et al.'s *Shuri* offer significant inroads into the decolonization of the comic book superhero as a less white, less hegemonic, and less patriarchal figure.[54] Burton's notion of the archive as a contact zone—as "the embodied experiences of the physical, emotional, intellectual, and political encounters between the scholar and the archive itself" (9)—can serve as a prompt to rethink the archives of the popular. If we read superhero comics as an evolving serial archive of fictional storytelling with real-world repercussions, the traditional contact zone would be the space in which creators and readers interact (the letter column since the late 1950s and now discussion boards and forums, blogs, and websites as well as related forms of networked digital interaction).[55] But perhaps comics like *Black Panther* can also be seen as archival agents that draw their creators and their readers into a globally accessible contact zone in which archives are continually mobilized to provide new perspectives on the global imaginaries of diasporic blackness.

If the *Black Panther* and *Shuri* series provide insights into a different kind of Black history in which Africa is central and where archives are shown to elicit dystopian futures as well as embodied memories, the graphic narratives examined in the next chapter return the gaze to the North American continent, mostly to the South, as a space of monstrous terror and racial trauma. While ancestors and memories play a significant role, these narratives foreclose any attempt to escape the horrors that continue to haunt Black life.

CH. 5

Chapter 5

MONSTROUS PASTS

In a mid-1990s interview with literary scholar Nelly McKay, Toni Morrison stated, "I am very happy to hear that my books haunt" (146). Couched in simple language, this statement presents a paradox that emerges from the alliterative contrast between the haunting powers of Morrison's stories and her happiness about this fact. To be haunted by literary portrayals of past and present suffering, Morrison seems to suggest, cannot be pleasurable, but the unpleasantness of this experience creates possibilities for celebrating Black life. This chapter investigates Morrison's paradox of haunted happiness, which is closely related to her "perfect dilemma" of forgetting and remembering as equally impossible tasks (qtd. in Chassot 197), by examining contemporary graphic narratives that invoke monsters and create scenarios of monstrosity to visualize the traumas of the past, account for their reach into the present, and unburden themselves of those traumas through consoling and sometimes celebratory (re)visions of Black history in graphic form.

The chapter returns to works addressed in earlier chapters—Tom Feelings's *Middle Passage*; Kyle Baker's *Nat Turner*; Jeremy Love and Patrick Morgan's *Bayou*; and Rebecca Hall, Hugo Martínez, and Sarula Bao's *Wake*—but broadens the scope by adding several more (and mostly more recent) texts—David F. Walker, Chuck Brown, and Sanford Greene's *Bitter Root*; Ayize Jama-Everett and John Jennings's *Box of Bones*; Jennings's *Blue Hand Mojo*; Jennings and David Brame's *The Mighty Struggle*; and Rob Guillory's *Farmhand*.[1] All of these works approach the traumas of the past as well as the traumas of everyday life in the Black diaspora through monstrous figures or figurations of monstrousness, utilizing the expressive potential of graphic narrative to challenge culturally pervasive associations of blackness and monstrosity (and vice versa) that have for centuries plagued Black communities. These works also draw on a wide range of cultural influences in their construction of monsters, incorporating and adapting elements from horror films to superhero comics and from Disney animation to gothic literature while being inspired by creators like Jack Kirby (as evidenced by Jennings's role in the *Black Kirby* project), Steve Bisette (especially his seminal *Swamp Thing*), and Mike Mignola (whose affiliation with monsters Scott Bukatman studies in *Hellboy's World*).

Morrison has argued that narratives of horror and haunting often introduce the trope of the ghost: trauma needs to find a form despite the generative tension between its inexpressibility and the urge to express it nonetheless.[2] Citing Morrison's statements in an interview with Marsha Darling (6), Joanne Chassot notes that to make readers "grasp the extent and significance of the 'carnage' and the 'devastation' that slavery caused in black people's lives and families, [. . .] loss and absence could not 'be abstract'" in *Beloved* "but had to be given a tangible form, had to appear literally in the text" (18; see also Gordon's reading of *Beloved*). Trauma must be presented, must appear literally (or visually in the context of graphic narratives), so that the loss and absence that cause it can become part of a broader effort toward cultural (re)memory and part of a larger project of (re)imagining—giving form to—historical experiences that official documents did not (and were never intended to) record.[3]

In *Monstrous Imaginaries* (2019), her study of the legacy of romanticism in comics, Maaheen Ahmed ponders the self-reflexive capacities of monsters and draws a connection to the historically maligned status of comics as a lowbrow medium: "What if monsters were also able to reflect their media contexts and the imaginaries giving them tangible form?" (6). At the center of this question is the process of translating monstrosities—of giving "form to the impossible" (3)—from the imagination to a particular medium shaped by specific limits and affordances. The works examined in this chapter underscore the significance of Ahmed's questions, shuttling between the imaginary and the tangible, the fantastic and the real, the speculative and the documentary within their storyworlds while displaying an awareness of the visual apparatus at their disposal and its potential to reshape the media contexts in which they appear.[4]

While Morrison's novels (especially *Beloved*) revolve around ghosts that haunt her characters during and after slavery, Ahmed is specifically interested in monsters.[5] Whereas ghosts as signifiers of "not only those who are absent because they are dead [. . .] but also those who are absent from the narrative of American History itself" (Chassot 17) are central to the project of (re)imagining and (re)memorizing Black history, monsters launch the "return of the repressed" (21) and do their haunting in a more spectacular fashion. According to Chassot, ghosts can simultaneously present and absent trauma:

> The ghost's presence aptly evokes the symptoms of trauma, in its uncontrollable and repetitive occurrence and its disruptive effect on temporality and chronology, as it collapses the past in which the traumatic event occurred and the present in which the traumatized subject lives. In destabilizing narrative and meaning, in keeping an irreducible absence at the heart of its presencing, the ghost also disallows a transparent rendering of the experience of trauma that would make it too accessible and a facile assimilation that would trivialize the loss and the suffering of its original victims. (24)

Monsters, especially those marked as racially deviant, perform similar functions, acting as disruptors and destabilizers of temporality and narrative meaning. Yet they intensify the ghost's haunting function, playing more aggressive roles in challenging discourses, visual and otherwise, of Black monstrosity that are entrenched in Western modernity and that cast the Black subject as an abject, uncanny, grotesquely ambivalent figure.[6] "Monsters do a great deal of cultural work," Asa Simon Mittman notes, "but they do not do it *nicely*. They not only challenge and question; they trouble, they worry, they haunt" (1).

The compatibility of ghosts and monsters becomes clear in light of Chassot's questions about the cultural functions of ghosts: "What social, political, theoretical conditions and anxieties do these ghosts address? What is their cultural specificity, and to what extent do they enter into dialogue with other ghosts outside African diaspora literature?" Chassot continues, "Beyond the poetic work that they perform as metaphors, what cultural, theoretical, and political work do these ghosts do?" (3). The same questions can be asked about the monster figures and monstrous histories analyzed in this chapter and the graphic accounts of anti-Black violence they (re)present. What poetic and what cultural work do these graphic narratives and their monsters do? What forms do the traumas of Black history take? And, harking back to Morrison, how can they transform haunted history into moments of happiness?

In asking these questions, I build on "Opening the Box," Stanford Carpenter's foreword to Jama-Everett and Jennings's *Box of Bones: Book One*. According to Carpenter, "the story of Black experiences [is] embodied in some . . . not quite living things. [. . .] They are trauma given form, crafted from the echoes of moments long gone and pain everlasting, named and identified." Moreover, "Too often we speak of trauma in terms of cycles, this idea that history is an ever-repeating set of stories. But the making of things, the giving of life to trauma is most horrific in its evolutionary implications. [. . .] What do we make of our traumas given form moving and multiplying through space and time? What do we make of these vehicles, these artifacts of our imagination that speed them along?" Carpenter's thoughts include a self-reflexive component, noting not only that "Black experiences" are traumatic and that the echoes and implications of historical traumas extend into the present but also that those who give these traumas form—for instance, by creating graphic narratives—face the difficult problem that visualizing the echoes of trauma may enable these traumas to evolve, accelerate, and multiply through space and time.

This phenomenon plays out in the final scenes of *Box of Bones*, which features a conversation between the story's main character, African American graduate student Lindsay Ford, who is pursuing a doctorate in folklore/African American studies at the University of California, Berkeley, and a Black Vietnam veteran who has seen the horrors unleashed by the box of bones, the magical artifact that contains the traumas of Black history and causes unspeakable violence when opened. For Lindsay, the box offers "access to a power, a means of self-determination," but for the veteran, "the box of bones ain't nothing you should trouble your college dumb mind over. That type of power ever come your way, you [...] bury that power before it bury you." The comic's final page shows Lindsay in her car, looking at a hand-drawn image of the hat worn by one of the monsters from the box, with the implication that the veteran's warning will not dissuade her from continuing her research. In the graphic narratives investigated in this chapter, trauma not only haunts and harms everyone within its orbit but also drives people to face it as well as to research and capture it in graphic form.

Theorist Cathy Caruth has noted the disruptive power of trauma and the impossibility of controlling its evolutionary effects, arguing that it "brings us to the limits of our understanding" (*Trauma* 4). Speaking of "the radical disruption and gaps of traumatic experience" (4), Caruth proposes "that the impact of the traumatic event lies precisely in its belatedness, in its refusal to be simply located, in its insistent appearance outside the boundaries of any single place and time" (9). For those who have been traumatized, "it is not only the moment of the [traumatic] event, but of the passing out of it that is traumatic; that *survival itself, in other words, can be a crisis*" (9). "To be traumatized," she concludes, is "to be possessed by an image or event" (4–5); those who speak of this image or event will do so from *"the site of trauma"* (11). Transcending boundaries of place and time, being possessed, struggling with survival, facing crisis—these are crucial elements of monster narratives, from gothic literature and horror fiction to contemporary graphic narratives. They are also central facets of life in the Black diaspora. They appear in all of the works discussed here, in which the site of trauma is more often than not a historical site: Tulsa's Greenwood district (*Bitter Root*), destroyed by white Oklahomans as part of a race massacre; the Deep South as the location of lynchings and other anti-Black violence (*Bayou, Box of Bones, Blue Hand Mojo, Bitter Root*) (see also Tillet).

Caruth's theory of trauma is valuable for but not entirely compatible with the analysis of graphic narratives that attempt to visualize the historical traumas of Black life. As Chassot observes, works of African American literature reveal "the limits and inadequacy of foundational but overly general theories that identify trauma in relation to a 'sudden, or catastrophic event,' an event that would moreover 'be outside the range of usual human experience'" (25, citing Caruth, *Unclaimed*). Writing from a diasporic perspective, Chassot continues, "Such definitions fail to account for experiences like slavery or ordinary racism, forms of trauma that are neither event-based nor exceptional but continuous and part of the usual, everyday life of the victims" (25). Saidiya Hartman's "afterlife of slavery" and Christina Sharpe's "living in the wake" posit racial trauma as a basic condition of modern Black subjectivity rather than as isolated instances of individual struggle. "While all modern subjects are post-slavery subjects fully constituted by the discursive codes of slavery and post-slavery," Sharpe suggests, "post-slavery subjectivity is largely borne by and readable on the (New World) *black* subject" (*Monstrous* 3). Or as Cullen Sangerye, part of the family whose members fight people transformed into monsters by racial hatred in *Bitter Root*, exclaims after a particularly vicious attack on the streets of 1920s Harlem, "There is no safe place" (95).[7]

Jennings, a graphic artist and scholar, emphasizes this ordinariness and the mundane impact of racialized trauma, addressing the need to create "speculative space[s]" (Chambliss, "Black Kirby" 23) of empowerment and healing: "When you don't see yourself reflected in the world, it causes a type of trauma" (Elysee 42).[8] Jennings also notes, "I carry a lot of the weight of the racism in our country in my own personal experience. It's a haunted existence sometimes" (Chambliss, "Soul," 51). On yet another occasion, he specifies the nature of this trauma and its propensity to haunt: "I c[o]me from Mississippi where racism is as natural as breathing. You are haunted, metaphorically, by Emmett Till's spirit on a day-to-day basis" (Hinds 101). This personal account recalls Audre Lorde's treatment of Till in her poem "Afterimages" (1981), in which the autobiographical speaker claims to have "inherited Jackson, Mississippi" as well as Till, whose "broken body is the afterimage of my 21st year / when I walked through a northern summer" and away "from each corner's photographies."[9]

Till is a central figure in the Black historical imagination, figuring as both cause and effect of a traumatic past that is still ongoing and that not only shapes the everyday sensibilities of creators like Jennings but also haunts the creative space of graphic narrative. Claudia Rankine suggests accordingly, "Historically, there is no quotidian without the enslaved, chained or dead black body to gaze upon or to hear about or to position a self against" ("Condition"). Black trauma thus enables the white norm, encapsulated in a sense of the quotidian so privileged that it tries to remain unfazed by the traumas it has historically conditioned and continues to cause until the monstrous effects of these traumas can no longer be contained and start to wreak havoc—for instance, in the form of the monsters unleashed from the box of bones or the Jinoo onslaught that transforms white supremacists into zombielike creatures in *Bitter Root*.[10]

As Jennings indicates, Black trauma is at once individual and collective, historically concrete and temporally diffuse. In her reading of Ron Eyerman's *Cultural Trauma* (2001), Maisha L. Wester connects trauma with cultural memory and thereby the broader project of remembering the past. "Cultural trauma, as a process of memory, proves integral to the (re)constitution and (re)negotiation of African American collectivity," Wester writes, "tracing the ways black cultural identity has repeatedly been constructed around the scene of slavery. In naming slavery as the original and principle [sic] trauma for black culture, Eyerman distinguishes between slavery as a real, experienced event and slavery as 'collective memory, a form of remembrance that grounded the identity-formation of a people'" (*African American* 154). The graphic narratives analyzed in this chapter are part of a larger effort to construct a more inclusive "mediated memory" that gives space to the experiences of the historically (and currently) marginalized but does not, as Wester criticizes Eyerman, limit "renegotiations of identity" (154) by always and solely returning to slavery as the nation's foundational trauma.

Although Jennings was born several years after Till's murder, he is still haunted by the teenager's spirit through a form of "epigenetic trauma," where "pain is passed through our DNA" (Woodward 129). Guillory's genetics-conscious *Farmhand* series, in turn, tells the story of Black farmer-scientist Jedidiah Jenkins's organic transplants, in which plants are grafted onto the human body to supply missing limbs or heal other physical ailments but turn out to be monstrous seeds that transform people into zombies. In these works, the passing on of race-based pain, initiated by the lynching of Jedidiah's grandfather in post-Reconstruction Louisiana, literally occurs through genetic transmission.[11] In both Jennings's life and Guillory's graphic narrative, the trauma transcends generations and is ingrained in people's bodies and psyches. It is not an external force they can evade or a history they can ignore.

Jennings's sense of epigenetic trauma is bolstered by his encounters with pop culture (where racist images proliferate), his research into Black history (including traumatic experiences), and his practice as a comics creator.[12] Working on his graphic novel adaptation of Octavia Butler's classic work of speculative fiction, *Kindred* (1979), which features a scene in which a female character is whipped, made him weep onto the original art pages and compelled him repeatedly to revisit that space of traumatic violence (98–99): "The entire book has to be broken down into panels, sketched out. Then you draw it. So you're giving it more form. Then you ink it, giving it more form. Then you color"

(Hinds 99). Creating the graphic narrative not only means giving trauma visual form but picturing it "over and over again," which results in a "retraumatization" that makes Jennings and his collaborator Damian Duffy feel "enslaved by the book" (99). There is obviously no easy escape from "vicarious trauma" (Monnica Williams qtd. in Bruce 34), a kind of secondhand traumatization that feeds on the repetitive processes of comics creation as much as on the creator's broader sense of being haunted as a Black Mississippian.[13]

Working through this retraumatization, Jennings has developed what he and Stanford Carpenter call the ethnogothic, an aesthetic that, according to Jennings, "uses gothic tropes like the ghosts, the haunted house, the doppelganger, haunted artifacts to deal with those traumas" (Woodward 129) and thus addresses the "complex tensions around the black experience in the United States and in particular the black southern experience. It's also dealing with how trauma acts as a revenant of our continually contentious narratives around race, class, and history" (Chambliss, "Soul" 51). The ethnogothic evokes a sense of intersecting geographical place and speculative space that is useful for understanding how monsters in contemporary graphic narratives populate the US South as a haunted *and* homelike space and how these narratives portray the North of the Great Migration as a region where Southern horrors (as Ida B. Wells titled her antilynching tract) become hellhounds on the migrants' trails (according to Robert Johnson's blues poetics).[14] Before considering the forms and functions of the ethnogothic, however, I discuss monster theory (especially its views on race) and the images and narratives of Black monstrosity with which contemporary graphic narratives grapple. I also explore the connection between Black death as a fixture of modernity and diasporic life and the trope of the living dead as a response as well as conjuring and root work as part of the "African American tradition of healing and harming" (Chireau, *Black* 4; see also Chireau, "Looking"; Chireau, "From Horror").

MONSTERS AND RACE

The relationship between race and monstrosity is a very old one, going back to the belief in "monstrous races" in the Middle Ages and evolving during the Enlightenment into a thought system that stabilized the distinction between the civilized and the primitive, the human and the not quite human, the white European ideal and the Black African deviation from that ideal (see Weinstock, "Introduction"; Asma; Gilmore; Strickland, *Saracens*; Strickland, "Monstrosity"). This belief system undergirded the transatlantic slave trade and the institution of chattel slavery. After enslaved Black Africans were defined as noncivilized, not-human cargo and as impervious to pain (as some theories held and as the brutal logic of the tight-packing ships indicated), transporting this "merchandise" across the ocean and forcing millions of people and their children (and their children's children) to work as chattel on American plantations could be characterized as a project of civilizing the uncivilized or taming the monsters rather than as a massive crime central to the establishment of Western capitalism.[15]

Approaching the figure of the monster from the perspective of the African diaspora and the foundational trauma of the Middle Passage means recognizing a dialectical notion of monstrousness whose significances and implications shift depending on the vantage point from which it is perceived.[16] First, there is the prominent conjunction of monstrosity with blackness that we find in Western discourse, a conjunction that takes on specific meanings in colonial and postcolonial North America as the subjugation of Black subjects had to be defended against the egalitarian rhetoric of the nation's founding documents.[17] What Stephen T. Asma calls "the myth of the black monster" (233) and all that it implies has ensured the continuation of racialized trauma from the first moment an enslaved African touched North American soil to the structural racism and anti-Black violence of the present day. As myths are wont to do, the myth of the Black monster—prominently propagated through the figure of the Black rapist in D. W. Griffith's *The Birth of a Nation* (1915) and evoked as a racist trope in *Bayou*—assigns negative characteristics to Black Americans to legitimize otherwise untenable fantasies of normative difference, of a superior whiteness that is everything the Black monster (which by definition is not human and therefore cannot be a citizen) is not.[18] This is why monsters are often evoked to embody racialized and/or sexualized Otherness, to display a deviance that may serve as a justification for violence against those labeled monstrous and as a legitimation for exclusionary tactics intended to keep the monsters at bay.[19] As Wells wrote, the accusation of having raped a white woman placed the Black victim "beyond the pale of human sympathy" because "the world accepted the story that the Negro is a monster which the southern white man painted him" (qtd. in Cone 127).[20] By enabling the distinction between human and not-human, discourses of monstrosity have performed horrendous cultural work in sanctioning binary forms of thinking and attendant practices of Othering.[21]

Yet as monster theory holds, monsters must be repeatedly elicited, and their monstrosity must be continuously claimed to satisfy the specific demands of their time and place. And even if they may be created to sanction binary thinking, they never fully succeed in doing so.[22] Writing in 1854, when the Kansas-Nebraska Act unsettled the balance between abolitionism and support for human bondage, pro-slavery Mississippi statesman Henry Hughes claimed in *Treatise on Sociology, Theoretical and Practical* (1854) that "hybridism is heinous. Impurity of races is against the law of nature. Mulattoes are monsters" (239–40).[23] But as Southern enslaver society knew only too well and as slave narratives and abolitionist literature made clear, the actual separation of the races was much less rigid than Hughes's treatise surmised, with cross-racial intercourse forced on Black women by their enslavers and with the one-drop rule acknowledging the existence of what racist discourse termed miscegenation or amalgamation.[24] The monster is evoked as a threat against white supremacy and fantasies of racial purity, brutally marking the human consequences of the sexual violence against Black women as monstrous while hiding the monstrous act (legally sanctioned rape) itself. Countering this denial, Feelings's *Middle Passage* visualizes the sexual horrors to which enslaved women were subjected by the crews of the ships, both indicating the source of the "monstrous intimacies" imposed on the Black female subjects that Christina Sharpe traces in her study and underscoring the monumental—indeed, biblical—accusation that informs her work: "In the beginning is sexual trauma" (*Monstrous* 56).[25]

Hazel V. Carby rightly notes that "the institutionalized rape of black women has never been as powerful a symbol of Black oppression as the spectacle of lynching" (39). This is true to some extent in the graphic narratives analyzed in this book, where the lynching of male characters is a recurring event but the sexual violence against women remains underdeveloped. The exceptions include Feelings's *Middle Passage* and Mat Johnson et al.'s *John Constantine Hellblazer: Papa Midnite*, which presents a rape scene as part of its depiction of the 1712 uprising in colonial New York, where the white colonists capture a group of Black rebels who have fled into a nearby forest.[26] Asked about what to do with the Black women, one of the white pursuers declares, "That's where the heap of fun comes in." The next panel shows one of the women kneeling on all fours in the snow and screaming "Noooooo!" (highlighted in red font). The following panel shifts the perspective toward the rest of the group but repeats the scream to signal the moment of rape. The violence is not represented but can be imagined through the process of closure. Moreover, the woman is depicted in a sexualized fashion, which might indicate the gaze of the perpetrators but also objectifies her.

If monsters in this racially and sexually charged discourse embody that which is positioned outside the norm as a way to mark the boundary between normal and abnormal, they are ultimately unknowable creatures, signifiers of the uncertain that prod the limits of the imagination and not only fascinate but also challenge the epistemic and ontological grounds on which they were designated as monsters.[27] "Monsters have power," Leila Taylor writes (*Darkly* 79), while Noël Carroll reads them as agents of "category-jamming" (194). As inherently transgressive and ambiguous figures, monsters can destabilize what they are meant to solidify. In the context of US race relations, it is no surprise, then, that the conflicted affect of the monster—what Asma calls "lure and repulsion" (6) and Jeffrey Jerome Cohen describes as "fear, desire, anxiety, and fantasy" or "repulsion and attraction" ("Monster" 38, 49)—resonates with the nation's troubled treatment of Black life as well as with Morrison's paradox of haunted happiness. Working in a medium whose "cross-discursive" nature (Chute and DeKoven 768) and precarious status as an image-text hybrid has often been taken as a threat—as illustrated by Fredric Wertham's notorious *Seduction of the Innocent* (1954)—and whose history of denigrating Black culture is substantial, African American creators approach the monster and its conflicted allure from a peculiar position. In these works, the anti-Black atrocities of the past emerge as "excesses [that] cry out for generic recasting into the horror gerne" (Wanzo, "On Monstrosity" 483)

We therefore need to account for two mutually constitutive notions of monsters and monstrosity. The first notion concerns the conjunction of blackness and monstrosity that underscores how people of color have been historically positioned outside the master narrative of American exceptionalism and how violence (physical, psychological, structured) against them has for centuries been sanctioned.[28] This conjunction pervades historical formations and systems of exploitation from the Middle Passage and chattel slavery to the Jim Crow era, the Harlem Renaissance, the civil rights movement, and Black Lives Matter and provides the traumatic impetus for these monster narratives. But these narratives also point to the second notion of monstrosity—the monstrous violence marshaled against Black Americans over many centuries and the traumatic effects of that violence.

THE LIVING DEAD

One of the most visually and affectively striking—and harrowing—images of racial trauma given graphic form occurs in chapter 2, "Wretched Blood," of Jama-Everett and Jennings's *Box of Bones*. It calls forth staples of racist iconography from America's visual archive (fig. 5.1). The opening splash page takes the form of a collage and shows a tree surrounded by green space, in front of which dangle various "coon" artifacts with nooses tightened around their necks and torsos. These artifacts include golliwog rag dolls, inspired by Florence K. Upton's late-nineteenth-century children's books (e.g., *The Adventures of Two Dutch Dolls and a "Golliwogg"* [1885]), as well as a figurine of a Black child eating a watermelon, two Black servant dolls, a mechanical coin bank in the shape of a grotesquely grinning Black face ("Jolly"), and a 1916 caricature of a Black child drinking ink ("[Caricature]"; see also Gilson). Jama-Everett and Jennings have supplanted the bodies and faces of the Black men and women

Fig. 5.1: "Wretched Blood," the opening splash page of chapter 2 in *Box of Bones: Book One*.

documented in so many lynching photographs with artifacts from the racist past that sanctioned the killing of Black citizens by designing them as either savagely monstrous or grotesquely infantile beings—as noncitizens who lack legal, social, and political protections.

At the bottom of the collage, a muscular Black man leaps out of the image's wooden frame, his hands partially shackled, a noose around his neck, and his face and torso obscured by an overlaid image of a gorilla baring its teeth. The figure recalls the description of Calvin Wagstaff as "a big and burly wretch, with long, sinewy, apelike arms and massive hands" in the fictional newspaper article featured in *Bayou* (vol. 1). The image also evokes the racist discourse, visual and otherwise, of African Americans as simian creatures. This is the ugly face of monstrous blackness, but it also plays into an issue central to graphic narratives: the issue of Black anger or rage and how these emotions, though justified in light of the long history of anti-Black violence, may end up consuming any sense of self and community.

With the collage setting the tone for the ensuing storyline, graduate student Lindsay Ford goes to New Orleans, where she encounters the city's voodoo culture. A flashback sequence informs her that the historical Madame Laveau, a voodoo priestess, had the box of bones until her sister Baptise stole it in the wake of her lover's lynching. Despite Madame Laveau's warning that "the box unleashes terror, not vengeance," Baptise insists on using its magic to wreak havoc on the murderers and their children: "I will punish the fruit of their loins," she exclaims, "those Stygian crevasses they crawled from, their drunken elders who did not teach them to fear proper power, and those who stay silent while me and mine swing from trees" (chap. 2). Opening the box, Baptise unleashes "a terror she'd soon regret" even though some of her targets "deserved the wrath," as Mister Alphonse, Madame Laveau's nephew who narrates the flashback sequence, concedes.

What ensues in the following fifteen pages can only be described as carnage based on racial trauma and its most brutal consequences. The sequence begins with a white family discussing lynching over dinner in a Southern cabin. The girl and boy are eager to attend their first lynching, but the father argues that it is "grown man business" and that "the responsibility of the white man to keep n*****s in check is a sacred" task. This is white supremacy in its most entrenched form, internalized as a civic and quasireligious duty by the region's poor white population and embraced as a legitimate practice by their children. The scene goes to the heart of Rebecca Wanzo's argument about the monstrous histories of white supremacy: "The refusal to see monstrosity in white supremacist violence is part of how racism does its work. People do not want to acknowledge that their ancestors committed monstrous acts, they do not want to admit that their loved ones are racist, or that structural racism continues. [. . .] Many people probably saw goodness in family pictures of family members smiling around lynched Black people" ("On Monstrosity" 482).

Box of Bones fractures this historical denial and the attendant whitewashing of whole family histories from the implications of a racist past. When one of the kids claims to have "heard tell somebody strung up one of them voodoo coloreds not two nights ago," the tree outside the cabin transforms into a gorilla-like creature with bared teeth and nooses hanging from its branches. On the next page, the monster tree snatches multiple family members from the cabin, wrapping nooses around their necks and violently transforming them into Black "coon" figures. The page design becomes more hectic, as if the panel grid is losing its hold, giving way to shaky panel frames and a monster that refuses to be confined by these frames. "I feel like . . . . . . like I got some black in me!" the daughter screams (a phrase with sexual connotations), as she, her brother, and her mother become "strange fruit," in the words of Mr. Alphonse, of the most grotesque sort, recalling the golliwog rag dolls from the chapter's opening page. They yell, "Zippidty Doo Dah!" "Why my neck hurt?" and "Isa wants sum watermelons!" evoking racist renditions of blackness that include Disney's *Song of the South* ("Zip-a-Dee-Doo-Dah," with lines sung by African American actor James Baskett about a "wonderful feeling" on a "wonderful day" in the Jim Crow South) and a stereotypical fondness for watermelons. The characters seem possessed by a grotesquerie so forceful that the coloring of their speech balloons switches from white to black. The members of the still-white father's family plead with him as if he was their enslaver, "Don't whip us none, massa!" referencing the reductive repertoire of Black suffering and white domination that still shapes many representations of slavery.

The next page reveals a remediated drawing of Lawrence Beitler's photograph of the 1930 lynching of Thomas Shipp and Abram Smith in Marion, Indiana (with the difference that only one victim appears in *Box of Bones*) (fig. 5.2). "There are stories of white families, around the same time, who went to see a lynching . . . . . . and were never seen again," Mr. Alphonse continues, with the accompanying images showing the tree ensnaring the spectators and transforming them into more strange fruit. The last multipanel of this speculative revenge fantasy, whose thick frames take on a liquid look that suggests dripping tar or blood and destabilizes the conventionally fixed frame of the photograph, depicts the grinning tree, blood flowing from its mouth onto the soil in recollection of Abel Meeropol's haunting lines: "Blood at the root / Black bodies swinging in the southern breeze / Strange fruit hanging from the poplar trees." Clustered around the figures are items from the lexicon of racist speech, including the more traditional *coon, tar baby, gator-bait*, and *burrhead* to more recent coinages such as *jungle bunny, porch monkey*, and *spearchucker* (see *Green's Dictionary*). It is as if all the racist hatred floating around the region must be brought out in the open to be exorcized, playing into a notion of gothic excess that involves seeing both too much and too little in Julia Round's sense: terrifying images of things that "*should not be there*" and the horrors of the unknown (76). As the graphic novel continues, the racial terror is not eradicated but evolves.

In the final pages of the sequence, the gorilla tree (which identifies itself as "I am Wretched") and its strange fruit begin looking for more victims, and they turn up at the Laveau house, uttering racist commands and attacking Madame Laveau, Baptise, and the rest of the household. "What kind of foul coonery is this?" asks Laveau's Black servant Bonita as she and others fight the demonic tree. Baptise ultimately takes a noose from the box of bones, places it around her neck, and allows herself to be pulled into the contraption because the box

Fig. 5.2: Remediated lynching imagery in *Box of Bones: Book One*. Page one of two.

"can only be sealed with the blood . . . . . . of its summoner." Before she dies, she muses, "I was so angry . . . I didn't realize what so much anger could destroy, could break." Racial trauma, this vignette suggests, may lead to justified anger, but this anger can become self-destructive, terrorizing those who cannot find

Fig. 5.2: Remediated lynching imagery in *Box of Bones: Book One*. Page two of two.

more productive ways of dealing with it. The better and perhaps only viable option, the comic suggests, is to deal constructively as well as creatively with the past and its ongoing impact on the present.

Carpenter's concept of the "not quite living things" works on two levels here. The first level entails the contents of the story, more specifically the contents of the box of bones—the US history of racial division and anti-Black violence—which may be temporarily contained but has not yet been put to final rest. The box is opened again and again throughout the narrative, and the traumas for which it serves as an unconventional archive break out in the open. The second level pertains to Jama-Everett and Jennings's work as visual-verbal storytellers whose contribution to the field of graphic narrative is their insistence on depicting violent parts of Black history routinely repressed in the national narrative and in comics. The creators highlight the image-text hybridity through their visual aesthetic, including the use of photographs in the collage on the opening splash page.

Jama-Everett and Jennings's work speaks to Leila Taylor's two provocative questions about "America's gothic soul": "How can you mourn the dead when the mechanics that made slavery possible are still churning? How do you get over the death of something that is still alive?" (104). Taylor's questions recall Hartman's emphasis on the effects of enduring historical violence and the evolution of trauma. "How might we understand mourning, when the event has yet to end?" Hartman asks. "When the injuries not only perdure, but are inflicted anew? Can one mourn what has [not] yet ceased happening?" ("Time" 758). Mourning the momentous loss of Black life, unfathomable as it is in its centuries-spanning scope, is complicated in both Taylor's and Hartman's interventions by the fact that there can be no closure as long as the trauma is still unfolding and the dying continues. Living in the wake of massive death has created a paradox of monstrous dimensions in Black diasporic culture that embodies the impulse to mourn the dead and celebrate their actions as a continuing inspiration—as ancestors, as heroes, as freedom fighters—for the present and the future.

Bitter Root positions this paradox at the heart of its narrative. Presenting a storyworld in which racial hatred turns white supremacists into actual monsters (the Jinoo) and unresolved racial trauma into a different type of monster (the Inzondo), *Bitter Root* is a powerful example of Carroll's "category-jamming," suggesting that more than one type of monster exists and making sure that these monsters do not correspond to the dominating discourse of "black monstrosity."[29] The members of the Sangerye family, the series's Black protagonists, not only fight the Jinoo (as they have since colonial times) as well as the Inzondo but also deal with racial trauma.[30] They do so through a "paradoxical mix of healing and harming" (Chireau, *Black* 57), providing shelter and cures for the needy and using spiritual and physical force against both types of monsters. There is disagreement over the means employed in this fight. While some family members, especially the matriarch and conjure woman Ma Etta, want to heal the monsters' souls with a special serum, others, among them the more aggressive Ford, want to kill the monsters with special bullets: "Divided over how to deal with the creatures, some of the Sangeryes felt it was their moral obligation to 'purify' the infected souls of the Jinoo, while others felt the only option was to 'amputate' the soul" (343). *Bitter Root* counters images of passive Black suffering without neglecting the impact of transgenerational trauma. The Sangeryes safeguard the nation's soul without succumbing to an all-consuming sense of rage (as the Inzondo do) and without giving up their resistance to white supremacy (as represented by the Jinoo).

Bitter Root negotiates the fraught territory of racial trauma by forming a sense of Black history that acknowledges but is not controlled by past and current suffering. The comic does so by showing the dangers of anger and rage while seeking to integrate trauma into the Sangerye family's life. As such, *Bitter Root* aligns with the conclusion offered in *Wake*, indicating a shared sense of purpose and a connected understanding about what comics can contribute to the project of commemorating Black history: "Living in the wake of slavery is haunting, and to experience this haunting is to be nothing less than traumatized," Hall's narrative voice acknowledges.

> Still, it is possible to heal from trauma. Or come to terms with it. At first, we try to block out the horrors of the past. To ignore them. To pretend they are not there. The next step is to acknowledge the past and its harm. [. . .] We reach the final stage of healing from trauma when we integrate the past into who we are. It becomes a part of us that we acknowledge and provides understanding of our world. The past is not a ghost we want to banish or exorcise. It is something we want to internalize.

Healing from trauma is a central concern in *Bitter Root*, and integrating the past into the present by internalizing its implications is exactly what different characters in the series struggle with. Walker, Brown, and Greene suggest that the dead cannot be brought back to life and that the nation's Black citizens must embrace the suffering caused by white aggression, however unbearable it seems, as a source of strength and resilience rather than allowing it to cause blind anger and rage.[31]

This idea plays out in a five-page sequence set in 1924 in a small Georgia town where a young Black boy has just been lynched (214–18). The evil creature Adro is taking Dr. Sylvester, who has lost his children in the Tulsa Race Massacre and is "possessed" (in Caruth's sense) by this event, haunted by the Greenwood rubble as the site of his life-defining trauma. At the site of the lynching, with the boy's corpse still hanging from the tree, Dr. Sylvester seeks supernatural aid to avenge the deaths and "liberate" other Black folk suffering from all-consuming grief.[32] This is yet another graphic remediation of lynching photography, another effort to rescue such images of Black vulnerability and white glee from the supremacist archive and transpose them into new contexts—another "refusal to disavow the monstrous pleasures" (Christina Sharpe, *Monstrous* 175) of the supremacist gaze.[33] Adro reminds Sylvester of his children—the victim of the lynching is "just a boy. Not much older than your son was when your children were taken from you" (214)—and pretends to empathize: "I know what you are feeling. The pain. The anguish. It claws at your soul." Suggesting that "the same pain and anguish claws at the souls of all who loved that child hanging from this tree" (215), Adro promises Sylvester and the townspeople "peace through retribution" and offers a devilish deal: "Just give us your pain, and we will deliver you from all of this suffering" (218). As the story continues, Adro brings the boy back to life (241), but as his parents embrace him, his yellow eyes betray his zombie status.[34] Still later, the grieving father is forced to acknowledge, "My boy was swingin' from a tree, and I prayed and prayed and prayed. I just wanted my son back, But this ain't him" (258). Sylvester, too, comes to a brutal realization that Adro is a false prophet whose promise to bring the dead back to life is wrong: "Trickster, the comfort you bring is merely a mask for chaos. The salvation you promise only leads to damnation" (261).[35]

Drawing on John S. Mbiti's *African Religions and Philosophy* (1969), critics like Chassot and Kinitra D. Brooks identify the living dead as apt figures through which to reconcile the urge to bring back the dead with the realization that they can only be mourned and remembered. "In the African conception of time and death a person's passing does not mark a break with the community of the living: the 'living-dead,' as [Mbiti] calls them, remain 'alive' in the memories of those who knew them as well as in the spirit world. The living give the dead 'symbols of communion, fellowship and remembrance' [...] in the form of sacrifices, offerings, libations, and food" (Chassot 8–9). For Mbiti, the living dead remain present and active, "'alive' in the memories of their surviving families, and [...] still interested in the affairs of the family to which they once belonged in their physical life" (104). Likewise, in Ta-Nehisi Coates's *Black Panther*, Shuri exists in "a petrified state known as The Living Death" (book 3), and the Djalia serves as a spiritual space that holds "Wakanda's past, present, and future." Moreover, there is also Necropolis, where king T'Challa summons "the legions. And the dead rall[y] one last time" and where he seeks counsel from his predecessors.

Mbiti's notion of the living dead ties in with the figure of the zombie, whose diasporic significance has been the subject of a number of studies and whose current popularity makes it an attractive trope for graphic representations of Black history (see Ackermann and Gauthier; Cussans; Lauro; Michel and Bellegarde-Smith; Sheller). "Of West African origin but today more generally associated with Caribbean, more particularly Haitian, culture, the zombi traditionally designates a dead person brought to 'that misty zone which divides life from death' [. . .] by a sorcerer or priest (a *bokor* or *houngan*), a master for whom it must work or perform certain tasks," Chassot suggests. "A body without mind, personality, memory, or desire, the zombi is thus an avatar of the slave, an empty husk whose only social utility is raw labor. While it seems a monstrous figure, the zombi is the result of alienation rather than the essence of otherness; its monstrosity therefore does not pertain to an intrinsic characteristic but points at the monstrosity of the forces that created it—the slavers, the slave trade, slavery" (51, citing Métraux 282). In popular fiction, "zombie infection [often] plays upon the racialized nature of contagion" and evokes "the disgust elicited by impurity, something that is categorically interstitial, incomplete, and/or formless" (Kinitra D. Brooks, *Searching* 4, 5). The zombie is, in many ways, a monstrous figure whose racialized underpinnings may evoke images of Black disease and infection as well as more positive notions of Black resistance and agency when characters resist confinement to a zombie status, such as Dr. Sylvester in *Bitter Root* or the blues detective/conjure man Half-Dead Johnson in *Blue Hand Mojo*.[36]

The reanimated young Black boy in *Bitter Root* is one instantiation of this monstrous figure. A different variation on the zombie as an undead figure emerges from Walker, Brown, and Greene's creation of the charismatic, physically massive, and intellectually inspiring Berg Sangerye. Berg's struggle with intergenerational trauma points beyond the zombie's nature as a mindless and memoryless body and a mere avatar of the enslaved. Yet it also complicates Mbiti's claim that the dead will live on in the memories of others and in the spirit world. Infected by the Inzondo, Berg accesses the ancestors' collective pain, which grants him a sense of transhistorical suffering but also threatens to overwhelm him with grief and prevent a healing internalization of trauma. Evoking Ralph Waldo Emerson's notion of the "transparent eyeball" from *Nature* (1836), Berg reveals,

> I can feel what [the Inzondo] felt. There is hatred and fear, but much, much more. But I felt so much more . . . The loss of my father. The death of my Aunt Bernice. And it is not just my own pain and loss that I feel—it is theirs. I feel what my father felt when he lost my mother in that Jinoo attack. The man who led the attack here in Harlem—I sense his loss. I sense the grief of his children, as if their sorrow is my sorrow. I hear it all. I feel it all. It calls out to me. It connects me to them—all of them. I just want to end all the pain and sadness. (236)[37]

Berg's turmoil, his transcendental rememory of family members' and other people's emotions—hatred, fear, pain, loss, sorrow, grief, sadness—may be understood as a connection to the Black diaspora, but it burdens him with the tremendous task of avoiding the destructive potential of such accumulated hurt. Berg's wish "to end all the pain and sadness" is laudable, but there is no viable way to fulfill it. Racial trauma cannot be ended, the passage suggests, as any sense of closure would erase a substantial part of Black history and render moot the ancestors' experiences.

If the notion of the living dead radically revises "two mainstream horror tropes—the ghost and the zombie," as Kinitra D. Brooks suggests (*Searching* 103), it does so by transposing Mbiti's focus on African religions to the Middle Passage as the fulcrum of the transatlantic slave trade. The limbo "that could sustain neither life nor death" (Smallwood 145; cf. Chassot 49–52) and that marks "a course or state between extremes" (Chassot 48, citing the *Oxford English Dictionary*) reduced the enslaved "to an existence so physically atomized as to silence all but the most elemental bodily articulation, so socially impoverished as to threaten annihilation of the self, the complete disintegration of personhood" (Smallwood 125).[38] Chassot cites Stephanie E. Smallwood's understanding "of the commodified captive as a creature reduced to its most basic bodily functions and emptied of all the social, psychological, and spiritual components that make up the self" as "strikingly evocative of the zombi." Chassot goes on to suggest that "the living dead and the zombi are apt tropes for the social death and the dehumanizing and commodifying processes that the Middle Passage initiates" (51). However, the Africans fighting enslavement on the ships in *Middle Passage* and *Wake* as well as in Baker's *Nat Turner* indicate that social death and dehumanizing commodification, while fatal for millions, did not erase all resistance against reduction to zombie-like status.

On American soil, where the ship as the (non)site of Black trauma is replaced by the plantation as the scene of monstrous intimacies and spectacular violence, the zombie remains very much relevant as an undead figure of racialized infection and embodiment of the living dead as ancestral companions whose death marks less a passing than a passage into "an afterlife, otherworld, ancestral gathering place, heaven, or home" (Bruce 16).[39] The trope appears in such narratives as Henry Bibb's *The Life and Adventures of Henry Bibb: An American Slave* (1849), in which he describes slavery as "almost a living death" and the slave states as "one of the darkest corners of the earth" (62, 114), and resurfaces in Guillory's *Roots of All Evil* (*Farmhand* vol. 3), where the main character, the infected Ezekiel, wakes up in complete darkness and exclaims, "Oh shit ... I'm dead," to which another character replies, "You ain't dead, boy ... but you ain't exactly alive either" (chap. 15).

This status of being neither fully alive nor completely dead can be traced to the violent displacement of Africans from their native soil and to a life in slavery on a new continent. "The gap between Africa and Afro-America and the gap between the living and the dead and the gap between the past and the present does not exist," Morrison said; "it's bridged for us by our assuming responsibility for people no one's ever assumed responsibility for. They are those that died en route. Nobody knows their names, and nobody thinks about them. In addition to that, they never survived in the lore; there are no songs or dances or tales of these people" (qtd. in Chassot 34). This idea reappears in the storyworlds of several graphic narratives as a conflict between forces from different realms—the physical world and the spiritual world, the world of the past and the world of the present. This spiritual realm becomes apparent if Sharpe's description of monstrous intimacies is combined with Morrison's thoughts. "Slavery and the Middle Passage were ruptures with and a suspension of the known world that initiated enormous and ongoing psychic, temporal, and bodily breaches," Sharpe writes, suggesting that monstrous intimacies "account for the long psychic and material reach of those passages, their acknowledged and disavowed effects, their projection onto and erasure from particular bodies, and the reformulation, reproduction, and recirculation of their intimate spaces of trauma, violence, pleasure, shame, and containment" (*Monstrous* 4).

Morrison's gaps in need of bridging and Sharpe's notion of ruptures and breaches between worlds (including her sonically sanctioned conjunction of breach/reach) could well be used to describe the storyworlds of *Blue Hand Mojo*, *Box of Bones*, and *Bitter Root*. In *Blue Hand Mojo*, Half-Dead Johnson is a conjure man haunted by the memories of the lynching of his wife and children and his narrow escape to make "a crossroad deal" with the devil, Brother Scratch. As part of this deal, Johnson (named after Robert Johnson, who allegedly sold his soul to the devil to become a beguiling bluesman) "reached into the Noir" and "pulled power right outta her"; as a result, part of him "now belongs to her." The deal bestows him with conjuring powers, concentrated in his blue mojo hand, which keeps him tied to The Noir. The Noir "is where all black magic and creativity begin and end" (chap. 2), the "living space where all Black Imagination lives and breeds" (chap. 6). Johnson imagines The Noir as a feminine space, assuming that the "power of my mojo and all my spells come from her strange and dark womb. She is the secret that black women pass on from one to another in the shadows" (chap. 6). The Noir offers a "secret way" and a "Strange Root system that connects all the world together as one" (chap. 6). Johnson uses this system to travel throughout the city. But The Noir also threatens to suck him in: "Frank, my love!" it exclaims, "Are you ready to join the others in my darkness? Your story would be legendary! Your pain, so epic!" (chap. 6).[40]

The Noir visualizes Morrison's gap and Sharpe's breach and graphically relays Patricia J. Williams's point that the suppression of Black history "leaves a void that will surely haunt us" and "into which so many lives disappeared without much trace." The Noir exists as a rift between reality and fantasy, the visible and the invisible, the physical and the spiritual, as a liminal space (in limbo) between past and present in which members of the African diaspora struggle with their position in the world. The Noir also exposes new spaces for the racial imagination—the "realm between earth and hell" (also called purgatory or Barzakh) in *Bitter Root* (197), the Djalia in *Black Panther*, the box of bones.[41]

Damian Duffy conceptualizes this liminal space as "the Hole" in "The Appetite for Hunger." This essay forms part of the paratextual apparatus of his collaboration with Jennings, *The Hole: Consumer Culture* (2008), a horror story centered on a New World reincarnation of the Yoruba trickster Papa Legba. "What is the Hole?" Duffy asks before answering his own question: "The Hole is everything. It is a floating signifier, that which has no stable meaning save what meaning is assigned to it. It stands at the crossroads of meaning, neither this nor that but both at the same time. One meaning the authors of this graphic novel ascribe to is the idea of the Hole as an open wound, the wound of the middle passage, slavery and racism. This is a perpetual wound, the profound and continual schism of race relations that continues unabated in the 21st century" (153). "The Hole," "open and perpetual wound," "profound and continual schism," "crossroads of meaning"—the semantics of Duffy's passage are suggestive in terms of the transgenerational racial trauma that shapes Black diasporic history and life in the present. These elements become explicit and take on monstrous forms in these graphic narratives, which feature actual wounds, both physical and mental, that torment those on whom they are inflicted and in some cases on those who inflict them.[42] *Bitter Root* is filled with blood-and-guts scenarios in which members of the Sangerye family fight Jinoo, Inzondo, and equally dangerous otherworldly creatures who call themselves "the harbingers of retribution" (106). The twist is that the Sangeryes fight either through healing (Ma Etta's purifying serum) or through killing. These otherworldly creatures from the "realm between earth and hell" (purgatory/Barzakh) feed on the pain and thus on the open and perpetual wounds of Black Americans, whose capacity to suffer has transformed into boundless rage, with the Sangeryes trying to close the "gateway" as Cullen is sucked into "that void" (104–8), where he will meet his living dead father and aunt. In *Blue Hand Mojo*, The Noir offers solace and redemption but ultimately threatens to consume Half-Dead Johnson (whose name recalls the zombie figure), while Johnson is the conjure man at the crossroads of meaning, burdened by the trauma of his family's lynching and enabled by his mojo to solve the crime and serve his community.

Notions of loss and absence and the urge to bridge the gaps, close the breaches, and fill the holes of Black history take on a different dimension in light of the vast repository of sonic metaphors and water imagery and their associations with monstrosity. Smallwood ponders the "traumatic echo" (7) of the Middle Passage in the lives of the enslaved and their communities, an observation that recalls the "dual figure of the living dead" (Chassot 54), Carpenter's definition of trauma as "echoes of moments long gone," and Sharpe's "living in the wake" in that it indicates the particular temporalities and spatialities of trauma as something that is never over, evolves across time and space, and can reach its targets indirectly. Moreover, sound can serve as a sonic bridge between divided spaces, a metaphor evident in Baker's *Nat Turner*, where Nat is retelling his mother's account of how a baby was thrown into the shark's mouth from aboard the ship that brought her to America. Nat's words, rendered not in language but as an image, function like a visual echo, repeating a smaller version of the image presented two pages earlier (55, 57). This earlier image is reframed by a speech bubble whose tail points to young Nat's mouth, identifying him as the speaker, as a protorevolutionary (some would have called him a monster) whose ability to repeat the ancestor's account of the Middle Passage equips him with the power to mesmerize many of the enslaved on the plantation.[43]

In *Bitter Root*, Berg's ability to hear others' "traumatic echoes" leads him to supplant more genteel ideas about silent suffering with a cacophony of monstrous horror: "It was Henry Wadsworth Longfellow who said, 'There is no grief like the grief that does not speak.' He was mistaken. There is a grief that cries out so loud it drowns out all sound. But when the screams fall upon deaf ears, the soul becomes tormented. I hear the screams of grief. All of them. And my soul . . . . . . it feels the torment" (255). Berg's connection to the past is represented not by the unrecorded silence of the grieving—a known trope in studies of marginalization and historical repression, archival and otherwise—but by the screams of the tormented, a phenomenon that the reader is invited to sense in a rectangular insert panel that shows a close-up of Berg's saddened eyes.

A particularly powerful passage in Hall, Martínez, and Bao's *Wake* declares, "Sound waves travel so slowly in water and the ocean is so vast, the sound can last centuries under water. Maybe, if we listen carefully, we can hear them." This association between water and sound is visually captured in the book's opening sequence, which shows Africans jumping off the ship into the water and toward death, and reappears at the end in a double splash page that depicts an African woman warrior, brandishing her spear as she rises from the water and says, "For the future." This image constitutes another visual echo and creates a graphic encapsulation of Mbiti's living dead. In *Wake*, water serves as a constant reminder that the past is not past and that the dead are not dead. For this reason, snapshots of Black history and the ancestors appear throughout the narrative in puddles on the streets of New York City.

In Love and Morgan's *Bayou*, water takes on an equally charged role, from the fearsome swamp from which Lee must retrieve Billy Glass's corpse and that houses the golliwog monster to the flood that sweeps away the juke joint and kills Lee's mother, Tarbaby, in a long flashback scene set in 1922. ("The bayou got her," Lee explains [vol. 1]) Swamp, river, and bayou appear as ambiguous bodies of water, serving both as potential routes of escape (Lee and Bayou raft on the river in a revision of Huck and Jim from Mark Twain's *Huckleberry Finn*) and as unpredictable sources of violence. According to Lee, the swamp is a "bad place" where "nuthin' good ever happened"; "Ain't nuthin' getting me back in that water again" (vol. 1). The swamp is the trap that allows Cotton-Eyed Joe to swallow Lily, and by causing the white girl's disappearance, the swamp initiates Calvin Wagstaff's arrest. It is the natural grave where Billy Glass's murderers sink his dead body as well as the place where Lee first encounters Billy's spirit and starts engaging with the spiritual world. While the flood at the end of the narrative drowns many people at the juke joint, including Lee's mother, whom Lee imagines soaking in a bathtub and talking to her about her "nappy" hair, it also washes away some of the crime and depravation that dominated the goings-on at the establishment (including a leering reverend in the form of an anthropomorphized bear who lusts over Lee and whose monstrous advances Bayou foils).[44] Moreover, Love and Morgan reference an African American spiritual in which water plays a significant role: Bayou sings "Wade in the Water" while looking wistfully at the Mississippi River, where his friend Rabbit drowned in the flood: "WAAAADE in the WaaAATUH' ... GAWD'S GONNA TROUBLE The WAAAATUH'" (vol. 2).[45]

In her study on pastoral returns to the South in contemporary African American culture, Stefanie K. Dunning discovers a connection between "Black precarity and water" and detects a "cartography of Black suffering traceable by water" (62), from the Middle Passage to the Great Mississippi Flood (1927) and the Okeechobee hurricane (1928) to Hurricane Katrina and the subsequent flooding of New Orleans (2005).[46] "Water iterates death, especially for Black people," Dunning argues, because "water is a kind of grave marker that exposes not only *where* the bodies are buried but also the means by which they got there" (62). The Atlantic serves as a mass grave, and ships functioned as "floating graveyards of the socially dead" (Bruce 4).[47] Whereas African grave sites on land may be rescued from oblivion when they resurface during urban construction, for example, the ocean constitutes a much more difficult dying space. "Can the sea be haunted?" Leila Taylor asks, focusing on the trope of ghosts of the past haunting Black life in the present. "How does a ghost inhabit that which has no borders, something formless that ebbs and flows?" (41).[48]

This borderless watery expanse, ebbing and flowing across the remains of the nameless dead, is symptomatic of the Middle Passage as the initial rupture of the modern Black world. This image captures the fundamental dislocation of Black subjects forcibly transplanted to the American continent. Hortense J.

Spillers observes that the enslaved "were literally suspended in the 'oceanic'" and "removed from the indigenous land and culture" but also were "not-yet 'American'"; they were "captive persons, without names that their captors would recognize, [...] in movement across the Atlantic, but they were also nowhere at all" (72).[49] For La Marr Jurelle Bruce, the "restlessness and rootlessness" that the Middle Passage instilled in the enslaved Africans "persist in many of their descendants" (3), indicating that a lasting sense of homelessness is another aspect of modernity's infliction of trauma on Black subjects. This sense is very much present in contemporary graphic narratives of Black history and manifests in Half-Dead Johnson's flight from the South to Depression-era Chicago in *Blue Hand Mojo*, in the Sangerye family's shuttling back and forth between their Northern base in Harlem and the Jim Crow South in *Bitter Root*, and in the appearances of monstrous stereotypes in *Box of Bones*.

ETHNOGOTHIC LANDSCAPES

If monsters embody the traumas of the racialized Other, then the Deep South ("the lynching states," as Walter White calls them [*Rope* 8]) might be their most natural habitat. Locating monsters in the South—including the imaginary South of popular myth—has been a staple of US American gothic literature, as scholars Maisha L. Wester and Leila Taylor have pointed out.[50] The graphic narratives discussed here exemplify Jerrold Hogle's "gothic matrix" and its four central elements—"an antiquated space, a hidden secret from the past, a physical or psychological haunting, and an oscillation between earthly reality and the supernatural" (Round 17)—albeit from Black diasporic perspectives. The antiquated space is the ethnogothic landscape these narratives present. The hidden secrets from the past are the system of white supremacy as well as the alternative worlds, real and imaginary, created by the enslaved and oppressed that seldom make it into mainstream accounts of America's past. The physical and psychological haunting are the wounds and traumas of centuries of anti-Black violence. The oscillation between earthly reality and the supernatural appears in the guise of living dead ancestors, conjuring practices, and the intersection of physical and spiritual worlds.

Leila Taylor calls the Deep South "the heart of America's Darkness" (43), a geographical place and sociocultural space rampant with "phantoms that haunt gothic narratives [about] the ramifications of racism, repressed gilt, social pariahs, and marginalized freaks" (44). Phantoms and freaks are well known in comic books, and when Wester labels the South America's Gothic Other, a place that anchors conflicted accounts of America's racist past in the national imagination, she essentially describes the setting of many graphic narratives: "The

South proves the location onto which we repeatedly abject histories of racial oppression, specifically between white Americans and African Americans," she writes. "Deemed both exceptional and abnormal for social, economic, and political reasons, the South is made to embody and speak America's horrific racial past" ("Southern"; see also Miles).

The gothic has long been recognized as a powerful mode of writing about the South as a peculiar space marked by "entire histories of racial ideologies and tensions" and as a genre "aware of the impossibility of escaping racial haunting and the trauma of a culture that is not just informed by racial history, but also haunted and ruptured by it" (Wester, *African American* 25). The life narratives of formerly enslaved Americans, on which several contemporary graphic narratives draw for inspiration, frequently expressed these tensions and ruptures, envisioning the South as a "haunted landscape, its darkness troubled by the wails and screams of the tortured" (30). After trying to escape enslavement and being captured, Henry Bibb recalled, "Things looked to me uncommonly pleasant: The green trees and wild flowers of the forest; the ripening harvest fields waving with the gentle breezes of Heaven. [. . .] I was conscious of what must be my fate; a wretched victim for Slavery without limit" (60–61). The South emerges from such depictions not only as a limitless place—as the sine qua non of the enslaved persons' bounded world, a place they can never fully escape because slavery's traumatic effects will haunt even those who flee—but also as a paradoxical place of natural beauty and human-made horror. It is a "location of ancestral origins and inherited horrors" (Wester, *African* American 102), and the enslaved and their descendants must struggle to make it home despite the prevalence of racism, exploitation, and oppression.[51]

If "the trauma of slave history," as Wester argues, is "written into both the landscape and the people" of the South (*African American* 108), and if, as Charles Johnson writes in *Being and Race*, Black culture is characterized by "the longing for a real and at times a mythical home" (qtd. in Wester, *African American* 102), then the gothic mode with its uncanny—scary/unhomelike—propensity for monsters provides a fitting framework for creators of graphic narratives seeking to (re)claim Black history by telling different tales of the South. Indeed, Carpenter and Jennings's notion of the ethnogothic landscape offers a useful lens for the study of contemporary graphic narratives invested in representations of the US South (see also Costello and Whitted). This landscape, Carpenter suggests, "serves as a warning to us all about just how dangerous our traumas can be. We bear witness to the transformation of experiences into things. Things forged from emotional turmoil and physical pain rooted in Black experiences" ("Opening"). For Jennings, the ethnogothic opens up "a storytelling space" and "centers racially oriented speculative narratives that actively engage affective racialized psychological traumas via the traditions of gothic tropes and technologies. These tropes include the grotesque Other, body horror, haunted spaces, the hungry ghost, the uncanny, the doppelgänger, and multivalent disruptive tensions between the constructions of memory, history, the present, and the self" (Donna-lyn Washington, "John" 140).[52]

Bayou, Box of Bones, Bitter Root, and *Farmhand* utilize many of these tropes to unpack what Jennings describes as "trauma around racial difference or around racial pain" (Woodward 129). These graphic narratives seek to reconcile Southern "pastoral and natural imagery with the overburdened history of racist violence in natural spaces" (Dunning 23). As such, they are part of a shifting sensibility in contemporary Black cultural production that appears in narratives by contemporary African American authors as a return "to rural, often (though not always) southern, agrarian settings through the tropes of self-discovery, coming home, healing, and communalism" (21). This return, Dunning maintains, necessitates a reckoning with the horrors of the past and includes redressing a sense of alienation from the Southern soil that stems from centuries of "forced agrarian labor" and from the racialization of the landscape during slavery and Jim Crow, including the "theft of the forty acres"—the unkept promise of Sherman's Field Order 15—at the tail end of the Civil War (6, 14, 16–17).[53]

Such racialization of the ethnogothic landscape appears most prominently in scenes of lynching that are combined with more celebratory visions of Black life and culture (especially music and folklore but also religion) as a corrective to the overdetermination of the South as a place of violence and suffering. Dunning argues that mob violence caused a "palpable rupture from nature" (17) and turned the pastoral self-image of the agrarian South (evoked, for instance, in the opening pages of *Bayou*) into "a mnemonic reminder of lynching" (18), enforcing a system of racist violence in one of the most brutal ways imaginable.[54] Setting their stories in this overdetermined space, graphic narratives participate in a project of contemporary Black literature that is intent on "reclaiming and recoding nature as contiguous with Blackness" (23) and that reimagines what would otherwise be "an irreducible relationship" among nature, "Blackness, and death" (84) as a more ambivalent connection of pain and pleasure, haunting and happiness, suffering and self-sustenance.

Visualizations of the terrorist practice of lynching are prominent in *Blue Hand Mojo, Bitter Root,* and *Farmhand* and figure in graphic narratives of Black history as a powerful signifier of the ethnogothic South. *Blue Hand Mojo* features a single lynching scene on the second page that positions the murder of Frank Johnson's wife and two children and his narrow escape as the protagonist's life-defining trauma (fig. 5.3).

While the setting is Chicago in 1931, Johnson's mind is in the South, and his story shows how the Southern ethnogothic landscape extends into the North and Midwest of the Great Migration. He is half asleep in bed on a Saturday morning after a night of "homespun blues" and "cuttin' up," plagued

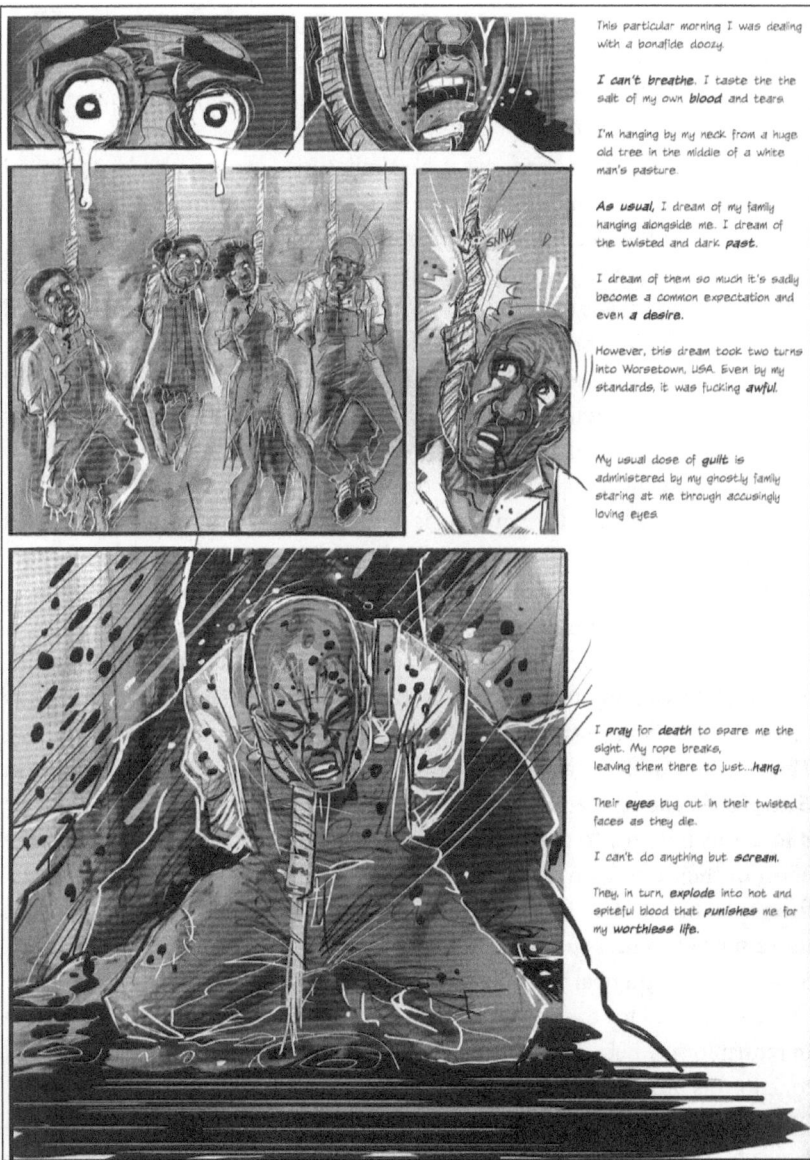

Fig. 5.3: Half-Dead Johnson's nightmare in *Blue Hand Mojo: Hard Times Road*.

by nightmares that come at him "hard, vivid, and full of anger and dread." On this morning, the dream takes him back to Mississippi:

> I can't breathe. I taste the [. . .] salt of my own blood and tears. I'm hanging by my neck from a huge old tree in the middle of a white man's pasture. As usual, I dream of my family hanging alongside me. I dream of the twisted and dark past. [. . .] My usual dose of guilt is administered by

my ghostly family starting at me through accusingly loving eyes. I pray for death to spare me the sight. My rope breaks, leaving them there to just . . . hang. Their eyes bug out in their twisted faces as they die. (chap. 1)

Frank's recurring nightmare makes him relive his wife and children's violent deaths as well as his own accidental survival. His family members "explode into hot and spiteful blood that punishes me for my worthless life," Frank recalls, evoking the Southern horrors present in so much antilynching literature: "The storm of blood makes the ground beneath the tree into a swamp of mud and hateful redness." Wrecked by survivor's guilt, he says, "I can't breathe," recalling Eric Garner's final words and evoking the Black Lives Matter movement, and ends up feeling tremendous rage: "I choke like I should have in that fucking tree some ten years ago. My rage shatters me."

This harrowing verbal recall is accompanied by equally horrific images. The double page visualizing the lynching is framed on the top left and bottom right page with a close-up of Frank's eyeballs as he stares in disbelief and horror at the murder of his family. In both panels, tears well from his eyes, trickling over the panel frame and flowing down the page—on the top left, they flow across the gutter and into the panel directly underneath, which shows Frank, his wife, and his children hanging from ropes wrapped around their necks. Frank's eyes evoke the tears Jennings tears shed while adapting Butler's *Kindred* (Hinds 99). This may not quite be a case of bell hooks's oppositional gaze, introduced in *Black Looks* and conceived as a self-confident look back at the oppressor, yet it forces us not only to gaze at the dying Black bodies but also to consider the effect of their dying on the atrocity's lone Black survivor.[55] While Frank will forever be haunted by the trauma, it does not incapacitate him or freeze him into a state of endless suffering. Rather, he makes a blues deal with devilish Mr. Scratch. "I made a deal with this two-faced muthafucka," Frank later explains. "My eternal soul for the power to avenge my family. [. . .] He kept half my soul in return for my help finding the right souls. Souls that resonate with the right tone for his ultimate blues song for the end times" (chap. 7).

While not beholden to a blues aesthetic, Guillory's *Roots of All Evil* (*Farmhand* vol. 3) tells a similar story of a Black family destroyed by lynching. Guillory includes a three-page family history and account of Freetown, Louisiana, that links the series's current events—paterfamilias Jedidiah Jenkins's crop of "fast-healing, highly customizable human organs" (back cover) that eventually go haywire and wreck this Southern community—with a history steeped in anti-Black violence. This violence includes the lynching of Jenkins's grandfather Isaiah (described as Jenkins's "ancestor"), who wanted to turn Freetown into an "oasis of peace" (chap. 1) but whose bloody, tormented body is shown hanging from a tree as a tableau of hooded henchmen (Klan members) are looking at their deed and as his little son weeps on his knees next to the tree (fig. 5.4).

Fig. 5.4: "A bitter root had been planted" in *Roots of All Evil* (*Farmhand* vol. 3).

The scene's visual arrangement pits the white Klan members against the group of angry Black men armed with rifles and farm tools that emerges from below the tree roots. The figures are enveloped by a yellowish background that seems to float or shine from Isaiah's body into the ground. This is another re-visioning of lynching photographs as well as of Meeropol's "Bitter Fruit": instead of "blood at the root," a luminous substance colors the ground beneath the tree and gives birth to Black resistance. The captions, which represent the conjure woman Auntie Jannice's recollections of Jenkins's ancestor, suggest that the lynching was meant to "drown" (another watery metaphor) the flame of hope and Black progress "in blood" and "to kill Freetown" along with Isaiah but that it was countered by "righteous men who beat back the Klan with fists and knives." However, as the page's final caption indicates, "A bitter root had been planted in the Jenkins bloodline." The next page (the final splash page in the three-page sequence) displays a mutated tree holding Jedidiah and a few other Black men in its claws as Auntie Jannice continues to narrate the Jenkins family history. "Isaiah's hope—the hope that birthed this town—it died on that tree with him," the conjure woman claims, concluding, "The Jenkins bloodline has grown more wicked every generation since. Your family tree today is a bloody stump of what it once was." The transgenerational trauma of Isaiah's lynching has become part of the family DNA and shapes the lives of its members long after slavery and Jim Crow have ended.[56] When Jedidiah's organic transplants ("zombie plants from the pit o'hell," as two schoolkids mockingly call them) start infecting people and turn them into monsters, the comic's ominous motto rings true: "Good fruit can't come from a bad tree" (chap. 1).[57]

Guillory revisits this lynching scene in *The Seed* (*Farmhand* vol. 4) with an unpaneled flashback sequence that narrates the young Black boy's relationship with his father in brutally short fashion. Such flashbacks graphically render the haunting effects of history and their function as a traumatic echo of a violence not yet past in a medium where the past always remains present—accessible by flipping back a few pages and always just a few panels away. In the first image, the son studies with his father, but right next to this rare glimpse at filial intimacy the boy sits below his father's lynched body, mourning his death. We then see the boy crying and hugging his dead father, whose face shows signs of a vicious beating and whose neck is still entangled in the noose. These sequences offer pertinent comments on the legacies of the post-Reconstruction South that visualize a history of racist violence and trauma, but neither *Farmhand*, with its focus on a modern Black family, nor *Bitter Root*, which celebrates a family of Black freedom fighters, allows this history to completely overwhelm or consume the characters and their stories.

The first occurrence of a lynching in *Bitter Root* is a failed 1924 event in Mississippi, where a group of Klansmen has congregated in the woods to kill a Black man. "This'll learn ya to not mess with no white women," their leader declares, while the Black man insists that he "didn't do nuthin'" and "didn't touch no white girl" (33). This sequence first evokes and then revokes the traditional lynching narrative as a hallmark of the ethnogothic South: the rape accusation and a close-up of a dangling noose tick off two plot points from the conventional storyline, while the last panel of the second page announces the unexpected retributive carnage on the next page: The Klansman's insistence that the Black man, infantilized through the racist address *boy*, needs to know his place is countered by the single word *wrong*, which appears in a speech bubble on the final panel that has a tail pointing outside the frame.[58] The source of this utterance is revealed on the next page, but this panel already contains a splattering of red dots in the middle, representing droplets of blood sprayed across the image and announcing incredible violence. On the following page, Ford Sangerye is depicted from a worm's-eye perspective, towering over a gaggle of shot Klansmen, one of whom lacks a hood, revealing monstrous facial features that identify him and the other men as Jinoo (fig. 5.5).[59] Overlaid on this image are five insert panels, four of which picture hooded Klansmen being shot in the head, while the fifth, in the middle, depicts the surprised and shocked Black man. Ford's dramatic sentiments accompany these images: "If anyone needs to know their place, it's you. [. . .] And I'm sendin' all of you to your place . . . . . . straight to hell" (34).[60]

Ford's amputative action and rewriting of the lynching script do not end the Jinoo plague, however. In fact, the Jinoo become more powerful over the course of the story as the Sangeryes battle the Inzondo. Yet the repeated appearance of lynching imagery, especially the lynching tree as a trope, captures the culture of the ethnogothic South. Later in the narrative, the infection spreads to Southern nature. Venturing into a stretch of woods in southwestern Tennessee outside Memphis, Cullen Sangerye finds himself entangled in the roots of a mysterious plant. "Never seen any plant like this," he exclaims. "Damn. This thing has some strong roots" (361). On the following double splash page, Cullen is chased by treelike monsters with mummy-like corpses swinging from the branches and evoking zombies returning to the place of their murder. "It never occurred to him that evil could infect far more than the soul of a human being" (364), the narrative box at the end of the sequence states. The next issue depicts Cullen fighting an increasingly violent and increasingly animated lynching tree and the monsters it has spawned (cf. 367–71).[61] In "Alabama Poem" (1976), Nikki Giovanni pondered, "if trees could talk / wonder what they'd say" (64): *Bitter Root* offers a revised sense of wonder that might be more fitting for an action-driven comic book but that nonetheless acknowledges the monstrous dimensions of the ethnogothic landscape. If trees could be infected with and act on racial hatred, what would they do? They would, as *Bitter Root*, *Bayou*,

Fig. 5.5: Ford Sangerye killing the Ku Klux Klan Jinoo in *Bitter Root Omnibus: Book One*.

Blue Hand Mojo, and *Farmhand*, suggest, bear strange fruit in graphic form and would generate from these fruit not only monstrous visions of the past but also poignant reimaginations of the ethnogothic South.

In these narratives, the South is both a cursed and an enchanted place. It is at once a pastoral space of natural beauty and a space haunted by the monstrous violence of slavery and Jim Crow.[62] It is, moreover, a divided space in which racial affiliation splits the population into a white segment, supported politically, socially, economically, and legally through the ideology of white supremacy, and a Black segment, where lives unfold "under sentence of death" (W. Fitzhugh Brundage's phrase) and where alternative ways of living have been created to escape this sentence. This split is evident in the depiction of nature in *Bayou*, *Bitter Root*, and *Farmhand*, especially in their construction of an ethnogothic landscape that transcends the border between the physical world and the spiritual realm.

Bayou signifies a sense of otherworldliness or the fantastic through its warm and intense color scheme, which invests the landscape with a mythical hue and suggests an alternative understanding of the world. The short summary of the storyline on the back cover of the first volume states that "South of the Mason-Dixon Line lies a strange land of gods and monsters that only Lee Wagstaff is aware of," suggesting that the world on the comic book page is seen through the eyes of a traumatized Black girl thrown into a life of racist terror where the bayou is a place of fear and the woods are dangerous. This may be Love and Morgan's most powerful speculative twist: what appears on the page is determined by Lee's split encounter with the world, her experience of the South as a space where reality and fantasy mix to a degree that makes it impossible to keep them apart, where the brutal facts of life are so hard to bear that the imagination shapes her perception. There is no world outside of Lee's imagination, and the comic presents the girl's attempt to find beauty in a life that seems to offer only horror. The many mythical creatures she meets during her quest to save her father (Bayou, the golliwog, anthropomorphic animals, the murderous Cotton-Eyed Joe, Jubal the Bloodhound, the badman Stagolee as well as the Disneyfied Uncle Remus and Brother Rabbit) are one indication of Lee's imaginative flight into fantasy.[63] That she is unable to keep her fantasy free from the monsters of the South (the lynched corpses she encounters, the physical and psychological violence she endures, the gigantic crow-like monster that invades her dreams and kills Mother Sista) foregrounds the horrific nature of the trauma of living in the Jim Crow South.[64] One of Lee's coping mechanisms is to imagine beautiful insects, such as butterflies, bugs, bumblebees, and fireflies, and Love and Morgan populate many panels, including extremely gruesome ones, with these creatures.[65] The insects provide a sense of solace, offering a reminder that although Lee's trauma may be all-encompassing, she has found ways to wrest moments of beauty from an otherwise horrible existence. The butterflies announce possibilities of transformation, however fleeting they may be.

Lee's flight into fantasy is predestined by the circumstances of her birth. She was conceived when her mother, Tarbaby, cheated on her husband, Calvin Wagstaff, with blues musician Mr. Rabbit on the same night that the Mississippi River flooded, breaching the levees and sweeping away the juke joint where Tarbaby is performing her music. This sequence from 1922, eleven years before the main narrative, is told in flashback. The flood constitutes the breach in the continuum between reality and fantasy, as the main characters (including Rabbit and even Bayou) are depicted as human before the catastrophe but subsequently as animal(istic) creatures.

Lee's enchantment with the spiritual world begins when she is diving for Billy's body. Seeing him at the bottom of the swamp, seemingly alive but with butterfly wings attached to his back, she concludes that she is witnessing "Billy's soul on his way to glory" (vol. 1). This impression comes shortly after Lee has found Billy's corpse, the noose still attached to his neck, thereby indicating that imagining the boy's body as animated by his soul, which is assumed to have outlived his physical existence, may be her way of dealing with the shock of finding the corpse. This embrace of the spiritual world—of an enlivened fantasy—continues when Lee and her white friend Lily play near the bayou even though Lee does not want to revisit this place of bad memories. As the two girls sit in the grass, their arms around each other, surrounded by butterflies and a ladybug sitting on a leaf, Lee imagines voices that Lily cannot hear: "You hear that? Folks singing. Like it's coming from the trees," Lee muses. "Maybe they angels. Maybe my mama is singing with 'em" (vol. 1). For Lee, the world looks and sounds entirely different than it does for Lily, and the fact that Lee associates the voices in her head with angels and her deceased mother indicates that she is again coping with trauma.[66]

This imaginative investment in the spiritual world, where people continue to exist as ghostly support figures after they have passed away and where Lee can find solace from worldly suffering, carries throughout the whole narrative. It is most forcefully present in Billy's repeated appearance whenever Lee is in trouble. When Lee falls into a trap and suffers serious injuries, surviving only thanks to Bayou's folk medicine and impromptu surgery, Billy appears in her half-conscious dreams and flatly states, "You dead, Lee." When Lee counters that "Bayou "is fixin' me," he responds, "Ha Ha Ha You got a few days to live" (vol. 1). Billy appears again in volume 2 to warn Lee that her dreams are real and that they can hurt her. He also tells her that she is being chased by "a terrible mucker straight from hell," released by the racist General Bog, and that she should chew a root Billy has stolen from Mother Sista to prevent dreams and provide protection against Stagolee (vol. 2).[67] Billy brings Lee fireflies to thwart off the golliwog. When Big Sis, another spiritual being and another person killed by anti-Black violence whose memory Lee embraces, catches him, Billy defends his actions: "I was just tryin' ta get Lee some dry clothes and medicine"; "I wouldn'ta been laid to rest proper if'n she didn't fish me out the bayou" (vol. 2). Mother Sista understands Billy's loyalty but worries about the balance between the physical and the spiritual worlds: "Bog wants that child. If you keep aiding her, there will be conflict... Conflict with Bog is no easy thing. What we do here makes a difference to our fleshly brothers and sisters. We can throw their world in chaos if we do battle here." There is no simple way out of Lee's predicament, no easy escape from the horrors of the Jim Crow South. The spirits can offer emotional support but lack the power to rescue Lee from her harrowing circumstances.

The preoccupation with the Southern landscape—with nature, roots and the soil, water—in narratives like *Bayou* is not surprising given the landlessness of the enslaved population and Black farmers' dependency on white landowners, the "Lords of the Land" (Richard Wright, *12 Million* 12), under the sharecropping system.[68] Guillory's *Farmhand*, too, is explicit about the difficult relationship to the land that shapes Southern Black culture. Instead of a Black-owned Oasis of the South, Freetown becomes the site of Jedidiah's dangerous experiments as well as the place "where his granddaddy got lynched" (*The Seed*, chap. 16).

The contrast between white landownership (and its accompanying social, political, economic, and legal power) and Black tilling of the earth (and all the precarity and hardship it entails) is exposed in two consecutive pages in *Bayou* (vol. 1). The page on the left shows a sunny afternoon, with Lily's mother sitting on the porch of her stately Southern home, reading the newspaper and smoking a cigarette amid green grass and blooming magnolias. The color scheme is bright, with lots of white, light yellow, and blue. It is in the middle of the day, and Mrs. Westmoreland is not working. On the facing page, Lee and Calvin plow the earth with the help of a mule; the sun has almost set, Calvin has taken off his shirt because of the heat, and their humble shack is visible at the top. The color scheme is darker, involving brown, gray, and dark orange. The Wagstaffs are poor but hardworking people, and subsequent images show them living a simple domestic life. But this life is disturbed when Mrs. Westmoreland arrives with the sheriff and demands Lee's arrest for stealing Lily's locket (though she is not guilty). Mrs. Westmoreland yells at Calvin and Lee, "I got half a mind to throw the both of you off my land!!" (vol. 1).

This conjunction of the soil, the plants whose roots it holds, and the control over human life legally inscribed into the Southern landscape is a recurring theme in these graphic narratives. They draw on a discourse of anti-Black violence that undermines notions of racism as the natural order of things by redeploying nature imagery. One of the most important examples of such discursive redeployment is Walter White's *Rope and Faggot*, where organic metaphors blossom into a full-blown semantic field. In "The Mind of the Lyncher," White ponders the impact of lynching on the mental and moral development of Southern children: "A careless word of approbation or reproof may find root in the mind of a child" and "bear unwholesome fruit many years later." Continuing the metaphor, he writes, "In the unconscious of these immature minds are thus sown the seeds of lynching" (3–4). White turns the table on white supremacy, reversing the discourse or "flipping the script on the narrative of Black monstrosity" (as Wanzo puts it ["On Monstrosity" 482]) to put the blame and the pain on the children of the white South, who are mentally and emotionally stunted by the lynching regime their parents uphold (as evidenced by the children in *Box of Bones* who urge their father to initiate them into the practice of lynching). When White writes that "the South witnessed bestialities that shocked the entire country and the world" (*Rope* 101), he reveals the identity of the real monsters.

White extends the agricultural metaphor through his discussion of additional economic concerns—white supremacist groups like the KKK "had their roots firmly grounded in economic advantage," and "the poor white [...] in his ignorance furnishes a fertile field for Ku Klux organizers" (*Rope* 121, 164)—and into the realm of politics and law: "If lynch-law fixed its roots in American soil" during the 1830s, 1840s, and 1850s "and plunged those roots to the very lowest layer of the national and especially the Southern soil during Reconstruction, its full flower was destined to be seen as the nineteenth century entered its last decade" (100–101). Nordic propaganda, with its investment in visions of a "blue-eyed, blond-haired [...] superman," might have waned after World War I, "but there is ample evidence that the seed sown did not fall upon barren ground" (121). *Bayou*, *Box of Bones*, *Blue Hand Mojo*, *Bitter Root*, and *Farmhand* transform White's semantics into the realm of the visual, populating the South (as well as Southern roots as they have extended into the North and Midwest) with monstrous, demonic, and woeful trees, with dead bodies in pastoral scenes, with hatred and suffering that reach across generations.[69] But these narratives do not end there, refusing to resign themselves solely to depicting trauma and horror. Some of the fruits they depict may be strange, and some of the trees they portray are demonic, rotten at the root, but these narratives also tell stories about the beauties of the ethnogothic landscape and the Black life and culture to which it has served as an inhospitable home. Bruce has a point when he writes that in what Michel Foucault has labeled a "fruitless expanse" (qtd. in Bruce 2), "the enslaved bore fruit. The pit held seeds, as pits sometimes do" (3).

CONJURE AND ROOT WORK

In a personal essay about her donation of family photographs, letters, and other documents from her "ancestors' archive" to Harvard's Schlesinger Library, Patricia J. Williams describes slavery as "the void into which so many lives disappeared without much trace" and suggests that the suppression of Black history "leaves a void that will surely haunt us." Calling her desire to rescue her ancestral archive from the "dumpster" of forgotten history and her effort to confront her family's past "gathering the ghosts," Williams concludes that preventing the erasure of Black history means releasing it from its confinement to the representational void, where Black lives do not matter and their stories remain untold. "This is a question of representation," she supposes, and then asks, "What part of a life after life lives on as 'papers'? What fiction will emerge, what wormholes to the future?"

Williams's remarks simultaneously evoke the haunting presence of ghosts as figures of traumatic recall and the voiding of the ancestor's agency as well as the powers of writing—and especially fiction—to imagine gateways (or wormholes) to a better Black future. Williams's essay resonates with one of the most prominent elements of several graphic narratives: their imagination of alternate realms and states of being where new cosmologies and epistemologies of Black being become possible and where the traumas of the past can be faced and fought. In doing so, these graphic narratives combine Black folklore, the recognition of Black people's (and especially Black women's) use of nontraditional expertise, and an interest in conjuring and root work as diasporic practices of harming and healing.[70] In these works, conjurers pass this knowledge down through the generations, acting as ancestral figures and fighters in the struggle for racial justice. "These ancestral figures," Chassot writes, "are the guardians of what Morrison refers to as the 'discredited knowledge' of black people, a knowledge that [. . .] is part of a way of looking at the world that productively blends an acceptance of, and reliance on, the 'supernatural' with practicality and 'shrewdness'" (110).

These ancestral figures function as emblems and agents of an alternative reality where Black suffering as well as Black joy serve as repudiations of popular racist stereotypes—from the "coon" or Black "buck" to the "mammy" or Black "Jezebel," already exposed as supremacist fantasies in *Box of Bones*. These figures indeed create wormholes to different representations of Black history that draw on African American traditions from musical expressions such as spirituals and the blues to literary works like Charles Chesnutt's 1899 novel *The Conjure Woman* and Zora Neale Hurston's collection of folk tales in *Every Tongue Got to Confess* (2001). These representations push the envelope in terms of graphic storytelling: through *Bitter Root*'s steampunk style (discussed in Duffy's "Deep Structures," which analyzes the Sangerye "conjurepunk crest" as a synthesis of technology, represented by the three cogs, and nature, emblematized by the roots at the bottom), *Bayou*'s fantastic coloring, and *Blue Hand Mojo*'s remix of horror, pulp conventions, and a blues aesthetic.[71]

Black conjurers and root workers have been "highly visible figures on the cultural landscape in black America" whose role has often been to foster "understandings of the supernatural as both theoretical and practical ideas by which members of black communities" interpret suffering and learn to bridge "the physical realm and the invisible world" (Chireau, *Black* 13, 7, 8). In particular, the ability to allow "black people to attain a measure of control over their lives" (17) made conjure women and root workers as well as other practitioners of the supernatural (e.g., hoodoo or witch doctors) important actors in Black life and mythical figures in African American folklore. Conjuring also provided a "resource for resistance" (18) in a system stacked against the Black population. Conjuring practices were geared to address traumas and heal wounds but also to defend and attack as "countermeasure[s] against oppressive forces" (75).[72]

This use of conjure as a resource for resistance and a means of countering oppression is evident in *Box of Bones*. The narrative's five chapters portray Black diasporic subjects in need of supernatural help—the young woman Gauge, who calls forth the contents of the box (given form through the monstrous figure of The Nobody) to take revenge on the white Southerners who raped her; Baptise Laveau, who opens the box to avenge her lynched lover and unleashes The Wretched; African immigrant Brother Kurumba, who becomes a spiritual mentor at the UMOJA House for African Upliftment and Unity in early 1970s Philadelphia and enlists the evil from the box (in the form of The Dark) to defend residents from police violence; the enslaved of the Beau L'eau Plantation in historical Haiti, whose hope for freedom lies in the rage let loose from the box (The Suffering) to support their rebellion; the Black soldiers in Vietnam, who are caught in an ambush and open the box and release The Burden in a quest to escape. In all five cases, the box of bones and the carnage it inflicts on everything in its path seems to be the only way out of in an impossible situation. Rage and suffering become manifest in monstrous figures that underscore the destructive potential of racial trauma, its tendency to consume the souls of Black folk, and its capacity to foreclose any chance for a wholesome future.[73] As Lindsay Ford explains to her doctoral committee, the box contains "demonic creatures," embodiments of Black trauma that "have only one proper designation ... evil" (chap. 1).

In *The Mighty Struggle: A Town Called Miracle*, this potential for destruction is embodied by a monstrous figure calling himself The Murder who initially appears as a flock of crows before he takes on his grotesque (or crow-esque) form. Set in Mississippi in 1920, the story begins with The Murder implanting dark thoughts (represented in black speech balloons) into the mind of a white Southerner, stirring his envy of Miracle, a prosperous Black town: "We are what you need. We are the feathered blood of the real America ... We are the righteous hate of all things not us ... We are the darkness and fear that drive this land ... We are the twisted engine that makes it all go ... We are the murder ... Hear us crow." The Murder embodies America's dark consciousness, encapsulating all the racism and rage against the nation's Black citizens and using it to summon white Southerners to a race riot that inflames the KKK into a lynch mob: "Let's get the word out now! Let's raise a perfect, Christian white army to destroy these uppity smart n*****. How dare they look down on us. Not want to socialize with us and share all that they've made! They wouldn't even be here making those things if it weren't for us. They'd be making things in straw huts if it weren't for us and dancing around like animals. Let's go teach them a lesson, fellas. Let's go show them their place." The Klansmen "terrorized, maimed and ended the lives of everyone they saw," the narrative continues. "It was another race massacre to add to the books. Nothing to see here." What follows is a revenge sequence in which a superhero figure, The Struggle, armed with a magic branch from an echo tree that had been used to lynch a Black man, vanquishes the Klansmen and drives away The Murder. The epilogue narrates the aftermath of the massacre and describes the trauma of the survivors, noting an absence in the historical record and a void in the ethnogothic landscape: "The only trace of anything was a massive hole where the town had been." Conjuring enables the Black characters to resist racial violence but often cannot prevent it.

In *Farmhand*, Guillory combines elements of traditional conjure—Aunt Jannice is a side character and is no longer practicing her craft, but she recalls the Jenkins family history and provides the account of the lynching of Ezekiel's grandfather—with a modern understanding of magical roots in the form of the organic transplants that infect human bodies (*transplants* takes on a double meaning here, as Ezekiel is a descendant of Africans "transplanted" onto the American continent through the Middle Passage). In *Bayou*, conjuring occurs through the figure of Mother Sista, who provides guidance from her position as the caring mother of the Southern spirit world. Mother Sista serves as an ancestral protector figure whose means are limited (she is killed at the end of the second volume), offering advice to the dying (Billy) and the struggling

(Lee) and using roots and other forms of folk medicine to keep the evil forces (Bossman and his henchmen and monsters) at bay whenever they threaten to harm Lee in her sleep. Mother Sista may be described as an earlier, less elaborate, and less powerful version of *Bitter Root*'s Ma Etta, who is not only a conjure woman in the tradition of African American folklore (which includes Chesnutt's Aunt Peggy and Hurston's "witch and hant tales" as well as Gloria Naylor's Mama Day and Walter Mosley's Momma Jo) but also the matriarch of the Sangerye family, having "learned the art of herb mixing and curing Jinoo when she was a runaway slave in the underground railroad" (7).[74]

In 1924, when the main action of *Bitter Root* takes place, Ma Etta is the head of the family business, Sangerye Tonsorial & Elixirs, which has made a name for itself by knowing "the roots better than anyone else," as Dr. Sylvester puts it (24). Her knowledge is particularly valuable for the Fiif'No serum, the only cure for Jinoo infection. But the Sangeryes now face a new threat beyond that of the Jinoo (whites infected by racism): the even more monstrous Inzondo (Black Americans who have suffered massive trauma; *inzondo* means "hate" in Zulu). The serum does not work properly against these novel monsters. Ma Etta says that she has "never seen a soul infected like this. [. . .] The Jinoo are souls sick with hate. But this soul here is sick with something else. [. . .] Pain. Fear" (283). Earlier in the story, she notes that "whatever's taken hold of Berg ain't of this world—that's why none of the roots are working. This is beyond root work. Beyond science" (69).

Bitter Root thus introduces the idea of a supernatural force, with evil creatures from an otherworldly realm that feed on Black suffering to seek retribution for racial trauma. Indeed, the Sangerye family struggles mightily against these forces as well as against the Jinoo, using Ma Etta's conjuring skills and root work to the best of their advantage and employing their fighting skills when spiritual means fail.[75] Facing Berg as he turns into a green-skinned monster with giant fangs and runs toward Ma Etta, threatening to attack her, the matriarch remains unfazed (fig. 5.6): "I'm a little too old to run. Beside, I ain't runnin' from my own kin. That's right, child, you my kin. And I ain't about to lose no more of my kin. If I can't cure you, I'm gonna put your soul to rest! Like I said—too old to run . . . . . . and too stubborn to quit" (76–77). As she utters these words, which suggest that her sense of family might be her most effective superpower, Ma punches Berg with a magic hand that recalls Half-Dead Johnson's mojo hand. She fights repeatedly, a skilled warrior who will stand her ground against even the most monstrous creatures. But she also works in the kitchen, preparing serums and tonics, and interacts with children, initiating them into the world of folk wisdom, teaching them herbal knowledge and root work (451), and familiarizing them with what Chireau calls "the apothecary of African American supernaturalism" (*Black* 48).

Fig. 5.6: Ma Etta confronting the infected Berg in *Bitter Root Omnibus: Book One*. Page one of two.

Ma Etta emerges from these scenes not only as the family matriarch, a conjure woman curing the sick, and a fierce fighter against monstrous evil but also as a teacher and inspirational figure who passes on the elders' knowledge and wisdom to the next generations. She guides and mentors her granddaughter Blink, whose head is filled with ideas about gender equality and

Fig. 5.6: Ma Etta confronting the infected Berg in *Bitter Root Omnibus: Book One*. Page two of two.

whom Ma Etta eventually picks to succeed her as the head of the family. Early on, Ma suggests that "fightin Jinoo ain't women's work," but Blink responds that "times are changing" and "women can do anything" (17). Nevertheless, Ma's philosophy is not as old-fashioned as it may seem: "In this family, men do the brawn work. Women do the brain work. Women only fight when we ain't got no other options" (17). True to her words, Ma is the brains of the Sangerye operation, producing the serum and using her magic—for example, by visiting and seeking advice from the elders in the spirit world when she realizes that "it's time to wade some dangerous waters" (428). But she also fights and keeps the family together, reminding her relatives of their humanitarian ethos: "The Sangeryes don't turn their backs on folks in need. That ain't the way we do things. We gonna fight the fight. But we also gonna feed the hungry, we gonna comfort them that's scared . . . . . . and we gonna heal the sick" (122–23).[76]

Alongside *Bitter Root*, *Blue Hand Mojo* offers the most extensive depiction of conjuring, although a conjure man (Half-Dead Johnson) replaces a conjure woman as the center of attention.[77] Half-Dead Johnson is a hoodoo detective in the tradition of Ishmael Reed's Papa LaBas (*Mumbo Jumbo*, 1972). Johnson calls himself "a black hoodoo man" and (in Ellisonian terms) a "strange spook in the wrong part of town" (chap. 7). A former colleague enlists Johnson to investigate a supernatural crime: the murder of a gang of criminals by what turns out to have been the monstrous reincarnation of a young man, Red, who was killed by one of the gangsters. "Hell-bent on revenge" and animated by "pain and rage" (chap. 4), the monster was conjured by a two-headed hoodoo doctor, Papa John Gooden, whom Red's mother, Sweet Liza Mae, had hired to cast a "very fucking, soul-destroying, powerful-ass hex" (chap. 4) on the murderer and his associates.[78] As in *Bitter Root*, Black trauma is the source of evil called forth to seek revenge against white oppressors. Here too, Black magic proves harmful for all, including those who enlist it in the struggle to gain control over their lives.[79]

Half-Dead Johnson is a fascinating character because he (in conjunction with Papa John and his Gooden Plenty store, which sells "the absolute best roots, herbs, and conjuring supplies around" [chap. 6]) represents what Chireau calls "the rise of urban magic" (*Black* 144) in Northern Black neighborhoods shaped by the arrival of people from the South as part of the Great Migration.[80] Johnson is also a comic book instantiation of the conjure man evoked in blues tunes such as "Mojo Hand Blues" (1927) by Ida Cox (cf. Chireau, *Black* 120). He draws on a wide arsenal of conjuring techniques, among them divination powder, gris-gris, magic smoke, goofer dust, jujus, and hexes. But as a hardboiled blues detective reeling from personal trauma, he remains bound to the devil and tied to The Noir. He is not entirely incapacitated but becomes an agent of his own fate at least to some extent. The magic of his mojo hand makes him a powerful figure in the world of urban crime, and he brings back Red "with a lot of magic and a lot of sweat and blood." This feat earns him half of Sweet Liza Mae's juke joint, which the two reopen as the Hard Times Road Café. He embraces Albert, suggesting that he will act as a surrogate father to the boy (chap. 10) and thus exemplifying the makeshift Black family just as Bayou did in protecting Lee.

MONSTROUS HISTORIES AND THE CRISES OF THE PRESENT

Cohen begins his essay "Monster Culture: Seven Theses" (1996) with the idea of providing "a new *modus legendi*: a method of reading cultures from the monsters they engender" and a promise to work "toward understanding cultures through the monsters they bear" (37, 38). Noting that the monster is "a construct and a projection," Cohen highlights the figure's etymology as "that which reveals" and "that which warns" and its cultural function as "a glyph that seeks a hierophant" (38). As a creature of "category crisis" (Garber 11), the monster has long constituted a marginal figure whose threatening power lies not so much in its propensity to cause physical harm as in its ability to destabilize the known world, to act as an agent of epistemic and ontological irritation that troubles binary thinking.[81] In *Box of Bones*, for instance, the monstrous contents of the box do not fall neatly into stable categories of good or bad; while Lindsay proposes that the demonic creatures can properly be designated only as evil, these creatures disturb the reign of white supremacy by ridding the world of rapists and racists. In *Nat Turner*, the line between monster and folk hero, murderer and revolutionary, is indeed thin and must be drawn quite differently depending on the interpretation of the relationship between white supremacy and Black trauma.

If monsters usually "exist in margins," as Allen S. Weiss suggests (125), and if they have traditionally been associated with racialized and sexualized Others, with what the dominant culture deems disgusting, deviant, abject, and grotesque, what do we make of the widespread popularity of monsters in twentieth- and especially twenty-first-century media, including graphic narratives?[82] "What does it mean that our historical monsters have moved from the margins to the mainstream?" Megen de Bruin-Molé asks (3), while Jeffrey Weinstock argues that "the overall trend in monstrous representation across the twentieth century and into the twenty-first has been toward not just sympathizing but empathizing with—and ultimately aspiring to be—the monster" ("Invisible" 277; see also Levina and Bui). In the contemporary graphic narratives, monsters stake out a claim, both diegetically and within the larger sphere of comics production, that resists marginalization. Readers are indeed invited to sympathize with characters like Dr. Sylvester and Miss Knightsdale in *Bitter Root* or Gauge and Baptise in *Box of Bones* by empathizing with their suffering. But rather than possessing aspirational qualities, these characters tragically succumb to their obsession with revenge. If Cohen's observation that "because of its ontological liminality, the monster notoriously appears at times of crisis" ("Monster" 40) is correct, then the question becomes what contemporary crisis the monsters in graphic narratives address, how they position themselves vis-à-vis the problems of present-day Black lives, and how they comment on the current status of race in US comics.

Following Cohen's assumptions, we should investigate what such contemporary crises can mean for historical (re)memory and the resuscitation of Black history from official oblivion. The renewed interest in the 1921 Tulsa Race Massacre is an intriguing case in point. Not only is it evoked in Hall, Martínez, and Bao's *Wake*, its centennial prompted the appearance of several graphic narratives, among them Alverne Ball and Stacy Robinson's *Across the Tracks: Remembering Greenwood, Black Wall Street, and the Tulsa Race Massacre*, as well as illustrated children's books like Carole Boston Weatherford and Floyd Cooper's *Unspeakable: The Tulsa Race Massacre* and Najah-Amatullah Hylton, Quraysh Ali Lansana, and Skipp Hill's *Opal's Greenwood Oasis*.[83] In *Bitter Root*, this massacre and its Red Summer precursors are central to the story, turning Dr. Sylvester and Miss Knightsdale into Inzondo. Losing their children in the massacre connects them as a couple in need. "Without you... ... I would have died in Tulsa with all the others," Dr. Sylvester tells Miss Knightsdale (50). He later states, "We were both dying, but in our pain and fear we found each other, and ... became something more"; Miss Knightsdale offers him her "pain and fear" and urges, "Let it feed you" (121). Over time, they realize that their pain makes them vulnerable to a hate that turns them into monsters and cannot be contained by the serum. "The fear. The hate. It's calling out from Harlem ... so strong," Dr. Sylvester exclaims in a splash panel that shows him with demonic eyes, fangs, and a screaming mouth. "This affliction that has claimed us both—I had hoped to find a cure for those like us" (67). That such depictions of monsters are tied to historical events long ignored in national memory marks a significant development in comic book publishing precisely because these portrayals connect old wounds with new grievances in the wake of Black Lives Matter and its critiques of structural racism.

The Tulsa Race Massacre receives its most extended treatment in the Red Summer issue, which proposes a genealogy of anti-Black violence and Black rebellion from the days of slavery to Chicago in 1919 and Tulsa in 1921. The opening segment shows Ma Etta with a family on the Underground Railroad in Maryland in 1850. They are attacked by vicious creatures supplanting the slave catcher's dogs and saved by Harriet Tubman ("Moses") and Metellus Sangerye, Ma Etta's future husband (155–60). The Chicago segment features Ford and Berg under attack by monstrous creatures with gaping mouths and giant tentacles. "We can't run from this! This is more than a Jinoo infestation," one Black Chicagoan (perhaps Ford's uncle) utters as Berg drags him away and Ford kills a monster with a stake, yelling, "This is for my family!" Ford emerges from the fight with a wound across his face and cannot save his aunt

Nora, who is squeezed to death by one of the monsters and whose dead body he carries away while crying (166–69).

The Tulsa segment is the most harrowing of the three historical flashbacks in this issue. It begins with a white farmer flying an airplane over the Greenwood district, lighting a pack of dynamite with his cigarette, and then dropping it on the district's Black citizens as they attempt to flee. The color palette is a mixture of browns and yellows that make the page resemble a war comic, an impression that is intensified by the combination of the running crowd and the explosion that throws people through the air in the final panel. As in the two preceding segments, the Black family bears the brunt of the attack, with Dr. Sylvester grabbing his son's and daughter's hands and telling them, "Run! Don't look back!" (171). The next two pages show the aftermath of the bombing: a cityscape in ruins, Dr. Sylvester holding onto his son as they realize that his daughter has been killed by the blast. While Dr. Sylvester mourns his "baby girl," Miss Knightsdale alerts them to the returning plane, which drops more dynamite, killing Dr. Sylvester's son (fig. 5.7). Lying in the dark ruins of the neighborhood, the Williams Dreamland Theatre sign dangling over a sea of brick and shattered wooden beams, and pleading for help and asking "Where ... are ... my children!" (175), Dr. Sylvester witnesses Miss Knightsdale's physical transformation. Staring at the bottom of the page and continuing over the next page, she turns into a crow-like monster, screaming in pain (yet without sound) and rescuing Dr. Sylvester from the rubble.[84] This kind of monstrosity is substantially different from racist discourse about African Americans as monsters; in fact, *Bitter Root* exposes the monstrosity of anti-Black violence and the anguish it causes. This marks a significant intervention into hegemonic narratives of US history, with their proclivity toward war heroes and visions of imperial greatness, suggesting that the nation has for centuries waged war on racialized minorities.

"The dead always return for a reason," Chassot argues, and the ghost "always responds to specific historical and cultural conditions and anxieties" (3). The same holds true for the monster. Graphic narratives like *Blue Hand Mojo* and *Bitter Root* not only intervene in ongoing debates about the significance and specifics of Black history but also reference current forms of resistance to racial oppression. At a moment in US culture when Black death has once again become a media spectacle (as Rankine's *Citizen* foregrounds), causing new wounds and reopening old ones that have never properly healed, it matters that creators like Jennings and Walker, Brown, and Greene connect the fantastic elements of their graphic narratives with the words of current victims of anti-Black violence: "I can't breathe" in *Blue Hand Mojo* and *Bitter Root* (when Nora is in the tight grip of an Inzondo [313]); "Don't Shoot!" as Berg yells in

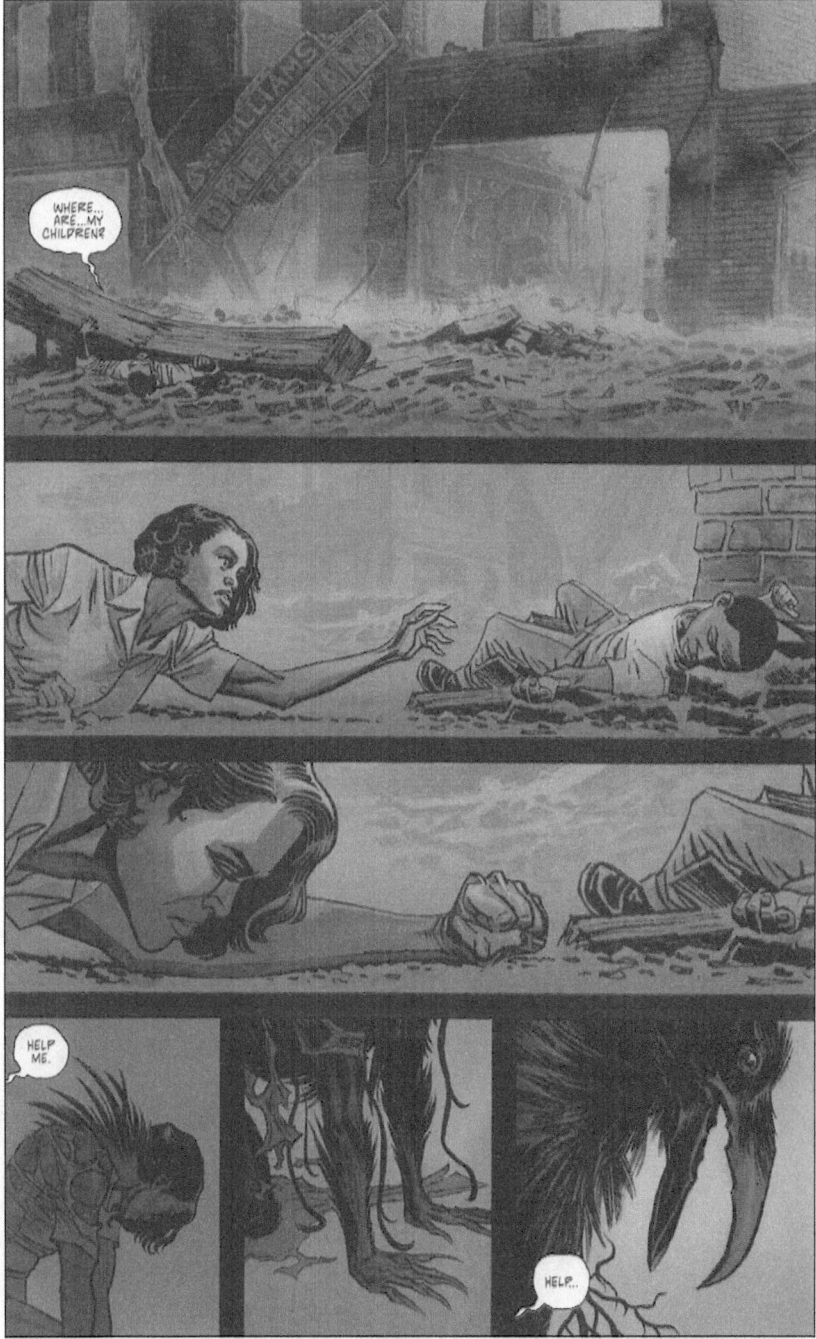

Fig. 5.7: Miss Knightsdale transforming into an Inzondo during the Tulsa Race Massacre in *Bitter Root Omnibus: Book One*.

Bitter Root (29) when two New York City cops hold him at gunpoint because they believe he and Cullen have attacked people in Harlem's St. Nicholas Park. Cohen is right to suggest that monsters "still serve as the ultimate incorporation of our anxieties about history, about identity, about our very humanity" ("Preface" xii). And Ahmed is correct in claiming that the medium of comics "is monstrous through its penchant for visual garishness as well as through the intensity of the hybrid, symbiotic—but also tussling—word-image relationships" (11). Several other comics pivot around the nexus of race and monstrosity—the *Killadelphia* series by Rodney Barnes et al. (2020–); David Crownson et al.'s *Harriet Tubman: Demon Slayer* (2017–); Chuck Brown, Prenzy, and Clayton Cowles's *On the Stump* (2020); Tananarive Due, Steven Barnes, and Marco Finnegan's *The Keeper* (2020); Nnedi Okorafor, Tana Ford, and James Devlin's *LaGuardia* (2019). They indicate the urgency of race as a monstrous crisis in US culture as well as its increasing recognition in this medium.

CODA

Fig. 6.1: The dedication page from *Uncelebrated Narratives from Black History* (*Strange Fruit* vol. 1).

Opening the cover of Joel Christian Gill's *Uncelebrated Narratives from Black History* (*Strange Fruit* vol. 1, 2014) reveals a stunning image (fig. 6.1). At the very bottom of the page, on a white plane with no background, appears an audience, some of whose members are shielding their eyes and looking away in horror while others gaze and point at something: a frayed and severed rope that is miraculously still, held up by an unknown force. For readers versed in US visual culture and cognizant of historical images of anti-Black violence, this illustration evokes the archive of lynching photographs and images in other media; like those images, this one includes children—a baby in what seem to be its mother's arms. By radically decontextualizing the audience and removing the center of the racist spectacle—the lynched Black body/bodies—from the image, Gill illustrates how deeply ingrained this imagery is in the wider US cultural consciousness, including visual culture. Most readers probably can mentally add the missing parts of the image through the process Scott McCloud calls closure.[1] Yet by absenting the tortured and tormented Black body/bodies and by uprooting the tree that traditionally bears lynching's iconic "strange fruit," Gill resists centuries of aggression, violence, and abuse.[2]

Gill's decision to allow the Black body to flee the lynching scene is powerful and historically trenchant. Not only does it point back to the many lynching photographs where the mangled body is at the center of attention, denying these photographs the last word on the representation of Black death, but it also evokes a painting from Jabob Lawrence's *Migration Series* (1941). As the online exhibition from the Museum of Modern Art and the Phillips Collection aptly summarizes (in comics-compatible language), "The emotional power of this panel hinges on absence" by leaving the noose at the center hanging empty from a single tree branch while to the lower left is a "huddled figure" with its "face turned from the viewer, head bowed, limbs tucked in." The description reads Lawrence's "grieving figure" as a "poignant manifestation of the lasting anguish produced by the murder of thousands of black citizens," suggesting that even those who manage to physically escape the lynchings remained bound to them psychologically ("One Way").

Gill's image encapsulates the idea that creators of graphic narratives invested in Black history insist on visually representing the horrors of the past and their lingering traumatic effects in the medium of comics while treating this representation as a prerequisite for recuperating, reconstructing, recreating, and reenvisioning more adequate and affirmative stories. The power of these efforts can be grasped by tracing Gill's image across a wider range of graphic narratives that offer additional takes on the empty noose.

A full-page image of a noose dangles from an unknown source outside the panel frame on page 27 of Blair Imani's *Making Our Way Home: The Great Migration and the Black American Dream* (2020), which accompanies his narrative of surviving massacres and lynchings in the 1920s and 1930s. Moreover, in Roland Laird, Taneshia Nash Laird, and Elihu "Adofo" Bey's *Still I Rise: A Graphic History of African Americans* (1997), an empty noose appears underneath a caption on page 74 describing the arrest of 139 people and the hanging of 46 participants in the 1822 Charleston revolt led by Denmark Vesey.[3] Blood is dripping from this noose, serving as a reminder that freedom is a long way off. Finally, the back cover of Ayize Jama-Everett and John Jennings's *Box of Bones* shows a noose that encircles the narrative's titular container of trauma against a deep red background. These examples present a different aftermath, afterlife, and afterimage—a different wake—of enslavement in which the victims have exited the scene to an unknown location.

Next to the top of the rope, where a branch would usually be, Gill's image has a handwritten dedication: "For all those who freed themselves by cutting the rope." With these words, the Southern-born Gill reimagines the troubled archive of Black history as the pretext for emancipation, elaborating on this notion in his introductory essay, "Why Strange Fruit?":

> As an undergrad, I had researched some ideas for paintings based on lynching photographs. Now, I felt, was the time to follow through. I listened to the song "Strange Fruit" by Billie Holiday, based on the poem by Abel Meeropol, and I decided to call my paintings "Strange Fruit Harvested: He Cut the Rope," showing me with a noose around my neck, holding the frayed end. I was trying to say that I was in some ways freed from the fear that had plagued my father and grandfather. However, I also wanted to convey that because the rope was still there, we still had a ways to go. (2–3)

These remarks, like Morrison's paradox of haunted happiness and her perfect dilemma of unacceptable forgetting and remembering, wrench a positive, life-affirming, and celebratory note from the dissonances of US race relations and thus work against a visual culture that has sustained the structures of white supremacy. According to Gill, his book "tells stories of people who, in spite of the 'Strange Fruit' society where they lived, liberated themselves from the magnolia trees and tried to do something amazing." He concludes, "Whether it was escaping from slavery in a box," as Henry Brown did, or emulating Bass Reeves and "chasing down outlaws, these people epitomized cutting the rope" (3).

Such creative reinterpretations of ropes and nooses (especially in lynching narratives), as well as of shackles and chains (in Middle Passage narratives and beyond) and of trees (the baobab in *Black Panther* and the tree of woe in *Farmland*) and bodies of water (the Atlantic Ocean in *Wake*, the swamp in *Bayou*), function as signifiers of oppression and atrocities. They further encompass the chains that bind together the huddled masses of enslaved Africans in Tom Feelings's *Middle Passage*; the rope and chains with which Nat Turner's mother is captured and restrained in Kyle Baker's *Nat Turner*; the chains smashed dramatically by the Black "cargo" in the ship's hold in Rebecca Hall, Hugo Martínez, and Sarula Bao's *Wake*; and the handcuffs around the wrists of peaceful civil rights protesters in John Lewis, Andrew Aydin, and Nate Powell's *March* trilogy as well as the ropes in Jeremy Love and Patrick Morgan's *Bayou* that are not only wrapped around the necks of the lynched men and women but also used to pull up and thus set free the body of Billy Glass.[4]

Yet there is more to the racially charged image and metaphor of the rope. In Alverne Ball and Stacey Robinson's *Across the Tracks: Remembering Greenwood, Black Wall Street, and the Tulsa Massacre*, the rope appears on a splash page that includes a facsimile of a 1 June 1921 article from *The Tulsa Tribune*, "Nab Negro for Attacking Girl in an Elevator," reporting the incident that set off the massacre. A young Black man, Dick Rowland, was arrested for allegedly attempting to assault a white elevator girl, and the comic shows outraged white readers pointing at the newspaper, shouting out the news to others. In the last panel on the page, a white man telephones the editor of Greenwood's Black newspaper, *The Tulsa Star*, urging him "to get word to the men of Greenwood that if they want to save Dick Rowland from a lynching, they better get down here soon." On the next page, the *Star*'s editor calls a member of the Greenwood community, setting in motion a chain of calls. As the communication unfolds, the phone cord, which resembles a rope, at once suggests the looming threat of the race-based lynching announced on the preceding page and the communal counteractivities of the Black Tulsans, who state, "We can't let this happen" and "There's been too many lynchings across this country. Enough is enough." Instead of encircling the neck of the lynched, the cord/rope frames the concerned, angry, and alarmed faces of the callers. It thus reframes the devastating history of race crimes and the long-standing practice of publicly mutilating Black bodies to envision a more affirmative and more emancipatory narrative of Black self-reliance. It imagines liberation where history tended to record subjugation and seeks reassurance in celebrating courageous acts of resistance.[5]

A third use of the rope appears in Arthur Flowers, Manu Chitrakar, and Guglielmo Rossi's *I See the Promised Land: A Life of Martin Luther King Jr.* (2010), a stunning reimagination of King's life through Flowers's vernacular poetics and Chitraka's Patua scroll art, which visualizes King and the civil rights movement through an Indian iconography that wrenches new meanings and affects from the otherwise well-known narrative. Ropes first appear in a segment headed "We talking slavery now," which is part of a longer section depicting Black diasporic history from the first enslavements and the Middle Passage to the twentieth century. In this segment, European and Arab enslavers are holding up ropes that, in the lower panel on the page, wrap around the necks and hands of four enslaved men (14–15). A few pages later, when the narrative turns to the Middle Passage, these ropes appear around the necks of the enslaved (18, 19,

24) but then become loosened (19, 20), floating unmoored through the panels and performing no obvious function. Still later, on North American soil, they recur as nooses around the necks of lynched men (32, 43–47).

This imagery offers emancipatory and liberating impulses that may be mobilized to overcome the suffering described throughout this book.[6] As comics and literary scholar Joanna C. Davis-McElligatt asks,

> How can we harness of the power of Black joy? How have Black thinkers, scholars, and artists turned their attention to forms of Black happiness as a critical and necessary affectual response to the logics of Black death? How can we describe—and make meaningful—the radical potential of Black happiness and joy as antidotes to the overwhelming logics of Black death and destruction? How have Black folk found and cultivated joy even in the midst of subjection, abjection, and the death-dealing logics of white supremacy? How are the affects and expressions of Black joy a life-affirming, rebellious, and meaningful counter to Black death? ("Rebellious")

This call stands in a tradition of what Christina N. Baker calls "the Black feminist praxis of understanding joy and pleasure as forms of resistance, self-care, and power," with joy and pleasure "broadly defined as a feeling of happiness, enjoyment, or satisfaction" (459). The call further evokes Imani Perry's claim that "Blackness is an immense and defiant joy" and resonates with Perry's reminder that "exhilaration in black life is not to mute or minimize racism": joy signals "not an absence of grief or rage, or a distraction. It is insistence." If, as Davis-McElligatt acknowledges and as Elizabeth Alexander argued decades earlier, "Black bodies in pain for public consumption have been an American national spectacle for centuries" (88), then Black joy can become a means of political resistance, "a real and imagined site of utopian possibility" (Javon Johnson 180). Javon Johnson holds that "house parties, backyard cookouts, and other spaces where black bodies gather in celebration [to] produce rich and profound moments in which black love and laughter" (180) serve as potentially utopian sites, while Matthew Jordan-Miller Kenyatta understands Black joy "as an oppositional practice of Black love in the face of hegemonic cultural injustice and racist disregard for the distinctive desires, dreams, and delimitations found within Afrodiasporic space" (218).[7]

Which rebellious affects, which kinds of joyful resistance, which imaginative possibilities, and which forms of Black joy, pleasure, and happiness serve as means of counterabjection in contemporary graphic narratives? At first sight, scenes of "unapologetic Black joy" (Christopher Paul Harris 11) appear to be few and far between—the past and present harm that the characters, their families, their sidekicks, and their communities must bear is too massive; the absence of these events in the pages of American comic books is too audacious; and the task of giving them visual form is too substantial. There are no elaborate celebrations of joy, no extensive depictions of pleasure in these works.[8] There are, however, brief moments of respite from racially motivated atrocities and scenes of harmonious life, though it is disrupted and often destroyed by violent onslaught. These scenes and moments, while scarce, are nonetheless significant and deserve to be recognized as attempts to "straddle the line between hope and Afropessimism" and to achieve some kind of "balance between black suffering and black optimism," as Rebecca Wanzo puts it ("How Long"). These scenes and moments can indeed be interpreted as what Wanzo describes as "struggles against state resistance to everyday black life," as indications that Black lives and Black forms of everyday living matter in a society that continues to stack the odds against its marginalized citizens (and even more so against noncitizens such as undocumented immigrants).

These narratives complicate the reduction of pained Black bodies put up for public consumption by remediating and reimagining hurtful historical visualizations such as lynching photography. Love and Morgan's fantastically charged South is home both to racial violence and to a sense of wonder—butterflies, the beautiful and colorful landscape, the loving swamp creature Bayou, the relatives who care for the wounded Lee. David F. Walker, Chuck Brown, and Sanford Greene flip the lynching script in *Bitter Root*: Ford Sangerye's timely intervention saves a Black man and results in the demise of white Klansmen. These examples may be understood as a gleeful sabotage of and signifying on white supremacist images that include Jennings's investment in revising conventional horror scripts and Baker's pop violence in *Nat Turner* as a fantasy of poetic justice.

These narratives contain four powerful recurring types of or occasions for Black joy. The first is spaces of pleasure and entertainment. In the second volume of Love and Morgan's *Bayou*, Lee and Bayou visit a jook joint, a place of wild music, dance, and sexual encounters that scares the girl and necessitates Bayou's intervention when she is about to be abused by a leering bear/reverend. Nonetheless, the patrons are having a good time, enjoying the raunchy atmosphere reminiscent of what Albert Murray calls the "Saturday Night Function." These scenes are connected to flashback sequences that portray Lee's mother performing as a blues singer and causing so many men heartaches and pain that one of them eventually kills her. In *Bitter Root*, the Sweet Pickin' Lounge in 1920s Harlem serves as a space for dancing, drinking, and socializing. Here, too, the pleasure of entertainment and the joyful atmosphere give way to the horrors of racialized violence when the Inzondo invade the lounge.

Jennings's *Blue Hand Mojo* and Ta-Nehesi Coates et al.'s *Black Panther & the Crew* offer a more hopeful outlook on Black spaces of pleasure and entertainment. In *Blue Hand Mojo*, Half-Dead Johnson solves the case with his conjuring powers and is rewarded with partial ownership of Liza's Hard Times Road Café, thereby allowing him leave behind his conjuring days and serve his community. Looking directly at the reader, he intones, "You should come through! We feed you, get you drunk, take your money and make you love us for it." In *Black Panther & the Crew*, Londell's Café connects the era of the civil rights movement with present-day Harlem, providing a place of refuge for "the crew" and allowing them to regroup and plan further activities.

The Southern jook joint, the Sweet Pickin' Lounge, the Hard Times Road Café, and Londell's are (semi)public spaces, but these narratives also feature more private spaces of familial and communal retreat. In most cases, these spaces can offer only a temporary reprieve from violence, but they are important parts of the narratives because they show that life in these spaces, though far from perfect, is nonetheless life and that happiness, though limited by the circumstances, is nonetheless possible, at least for a time. Living in the racially segregated and violent Jim Crow South, people like the Wagstaffs have built homes in which they can enjoy their lives despite their general hardships. Lee and Calvin till the earth in front of their cabin, and Lee prepares chicken soup before they are disturbed by the sheriff. Once the interruption is over, father and daughter sit down at the dinner table. "This is some good eatin', babygirl," Calvin says before the conversation turns to the serious business at hand: the accusation that Lee has stolen a locket from Lily and Lee's question about why her father did not defend her in the face of the allegations. "You got a roof over your head. Place to grow. Go to school," Calvin tells his daughter, reminding her of their humble and precarious achievements (vol. 1).

Such precariousness is omnipresent in these graphic narratives: in Baker's *Nat Turner*, enslavers raid an African village. In Rob Guillory's *Farmhand*, the Freetown community, planned as an oasis for Black folk after Reconstruction, is destroyed when Ezekiel's ancestor is lynched by the KKK. The *March* books show Lewis's poor country upbringing, including the discovery of the Bible and his preaching to the chickens that his family will eventually eat. In *Wake*, recurring scenes of a beach vacation where Hall spends time with her wife and son indicate how the joys of family life mingle with her thoughts about her research into the transatlantic slave trade. Ho Che Anderson's *King* offers a look behind the popular image of Martin Luther King Jr. and into his home, with children roaming around and the family trying to cope with his increasingly dangerous activities. In *Bitter Root*, the members of the Sangerye family do not always see eye to eye but nevertheless band together to fight monsters and feed the hungry. All of these scenes feature what Christopher Paul Harris calls an "ethics of care" that extends from the individual to the collective (14).

In these narratives, intimate moments between romantic partners or between parents and children occur relatively frequently and constitute a second trope of Black joy.[9] Though less common than situations shaped by violence, these moments occur persistently and signal a sense of resistance against the destruction of romantic and familial intimacy. Half-Dead Johnson has a symbiotic relationship with his lover, Sophie, a "rootworker" who is "as sweet as honey and loves me more than I think she even knows" (chap. 2). They sustain each other with their conjuring powers: Sophie makes a tonic that helps Johnson control his mojo hand; Johnson gives blood for the potion that allows Sophie to pass as a white woman. *Wake*, *Box of Bones*, and several *Black Panther* renditions feature homoerotic and homosexual relationships between women as well as a heterosexual relationship between T'Challa and his lover and later wife, Ororo. In *King*, Anderson narrates Martin's courtship of Coretta, their wedding, and their increasingly troubled marriage, including King's infidelities. While all of these relationships have problems and thus cannot be categorized as exclusively joyful, they remove Black lives from the specters of the spectacular and the monstrous and cast these characters—some invented, some historical—as human beings dealing with mundane interpersonal conflicts as well as with the challenges of living in racist environments.

From such interpersonal relations, it is only a short step toward family relationships as a third trope of Black joy, sometimes involving whole families but often involving only one parent and child. Lee has a loving relationship with her father, Calvin, and tries to rescue him when he is jailed and in danger of getting lynched. Hall escapes the horrors of archival research by spending time with her wife and son. Anderson's comics biography offers glimpses into the King family's life. Feelings's *Middle Passage* and Nnedi Okorafor, Tana Ford, and James Devlin's *LaGuardia* depict pregnant women, indicating the possibility of new Black life. Baker's *Nat Turner* allows Turner and his family brief moments of joy before patrollers snatch Turner. *Farmhand* centers on a family narrative, with Ezekiel struggling to get along with his wife and rambunctious kids as well as with his reckless grandfather. *Blue Hand Mojo* begins with Half-Dead Johnson dreaming of the murders of his wife and children and ends with him embracing the illiterate boy Albert, for whom he and Sophie might become foster parents. Finally, *Bitter Root* contains perhaps the most elaborate cluster of family scenes, since the narrative concerns the Sangeryes as a family unit. Particularly remarkable are the scenes in which matriarch Ma Etta conveys to her granddaughter Blink that she should serve as the new leader of the family because she is strong and smart enough to take on that responsibility (372–73,

409). Moreover, Berg falls in love, marries, and cradles his newborn daughter, Mariah, as he tells his wife, "She is my life. You and she" (400).

Finally, music serves as a fourth trope and source of joy in these narratives. This should come as no surprise: music is foundational to African American cultural production and is played in spaces of pleasure and entertainment. But this musical connection also invests several of the stories with a blues aesthetic that goes beyond the beautiful and sonically suggestive scenes of Harlem Renaissance musicking in *Bitter Root* or the moments of jooking and jiving in *Bayou*. Rather than seeing and imagining music in *Blue Hand Mojo*, readers encounter the life story of a hoodoo detective whose traumatic past and burdensome present are steeped in the blues: the loss of his wife and children, the escape from the lynching, the migration from South to North, and the continuing threat of racially motivated violence that so many blues songs lament. *Bayou* spotlights the not-so-glamorous life of Tarbaby, whose sultry blues voice and sparkling red dress may have mesmerized audiences but whose infidelity results in her untimely death. Derek McCulloch et al.'s *Stagger Lee* is based on folk versions of the badman's life story, many of them captured in the form of song lyrics, which explains why many scenes involve bars and other places of music-making. Both Bayou and Berg sing the spiritual "Wade in the Water" in moments of temporary peace, and Bayou appears as a blues musician in Love and Morgan's narrative.

The most elaborate depiction of music (besides the multiple moments of singing in *March*) occurs in *Bitter Root*'s repeated scenes in the Sweet Pickin' Lounge, where happy people enjoy themselves dancing and the jazz band plays what must be a lively up-tempo song since the notes are flying around. This scene's placement at the opening of issue 11 (343) and the fact that the band, including a female singer whose pearl necklace and gardenia evoke Billie Holiday, is part of the massive splash-page tableau that encapsulates the Sangerye family saga and the current threats indicate the centrality of music to this graphic foray into Black history.

• • •

The continuing investment of contemporary creators in graphic narratives of Black history is a subject that must necessarily remain open, and the archive of racist images and narratives functions both as a lasting reminder of historical oppression and anti-Black violence and as an image bank to be undesigned and remediated for more affirmative visions of Black life. In that light, two avenues for further research seem particularly promising.

First, nonfiction graphic narratives about Black history are growing in significance. For example, Trevor R. Getz and Liz Clarke's *Abina and the Important*

Men (2012), Rafe Blaufarb and Liz Clarke's *Inhuman Traffick: The International Struggle Against the Transatlantic Slave Trade* (2015), and Karlos K. Hill and David Dodson's *The Murder of Emmett Till: A Graphic History* (2021) were written by professional historians and include substantial historical apparatuses that make them useful for classroom use. More outspoken and self-consciously "Black" works include Gill's graphic adaptation of Ibram X. Kendi's *Stamped from the Beginning* (2023), which traces the "history of racist ideas in America" and, like many of the works analyzed in this book, combines didactic and political concerns.

While the graphic narratives examined in this book have paved the way for Black history as a significant *sujet* for comics, such historicist works aim to make an impact on the historical profession and reshape how history can be studied and taught. Gill's work may serve as a bridge between these approaches, transforming elements from the racist visual archive into a new graphic discourse that acknowledges the archive's lasting power but nonetheless wrenches from it a more positive sense of Black history. In *Robert Smalls* (*Tales of the Talented Tenth* vol. 3), Gill tells the story of the enslaved man who stole a Confederate ship and sailed himself, his family, and a few companions to freedom. As in *Stamped*, Gill uses a racist caricature of a Black boy's head to visually bleep the N-word whenever racist white Southerners use it. By transposing the verbal racist epithet to an equally racist visual icon, Gill self-consciously censors himself, purposely avoiding any replication of the racist language of the time while indicating that this language has a visual counterpart. Though the image may seem less hurtful (the boy's head is rendered in a cutesy style), it nonetheless foregrounds the pervasiveness of racist representations across media. What we find here in condensed form and in greater variety throughout the contemporary graphic narratives analyzed are the joys of graphic storytelling itself, including not only subject matter, characters, and scenes but also a sense of stylistic exuberance and innovative page and panel design that make these works fascinating, though they are troubling as well as tantalizing, haunting as well as pleasurable.

A second pathway for future exploration winds through parts of the Black diaspora outside the US context. How could contemporary graphic narratives of Black history written and illustrated by non-US authors and artists offer new perspectives and expand the scope of inquiry? Marguerite Abouet and Clément Oubrerie's *Aya: Life in Yop City* (2007, 2008, 2009) depicts life in the late-1970s Ivory Coast, focusing on the lives of African girls and women. Marcelo D'Salete's *Run for It: Stories of Slaves Who Fought for Their Freedom* (2014) and *Angola Janga: Kingdom of Runaway Slaves* (2017) take on the maroon communities of late-sixteenth- and early seventeenth-century Brazil.[10] D'Salete's comics show how expanding beyond the US context will lead to different timelines, different terminology (African words and concepts as well as Catholic and Portuguese terms), different geographies and cosmologies (Palmares, a maroon community). The United States, which imported substantially fewer enslaved persons than Brazil did, arguably outstrips the former Portuguese colony in terms of comics production, including comics about Black history, precisely because the US system of nation building and its capitalist economy have proven globally more powerful than those of Brazil (which remained under colonial rule until 1822 and did not abolish slavery until 1888). *Run for It* and *Angola Janga* share a visual vocabulary with representations of slavery in US comics (see *Angola Janga* 110–12 [depicting the Middle Passage] and 118 [featuring shackles as instruments and icons of slavery]) as well as contain long wordless passages (as do Feelings's *Middle Passage* and Baker's *Nat Turner*), thus indicating the potential fruitfulness of a transnational perspective on these issues.[11] To include works like *Run for It* and *Angola Janga*, as well as *Aya: Life in Yop City*, Matthew Clarke and Nigel Lynch's Afro-Caribbean *Hardears* (2021), and Brazilian creator Hugo Canuto's *Tales of the Orishas* (2023) in follow-up studies would provide a fuller account of the many Black histories in contemporary graphic narrative yet to be uncovered.

NOTES

INTRODUCTION. STRANGE FRUIT AND BITTER ROOTS

1. Cf. Stuart Hall and Sealy: "'Black' does not reference a particular group, with fixed characteristics, whose social being or artistic imagination is determined by skin colour, genetic make-up or biological inheritance. It does not invoke an essentialized cultural identity, frozen in time, which is automatically transmitted into the work, and can thus be held to 'represent' collectively all those who belong to a particular 'race,' ethnic community, or tradition. 'Black' [...] is a politically, historically and culturally constructed category; a contested idea, whose ultimate destination remains unsettled" (35).

2. Christopher Paul Harris uses a mixed metaphor to describe this interconnection of past and present when he speaks of "the open wound of an anti-Black past whose shadow has yet to subside" (4). For further analysis of BLM, see Christopher Paul Harris; Keeanga-Yamahtta Taylor. On comic depictions of anti-Black violence and the BLM movement, see Haddad.

3. On sundown towns, see Loewen. See also Carlson.

4. For historical context and information about this lynching, see Carr; Madison. For a survivor's account, see Cameron.

5. For additional photographs of the massacre and its aftermath, see "1921 Tulsa Race Massacre."

6. While most creators covered in the book are male, gender nonetheless plays a central role in terms of constructing Black masculinity, the function of female characters for reimagining Black history, and the gendered implications and consequences of anti-Black violence as they are depicted in contemporary graphic narratives. On Black women in comics, see Whaley. See also Christopher Paul Harris's call for "intramural solidarity" in "a political culture that is at once feminist in its frame and abolitionist in its core objectives" (27, 20).

7. My corpus selection is inclusive to avoid any sense of racial essentialism and to recognize the many fruitful collaborations between African American and non–African American creators such as Derek McCulloch and Shepherd Hendrix; Mat Johnson and Warren Pleece; John Lewis, Andrew Aydin, and Nate Powell; and Rebecca Hall, Hugo Martínez, and Sarula Bao.

8. On visual culture and struggles for racial equality, see Gonzales; Jackson.

9. For examples from the racist history of "black images in the comics," see Strömberg.

10. Cf. Fanon: "It is the colonist who *fabricated* and *continues to fabricate* the colonized subject. The colonist derives his validity, i.e., his wealth, from the colonial system" (2).

11. Wallace writes that for "modern westerners of African descent," the "universe of inscription has always been much smaller and more exclusive than the world most of us have always inhabited" and that "Afro-Americans (and others of the African diaspora in the Caribbean, Latin America, and Canada as well) find ourselves with one foot in and one foot out of the modern world" (5).

12. On the Black Atlantic archive and the archives of slavery, see Elmer; Best. On the Black Atlantic in twentieth-century art, see Erikson. For early accounts, see Zuck.

13. Christopher Paul Harris speaks of the urge to "escape the shadow of Black death and lead a life worthy of the term" (6, 7).

14. On the ethics of looking at such scenes of suffering and death, see esp. Courtney R. Baker. For a critique of popular narratives that seek to humanize Black Americans through stories of suffering and triumph, see Russworm.

15. On frames and framing in comics, see Chute; Schmid, *Frames*.

16. Wanzo speaks of a "visual grammar about citizenship" (*Content* 4) that has historically excluded African Americans. On memorializing the transatlantic slave trade, see Araujo; Rice, *Creating*; Rice, *Radicals*.

17. This is not to say that there were no comics about Black history before the 1990s. Examples are Feelings's *Tommy Traveler in the World of Black History* (1958–59), where the youthful protagonist travels back in time to meet figures from Black history such as Phoebe Fraunces, Crispus Attucks, Frederick Douglass, and Emmett Till, and the *Golden Legacy* series (16 issues from 1966 to 1976) of comic book biographies about the lives of Black leaders such as Douglass, Harriet Tubman, and Martin Luther King Jr. Morrie Turner uses a similar biographical approach in *Explore Black History with Wee Pals* (1998). On early Black creators, see also Goldstein; Quattro.

18. For more on Afrofuturism, see Reynaldo Anderson and Jones.

19. In Mat Johnson et al.'s *John Constantine Hellblazer: Papa Midnite* (2006), one Black man finds the symbol on a coffin at the African burial ground in New York and explains, "It's the Sankofa. [. . .] It's an Akan symbol, from what we call Ghana, where a lot of the enslaved in 18th century New York came from." When asked what the symbol means, he responds, "Literally, 'Go back and fetch it.' Figuratively, that you must look to the past to build the future" (10). On Sankofa in Coogler's first *Black Panther* movie (2018), see Osei.

20. On the history of the poem and song, see Margolick. For a close reading and analysis of its didactic potential, see Stein, "Teaching."

21. On aesthetics and race, see Al-Saji; Paul C. Taylor. In *Black Gaze*, Campt sees a shift from the still photograph as the medium to "talk back to power" and "around and in between its silences and absences" to digital moving images as means of capturing "the precarious circumstances of Black people and the increasing prevalence of premature Black death" and ways to "document, archive, and disseminate the mounting threats to Black communities" (4). Comics occupy a middle position here.

22. Christopher Paul Harris uses the tree metaphor when he speaks in Fanonian terms of "the Black Diaspora's family tree" as "a chronicle of the wretched of the earth" (7).

23. For a more recent perspective, written from within an African context, see Mbembe.

24. On the tension between Afro-pessimism and forms of Black optimism, see Sexton; Weier.

25. On the "vexed relationship to the land" in African American culture, see Dunning (18).

26. For more on the poem and postwar "American lynching culture," see W. Jason Miller.

27. Cf. Wright's sense of epiphenomenal time as "the 'now,' through which the past, present, and future are always interpreted" in narratives that avoid an "overreliance on the exclusive use of linear progress narratives to define Blackness" (*Physics* 5).

28. Due to the workings of the comics industry, including reservations about work by Black creators, some graphic narratives have had difficulty getting published. Baker self-published *Nat Turner* in four installments before it was picked up by Abrams; Jama-Everett and Jennings raised money on Kickstarter for *Box of Bones*.

29. On theorizing the Black Atlantic and the tradition of diasporic thought, see Henry Louis Gates Jr., *Tradition*. On recharting the Black Atlantic from current perspectives, see Oboe and Scacchi. The classic study remains Gilroy.

CHAPTER 1. MIDDLE PASSAGE EPISTEMOLOGIES

1. For analysis of the Middle Passage poetics in some of these works, see Chassot; Charras; Lambert; Plasa. On the Middle Passage in the "Black imagination," see Diedrich, Gates, and Pedersen. On "middle passages" in Black women's writing, see Brown-Guillory.

2. On trauma literature's struggles to "narrate the unnarrateable," see Whitehead 4. On the divergent politics of Black grief (or loss) and white grieving (white victimhood), see Hooker.

3. Hartman, for instance, aims "to tell an impossible story and to amplify the impossibility of its telling" ("Venus" 11). Cf. Gray: "The magnitude of these atrocities can never truly be apprehended or appreciated—even as [artists] plumb these sites of trauma for narrative inspiration" ("Commence" 193).

4. On the memorial that marks this departure, the "Door of No Return," and its troubled histories, see Brand, *Map*. Browne writes, "Branding was a practice through which enslaved people were signified as commodities to be bought, sold, and traded. At the scale of skin, the captive body was made the site of social and economic maneuver through the use of iron type" (93). As such, "branding was a racializing act. By making blackness visible as a commodity and therefore sellable, branding was a dehumanizing process of classifying people into groupings, producing new racial identities that were tied to a system of exploitation" (94). Blaufarb and Clarke combine conventional historical narrative with graphic storytelling, including primary sources and questions for students, but do not visualize the branding process.

5. This practice derives its legitimation from the law of *partus sequitur ventrem* (1662), which stipulates that children of enslaved women inherit their maternal status, and its application in the North American colonies and later the United States (cf. Lowe 94). Addressing his son, Ta-Nehisi Coates maintains in *Between the World and Me*, "Remember that you and I [. . .] are the children of trans-Atlantic rape" (128). On the sexual vulnerability of Black women, see Hine; hooks, *Ain't*; Michele Mitchell; Mustakeem; Christina Sharpe, *Monstrous*.

6. Gilroy seeks to overcome this dynamic though the "theorisation of creolisation, métissage, mestizaje, and hybridity," which "exceed racial discourse and avoid capture by its agents" (2).

7. Green defines "the Middle Passage as a site for, if not the origin for, both blackness (as a state of being) and white supremacy (a social myth)" (3). See also Michelle M. Wright, *Becoming*, especially the introduction and chap. 1. On "western modernity's construction of racial blackness" (Rowe), see Barrett.

8. On the connection between *Beloved* and Feelings's *Middle Passage*, see Wyman.

9. On contemporary literary engagements with slavery, including neoslave narratives, see Keizer; Rushdy, *Neo-Slave*. On graphic neoslave narratives, see Godfrey.

10. Cf. Emanuel's ancestral gesture in his poem "The Middle Passage Blues," where the speaker describes himself as "rememberin' Grandma's chair / she had slave-girl mem'ries, and she rocked and hummed 'em there."

11. This project entails "listening for the unsaid, translating misconstrued words, and refashioning disfigured lives" (Hartman, "Venus" 2–3).

12. A recent example from the realm of illustrated children's books, Hannah-Jones, Watson, and Smith's *The 1619 Project: Born on the Water* (2021), devotes ten pages to the Middle Passage (including the moments of entering and exiting the ship). See Stein, "Breaking." Laird, Laird, and Bey includes a five-page sequence on the Middle Passage (27–31).

13. Cf. Christina Sharpe on "forms of Black expressive culture [. . .] that do not seek to explain or resolve the question of this exclusion in terms of assimilation, inclusion, or civil or human rights, but rather depict aesthetically the impossibility of such resolutions by representing the paradoxes of blackness within and after the legacies of slavery's denial of Black humanity. I name this paradox the wake" (*In the Wake* 14).

14. The strips collected in *Tommy Traveler in the World of Black History* (1991) offer vignettes about historical figures (Phoebe Fraunces, Emmett Till, Aesop, Frederick Douglass, Crispus Attucks). Different in style and narrative from *Middle Passage*, these vignettes speak to an earlier historical moment (the late 1950s) and to the constrictions of newspaper publication (they originally ran in the *New York Age*). The single-page story about Till relates the moments that led up to the youngster's alleged whistling at a white woman in Money, Mississippi, in 1955 but uses a text-only panel to recount his kidnapping and lynching. Douglass's mistreatment at the hands of the overseer Edward Covey, documented in *Narrative of Frederick Douglass*, and subsequent retaliation is shown in a manner that only hints at the brutality of the beatings.

15. The scene foreshadows a panel on one of the narrative's final pages that remediates a photograph from the Tulsa Race Massacre, which destroyed the affluent Greenwood neighborhood popularly known as Little Africa before Booker T. Washington christened it "Negro Wall Street" (Messer, Shriver, and Adams 791).

16. The scene also recalls a passage from James Baldwin's short story "Come Out the Wilderness" in which the female protagonist looks over the "furious streets" of New York "on which, here and there, like a design, colored people also hurried, thinking, *And we were slaves here once*" (191–92).

17. Cf. Crucifix's notion of "undrawing" in comics as the "transformative processes" involved in "tapping into sundry archives of comics" (155).

18. On kinship relations in a Black Atlantic context, see Adair; Jennifer L. Morgan, *Reckoning*.

19. See also Fuentes, a study of "the distortions of enslaved women's lives inherent in the archive" (1). Lowe conceives of such efforts of archival and historical recovery as a paradoxical praxis. The promise of recovery, she argues, is set "within the limits of an archive that authorizes knowledge about the history of slavery and freedom in terms of particular interests—those of slave owners and citizens, and not the enslaved—which denies enslaved people the humanity and presence it accords free liberal persons and society" (85).

20. Finley discusses writers and artists such as Miguel Covarrubias, Amiri Baraka, Betye Saar, Romare Bearden, Keith Piper, María Magdalena Campos-Pons, Godfried Donkor, Hank Willis Thomas, and Romuald Hazoumé. She devotes two pages to *Middle Passage* but does

not consider its visual construction, instead categorizing it, somewhat surprisingly, as a "children's book" and as an "accessible visual narrative" that has "easy-to-read, yet excruciatingly painful, visceral images" (222).

21. Gray's introductory statements abound with references to the horrific nature of Turner's and his followers' acts but remain silent about the cruelties of the system of slavery. He contrasts the rebels' "most atrocious and heart-rending deeds" with "the policy of our laws in restraint of this class of our population" of violent slaves and appeals to "each particular" white community to "look to its own safety" (Nat Turner, *Confessions* 246, 247).

22. Cf. Finley: "The slave ship icon frequently has been likened to a coffin and to a womb. It is a site of death, of dying Africans, and of new life, of a people who would persevere in the face of slavery and unspeakable cruelty to become a free people who helped define the modern era" (6).

23. Cf. Meeropol's commemoration of the victim's "twisted mouth."

24. On visual art and paintings of the Middle Passage, with a focus on the twentieth and twenty-first centuries, see Bernier. In a two-page spread, Feelings adds graphic scope and depth to Turner's painting, showing an emblematic ship with floating corpses in its wake at the center. To the left and right of the vessel, mirrored by otherwise identical images, the ship's white crew is hurling dead bodies overboard, while sharks are circling the dead in the image below. Gilroy notes that Martin R. Delany's *Blake; or, The Huts of America* (1859–62) includes a similar scene that constitutes "one of the few representations of the middle passage and life in the barracoons to be found in nineteenth-century black writing" (27).

25. Feelings has also stated, "I clearly did this book for black people so it would be something that inspires them. This book is also for whites who claim they can't recognize what racism feels like" (qtd. in Finley 223).

26. Cudjo Lewis, the last surviving witness of the Middle Passage, stated in the late 1920s, "We lookee and lookee and lookee and we doan see nothin' but water. Where we come from we doan know. Where we goin, we doan know" (Hurston, *Barracoon* 55). Lewis had been brought illegally to the United States in 1859 with a group of more than one hundred men and women.

27. "I can't find her," Hall's narrator states. "I'll never know what happened to Sarah or Abigail," two Black participants in the 1712 New York revolt. For more on the history of Black women in the United States, see Berry and Gross; on everyday forms of resistance among enslaved women, see Camp.

28. Enslaved women faced the added prospect of sexual violation, as Feelings shows in several of his images and as Alexis Wells-Oghoghomeh acknowledges when she writes about white male crew members abusing their female "cargo": "Experiencing and witnessing sexual assault in the holds of coastal slaving outposts and aboard slaving vessels awakened women to the cultural meanings surrounding the exposure of their legs and breasts in their new contexts. Naked and surrounded by the lustful, ever watchful eyes of their captors, they endured the psychological torture that accompanied existence in a constant state of sexual terror" (99).

29. In Emanuel's "The Middle Passage Blues," such haunted memories are cast in a blues ethos: "'MIDDLE PASSAGE': The WORD means blues to me. / Look at it front or backside, it still means BLUES to me." In the end, however, the lament has reinvigorated the speaker: "I got the Middle Passage Blues, but my folks gave me a plan / (Grandma said it, 'When you grow up you be a Middle Passage man') / I'm a stand-up sailor / I'm a Middle Passage man."

30. Cudjo Lewis recalled his capture in Africa by another tribe: "Dey come and tie us in de line" (Hurston, *Barracoon* 54).

31. Reception studies could provide insights on how viewers position themselves vis-à-vis this image. Rambsy analyzes the reactions of Black male college readers to Baker's *Nat Turner*; Connor studies the responses of adolescents to Feelings's *Middle Passage*. Cf. Christina Sharpe's distinction between white viewers' reactions to the work of silhouette artist Kara Walker, which frequently entail "a seduction by or complicity with violent acts of reading, seeing, naming, and fixing into stereotype that resolves in disavowal and projection," and the responses of Black viewers, for whom "this looking can mean encountering shame and violence and sometimes refusing this representation or sometimes being seduced into and complicit with violent acts of reading, seeing, naming, and fixing into stereotype" (*Monstrous* 156).

32. Cf. Christina Sharpe's point on monstrous intimacies in which "black and white viewers alike find themselves, perhaps in different ways, participants" (*Monstrous* 175).

33. Feeling's title also evokes the title of Sekora's "Black Message/White Envelope." I thank Pia Wiegmink for this suggestion. On the slave ship as a modern technology and institution, see Rediker, *Slave Ship*.

34. Robert Hayden's poem "Middle Passage" contains an adapted quotation from a dated entry in a ship's log: "Blacks rebellious. Crew uneasy. [. . .] / Lost three this morning leaped with crazy laughter / to the waiting sharks, sang as they went under" (48).

35. Hall, Martínez, and Bao's enlarged images of the diagram, portraying individualized facial and bodily features, is anticipated by the original sketch and its early adaptations, as Browne's and Finley's analyses indicate. Browne cites Spillers's reference to the "tiny black figures" of the diagram looking "like so many cartoon figures" (72) but then suggests that a closer look at the diagram reveals "that each of the tiny black figures are not replicas of each other; rather, some have variously crossed arms, different gestures, or seem to face one another, while some stare and look back at the gaze from nowhere" that marks the outside viewer's perspective on the drawing (Browne 50).

36. The iconic image of the *Brookes* was first published in December 1788 by the Plymouth chapter of the Society for Effecting the Abolition of the Slave Trade; it was also sold by bookseller James Phillips. Most central to its early dissemination was a broadside, *Description of a Slave Ship*, printed and distributed by the London Committee in April 1789. A year later, six British and American versions of the image had appeared (Finley 27). See "*Brookes*"; Browne 45–50. Finley provides the most intricate genealogy of the image to date, including analyses of its image-text hybridity, form, and circulation; she also studies its reappropriation in the twentieth century.

37. On these minstrel echoes, cf. Kunka 178; Singer, *Breaking* 209; Wanzo, *Content* 89–91.

38. For an analysis of strategic impersonations of racist stereotypes during slavery, see Blassingame.

39. On the nexuses among race, citizenship, and graphic narrative, see Wanzo, *Content*.

40. As Hartman observes, "There is not one extant autobiographical narrative of a female captive who survived the Middle Passage" ("Venus" 3), which means that there is no written record that could contradict Canot's memoir from a female perspective.

41. As Singer points out (*Breaking* chap. 6), Baker's claim about the lack of sources on Turner ignores scholarship (Oates; Stone; Greenberg) and neglects the controversy surrounding William Styron's 1967 novelization of Turner's life (titled, like the nineteenth-century

account, *The Confessions of Nat Turner*; see John Henrik Clarke). Compared to the lives of the lesser-known African Americans celebrated in Gill, *Uncelebrated*; Gill, *More*; Gill, *Bass*; Gill, *Bessie*; and Gill, *Robert*, Turner is a rather well-known figure, especially since Nate Parker's film adaptation *The Birth of a Nation* (2016).

42. Singer finds a problematic causality between sentimental family scenes, their brutal disruption by the enslavers, and Turner's retributive violence because it removes the issue from "moral judgment" (*Breaking* 229). On Baker's Turner as Christlike and messianic, see Bruno; Whitted, "And the Negro." On Turner as a figure of "epistemic alterity" (prophet, madman, genius), cf. Bruce 19–20.

43. Cf. Hartman's association of the archive of slavery with the hold of the ship: "The archive is, in this case, a death sentence, a tomb, a display of the violated body, an inventory of property, a medical treatise on gonorrhea, a few lines about a whore's life, an asterisk in the grand narrative of history" ("Venus" 2). Here, "the unexpected connections, surprise finds, and serendipitous (in)sights that constitute the archive's lasting allure" (Stein, "What's" 339) turn traumatic.

44. Singer accuses Baker of creating a "cinematic spectacle" that violates the principle of "historical fidelity" (*Breaking* 195). That Singer misses the reference to *The Birth of a Nation* indicates that he may be underestimating Baker's practice of revising popular representations of Black history.

45. Hurston's recovery of Lewis's testimony, in turn, emerges as an attempt to bring a "Black" sensibility and language to the atrocities that left Lewis so deeply traumatized that he cries internally many decades later.

46. Mat Johnson et al.'s *John Constantine Hellblazer: Papa Midnite* includes a splash page with a collage that depicts the violence inflicted by ship crews against the enslaved Africans. One scene shows a crew member smashing a Black baby against a bloody post and telling the infant's screaming mother, "Give it a rest, cow. It won't make the journey" (17). A later segment shows the collective suicide of the rebel posse that revolted in colonial New York and was caught and whose members then decided to kill each other because "our lives are lost already" (51). The scene ends with a mother raising a knife to kill her newborn son, Fortune, and saying, "Forgive me, but I must rescue you from crueler fate" (51). Fortune's mother is shot before she can kill him, and he becomes Papa Midnite.

47. Cf. Chaney ("Slave" 287, 291–92). Green writes, "It was there—in the Middle Passage—that forms of Black resistance to social death were born" (4). Hartman speaks of "*the anomalous intimacy of cargo*" ("Dead" 209) and asks, "How does one conceive the possibility, chance and contingency of life as it is structured by death? What is the imagination and practice of freedom in the belly of the ship or on the plantation?" (213).

48. The broader visual history of sharks and the Middle Passage includes J. M. W. Turner's *Slave Ship (Slavers Throwing Overboard the Dead and Dying, Typhoon Coming On)* (1840) and Winslow Homer's *The Gulf Stream* (1899). For further historical, literary, and visual analysis, see Rediker, "History"; Santana.

49. Hirsch defines postmemory as "a *structure* of inter- and trans-generational transmission of traumatic knowledge and experience" and maintains that "it is a *consequence* of traumatic recall but [. . .] at a generational remove" (106). She adds, "Postmemory's connection to the past is thus not actually mediated by recall but by imaginative investment, projection, and creation" (107).

50. Scenes of family separation loom large in graphic accounts of slavery. Walker, Smyth, and Louise's *The Life of Frederick Douglass* depicts young Frederick's mother visiting him at Captain Anthony's, where his grandmother had brought him as soon as he was old enough to work. After feeling his mother's love for him at night, Frederick wakes up in the morning to find that she has already returned to the plantation where she is enslaved. The caption notes, "That was the last time I saw my mother. She died shortly after her visit. I was not present during her illness, her death, or her burial" (20).

51. Cf. statements from *The Confessions of Nat Turner* such as "we were strong enough to murder the family" (254); "the murder of this family [. . .] was the work of a moment" (255); "all the family were already murdered" (256); "having murdered Mrs. Waller and ten children" (257). On the child killings in Baker's *Nat Turner*, see Lockard.

52. Lockard comes to a different assessment: "*Nat Turner* is not about revenge" but rather "about equalizing the pain and terms of death" (111).

53. Greenberg suggests that Turner may have "engaged in a kind of self-censorship" (11). Holden reconstructs the larger social network around Turner and his fellow rebels, including enslaved as well as free Black women and children.

54. Whitted's analysis of this scene takes up the notion of the metapicture from W. J. T. Mitchell: "This concluding image replicates the cover page illustration of the white, glowing cover and dark hands, but with a difference. The image is now a startling metapicture, a *mise-en-abîme* that depicts a nineteenth-century slave reading the very book in which she appears, seeing herself in a series of nested recurrences" ("And the Negro" 92).

55. Arthur Flowers, Chitrakar, and Rossi also include a visual re-creation of a "slave castle" captioned, "Warehoused in the coastal castles of shame, Ghana's Cape Coast, Senegal's Goree Island, these must be experienced to be believed, to be understood, our ancestors warehoused like produce until they are stacked onto slaveships packfat w/ human cargo" (16).

56. Feelings's depiction of these women differs from the history of the white colonial gaze at breastfeeding women, but his images nonetheless expose this intimate moment. Feelings depicts the naked torsos of African women at least five times. For further analysis, see Jennifer L. Morgan, "Some"; Wells-Oghoghomeh.

57. These images also give visual form to the lines from Hayden's "Middle Passage" that speak of the "stench" and "effluvium of living death" and conceive of the hold as a space "where the living and the dead [. . .] lie interlocked, lie foul with blood and excrement" (51).

58. The image is also reprinted in Baker's *Nat Turner*. In the context of Feelings's narrative, the image recalls Smallwood's point that "human commodities" in the Middle Passage "followed a relentlessly linear course: the direction of their transatlantic movement never reversed. Ships traced circles. Commodities traveled in a straight line" (6).

59. Bruce calls the slave ship an "icon of abject blackness" (5).

60. Laird, Laird, and Bey note that the enslaved Africans "were shackled and packed together on the slave ships like rats" (27).

61. hooks mentions the ship *Pongas*, which transported 250 women, many of them pregnant and forced to give birth under horrifying conditions (*Ain't* 18). Cf. Christina Sharpe: "The history of capital is inextricable from the history of Atlantic chattel slavery" (*In the Wake* 5).

62. hooks provides no source for the quotation. It does not appear in Drake. By the time they docked on American shores, the enslaved "had already become enmeshed in a matrix of race- and gender-based labor regimes" (Wells-Oghoghomeh 48).

63. Cf. Gikandi: "To say that slaves couldn't speak is not the same as saying that they had no voices" (92).

64. Schmid finds echoes of Romantic painter Caspar David Friedrich's *Wanderer Above the Sea of Fog* here ("American"). There is a related image in Walker, Brown, and Greene's *Bitter Root* at the opening of the series's "Red Summer" issue. It shows the armed members of the Sangerye family (Enoch, Ford, Blink, Berg, Cullen, Ma Etta) on a rooftop, in an over-the-shoulder shot, as they are contemplating a cityscape with burning buildings toward the horizon from which a dark cloud creating a monstrous face is emerging (154).

65. Laird, Laird, and Bey title their graphic history of African Americans *Still I Rise* after Angelou's poem and include the poem's last two stanzas as a prologue.

66. On the silencing of Black female voices, see Higginbotham; Michele Mitchell.

67. Mat Johnson et al.'s *John Constantine Hellblazer: Papa Midnite* visits some of the same narrative territory presented in *Wake*. It opens with and repeatedly returns to scenes set at this New York African burial ground and depicts the 1712 rebellion covered by Hall, Martínez, and Bao.

68. On slavery as a "spectre from the past" in West African and African American literature, see Owusu.

69. *Wake* reserves portrayals of queerness to the contemporary frame narrative rather than investigating queer Black histories. By revealing Hall's lesbianism, it still works against a trend that Monalesia Earle describes: "Queer women of color are still often nothing more than props in the over-representational world of whiteness or even black masculinity" (3). By focusing on the experiences of enslaved women, *Wake* continues a tradition of Black feminist writings about slavery, the Middle Passage, and the lives of African (American) women. Michele Wallace once described Black women as "the Other of the Other" and as "dangerously unspeakable" ("Variations" 69).

70. While Baker's *Nat Turner* focuses on the figure of the male resurrectionist hero, it does pay attention to female experiences by focusing on Turner's mother's life and presenting her resistance against her enslavers (especially in the "Home" section) and by including at least one image of a young Black woman aiming a pistol at an enslaver and shooting him during the revolt (153). Feelings's *Middle Passage* depicts a shipboard revolt but includes only male figures in the group of Africans seeking to take control.

71. This statement matches Bernier and Wilson's title: "We were brave, We Were Strong, We Survived: Acts and Arts of Liberation in the African Atlantic Imaginary."

72. Mat Johnson et al.'s *John Constantine Hellblazer: Papa Midnite* (24–52) suggests that the Black rebels were male. The leader Cuffee's speech recalls Nat Turner's rallying of his followers but lacks the religious rhetoric and justification: "Today, we [. . .] form a new resistance. We, the survivors of kidnap and torture, the time for us to stand up has arrived. In other lives, we were farmers, and teachers, and traders. But today, we are warriors. New York is ours!" (25). Cuffee's speech is accompanied by an image that shows the rebels' arms raised, brandishing their weapons in a gesture of military strength. Through the thicket of arms and weapons, Cuffee appears as a grim and defiant leader. The image recalls Baker's Turner on horseback surrounded by his posse, arms and weapons raised in a show of force (140–41).

73. In her study of enslaved women in the Caribbean, Marisa Fuentes wonders "about the nature of history and the difficulties in narrating ephemeral archival presences by dwelling on the fragmentary, disfigured bodies of enslaved women" (1). Each chapter explores one or

more enslaved women's lives, including their names (Jane, Rachael, Joanna, Agatha, Molly, Venus) in her chapter titles.

74. The speaker of Clifton's "Slaveships" asks, "can these be men / who vomit us out from ships" (121).

75. Hine and Thompson open with a similar gesture of providing a name for the nameless enslaved: "A young woman stood on the shores of the New World. The place was Jamestown, Virginia. The year was 1619. [. . .] We do not know this woman's name, but we will call her Oni. She will be, for us, not a number—one of twenty slaves who were the first to be brought to North America—but the real woman she was" (8).

76. Arthur Flowers, Chitrakar, and Rossi's *I See the Promised Land* renders the corpses of enslaved Africans trailing the ship in a starkly different iconography, using a simplified Patua art style to show disembodied heads and a single full body floating around a tight-packing ship (19, 20). Formally separating image and text, the accompanying caption, placed over a completely blackened page, reads, "How many million dead, tossed overboard to feed wily sharks that follow each ship, how many leap of their own accord?" (21).

77. The dream of an underwater presence for those who died during the Middle Passage was developed more fully by the Detroit electronic music producers Gerald Donald and James Stinson, collectively known as Drexciya, in the 1990s. Haqq et al.'s two-volume graphic novel, *The Book of Drexciya*, gives the myth a visual appearance. The opening scenes show a dying Black woman being thrown into the sea and giving birth to a baby boy in the final moments of her life. The boy is rescued by an underwater sorceress and taken to the Ancient Atlantic School of Sorcery, where he and other rescued boys are raised as oceanic beings (Drexciyans) animated by the life force given to them by a group of sorceresses.

CHAPTER 2. LEGACIES OF LYNCHING

1. Hiatt opens with these quotations. The subject of his essay is the *Watchmen* television series, based on Alan Moore and Dave Gibbons's graphic novel of the same title, which features the superhero Hooded Justice and confronts the genre's racial history via the depiction of the 1921 Tulsa Race Massacre.

2. According to the Equal Justice Initiative's *Lynching in America* report, in 1940, when North published his piece, four African Americans were lynched; in 1948, when Legman's article appeared, one lynching was recorded. In the time between these articles, the number is twenty-eight. Lynching peaked between 1880 and 1940 and by the beginning of the twentieth century was widely understood "as a form of white supremacist violence, perpetrated largely in the South" (Wood and Donaldson 11). The Equal Justice Initiative has documented at least forty-four hundred "racial terror lynchings" (4) in the United States, of which approximately 90 percent involved white mobs killing Black men (Wood and Donaldson 11). Studies of individual lynchings include Madison; Patricia Bernstein; Arnold; McGovern. Bailey and Tolnay focus on lynchings in the South; Pfeifer considers the impact of lynching on American society more generally.

3. Francis suggests that "it is entirely possible that a successful black American superhero is impossible because it seeks to combine two ideals that are antithetical to each other: superheroes and American racial thinking" (138).

4. Ryan discerns "a paradoxical mixture of physical vulnerability and social insight" in Black superheroes that differs from the perceptions of white superheroes (68). See also Cunningham.

5. For a historical overview, see Austin and Hamilton. On Black comic book superheroes and superheroines, see Jeffrey A. Brown, *Black*; Nama; Whaley. Davis identifies Lion Man from Orrin C. Evans's *All-Negro Comics* (1947) as the first Black superhero.

6. See chapter 5 for my remarks on equally significant works—Rob Guillory's *Farmhand*, John Jennings's *Blue Hand Mojo*, Ayize Jama-Everett and John Jennings's *Box of Bones*, and Walker, Brown, and Greene's *Bitter Root*. Additional graphic narratives with lynching scenes include Gill, *Bass*, which tells life story of the African American marshal Bass Reeves and includes a scene where he saves a Black man from a lynching (one panel on page 75 is a close-up of his hand holding a knife and cutting the rope); Laird, Laird, and Bey; Helfer and DuBurke; Colomba and Levy; Tommie Smith, Barnes, and Anyabwile.

7. For scholarship on these issues, see Jeffrey A. Brown, "Panthers"; Whaley.

8. Armstrong's *Mary Turner* discusses Turner's lynching and its broader contexts, both in terms of its historical unfolding (it was part of a larger lynching spree) and its discursive, literary, and artistic echoes, including a report by the NAACP's Walter White and an article in the organization's *Crisis* magazine ("The Work of a Mob," September 1918) as well as a short story by Angelina Weld Grimké ("Goldie," 1920), a poem by Carrie Williams Clifford ("Little Mother," 1922), and the "Kabnis" part of Jean Toomer's *Cane* (1923). See also Armstrong, "Afterword"; Stein, "Lynching."

9. On lynching's gendered implications, see also Apel; Simien. Wiegman reads lynching as a "disciplinary tool that took on over time an ideological narrative [. . .] that both propelled the white crowd to action and defined the methods of torture subsequently imposed: that of the mythically endowed rapist, the flower of civilization (the white woman) he intended to violently pluck, and the heroic interceptor (the white male) who would restore order by thwarting the black phallic insurgence" (93). Armstrong argues that Mary Turner is one of many Black women "whose stories have received insufficient attention in a history of racial violence that for too long has been triangulated between white men, black men, and white women." According to Armstrong, "Black women played multiple roles: as victims, as loved ones left behind, and as those who fought back using grassroots, institutional, and artistic forms of resistance" (*Mary* 3).

10. Cloutier uses *shadow archive* to describe the "absences, removals, and delayed restorations [in] the history of the black literary archive" (1). Kimberly Juanita Brown reads these postcards as examples of "vicarious murder" (*Mortevivum* xxv). For Allen Feldman, these postcards and other lynching souvenirs eventually became part "of the American political unconscious and subjected to a pseudo-slave trade as curios and antiques," providing "American technological modernity with a dark underside" (373). On literary treatments of lynching by authors such as Carrie Williams Clifford, Countee Cullen, W. E. B. Du Bois, Angelina Weld Grimké, Lorraine Hansberry, Robert Hayden, Langston Hughes, Claude McKay, Lillian Smith, and Jean Toomer, see Armstrong, *Mary*.

11. Jesse Washington's 1916 lynching in Waco, Texas, was attended by fifteen thousand spectators; body parts were sold as souvenirs (Apel and Smith 47). Lynchings were often advertised in local newspapers, ensuring an audience for the murder. Walter White, who also documented the taking of body parts as souvenirs (*Rope* 35), recalled how the killing of Henry

Lowry on Christmas Day 1920 in Nodena, Arkansas, was announced by newspapers, which printed "early afternoon 'extras' giving full details as to time, place, and other arrangements for the forthcoming lynching" (23). The lynching itself was also covered in *The Memphis Press* and in *The Nation* (24–25). According to James H. Cone, *The Atlanta Constitution* and other newspapers regularly "announced to the public the place, date, and time of the expected hanging and burning of black victims" (9).

12. See also "The Shame of America," an NAACP ad that appeared in *The New York Times*, *The Atlanta Constitution*, *The Chicago Daily News*, *The Nation*, and other white-owned publications on 22 November 1922. Offering facts about lynching, the ad was intended to push the Senate to pass antilynching legislation. For extensive analysis of the NAACP's efforts and of related antilynching activities, see Raiford, *Imprisoned* chap. 2.

13. Carbonell holds, "The unmediated documentary value of lynching photographs is complicated by the fact that photographers often 'compulsively composed silvery tableaux (natures mortes) positioning and lighting corpses as if they were game birds shot on the wing'" (200, citing Allen).

14. On the ritual aspects of lynching, both historical and literary, see Trudier Harris.

15. The title of Brundage's essay collection on lynching, *Under Sentence of Death*, underscores this sense of permanent surveillance and emphasizes the precariousness of Black life shaped by a predetermined guilty sentence based merely on the color of the person's skin. On the long history of surveillance and control of Black Americans, see Browne.

16. Cone cites a Black teacher's response to Allen's exhibition of lynching photography, *Without Sanctuary*: "When I look at those pictures I don't see a lifeless body. I look at those pictures and I see my son, I see my brother, I see my father. If I look at that lifeless body long enough, I see myself" (121). Cf. Clifton's poem "The Photograph: A Lynching" (2000), which ponders in the final stanza whether all Black Americans are "captured by history into an / accurate album" and wonders whether they will all be "required to view it together / under a gathering sky?" (19).

17. Cf. Wanzo's concept of a Black identity hermeneutic (*Content* 4) and Campt's notion of the Black gaze (*Black*). Baldwin's "Going to Meet the Man" (1965) provides a sense of interiority lacking in lynching photographs. The story is at once ekphrastic, narrating many of the elements documented in these photographs, and revisionary, supplementing the effect of the lynching on the white child.

18. For additional considerations, see Courtney R. Baker.

19. Jackson uses similar wording when asking "how scholars might explore this imagery without replicating it" (10).

20. Wood has recently suggested that "lynching photographs also create the possibility of a white sympathetic encounter with the historical memory of lynching": "While for many black Americans the memory of lynching is visceral and ever-present[, . . .] for many white Americans it is hazy, distorted, or forgotten. Yet that misremembering can be disrupted through self-reflective acts of displaying and looking at lynching photographs" ("Somebody" 4).

21. One critique of Allen was that it "held the black victim in permanent tableau as a desecrated other" and "reified black victimhood" (Wood and Donaldson 17).

22. Allen was instrumental in this development.

23. For a survey and investigation of Emmett Till representations in comics, see Whitted, "Comics." According to Whitted, *Bayou* also alludes to George Stinney Jr., a fourteen-year-old

boy who was falsely accused of murdering two white girls and executed by South Carolina authorities in 1944 ("Comics" 198–99). On the Till photographs, see Alexandre chap. 5; on his lynching, see Whitfield; Metress; on the role of newspapers and journalism in making the local case a national concern, see Houck and Grindy.

24. Walker and Anderson's *The Black Panther Party* dedicates a whole page to Till's murder and burial. It includes a remediated photograph of young, well-dressed Till and ends with his grieving mother standing over his open casket. Yet instead of depicting Till's face, Walker and Anderson present an empty casket, referring verbally to the "photos of Till's horrifically disfigured corpse [that] appeared in newspapers and magazines all over the country" (9) while preventing the reproduction of visually encapsulated historical pain. They choose a related technique a few pages earlier by picturing the victim of a race-based lynching as a Black silhouette (4). Laird, Laird, and Bey devote a panel to Till's murder, calling the motivation for the killing what "white folks" called "reckless eyeballing" over an image of the teenager's mutilated body (181). Joel Christian Gill captures Till's murder and funeral in a single panel (193) in his graphic adaptation of Ibram X. Kendi's *Stamped*, which shows Till-Mobley from behind as she is standing in front of the open casket, sobbing. The image does not show Till's face but provides a glimpse of the now-famous photographs of him pinned to the inside of the casket.

25. Hagood offers a more critical take when he suggests that *Bayou* presents a "paradoxical blend of nostalgia and realism" (41).

26. On African American variations of the Southern gothic, see Wester, *African American*.

27. Another subtle hint appears in volume 1 when Bayou is shown in a polyptych splash panel as he is trying to decide whether he will follow the Bossman's orders to avoid causing trouble or help innocent Lee. In the middle section of the image, he states, "She just a chil'. Chilluns ain't got no mind fo' nuthin. Ain't got no sense yet. Ruh-Reminds Bayou of . . . of . . . ." Bayou seems to be comparing Lee to his lost children but apparently cannot bear to speak their names.

28. I build on some of Polak's analyses of these and other key scenes from *Bayou*. On the multimedia history of such pastoral scenes, see Stein, "From *Uncle Remus*."

29. James Baldwin's short story "Going to Meet the Man" depicts the lynching of a Black man through the eyes and mind of a white boy, Jesse (as recollected by his older self), to indicate the devastating effects of lynching on the psyches of white Southerners.

30. Chaney criticizes what he calls *Incognegro*'s "politics of viewer positioning in plenary scenes of lynching"—that is, the narrative's formal allowance of readerly distancing and affective disinvolvement (*Reading* 154). Anwer suggests that *Incognegro* provides "behind-the-scenes documentation of lynching—an 'inside view' that the photographs, despite their claimed reliance on a facticist projection of 'objective reality,' often fail to do" (15). For further analysis, see Cutter; Fine; Davis-McElligatt, "White"; Moynihan.

31. This perspective can be connected with the view of Black witnesses, such as those mentioned in Walter White's account of the lynching of Henry Lowry: "The mob brought his wife and little daughter to see him burning" (*Rope* 25).

32. Children appear in a photograph of Rubin Stacey (Fort Lauderdale, Florida, 19 July 1935) reprinted in Apel and Smith 5.

33. Christina Sharpe offers a broader consideration of "monstrous intimacies" as "the horrors enacted on the Black body after slavery and the periods of emancipation" (*Monstrous* 3). See also chap. 5.

34. Something similar happens in Arthur Flowers, Chitrakar, and Rossi's *I See the Promised Land*, which shows lynchings in its buildup to its treatment of Martin Luther King Jr. Here too, the Indian artist's bright color scheme, with its shining red, orange, yellow, blue, and green hues as well as the decision to show the bodies of the victims without any signs of physical wounds turns the victims into serene and transcendent figures who remind readers of past atrocities without reexposing and potentially debasing the victims (32, 43–47). In the second and third lynching scenes (43–47), most of the lynched Black men have their eyes closed, as if they are asleep or perhaps meditating; one of them has his eyes open and his hands folded in prayer, which undermines the charge of monstrosity lynch mobs commonly directed at their victims.

35. Polak discerns a permeable border between the real world and an alternative world, "half afterlife and half fever dream," where Lee confronts intergenerational trauma. Polak reads the bayou as the passage through which Lee enters this alternative world (150, 173). Cf. Polak's close reading of Lee's underwater recovery of Billy's body (152–53).

36. Whitted notes how "the comic's aesthetic choices produce a striking visual tension between the romanticization of the pastoral slave-holding South and counter-narratives of black oppression and resistance" ("Intertextual" 195). Like Walker, Love and Morgan revise the tradition of the plantation romance, where the swamp figures as an ideological threat to the myth of the plantation as the locus of the gallant South (see Cowan). Lee is also a critical reformulation of the stereotypical pickaninny. *Bayou*'s swamp creatures—the Golliwog, Cotton-Eyed Joe—evoke racist representations of blackness, including images of Black children being eaten by alligators (Tompkins). On *Bayou*'s engagement with the "aesthetic legacies of blackface minstrelsy," see Hershini Bhana Young 281. On representations of Black children in comics and beyond, see Robin Bernstein; Saguisag; Wanzo, *Content* (chap. 4).

37. Feldman associates lynching with blackface minstrelsy: "These encindered and hanging bodies are caricatures in which the capital penalty is transmuted into minstrelsy, composed of a final, fatal 'corking up' (burning) and the *danse macabre* of the hanging, swaying, and charred body. This minstrel aesthetic is a political taxidermy by which black bodies are recaptured in being theatricized, occupied, and imagined as consumable substances of pleasure and commensurability" (379).

38. Another possible reference is a 1908 photograph taken in Kentucky (repr. in Alexandre 37). Feldman suggests that images of multiple lynched bodies evoke scenes of hunting that assign animal status to the victims: "The hunting-animality iconography is particularly explicit when multiple bodies of victims are clumped together, like a brace of wild game" (375).

39. Cf. Polak's reading of this scene: "We are seeing over Lee's shoulder the eruption of a traumatic memory, but it is not her *own* memory. While she has seen the result of a single lynching while pulling Billy Glass's body from the bayou, an entire forest of hanged men [and women] is something distinct: this is not a reminder of something Lee herself has seen but rather a pastiche of what her ancestors have witnessed" (159).

40. Moten writes about the "phonic substance" of images like those of Emmett Till: "arrangements of the photograph [. . .] anticipate a looking that cannot be sustained as unalloyed looking but must be accompanied by listening [. . .] even though what is listened to—echo of a whistle or a phrase, moaning, mourning, desperate testimony and flight—is also unbearable" (197, 200). See also Campt, *Listening*.

41. Like Whitted, Henry Jenkins reads the men as white; he also notes the contrast between the individualized faces of the onlookers and Billy's featureless face (311).

42. For Jackson, "The power to look is also the power to police and govern that body, imbuing it with an erotics of control" (5). She notes how in some images, the "body refuses to be the static object but instead strikes back at the viewer's vision" (5). Jacquelyn Dowd Hall remains critical of lynching's "folk pornography" (*Revolt* 150)—its attraction for the spectators who attended the atrocities or later encountered them in writing or photographs.

43. Billy's sinking body also recalls the sinking or diving bodies of the enslaved who jump off the ship because they prefer death to slavery in Feelings's *Middle Passage* as well as the diving warrior women in Rebecca Hall, Martínez, and Bao's *Wake*, who will, like Billy, eventually emerge from the water again as mythical figures.

44. Wiegman speaks of an "overdetermination of punishment in the lynching scenario" that aims to transform the victims into figures of the "culturally abject" (81–82).

45. Baker also turns to Black history in his treatment of *Captain America: Truth*, a collaboration with Robert Morales, which tells the story of Black Captain America before Steve Rogers. Elijah Bradley is a Black superhero who witnesses several atrocities against Black bodies (when experiments with the superserum go wrong, for instance). Morales and Baker suggest a connection between the horrors of the Holocaust and the treatment of African Americans. For analysis, see Ryan; Wanzo, *Content* (chap. 3).

46. For an extended version of this argument, see Singer, *Breaking* 197.

47. Eve L. Ewing, Luciano Vecchio, Kevin Libranda, et al. introduce the Black superheroine Ironheart airborne, marveling at her elevated position as a superheroine and student at MIT and quoting from Maya Angelou's "Still I Rise": "I was never meant to fly. But how does that poem go? 'Into a daybreak that's wondrously clear . . . . . . I rise'" (6–7).

48. Cf. Darieck Scott's analysis of "Turner's apotheosis-via-hanging" ("Not-Yet" 345). At least one panel (Baker, *Nat Turner* 66) also uses the visual trope of the bloodied feet dangling over the earth, an image that also appears in Love and Morgan's *Bayou*. In *Nat Turner*, the bleeding slave is alive and will be crippled by Will's axe. This trope is revised on the cover of Lewis, Aydin, and Powell's *March: Book One*, where the images of feet designate protest against racial injustice.

49. Baker's style seems influenced by Reginald Marsh's cartoon *This Is Her First Lynching* (1934), which was part of *An Art Commentary on Lynching*, a 1935 exhibition organized by Walter White and the NAACP in New York. Baker's line work and shading evoke Marsh's style, although Baker uses a more cartoony approach. The image of the hanging Turner with the audience at his feet that precedes the title page of "Triumph" recalls the composition of Marsh's antilynching cartoon. In both images, a white child is held up to witness the atrocity; while Marsh's onlookers face left, Baker's face right, seeming to reverse the image with the lynched body added. Marsh captures the manic grins on the onlookers' faces, which Baker amplifies in the following pages. For more on Marsh's cartoon, see Teutsch, "On Racism."

50. *King* offers a complex conglomeration of voices that includes, in a passage about the 1961 Freedom Rides, a white supremacist Southerner whose narration overlays the graphic depiction of the events: "these n******, these goddam—strung up from a fucking tree—burning—eyes bulging" (95).

51. By associating Turner's lynching with Christ's crucifixion, Baker is tapping into a visual and philosophical discourse that equates what Cone theorizes as the cross as "the universal symbol of Christian faith" and the lynching tree as "the quintessential symbol of black oppression in America" (xiii). There is irony in the fact that Turner was hanged in Jerusalem,

Virginia, evoking Christ's crucifixion in Golgotha, near the historical Jerusalem. McGregor and Graham's "A Cross Burning Darkly Blackening the Night!" begins with the Black Panther tied to a burning cross by members of the Ku Klux Klan. While this is clearly a crucifixion scene, the comic seeks to be taken literally: "He is not a symbolic Christ," the captions exclaim. "Forget about turning his flesh and blood into some esoteric allusion to the persecution of contemporary man. This is the Black Panther . . . known as T'Challa. And he is made of flesh and blood, and the flames which consume the cross and his body prove his humanity."

52. Walker, Smyth, and Louise's *The Life of Frederick Douglass* portrays the hanging of John Brown, who was executed as punishment for his leadership in the 1859 raid on Harper's Ferry (123). The image of the dignified Brown hanging still from the rope around his neck is juxtaposed with an image of Frederick Douglass's family grieving the death of his daughter, Annie, while he was in England. Bridging the gap between the two scenes is Douglass, whose smallish figure stands in the middle at the bottom of the page, dwarfed by captions that express his sense of unworthiness in the face of these deaths.

53. White published his reports in the NAACP magazine *The Crisis* as well as in a variety of other venues, including *The Daily News*, *The Chicago Defender*, and *The Nation*. He also analyzed the "lynching industry" in *Rope and Faggot* and recalled many of his experiences in his autobiography, *A Man Called White* (1948).

54. Black avengers have historically been subject to a different narrative logic (see Pierrot).

55. For different readings, see Caron; Davis-McElligatt, "White"; Kunert-Graf.

56. This photograph has been discussed extensively (Madison; Apel and Smith). Laird, Laird, and Bey remediate a similar scene (70): three Black men hanging from a tree with a grinning white spectator staring directly at the reader (or the camera lens, if this image is read as a cartoony version of a lynching photograph). See also my analysis of Jama-Everett and Jennings's *Box of Bones* in chapter 5.

57. Cf. Cone: "Slaveholders whipped and raped slaves, violated them in any way they thought necessary, but they did not lynch them, except in the case of those who threatened the slave system itself, such as Gabriel Prosser, Denmark Vesey, Nat Turner, and other insurrectionists" (4).

58. Lee's uncle in Love and Morgan's *Bayou* fears that Lee's father will soon be lynched by a white mob and that trying to intervene would aggravate the situation: "You got white folks coming from Desoto, Washington, and now even all the way from Neshoba. We go down there [to rescue Lee's father] raising Cain and it'll be open season on every n***** in town" (vol. 1).

59. Cf. Blind Lemon Jefferson's "Lockstep Blues/Hangman's Blues" (1928), which is told from the perspective of a Black murderer sentenced to death, taken from the courthouse, and hanged. The final verse contains the haunting lines "Lord, I'm almost dyin', gasping for my breath."

60. Raiford emphasizes the multiplicity of Black gazes at such images. Speaking of a "spectatorial fluidity," she writes, "Though lynching photographs may hail black audiences as a singular 'other,' black spectators are not so easily interpellated" (*Imprisoned* 49).

61. Whitted sees "a bridge that connects the two realities" ("Blues" 239).

62. This version of events is based on Thompson and Dustin Crawford. Crawford includes photographs of Hughes in police custody and of his burned corpse (both by unidentified photographers; *Body*). Apel and Smith claim that Hughes shot his employer and was wrongfully accused of raping the man's wife (50–51).

63. Laird, Laird, and Bey offer a rare depiction of a burned Black body—an image most graphic narratives refuse to depict—being consumed by flames over a pile of wood, with four hooded Klansmen watching the scene and one of them spewing racist sentiments (115).

Mat Johnson et al.'s *John Constantine Hellblazer: Papa Midnite* depicts the burned bodies of Caesar and his white wife, Peggy (116), and features a splash page that encapsulates a vision of anti-Black violence and historical trauma, including three lynched men hanging from a tree and another dead man chained to the trunk, Klansmen, and a burning cross (88). Duffy and Jennings's *The Hole: Consumer Culture* (2008) includes two images of a scorched Black body that seem indebted to lynching photographs (120, 121).

64. This variation is complicated by the fact that the Captain America in the story is Sam Wilson, another African American character.

65. The killings of Black citizens by other citizens (as in Trayvon Martin's case) and by police officers can be understood as modern-day forms of lynching (including a frequent lack of accountability). Christopher Paul Harris, for example, notes "George Floyd's lynching in 2020" (10).

66. Assessing the connection between these references and what Christopher Paul Harris calls "the digitally driven Black counterpublic," where social media serves "as both the primary means of disseminating information and a central mechanism for collective action and community-centered dialogue" (19, 17), exceeds the scope of this chapter. Cf. Kimberly Juanita Brown's reference to photographic production as a "ghostly apparatus" in which "photography and antiblackness" have historically been "conjoined" (*Mortevivum* xii).

67. See Gonzales-Day, *Lynching*; Villanueva. For a broader historical perspective, see Berg. Two graphic narratives acknowledge the persecution and oppression of other racialized minorities, such as the Indigenous population. In *Bayou*, Love and Morgan spin a lineage for Lee that entails the ancestral figure Enoch, her uncle Bedford's great-grandfather who was the son of a "runaway slave" and a "Choctaw warrior" and thus "part Choctaw Indian." This backstory includes life in Spanish Florida, where "Choctaw, Seminole and Negroes who run off from slavery [. . .] made a good life for themselves in that swamp" (vol. 1). Walker, Brown, and Greene's *Bitter Root* imagines a multicultural community of Harlemites, including Native, Asian, and African American families, fighting the monsters. Another storyline brings Dr. Sylvester to northern Oklahoma's Osage Nation, where members help heal the injuries he sustained during the Tulsa Race Massacre.

68. Monique Guillory uses the phrase in her analysis of the gender politics of jazz.

69. For Campt, "the choice to 'listen to' rather than simply 'look at' images is a conscious decision to challenge the equation of vision with knowledge by engaging photography through a sensory register that is critical to Black Atlantic cultural formations: sound" (*Listening* 6).

70. On lynching as a modern phenomenon, cf. Raiford, *Imprisoned* 37–38. On the connections among superheroes, modernity, and race, see Regalado.

CHAPTER 3. CIVIL RIGHTS PEDAGOGY

1. Hamlin and McKinney tackle "the evolution of the black freedom struggle" from "rights" to "lives" (i.e., from the civil rights movement to the Black Lives Matter movement).

2. On police brutality against African Americans in New York City, see Clarence Taylor.

3. On the trajectory "from enslavement to Obama," see Obenland et al.

4. Other biographies of civil rights activists or biographically inflected accounts of civil rights history include Helfer and DuBurke; Walker and Anderson; Frank Smith, Reimuth, and Améziane. On graphic civil rights biographies, see Boykin.

5. Some of this optimism is absent from the sequel to the trilogy, *Run* (2021), which "recounts the lost history of what too often follows dramatic change—the pushback of those who refuse it and the resistance of those who believe change has not gone far enough," as the back-cover blurb by the Democratic politician and voting rights activist Stacey Abrams indicates.

6. Cf. Maegan Parker Brooks: "The master narrative's focus on a few larger-than-life leaders, its emphasis on national victories, and its triumphalist overtones belie the work that remains to be done, conceal the range of advocates with the potential to participate, and mask the ideologies that perpetuate white privilege and continue to disempower African Americans" (4).

7. Jacquelyn Dowd Hall attributes the term "classical" phase to Bayard Rustin and identifies 1954–65 as the timeframe ("Long" 1234).

8. See also Raiford, *Imprisoned*; Berger. On the political ontology of photography, see Azoulay, *Civil Imagination*. Walker and Anderson reiterate stock elements of the "master" narrative and foreground its limitations—for instance by mentioning the arrest on a Montgomery bus of fifteen-year-old Claudette Colvin nine months before Rosa Parks's more broadly memorialized arrest (10).

9. Capshaw reads the photographs in the *March* trilogy as an expression of dissent. *Run* offers more historical annotation than is found in the *March* books, which foregrounds the book's self-awareness as a graphic teaching guide to the civil rights movement: a section with biographies of movement members, explanatory notes, a list of sources, remarks by Powell about the graphic construction of individual characters and scenes, and a section about the authors.

10. The roots of the word *pedagogy* make it a particularly fruitful concept for thinking about what graphic narratives of the civil rights movement might teach us. In ancient Greece, the word *paidagogos* described a slave who was responsible for bringing boys to school and for tutoring them ("Pedagogy").

11. I base this list of didactic goals on Armstrong et al. xii; Raiford, "Come" 1151. On teaching comics, see Alissa Burger; Dong; Tabachnik.

12. The other members of the Big Six included A. Philip Randolph, Martin Luther King Jr., James Farmer Jr., Whitney Young Jr., and Roy Wilkins. Lewis was diagnosed with pancreatic cancer in December 2019 but vowed "to do what I know to do and do what I have always done: I am going to fight it and keep fighting for the Beloved Community" ("Rep. John Lewis"). He died on 17 July 2020.

13. Lewis's author bio at the end of *March* mentions his autobiography but does not identify it as a source text (cf. Oppolzer 231–32). For the photograph, see "Movement Photographs"; for the poster, see "SNCC Poster."

14. In Raiford's words, "Photography constituted one cog of the vast cultural work through which SNCC framed and popularized the movement" ("Come" 1140).

15. As some of my students noted, the image of the kneeling protesters also resonates with similarly framed photographs of Colin Kaepernick and fellow football players kneeling before games. One student remarked that Lyon must have been kneeling when he took the photograph so that he could position the camera—and thus the viewer's gaze—at approximately the level of the protesters' heads.

16. Jacquelyn Dowd Hall criticizes the "trope of the South as the nation's 'opposite other,' an image that southernizes racism and shields from scrutiny both the economic dimensions of southern white supremacy and the institutionalized patterns of exploitation, segregation, and discrimination in other regions of the country" ("Long" 1239). On movement photography

beyond the South, see Speltz. On extending the story of the movement to Northern campaigns, see Patrick D. Jones. *King* covers King's attempts to bring the movement to Chicago.

17. On African American reformulations of previously "frozen" imagery of civil rights leaders like King, see Wanzo, *Content* 95–110. Cf. Singer: "The stereotypes through which American popular culture often interprets and represents racial identity operate not only as tools of defamation but also as vehicles for far more subtle manipulations of race" ("Black" 107).

18. Protesters did not cross the Edmund Pettus Bridge until their third attempt. On 7 March, the protest ended in bloodshed. Two days later, King led another attempt, which was aborted. Finally, on 21 March, approximately thirty-two hundred people successfully crossed the bridge. The bridge was named after Edmund Winston Pettus, a brigadier general in the Confederate army, a grand dragon in the Ku Klux Klan, and a US senator at the turn of the twentieth century.

19. In *Run*, the authors acknowledge that the Voting Rights Act was only a first step toward racial equality: "The ink was barely dry . . . , but already forces were gathering to fight back, using our own tactics," state the captions that accompany images of the Georgia Ku Klux Klan getting ready to march. The next sentence—"And America's cities were ready to explode . . ."— looks ahead to the race riots of the mid- to late 1960s (7).

20. My analysis of the covers is indebted to Chaney, "Misreading."

21. Baker's *Nat Turner* includes a panel showing only the bare Black feet of the enslaved as they train for the rebellion (123). Here, marching takes on a military dimension, as the enslaved transform into members of a makeshift revolutionary army. In addition, the truncated feet in Love and Morgan's *Bayou* serve as a metonym for lynched Black bodies.

22. This perspective complicates the narrative's otherwise prominent call for empathy with the marchers and activists. On empathy in the *March* books, see Milne.

23. The comic contains a graphic biography of King, a story on Rosa Parks's role in the Montgomery Bus Boycott, and information on the "Montgomery Method" of nonviolent resistance. Oppolzer calls it "a primer that explained the philosophy and the necessary steps involved in organizing protests" (232); see also Davis-McElligatt, "Walk"; Santos, *Graphic* 53–56.

24. For historical context, see Rabaka; Maurice O. Wallace. On using music to teach civil rights history, see Freeland; Charles L. Hughes.

25. Cf. Santos's reading of these images (*Graphic* 71–74).

26. Anderson does not mention the *Martin Luther King Jr. Golden Legacy Magazine*, which features all the key scenes of the civil rights movement one would expect from a comic published in 1972: images of King preaching, Parks getting arrested on the bus and the ensuing Montogomery Bus Boycott, the lunch counter sit-in, protesters marching and in jail, Bull Connor's police dogs, King delivering the "I Have a Dream" speech at the March on Washington, and Bloody Sunday.

27. Anderson acknowledges in the "Gallery" at the end of the 2010 edition of *King* (290) that he was inspired by photographs from Mark Miller.

28. Douglas was one of Anderson's inspirations (Dale Jacobs 364). For Anderson's reflections on his stylistic evolution over the course of drawing *King* and about revising certain elements of the narrative when the story was published as a collected volume, see Dale Jacobs 376–77.

29. According to Anderson, the witnesses "offer a running commentary on the action, sometimes providing context, other times a counterpoint to the unreliable characters who were the story's primary players" (Dale Jacobs 378).

30. Earlier in the narrative, King explains his understanding of civil disobedience to television host Murray Myron: "Rauschenbusch, Gandhi—Thoreau, I was infatuated with Thoreau's argument that a creative minority, even a minority of 'one honest man,' could set in motion a moral revolution" (60). Apart from revealing King's philosophy, this passage invites readers to consider his source texts, including Thoreau's essay "Civil Disobedience" (1849).

31. Anderson speaks of "that jittery layering of meaning and effect that you get from collage" (Dale Jacobs 379).

32. In 2021, Anderson donated his original artwork and manuscripts to the Billy Ireland Cartoon Museum & Library at Ohio State University (McGurk). Studying these materials should provide additional insights into his artistic process and use of historical materials.

33. Writing about *March*, *King*, and Helfer and DuBurke's graphic biography *Malcolm X*, Boykin maintains, "These three comics challenge the perception of these men as superheroic vigilantes defeating racism and instead depict these highly-mythologized figures as complex individuals working within networks of activists" (69). Helfer and DuBurke offer a single-page overview of Black history that offers a good starting point for a discussion of alternative narratives of US history. The five panels propose a trajectory from the Middle Passage through Emancipation, the post-Reconstruction backlash, and Jim Crow segregation to Ku Klux Klan terror and lynching. The final panel remediates a lynching photograph and states, "Race riots, lynchings, and state-sanctioned discrimination achieved the Southern white racists' goal of subordinating African Americans. Searching for work and respect, millions of blacks moved North" (5).

34. According to hooks's notion of teaching to transgress, we should view "the classroom always as a communal place" and facilitate "collective effort in creating and sustaining a learning community" (*Teaching* 8). Davis-McElligatt's reflections on her teaching career, including a period when she was a "well-educated college professor *and also* poor and black and woman," underscore the need to reflect on the biographical, social, political, and economic factors impacting the classroom experience on the side of the students and on the teacher's side, what she describes as a "political praxis" that "extends far beyond the academic into the realm of the personal and political" ("On Being" 48, 44, 43).

35. Cf. Armstrong's suggestions for teaching the movement through the lens of literature ("Stay").

36. For teaching guides, see Meryl Jaffe; Haskins and Benson; Whitaker and Kallenborn. The Anti-Defamation League provides instructions for teaching all three books ("March: Book One"; "March: Book Two"; "March: Book Three"). Michelle J. Bellino and Darin Stockdill of the University of Michigan developed a forty-seven-page reading guide for *March: Book One* geared toward teaching the book in college. The website Teachers Pay Teachers offers additional lesson plans.

37. For Lewis's speech, see "Rep John Lewis' Speech." Walker and Anderson present a two-page portrait gallery of some of the forty-one "civil rights martyrs" who became victims of racial violence between 1955 and 1968 (13–14).

38. A comparative analysis of *March*'s depiction of Hamer and scholarly biographies such as Maegan Parker Brooks's *A Voice That Could Stir an Army* (2014) could enable cross-examinations of the gender implications of the movement.

39. According to Toni Cade Bambara, during the 1960s, "It would seem that every [Black] organization you can name has had to struggle at one time or another with seemingly

mutinous cadres of women getting salty about having to man the telephones or fix the coffee while the men wrote the position papers and decided on policy" ("On the Issue" 107).

40. Weaver remediates pages from the revisionist textbook *Know Alabama* that she encountered in school. These remediations could be used to encourage students to critically examine their present textbooks. For further analysis, see Breckenridge and Peterson; Rifkind.

41. Including Howard Cruse's *Stuck Rubber Baby* about growing up white and gay in the South could introduce questions of sexual orientation and their intersectional significance for civil rights movement history. See Santos, *Graphic* chap. 5.

42. For more extensive discussion of these issues, see Schmid, *Frames*. On framing in mass media and government accounts of racial conflicts, particularly the 1921 Tulsa Race Massacre, see Messer and Bell.

43. Chaney discerns "messianic [. . .] exceptionalism" ("Misreading" 31). Arthur Flowers, Chitrakar, and Rossi's *I See the Promised Land* offers opportunities to complicate celebrations of King's roots in the Black Baptist church by introducing African spirituality and its American offshoots. This includes references to Lord Legba and hoodoo religion as well as Dahomean notions of Fa, which narrator Ricky Trickmaster defines as "a funny thing—fate, free will, all that—I'm not quite sure how that work but I do claim with all my power that it was Martin Luther King's Fa to be in the temple" on the night before his assassination. "He say he seen the promise land. [. . .] I claim he was fated to be the ancestral call he is to us now. It is his Fa" (10–11).

44. On teaching the civil rights movement through #BlackLivesMatter, see Shannon King.

45. On gender in the civil rights movement, see Houck and Dixon; Collier-Thomas and Franklin; Vicki L. Crawford, Rouse, and Woods.

46. See also Bright; Hillstrom. This triple oppression evokes Kimberlé Crenshaw: "Because the intersectional experience is greater than the sum of racism and sexism, any analysis that does not take intersectionality into account cannot sufficiently address the particular manner in which Black women are subordinated" (140). Patricia Hill Collins argues, "Because violence permeates all segments of American society, it routinely supports hierarchies of race, gender, class, age, ethnicity, nation and sexuality" (917).

47. For extensive analysis of bleeds in *March*, see Santos, *Graphic* 64–77.

48. Cf. Boykin's reading of this scene (81–83).

49. Not all graphic narratives about Black history are equally useful for teaching. Singer, for instance, has mixed feelings about teaching Baker's *Nat Turner*: "I don't know that I'd recommend that other scholars not teach it," he explained. "But if they do I would hope that they'd teach it with more of an awareness of all of the inventions and fabrications and falsehoods that Baker has put into that book, instead of just assuming or taking it for granted that it's historically accurate" (Berlatsky). I would suggest that *Nat Turner* be taught like any biographical work about a historical figure (and perhaps alongside a biography like *King*): as a narrative construction that picks a certain emplotment to deliver a specific interpretation of that figure's life. Baker's narrative is rich in pop culture and other references: tracing these references and critically comparing his fabrications with historical documentation could be a productive approach to teaching *Nat Turner*.

50. Another productive approach to teaching Anderson's *King* would be to read it alongside other graphic biographies of King to discover and discuss differences in narrative perspective and structure, graphic visualization and style, and so forth. One particularly

productive companion biography is Arthur Flowers, Chitrakar, and Rossi's *I See the Promised Land*, which combines Flowers's poetic prose with Chitrakar's Bengali Patua art to create a visual narrative beyond the conventions of US-inspired comics.

51. Noting that some Bible editions print Jesus's words in a different color, Chaney reads this use of the colors of the American flag as a biblical reference that turns King into a messianic figure ("Drawing" 181).

52. The "Gallery" at the end of the book edition of *King* includes a draft version of this image from 1991 under which Anderson wrote, "This is taken directly from a photo of King during his 'I Have a Dream' speech. Y'know, doesn't he look a bit like Hitler?" (284). The *Martin Luther King Golden Legacy Magazine* depicts King in an identical posture, his right arm raised in the air and the American flag waving next to him.

53. Morales, Baker, et al.'s *Captain America: Truth* makes a similar connection, as does Walker, Brown, and Greene's *Bitter Root*, which ends with the Sangeryes rescuing inmates from a Nazi concentration camp. Cone speaks of "the tragic memory of the black holocaust in America's history" (159–60), and a similar reference occurs in McGregor and Graham's "A Cross Burning Darkly Blackening the Night!," where Klan members have tied Black Panther to a burning cross. "He is the Black Cat," the caption reads, "and given any choice, the Black Cat will flee the Holocaust."

54. This reference also appears in the *Black Panther & the Crew* miniseries scripted by Coates and Harvey. In issue 1, a relative of a Black man who has died under mysterious circumstances while in police custody asks the detective in charge to allow a peaceful protest: "Why don't you collar the Gestapo thugs who killed my uncle?"

55. Murakawa begins her book on the civil rights movement and the prison-industrial complex with a provocative statement: "One black man in the White House, one million black men in the Big House" (1). On the mass imprisonment of people of color as a new form of racial segregation, see Michelle Alexander.

56. A similarly gratuitous scene appears at the end of *Bitter Root*, when Cotton Sangerye kneels down to pat the shoulder of a rescued death camp survivor, a Jewish child wearing a Star of David armband, and offers reassurance: "My name is Cotton. Cotton Sangerye . . . . And as long as my family and I are here, nothing bad will happen to you" (464–65).

57. Discussing the potential symbolism of "the missing face of Christ on the stained glass window, which survived the bombing," theologian Reinhold Niebuhr and James Baldwin saw an allegory of white Christianity's failure to reconcile its religious principles with the subjugation and discrimination of the Black population (Cone 53). The bombing is also the subject of *Hell to Pay*, a short comic by Marcus H. Roberts, Jamal Williams Jr., Iwan Joko Triyono, and Hector Negreto in which two scientists create a time-traveling contraption that is supposed to send them to the church just in time to save the girls. The scientists soon realize that they have been sent to hell, where the "spirits of the klansmen" who murdered the girls are "getting tortured over and over."

CHAPTER 4. AFRODIASPORIC ARCHIVES

1. For more elaborate analyses of Black superheroes, see Burke; Nama; Darieck Scott, *Keeping*; Benson and Singsen; Gateward and Jennings; Howard and Jackson. Coates's first work of fiction, the novel *The Water Dancer* (2019), was published after the initial media hype around *Black Panther*.

2. Coates was aware of this genealogy, telling Evan Narcisse: "Before my run, there were several things that happened at Marvel. [...] First of all you've got Priest. Priest's job is to get white folks to take T'Challa seriously. T'Challa ain't no chump. He established that pretty well. After that, Reggie comes in, he says, 'Not only is T'Challa not a chump, but Wakanda ain't to be fucked with, period.'" On Shuri and the Dora Milaje (wives in waiting according to the Wakandan tradition) as intersectional (Black, female, queer) complications of the superhero formula, see FitzMaurice.

3. Hudlin's *Black Panther* 18 (September 2017) features Isaiah Bradley, Morales, Baker et al.'s Black Captain America, who has witnessed medical experiments reminiscent of the Tuskegee syphilis study and encountered emaciated inmates in the fictional (and ironically named) German concentration camp Schwarzebitte during World War II. In Hudlin's *Black Panther*, Bradley appears in a wheelchair at the celebrity wedding of King T'Challa and his mutant bride, Ororo Munroe (Storm). An editorial footnote at the bottom of the page directs the reader to *Truth*. For analysis of Morales, Baker, et al.'s work, see Carpenter, "Truth"; Ryan; Wanzo, *Content* chap. 3.

4. The paperbacks that collect Coates's run subdivide it into three parts: books 1–3, *A Nation Under Our Feet*; books 4–5, *Avengers of the New World*; and books 6–8, *The Intergalactic Empire of Wakanda*.

5. Jonathan W. Gray picks up on the connection between journalism and comic book writing in his interview with Coates ("Conflicted").

6. "You think Bandung is a great victory—I say that the game has just begun," the representative declares. "The empire is building an army to end all armies. So must we." A friend maintains, "All of us—Asia, Africa, Harlem—got the same enemy. But our brothers here got power, and all we got is prayer."

7. On the "Black fantastic," see Iton.

8. On archives in graphic narrative, see Jared Gardner chap. 5; Ahmed and Crucifix; Crucifix; Stein, *Authorizing* chap. 4.

9. A fuller placement of Coates's *Black Panther* run within his larger oeuvre would have to map the many theoretical and rhetorical overlaps between his literary writing (fiction and non-fiction) and his comic book activities. One example is Coates's interest in archives in *Black Panther* and his father's engagement with Black history, including efforts to republish books by Black writers. In *The Beautiful Struggle*, Coates writes that works by such writers as J. A. Rogers went out of print because "these were words that *they* [white America] did not want us to see, the lost archives, secret collections, folders worn yellow by water and years. But Dad brought them back" (13).

10. For Hartman, critical fabulation advances "a series of speculative arguments" and exploits "the capacities of the subjunctive (a grammatical mood that expresses doubts, wishes, and possibilities), in fashioning a narrative, which is based upon archival research" ("Venus" 11).

11. Appadurai understands popular archives as "the creation of documents and their aggregation into archives" as "part of everyday life outside the purview of the state. The personal diary, the family photo album, the community museum, the libraries of individuals are all examples of popular archives" (16).

12. Whether this Black diasporic imaginary remains US-centered or whether it is embraced by and recognized as valid by audiences abroad remains an open question. Research on the reception of Coogler's first *Black Panther* film (Sewchurran; Omanga and Mainye) suggests that African audiences welcomed the Wakandan fantasy and developed discursive

and creative ways of making it their own. On neoslave narratives that "stopped being only African American [...] and became transnational and global" (39), see Misrahi-Barak. Coates's *Black Panther* includes one such transnational slave narrative in the form of the embedded life story of Ifé, told by the griot (in the guise of Ramonda) in book 2. Black enslavers carry Ifé "out of Wakanda and across the burning sea" to be "sold in the market of Eram like an ox or a bushel of wheat" and serve as an enslaved wife to an older Black man.

13. Commenting on "national or imperial state collections," Lowe reads these records in Foucauldian terms "not with the aim of recovering a presence but, rather, to study the archaeology of knowledge through which the archive subjects and governs precisely by means of instruments that absent the humanity of the enslaved" (87).

14. By calling the rebels *maroons*, Coates suggests a lineage from the historical maroon societies of escaped slaves who established communities, often in conjunction with Native Americans, in hidden parts of the US South (such as swamplands) and to the future fighters against the empire. Volume 1 of Love and Morgan's *Bayou* imagines a backstory to the Wagstaff family that includes a maroon community of "Choctaw, Seminole and Negroes who run off from slavery" in Florida that Andrew Jackson and his troops attacked during the Seminole Wars in the first half of the nineteenth century. For further analysis, see Diouf.

15. The headline "Nigeria's Literary Lion Flies Home from Exile" on a *New York Times* story about Soyinka's return even sounds like a potential Black Panther title.

16. Walters sees "new imaginings which confront the gaps, spaces, and the master's pinning discourse by refusing to see this archive as finite or definitive, but rather open to rereading" (5). For Appadurai, the diasporic archive "is increasingly characterized by the presence of voice, agency and debate, rather than of mere reading, reception and interpellation" (22).

17. I thank an anonymous reviewer for reminding me that Tommy travels in time through the old man's magical library as well as for the Washington reference.

18. Cf. Koh: "Archives are not sites of knowledge retrieval but of knowledge production" (385).

19. *Plunder* is a central term in Coates's nonfiction oeuvre. In *Between the World and Me*, he discerns "plunder everywhere around us" (21) and warns, "Beware the plunderer!" (87–88). In *We Were Eight Years in Power*, he asserts, "America is literally unimaginable without plundered labor shackled to plundered land, without the organizing principle of whiteness as citizenship, without the culture crafted by the plundered, and without that culture itself being plundered" (85).

20. For a related distinction between comics in archives (e.g., research libraries, private collections) and comics as archives (i.e., comics acting as archiving institutions), see Stein, "Comic."

21. Ahmed and Crucifix discern "various types of archival work in comics unfolding at different scales, from the archival function of drawing to institutional strategies of memory management" (8). On archives and comics memory in contemporary graphic narratives, see also Crucifix.

22. Bibi Burger and Engels take the concept of a "metaphorical Mecca" from Coates's earlier work as a critical framework to suggest that the "fictional African country of Wakanda functions as a metaphorical Mecca" (1). Coates introduces the notion of Howard University as the mecca and "incredible cosmopolis of blackness" in *The Beautiful Struggle* (132) and calls it "the crossroads of the black diaspora" in *Between the World and Me* (40).

23. Coates includes "various ideological and philosophical debates" that play "out metaphorically" in the comics, such as Zenzi's populism, the "Midnight Angels' radical feminism and the philosopher Changamire's pacifist anti-monarchism" (Bibi Burger and Engels 3). Burger and Engels suggest that "the various characters in *a nation under our feet* [sic] represent different and conflicting ideological positions. These positions are metaphors for real world political views and in playing out the consequences of these ideologies" (1).

24. In Jennings and Brame's *The Mighty Struggle: A Town Called Miracle*, this function is performed by the mythical figure Tome: "I am the keeper of the secrets, the follower of the weight, the recorder of the takers and all of their exploits throughout time and space."

25. According to Dando, *griot* translates as *blood* in the Mandinka language, and the "griot embodies an explicitly socio-cultural and particularly political role in African diasporic tradition as an individual who is deeply connected to the soul and spirit of a people" (331). In my reading of *Black Panther*, the role of archivist can be added to the griot's functions as artist, author, and activist.

26. Hartman emphasizes the discrepancy between "the twelve or fifteen or twenty million or more who endured the Middle Passage [and] the few who went on to write about it" ("Dead" 211). The Djalia is an "immaterial archive" (see Jenny Sharpe).

27. In *Between the World and Me*, Coates counters notions of American exceptionalism via Hannah Arendt, referring to the country's long history of anti-Black repression as "this banality of violence" and maintaining that it "can never excuse America, because America [. . .] believes itself exceptional, the greatest and noblest nation ever to exist." He concludes, "One cannot, at once, claim to be superhuman and then plead mortal error" (8).

28. Okorafor et al.'s *Shuri* series is set in the same universe, as footnotes referring to Coates's run indicate. The central memory space created by Coates, the Djalia, appears there as well, and Shuri serves as the Aja-Adanna (see issue 8).

29. The mutant Muti also quotes Yeats's phrase in issue 10 of Okorafor et al.'s *Shuri*.

30. The Wakandan government also relies on more Westernized institutional archives, according to Okorafor et al.'s *Shuri*, where the title character explains in issue 7 that she has offered a friend's mother a job as "assistant archivist for the Wakandan Embassy here in New York."

31. Locating the story arc within the field of African American science fiction goes beyond the scope of this chapter, especially since Coates seems more interested in reimagining the past than in providing glimpses of "diverse futures" (Sanchez-Taylor 2021).

32. Patterson describes this transformation of the enslaved as a form of "social death," while Gikandi speaks of the Middle Passage as "the ground zero of signification" (88).

33. Cf. Walters: "The archives of the nation-state too often fix subjects in an abject status of wounding, absence, and violence" (5).

34. For an Afrofuturist take on these issues and "Astro-Blackness" as a concept that "represents the emergence of a black identity framework within emerging global technocultural assemblages," see Reynaldo Anderson and Jones vii. Jennings suggests, "The first true Afrofuturist was the first slave that said, 'You know what? I don't think I like this slavery thing. I think perhaps I should follow that star, and I shall go because I deserve a better future'" (Watt 72). On Afrofuturism, see also Gunkel and Lynch; Lavender; Lavender and Yaszek; Womack, *Afrofuturism*. For an Afropessimist take, see Murillo.

35. Ayo and Aneka recall Rebecca Hall, Martínez, and Bao's Dahomeyan women Alele and Adono, connecting African women warriors in nonfiction graphic narratives with superhero comics and vice versa. On Storm's connection to the African diaspora, see Jonathan Flowers.

36. On the Black Panther's performative embodiment of blackness and spectacles of race in the 1960s and 1970s, see Peppard.

37. For interrogations of Lee and Kirby's original version of the character and its political implications, see Darowski; Lund. For a historical account from the earlier appearances to Coates's run, see Burroughs. For increasingly diverse fandoms that reimagine popular comic book characters and narratives from previously marginalized perspectives, see Pande, *Squee*; Pande, *Fandom*.

38. Walker, Brown, and Greene's *Bitter Root* goes one step further by appending extensive bonus sections, "Bitter Truths," to the issues collected in trade paperbacks as well as in an Omnibus edition. Curated by John Jennings and featuring short essays mostly by African American scholars and comics practitioners, these sections historicize and contextualize the series's subject matter, character constellation, and visual styles. Acting as popular archives and incorporating both academic and fan work into the comic's paratext, these curated spaces also lead readers into a much bigger and much more dispersed archive of Black intellectual thought. For further analysis, see chap. 5.

39. Aneka's mother says, "Have you so soon forgotten the parable of Zami: 'A free house is not built with a slave-driver's tools'"; see also Coates et al.'s *Black Panther & the Crew*: "Frank thought he could dismantle the empire with the empire's tools" (issue 6).

40. *Black Panther & the Crew* retcons US history when it reveals the attempt to enlist superheroes in the fight for racial justice in Harlem as a ploy by the terrorist organization Hydra in an attempt to create social unrest and enable the organization to use Harlem as a base to increase its power. "Hydra had us made from jump," the dead Ezra Klein's voice intones toward the end of issue 6. "From Bandung to Harlem, they'd played us. What a scheme."

41. Several cover variants reprinted in the *Black Panther* graphic novel collections evoke Coogler's film, acknowledging the superhero's growing significance as part of Marvel's transmedia franchise.

42. "It was a heck of a challenge merging the Shuri from the comics and the Shuri from the film," Okorafor writes in remarks appended to the *Shuri: 24/7 Vibranium* graphic novel edition. For analysis of the movie as a decolonial film, see Osei; McSweeney; Bukatman, *Black Panther*; Howard; Ward; Womack, *Black Panther*. On Miles Morales as a mixed-race superhero, see Santos, "Talented."

43. For the larger process of genre evolution, see Stein, *Authorizing*.

44. Cole's critique of Coogler's *Black Panther* only partially applies to Coates: "There are fifty four African countries. What would it mean to dream with these already-existing countries themselves? What would it mean to dream with Mozambique, Sudan, Togo, or Libya, and think about their politics in all their hectic complexities? What would it look like to use that as a narrative frame, even for works of fiction? Wakanda is a monarchy. [...] Why are monarchies the narrative default? Can we dream beyond royalty?" ("On the Blackness"). Coates is struggling with some of these questions, and his attempts to transform Wakanda into a democracy and show the country's ethnic and cultural diversity address this critique at least in some ways.

45. These words recall the famous chiasma from Douglass's *Narrative of the Life of Frederick Douglass*: "You have seen how a man was made a slave; you shall see how a slave was made a man" (47).

46. In Okorafor's "Keeping Your Friends Close, Part 1," collected in Okorafor et al.'s *Black Panther: Long Live the King*, Shuri is presented as a master scientist surrounded by computers who wears tight-fitting African-style clothes that show off her muscled midriff and accentuate her breasts. For a critique of female Black comic book characters as stereotypically gendered "signs" of Africa, see Whaley, chap. 3. The visual depictions of these characters are not per se Coates's but rather those of his pencillers, inkers, and colorists, and Coates, though the main writer for the series, would not have independently overseen the graphic artists' aesthetic decisions. A broader analysis would have to consider the roles of editor Wil Moss and executive editor Tom Brevoort.

47. In book 5, Tetu voices his challenge to T'Challa's rule in a patriarchal language that simultaneously questions and reproduces colonial discourse by rejecting binaries while associating Africa with feminine beauty: "Your problem is the dualities and binaries. The unswerving lines. The boxes. The obsession with fitting a round world into a square Wakandan mind. It is not African." He continues, "Africa is a beautiful woman—round and lush. But Wakandans are trapped in the binary. So strict. So western. Boxes where there should be circles. Stasis . . . when what we need is revolution. [. . .] What would it mean to expand beyond the binaries?"

48. These ancestral figures are not always sources of wisdom. Sometimes, they pester Shuri with clichés: "knowledge is power" (issue 2), "travel changes everyone" (issue 3), and "there's always a give and take" (issue 8).

49. As the superhero mutant Queen Ororo of Kenya summarizes in a television interview in issue 7, "From the slave trade to Apartheid, Africa has been a victim of a series of moral abominations condoned by world governments, religions and businesses."

50. Okorafor details her personal investment in these debates in a paratextual statement: "I'm Igbo (a Nigerian ethnic group) and amongst the Igbo there's a popular saying, 'Igbo enwe eze,' which means, 'The Igbo have no king.' Being a more democratic society consisting of many small independent communities, historically, Igbos never had a centralized government or royalty. I've grown up hearing this phrase and between this and also being an American, any type of monarchy gets my side-eye of disapproval . . . even a mythical one" (Okorafor et al., *Black Panther: Long Live the King*).

51. Alitha E. Martinez and Roberto Poggi's illustration of the Dora Milaje's training clothes includes a sports-bra-type garment that accentuates the women's upper-body physique as well as pants cut ridiculously far below the women's navels.

52. Neither Pinto nor Goyal, *Runaway Genres*, includes any discussion of graphic narratives. Ashe and Saal contains an essay on Duffy and Jennings's adaptation of Octavia Butler's *Kindred* (Godfrey). Raiford and Raphael-Hernandez, *Migrating*, features a chapter on Baker's *Nat Turner* (Darieck Scott, "Not-Yet").

53. Coates has written the *Captain America* series in addition to *Black Panther* (see Coates, "Why"), and his comic book work and his nonfiction writing can be situated in a post-civil-rights era that Ashe and Saal describe as "post-soul or post-black." Drawing on a growing body of scholarship on these issues, they associate this era with "recent African American cultural productions" that "partake in a larger poetics of literary and visual narratives of slavery marking the circum-Atlantic world" (5).

54. Chambliss speaks of "the decolonization of *Black Panther*" ("Different" 204). On the whiteness of the superhero, see Guynes and Lund.

55. It is no coincidence that popular series like *Black Panther* weave storylines around the idea of archives of enslavement at a time when "digitization transforms slavery's status

as a particular—even peculiar—object of knowledge within and beyond literary studies" (Rusert 268).

CHAPTER 5. MONSTROUS PASTS

1. The graphic narratives examined in this chapter have been produced primarily by male creators, which is no surprise since body horror and monster fiction have traditionally been configured as male (a tradition criticized by Kinitra D. Brooks's *Searching for Sycorax*). I counteract this bias by using Morrison's sentiments as an organizing framework, by focusing on strong female characters (especially in *Bitter Root*), and by gesturing toward other narrative possibilities offered by Black women, among them graphic works written by Nnedi Okorafor (*LaGuardia*, 2019) and Tananarive Due, Steven Barnes, and Marco Finnegan (*The Keeper*, 2022).

2. Recall Hartman: "I intended both to tell an impossible story and to amplify the impossibility of its telling" ("Venus" 11). On Morrison's "impossible stories," see Spatzek.

3. Cf. Chassot on the ghost's prosopopoeia: "the ghost thus voices that which remains unspoken in the historical narrative because it was not recorded, as well as that which remains unspoken because it was silenced, written over by other voices whose interests lay elsewhere or required that the slaves' perspectives and subjectivities be repressed" (19).

4. On monsters in visual culture more generally, see Alexa Wright.

5. Wester's description of *Beloved* as a "narrative of haunting, monstrosity, murder, madness, and abandonment" (*African American* 187) underscores the connection between ghostly haunting and monstrous violence. Ghosts are common in African American literature by women, including Toni Cade Bambara's *The Salt Eaters* (1980), Paule Marshall's *Praisesong for the Widow* (1983), Morrison's *Beloved* (1986), Gloria Naylor's *Mama Day* (1988), and works by Due such as *The Between* (1995), *The Good House* (2003), and *Joplin's Ghost* (2005). Chassot (2–3) also mentions Julie Dash's film *Daughters of the Dust* (1991).

6. Julia Kristeva's conception of the abject and Sigmund Freud's theory of the uncanny loom large in theories of monsters. Wester speaks of "grotesque ambivalence" (*African American* 39). Cf. Bruce: "Antiblack discourse constantly codes black people as savage, irrational, subrational, pathological, and effectively mad" (12).

7. Cf. Rankine: "Something is wrong everywhere and all the time" (qtd. in Leila Taylor 98).

8. For Due, horror is "an entertainment on the surface that has a deeper mission and goal, which is to heal trauma" ("Healing" 133). On "the terror of the mundane and quotidian," cf. Hartman, *Scenes* 2. On the speculative element in Black comics and particularly in *Bayou*, see Whitted, "Intertextual."

9. The poem continues with the media coverage of Till's murder, including the open-casket funeral that had shown "a black child's mutilated body" to be gazed at by voyeuristic eyes. The lesson the speaker takes away from the mediatization of the boy's death is harrowing because it has taught her "to be at home with children's blood" and intimately familiar "with pictures of black broken flesh." For analysis of the poem, see Kimberly Juanita Brown, *Repeating* 1–2.

10. The Jinoo are relatives of Afro-Caribbean vampires (see Anatol; Jerry Rafiki Jenkins; on monsters in a Caribbean context, see Braham). This is an apt reminder that the Black diaspora extends beyond Africa and North America, as Gilroy suggests. A broader investigation would account for graphic narratives from these regions, such as Matthew Clarke and

Nigel Lynch's Afro-Caribbean *Hardears* (2021), which is set on what Cathy Thomas calls "an ethnosurreal Caribbean nation" named Jouvert Island and pays tribute to the specifics of "Caribbean Afro-diasporic culture" (179). Brazilian creator Hugo Canuto's *Tales of the Orishas* (2023) "fuses the pantheon of the African diasporic religion of Candomblé with the Silver Age comic aesthetics" (cover blurb). Marcelo D'Salete's *Run for It* (2017) and *Angola Janga* (2019) feature a late-sixteenth- and early seventeenth-century independent kingdom founded by runaway slaves in Brazil.

11. Okorafor, Ford, and Devlin's graphic novel *LaGuardia* offers an Afrofuturist take on sentient, living, and even speaking plants in a future world of humans and aliens. In the story, a pregnant Nigerian doctor, Future Nwafor Chukwuebuka, travels to New York City and fights for social justice.

12. Jennings discusses "the materiality of blackness distilled through a pop-culture lens" in Barber 61.

13. As Bruce notes, Williams "suggests that watching and listening to loops of mediatized black death inflicts 'vicarious trauma': empathic secondhand trauma born of witnessing others' pain, especially others with whom one holds affinity or shares identity" (34).

14. Joel Christian Gill defines the Great Migration as "the Black diaspora fleeing White terrorism" in his graphic adaptation of Ibram X. Kendi's *Stamped from the Beginning* (172).

15. Harriet Jacobs criticizes the treatment of the enslaved as "merchandise" (see chap. 1) and describes slavery as a "demon" and "monster" (800). Lydia Maria Child evokes slavery's "monstrous features" in her introduction to Jacobs's narrative (748). Cf. Leila Taylor on the "invention of Blackness [as] a crucial marketing tool of chattel slavery": "To justify the buying and selling of human beings, the enslaved had to be diametrically oppositional to the slavers, all the way on the other side of their cultural chroma" (89–90).

16. Cohen speaks of the monster's "function as dialectical Other" ("Monster" 41).

17. Cf. Wester's reminder that "individualized dramas and traumas can act as a synecdoche for the nation and its relation to various Others" (*African American* 13).

18. This is also constitutive of (African American) gothic fiction, as Wester suggests: "The gothic blurs the distinctions between the 'monstrous'/unlawful and the normative" (*African American* 13).

19. Cohen writes, "The monster is difference made flesh" ("Monster" 41).

20. Cf. Leila Taylor: "The monster is despised and feared by the very nature of its monstrosity. The monster is dangerous and threatening and therefore can be tortured, killed, or maimed with impunity." She concludes, "The process of dehumanization is a process of monster-making" (79). *Bayou* exemplifies this process through a newspaper article about Calvin Wagstaff, who is accused of kidnapping and raping Lee's white friend Lily, that maligns him as "apelike" and "devoid of feeling and humanity" and refers to "the white girl's undoubtedly violated body" and concludes, "One finds it hard to empathize with this criminal" (vol. 1).

21. As Wester writes, the black body "is always and already outside of the norm" (*African American* 20).

22. Cf. Cohen: "The monster resists any classification built on hierarchy or a merely binary opposition, demanding instead a 'system' allowing polyphony, mixed response (difference in sameness, repulsion in attraction), and resistance to integration" ("Monster" 40).

23. Hybridity is a central characteristic of the monster. Cf. Cohen's Foucauldian argument: "This refusal to participate in the classificatory 'order of things' is true of monsters generally: they are disturbing hybrids whose externally incoherent bodies resist attempts to include

them in any systematic structuration. And so the monster is dangerous, a form suspended between forms that threatens to smash distinctions" ("Monster" 40).

24. According to Wester, the fear that "white and black relations would inevitably degrade, if not destroy whites" and the "obsessive need to ensure the maintenance of boundaries" resulted in a "preponderance of segregationist laws" after the Civil War. "Racial transgression embodied in 'half-breeds'" resulted in a discourse of the "miscegenated and miscegenating monster" (*African American* 19).

25. Sharpe defines monstrous intimacies "as a set of known and unknown performances and inhabited horrors, desires and positions produced, reproduced, circulated, and transmitted, that are breathed in like air and often unacknowledged to be monstrous" (*Monstrous* 3).

26. *Box of Bones* also acknowledges racially motivated sexual violence. The act that drives Lindsay's research on the "demonic creatures of folklore that have plagued the African diaspora for centuries" (creatures that she identifies as The Suffering, The Wretched, The Nobody, The Burden, The Night Doctor, and The Dark and that take on a variety of monstrous appearances) is the rape of her grandfather's girlfriend, Gauge, by two young white men (chap. 1). Gauge retaliates when she opens the box of bones she has taken from her mother, turning herself into a monster that murders her rapists and their families.

27. On the monster's "ontological liminality" and on failed attempts "to incorporate the monstrous races into a coherent epistemological system, [as] the monster always escaped to return to its habitations at the margins of the world," cf. Cohen, "Monsters" 40. Weiss suggests that "monsters are indicators of epistemic shifts" (125).

28. Kinitra D. Brooks speaks of the "intersections of blackness and monstrosity" (*Searching* 23); Wester notes "the nation's tendency to exclude and repress counter narratives from its dominant metanarrative" (*African American* 4); Leila Taylor acknowledges "the ghosts of our history, the spectral remnants of our nation that were too often forgotten and dismissed" (10).

29. Enoch, one of the Sangerye elders, maintains, "Souls tainted by hate become Jinoo. But there's some that believe a soul ravaged by great sorrow and pain can also become infected" and become an Inzondo (97).

30. Ford Sangerye explains, "Jinoo been runnin' wild in this country since before it was a country, but folks like me and my family kept 'em in check—fighting and curing 'em" (79). See also Brand's remarks on the "chronic fever of antiblack racism" with which generations have struggled and on the "dis-ease" of "living a pandemic" that "is structural rather than viral; it is the global state of emergency of antiblackness" ("On Narrative").

31. Cf. Bruce on "Black rage" as "at once a symptom of antiblack trauma, a defense against antiblack trauma, and a mighty force in battles against antiblackness" (24).

32. On Black avenger figures in Atlantic culture, see Pierrot. In Jennings and Brame's *A Mighty Struggle: A Town Called Miracle*, the family of a lynched Black man decides "to devote their lives to making things better in the world for black people" after his wife creates a magical weapon from a tree branch and uses it to kill the murderers. "They all gave up their identities and put them into mystical Mason jars to protect them," the prologue reads. "Simply calling themselves 'the family', these brave black men and women used their abilities, resources, and will to push the needle forward for black people across the world."

33. The boy's body is depicted from a worm's-eye perspective, placing the viewer on the ground and thus at the root of the lynching tree (as in one of the opening images in Love and Morgan's *Bayou*) and allowing a glimpse at the destroyed area surrounding the tree. Among

the wooden ruins, a cross-like structure is located directly underneath the boy's feet, an iconography and placement that evoke Cone's thoughts on the cross and the lynching tree as two interconnected symbols of death, one representing "a message of hope and salvation" and the other signifying "the negation of that message by white supremacy" (xiii). Cf. Cone on Black religion's potential to "transform ugliness [...] into beauty" and to "discover the 'terrible beauty' of the cross' and the 'tragic beauty' of the lynching tree" (162).

34. In *Blue Hand Mojo*, Half-Dead Johnson uses his magic powers to reanimate juke joint owner Sweet Liza Mae's murdered son, Red, who returns from the dead as a patched-up, zombified creature.

35. On African diasporic visions of witches, goddesses, and other angry spirits, see Marouan.

36. Morrison's *Beloved* describes Paul D and his fellow prisoners as "like the unshriven dead, zombies on the loose" (130) when they escape a flooded area. On the deep connection between blues and conjuring, see Kinitra D. Brooks, *Searching* 10, 120.

37. Berg's recollection of his father's and aunt's deaths is accompanied by an image of a family photograph, not only underscoring the importance of family and ancestors but also associating a particular narrative of familial suffering with the archives' many silent photographs of Black families, which often exist without any context.

38. Leila Taylor argues that "for those who survived" the transatlantic slave trade, "it must have felt like a living purgatory, something in between life and death, here and there, the known and the unknown. Limbo is supposed to be a space of waiting, something in between heaven and hell. But limbo also represents a state of oblivion and nothingness. It's both a transition and a place of imprisonment, a home for the disappeared" (38).

39. As Bruce notes, "By the nineteenth century, the slave ship gave way to the plantation as the paradigmatic site of black abjection and confinement in the Western Hemisphere" (16). Looking beyond slavery, hooks writes that Black domestic workers during Jim Crow were "reduced to the machinery of bodily physical labor, [as] black people learned to appear before whites as though they were zombies, cultivating the habit of casting the gaze downward so as not to appear uppity" (*Black* 168).

40. This description of The Noir recalls Chassot's understanding, derived from Édouard Glissant, of the "the hold as both tomb and womb" (54).

41. *Barzakh* is a Persian word meaning *limbo*, *barrier*, or *partition*; in Arabic, the word means *obstacle*, *hindrance*, *separation*, or *barrier*. In the Islamic faith, the term denotes a phase or stage between death and resurrection (Karbassian 86). The usage of *barzakh* ties in with Walker, Brown, and Greene's explicit multiculturalism: the Sangeryes join forces with Chinese and Native American families to fight the monsters.

42. As such, the narratives complicate Caruth's understanding of trauma as "a wound inflicted not upon the body but upon the mind" (*Unclaimed* 3).

43. Round distinguishes reflecting echoes, which are "echoes of word and image that come from within the comic book," and absorbing echoes, which are acts of overwriting that offer alternate perspectives on the characters that may also entail references to "real world events" (109, 110). *Nat Turner*, *Wake*, and *Bitter Root* combine both types of echoes, creating intradiegetic echoes between images through what Groensteen calls "braiding" and extradiegetic echoes between their storyworlds and the historical worlds they reconstruct and reimagine in graphic form.

44. Lee's unhappiness about her hair runs through the story and offers a running commentary on white hegemonic notions of beauty and their effects on the self-consciousness of

Black girls, a phenomenon Morrison explored in *The Bluest Eye* (1970). At the beginning of the story, Lee plays with Lily's hair and says, "Your hair is pretty, I wish I had hair like yours" (vol. 1). When combing her mother's straight hair, Lee asks, "Mama, how come my hair ain't pretty like yours?" and her mother replies, "You take after ya daddy. Them Wagstaffs are some nappy headed Negroes" (vol. 2). After Mrs. Rabbit has straightened Lee's "steel wool" with a "hot comb" and "pressin' oil," Lee looks at her reflection in the river and concludes, "I don't think my hair ever looked this pretty" (vol. 2). For an extended graphic treatment of the significance of hair and hairstyles in the lives of Black women, see Ebony Flowers; for scholarship on Black hair, see Banks; Byrd and Tharps; Dabiri.

45. This spiritual also pops up in *Bitter Root*, where Berg is singing it as he is about to embrace his baby daughter (399). The song lyrics were first published in 1901 in Work: "Wade in the water / Wade in the water, children / Wade in the water / God's gonna trouble the water" (8).

46. Among the many blues songs that memorialize the flood are Big Bill Broonzy's "Mississippi River Blues" (1934) and Charlie Patton's "High Water Everywhere, Part 1 and 2" (1930).

47. Portuguese captains referred to ships under their command as *túmolos fluctuantes* (floating tombs) (Joseph C. Miller 314; cf. Chassot 46).

48. Cf. Wardi's recognition of "bodies of water as haunted by the bodies of those who lost their lives in their currents. Water, then, the course of travel, marks severed paths to home, family, landscape, and life" (4). Mayer defines the sea as a "paradigmatic space of openness and indeterminacy" that gains "radically contradictory connotations once it becomes the setting for abduction, violation, enslavement, and revolt" (561). See also Dawson.

49. Cf. Leila Taylor: "All horror stories start with [...] the nothingness of the space between places," and "Blackness in America is still in the middle, residing in the place between opposites: living in the present while carrying the past, being human but perceived as other, considered both a person and a product, both American and foreign, neither here nor there" (37).

50. For queer takes on gothic literature and film, see Halberstam; Jones and Harris.

51. Wester adds elsewhere, "For Black writers the South is a gothic location of contradiction—detestable hell and comforting home, unspeakable violence and undeniable beauty, ancestral loss and ancestral origins" ("Southern"). Bruce describes this as a process of making "homeland in wasteland" (2).

52. McKittrick criticizes the gendered nature of what she calls "black women's geographies" (xi) and their attending "cartographies of struggle."

53. According to Dunning, "The theft of Black land in the United States presses upon an old and enduring wound of the Black person in America—that of placelessness. [...] Though one way to understand slavery is to see it as the theft of Black persons-as-bodies, it was also simultaneously a theft of land, a literal 'taking' of Africa from enslaved Africans" (104). In *12 Million Black Voices*, Richard Wright calls the enslaved and their descendants "the landless upon the land" (93). See also Coates, "Case."

54. Sexual abuse of Black women marks a second stream of violence, but it often took place in the domestic sphere, hidden from public view in scenes of everyday atrocities, whereas lynchings (most of whose victims were male) were often committed in nature, making the lynching tree "the most potent symbol of the trouble nobody knows that blacks have seen but do not talk about because the pain of remembering—visions of black bodies

dangling from southern trees, surrounded by jeering white mobs—is almost too excruciating to recall" (Cone 3).

55. hooks's oppositional gaze "'looks' to document" (*Black* 116). Considering the digital creations of contemporary Black fine artists, Campt posits a Black gaze that does not depict Black folks or Black culture but instead "forces viewers to engage blackness from a different and discomforting vantage point." It "shifts the optics of 'looking at' to a politics of *looking with, through, and alongside another*" (*Black* 8).

56. The first chapter of *Reap What Was Sown* (*Farmhand* vol. 1), like *Blue Hand Mojo*, begins with a nightmare in which Jedidiah tells his son Ezekiel, "The seed was sown long before us. The roots are deep into black soil. Black as the heart of man. Our family tree." The next page shows a giant tree studded with human bodies that scream, "We're just branches on a tree of woe." Visibly disturbed by these nightly visions, Ezekiel wakes up in horror. Cf. a splash page at the beginning of *Bitter Root* 11, which tells the saga of the Sangerye family in the shape of a tree made up of its members, with Ma Etta as the stem above the roots and the rest of the family branching out above her and with Jinoo (representing racism) to the left, a Harlem Renaissance jazz band (celebrating Black happiness) to the right, and Dr. Sylvester and Miss Knightsdale in their nonmonstrous human form (signifying Black suffering) on top (343).

57. As Chassot points out, "The term 'diaspora,' as Stefan Helmreich has remarked, is etymologically and symbolically linked to paternity, as it 'summons up the image of scattered seeds,' a metaphor for 'the male "substance" that is traced in genealogical histories.' In this respect, diaspora 'refers us to a system of kinship reckoned through men and suggests the questions of legitimacy in paternity that patriarchy generates" (149, citing Helmreich 245).

58. Walter White argues that rape accusations also impacted the white accusers: "The creation of the bogy of sex crimes as a defense of lynching has made the South the terrified victim of the fears of its own conjuring. [. . .] Having created the Frankenstein monster (and it is no less terrifying because it is largely illusory), the lyncher lives in constant fear of his own creation" (*Rope* 56–57).

59. The details become clear in the aftermath of Ford's intervention, when he explains to the only survivor, the young white Johnnie Rae, who has not yet lynched anyone, that the Klansmen, including Johnnie Rae's entire family, had to be killed because they were "lynch-happy peckerwood[s] turned Jinoo" (47). For a similar revenge narrative in which a demonic old Black man raises the undead zombies of lynching victims to massacre Klansmen, see Barnes, Brame, and Negrete.

60. In Jennings and Brame's *The Mighty Struggle*, the prologue remembers a Black man whose wife uses conjure and rootwork to turn the branch on which he was hanged into a powerful weapon with which she smites the men who killed her husband.

61. Cf. *Farmhand*'s "tree of woe," described to Ezekiel as "a demon tree. A tree that countless men have died upon. It's what kept your ancestors in chains for generations and keeps men in chains to this very day. [. . .] It's been waiting. Looking for any inroad to take back this town. It used your daddy. Now it wants to use you" (*The Seed*, chap. 19).

62. Cf. Wester on the "horrific contrasts implicit in the definition of Southern beauty in the song 'Strange Fruit' as speckled by mangled black bodies" and the "the seeming beauty of the American scene [that] masks its true, monstrous face" (*African American* 72).

63. Stagolee, the ultimate badman figure from Black folklore, exclaims as he is about to kill Mrs. Meadows and Mr. Rabbit, "No deals, no tricks, no BRIAR PATCH, no LAUGHING PLACE" (vol. 2).

64. *Bitter Root* also uses crows to represent monstrosity in a process of transubstantiation through which the pained and enraged victims of anti-Black violence, such as Dr. Sylvester and Miss Knightsdale, become monsters with pointy beaks and sharp claws whenever they run out of serum. These monsters flip the script on the lynching narrative by depicting Black families rather than "monstrous" figures like Thomas Dixon Jr.'s Black "rapist" Gus, whom *The Clansman* describes as "a 'beast' [that] sinks his 'black claws' into the 'soft white throat' of a symbol of pure white southern womanhood" ("Wanzo, "On Monstrosity" 482).

65. Wells-Oghoghomeh would call this a case of the "trans-sense—the realm of, beyond, and between the visible and invisible" (162) triggered by memories of the dead.

66. Lee does not know that Calvin, whom she loves dearly, is not her biological father. The anthropomorphized Miss Meadows tells the unfaithful Mr. Rabbit, "Here you are abandonin' the only chil' you got left alive. [...] You mean you don't know? Dat nappy headed" girl may have a black "hide [...] like Tarbaby, but she got da eyes of Bruh' Rabbit!" (vol. 2).

67. The dreams alleviate the effects of Lee's trauma by reinstating or at least reinvigorating her mental defense mechanisms, helping her to ward off, however imperfectly, what Freud would define as the neurosis following from trauma, "a consequence of an extensive breach being made in the protective shield against stimuli" (35). Instantiating this breach, "traumatic events create conflicts in the ego which 'split off' from the unity of the ego and are repressed but return later often in dreams" (Mambrol; cf. Freud 8).

68. Richard Wright unmasks Jefferson's agrarian ideal: "More than one-half of us black folk in the United States are tillers of the soil, and three-fourths of those of us who till the soil are sharecroppers and day laborers" (*12 Million* 31).

69. Half-Dead Johnson identifies the hoodoo source of the hex that caused the monster to kill the white mobsters by noting that the red substance at the crime scene is not blood: "I'd know this mud anywhere. This is the muddiest Mississippi mud I've ever seen" (chap. 3). These narratives also have a biblical dimension that includes the tree of life and the tree of the knowledge of good and evil from Genesis. Each of the four volumes of *Farmhand* published to date ends with a quotation from the Bible, and the deluge that sweeps away the juke joint in *Bayou* and the purgatory in *Bitter Root* have biblical connotations.

70. According to Wells-Oghoghomeh, conjuring refers to practices of creating spells, whereas root work most frequently involves breaking spells (184). For Chireau, harming and healing are ways in which "black communities interpreted suffering" and practitioners "bridged the physical realm and the invisible world" (*Black* 7, 8). Cf. Kinitra D. Brooks: "Rootwork is a semi-formal manifestation of black folks' practical need for healing through the making of medicines intertwined with the highly theoretical process of world-building and creating an inheritance of knowledge steeped in spirituality" ("Root" 141).

71. These works speak to folk horror and African American interventions into the horror genre as well as to Afrofuturist and speculative fiction. Kinitra D. Brooks defines "folkloric horror" as "texts of black women horror creators [that] revise and reimagine African diasporic folklore as a mode of participating in and interrogating contemporary mainstream horror" (*Searching* 12). She locates it in the "'Devil Tales' and 'Witch and Hant Tales'" that highlight "black interest in horror as a long-established reality in its communal literature—the rich oral folk culture and tales passed down through familial generations" (14). On folk horror in comics, see Chamberlin. On "Black American horror," see Coleman.

72. Martin defines conjure as "the healing and harming ritual practices of African-derived religious practices that evolved in the New World" and "communication with supernatural

entities that [...] may be referred to as ghosts, ha'ints, specters, or apparitions but across the African diaspora are known as the Ancestors, loa, orisha, or simply Spirit" (1–2).

73. According to *Box of Bones*, "The sum of the suffering on the plantation became manifest" (chap. 4). The monster, a hypermuscular Black man dressed in overalls with a noose around his neck and a hat with three cross-stitches pulled over its face, kills everything in its path.

74. On the conjure woman as a healer and spiritual counselor in *Mama Day*, see Kinitra D. Brooks, *Searching* 104–9. Due, Barnes, and Finnegan's *The Keeper* "uses horror as a way to talk about generational trauma" (inside flap). A young Black girl, Aisah, has lost her parents in a car accident, and her dying grandmother summons a dark spirit, The Keeper, that has protected the family for generations, to watch over the girl. But The Keeper sustains itself by killing people from Aisha's apartment building, and Aisha and her friends must defeat the monster.

75. This resonates with Carole Boston Weatherford's introduction to Whit Taylor and Kazimir Lee's graphic biography, *Harriet Tubman: Toward Freedom* (2021): "Harriet emerges from this action-packed epic—pitting freedom against slavery, good against evil—as a superhero of sorts," but readers also learn that "as a nurse, she used folk remedies to treat soldiers." For a fantastically monstrous take on Tubman, see Crownson et al., *Harriet Tubman: Demon Slayer* (2017–).

76. On conjure as "a magical tradition in which spiritual power is invoked for various purposes, such as healing, protection, and self-defense," see Chireau, *Black* 12.

77. Johnson's lover, Sophie, is a "strong rootworker" who mixes the magic tonic that Johnson calls his "saving grace" and that keeps his mojo under control and The Noir at bay (chap. 2). Johnson donates blood for her "passing potion," an elixir that enables her transformation to a white woman to reap the benefits of whiteness in a world of racial exclusion (chap. 1).

78. On good and bad hoodoos and on conjure harming as "the malign use of supernatural power by practitioners," see Chireau, *Black*, 30, 31.

79. Equally reminiscent of *Bitter Root* is the passage that depicts Red's murder and his mother's grief, which are revealed in a flashback narrative by gangster Mac the Shark: Red "died right there in his mother's arms. I never heard wailing like that. Never. [...] Then, all of a sudden, she stopped and stared at us with this ... look. She didn't say a word. She just ... looked right through us like we weren't there" (chap. 4).

80. *Blue Hand Mojo* can be characterized as an African American migration narrative (Griffin).

81. Garber's "category crisis" describes "a failure of definitional distinction, a borderline that becomes permeable, that permits of border crossings from one (apparently distinct) category to another: black/white, Jew/Christian, noble/bourgeois, master/servant, master/slave" (16).

82. See Bukatman's analysis of Mike Mignola's *Hellboy* series, programmatically titled *Hellboy's World*.

83. Ball and Robinson remediate photographs of iconic buildings, such as the Dreamland Theatre and the Stradford Hotel, and signal their stake in historical verisimilitude by presenting a facsimile of the newspaper article that sparked the massacre and including endnotes as well as a list of sources. For historical context, see Eddie Faye Gates, *Riot*; Johnson, *Black*.

84. The event is retold in a double-page spread several issues later, when Dr. Sylvester's doubts about his Christian faith are accompanied by images of smoking rubble, dead children, and Miss Knightsdale moments after her monstrous transformation (224–25).

CODA

1. See also Gonzales-Day, "Erased," a project that erases the murdered bodies from lynching photographs.

2. A similarly powerful use of the cut rope as a signifier of slavery and lynching's continuing grasp on Black lives is Andrew Burton's 2014 photograph of a neatly dressed young Black man standing in the middle of Times Square with the body of an acoustic guitar visible behind his right arm and a noose around his neck and looking somberly up toward the sky. The noose evokes the legacy of lynching and its photographic reverberations, while the guitar calls forth the sounds of the blues and its bittersweet take on life. For analysis, see Schneider. For the image, see https://d.ibtimes.co.uk/en/full/1411614/black-lives-matter.jpg?w=980&e=b87a03eaf6433b2953cadcb120790e39 (accessed 29 May 2025).

3. Kendi depicts the lynchings of Gabriel and Nancy Prosser (85), Vesey (91), and Nat Turner (105).

4. Cf. Wester, "Southern," which mentions Jean Toomer's poem "Portrait in Georgia" (1923): "Hair—braided chestnut, / coiled like a lyncher's rope, / Eye—fagots, / Lips—old scars, or the first red blisters, / Breath—the last sweet scent of cane, / And her slim body, white as the ash / of black flesh after flame."

5. Telephone cords also surround speech balloons in *March: Book Three*'s depiction of the Lyndon Johnson administration's back-channel effort to prevent the representatives of the Mississippi Freedom Democratic Party from being seated at the 1964 Democratic National Convention (121). The phone cord may also be read as a reference to Booker T. Washington's "'grape-vine' telegraph" (14): an alternative communication network used by Black Americans to alert each other of impending dangers.

6. Haensell observes the urge in contemporary Afropolitan literature to "open history's violent chapters first and foremost with the hope of opening up a different, better future" (216).

7. Campt writes of "the frequency of radical Black joy" and celebrates the "depiction of Black flow—the countergravitational capacity of Black folks' ability to defy the deadly downward pull of white supremacy," which manifests in "a defiant refusal to capitulate or be subdued" (*Black* 200).

8. This statement may not hold true for narratives addressed to teenage audiences, especially works written by women, such Magruder; McKinney and Smith; and Gibbs, Gibbs, and Cannon. But these works do not engage deeply with history.

9. On the (im)possibilities or romance in Black Atlantic literature, see Goyal, *Romance*.

10. *Angola Janga* was translated into English, French, and German from the original Portuguese; *Run for It* received the Eisner Award for the Best US Edition of International Material in 2018.

11. In ways rarely seen in US comics, *Angola Janga* juxtaposes images of African sacrificial scars with the branding of the enslaved and the scars inflicted by enslavers through whipping or cutting off fingers. D'Salete also depicts female nudity more openly than do US creators and references the scourged back photograph in *Angola Janga* (244–46, 255, 260, 267) as well as the practice of rubbing salt into wounds (also shown in Baker's *Nat Turner*). References to babies and family (23–24, chap. 2, "Birth"; 55–57, 61, 64–65, 69, 70, 72–74, 235, 257) connect *Angola Janga* with Baker's *Nat Turner*, while depictions of women warriors on the covers of *Angola Janga* and *Run for It* evoke the protagonists of *Wake*.

WORKS CITED

Abouet, Marguerite, and Clément Oubrerie. *Aya: Life in Yop City*. 2007, 2008, 2009. Drawn & Quarterly, 2021.
Achebe, Chinua. *Things Fall Apart*. Heinemann, 1958.
Ackermann, Hans-W., and Jeanine Gauthier. "The Ways and Nature of the Zombi." *Journal of American Folklore* 104.414 (1991): 466–94.
Adair, Gigi. *Kinship Across the Black Atlantic: Writing Diasporic Relations*. Liverpool University Press, 2019.
Ahmed, Maaheen. *Monstrous Imaginaries: The Legacy of Romanticism in Comics*. University Press of Mississippi, 2020.
Ahmed, Maaheen, and Benoît Crucifix, eds. *Comics Memory: Archives and Styles*. Palgrave Macmillan, 2018.
Alaniz, José. *Death, Disability, and the Superhero: The Silver Age and Beyond*. University Press of Mississippi, 2014.
Alaniz, José. "Wakanda Speaks: Animals and Animacy in 'Panther's Rage.'" *The Ages of the Black Panther: Essays on the King of Wakanda in Comics Books*, ed. Joseph J. Darowski. McFarland, 2020. 76–98.
Alexander, Elizabeth. "'Can You Be Black and Look at This?' Reading the Rodney King Video(s)." *Public Culture* 7.1 (1994): 77–94.
Alexander, Michelle. *The New Jim Crow: Mass Incarceration in the Age of Colorblindness*. 10th anniv. ed. New Press, 2020.
Alexandre, Sandy. *The Properties of Violence: Claims to Ownership in Representations of Lynching*. University Press of Mississippi, 2012.
Allen, James. *Without Sanctuary: Lynching Photography in America*. Twin Palms, 2000.
Alridge, Derrick P. "Teaching Martin Luther King Jr. and the Civil Rights Movement in High School History Courses: Rethinking Content and Pedagogy." *Teaching the American Civil Rights Movement: Freedom's Bittersweet Song*, ed. Julie Buckner Armstrong, Susan Hult Edwards, Houston Bryan Roberson, and Rhonda Y. Williams. Routledge, 2002. 3–17.
Al-Saji, Alia. "Glued to the Image: A Critical Phenomenology of Racialization Through Works of Art." *Journal of Aesthetics and Art Criticism* 77.4 (2019): 475–88.
Altınay, Rüstem Ertuğ, and Olivera Jokić. "Archival Lives of Popular Culture: Our Introduction." *Journal of Popular Culture* 53.6 (2020): 1261–72.

Amistad. Dir. Steven Spielberg. HBO Pictures/DreamWorks, 1997.

Anatol, Giselle Liza. *The Things That Fly in the Night: Female Vampires in Literature of the Circum-Caribbean and African Diaspora*. Rutgers University Press, 2015.

Anderson, Ho Che. "Creating King: Personal and Professional Reflections." *King: A Comics Biography: The Special Edition*. Fantagraphics, 2010. 235–42.

Anderson, Ho Che. *King: A Comics Biography: The Special Edition*. Fantagraphics, 2010.

Anderson, Reynaldo, and Charles E. Jones, eds. *Afrofuturism 2.0.: The Rise of Astro-Blackness*. Lexington, 2015.

Andrade, Emmanuel. "Black Panther Fan Art." *Emmanuel Andrade: Freelance Artist and Illustrator*. https://angar2.artstation.com/projects/baZBkr. Accessed 26 April 2025.

Angelou, Maya. "Still I Rise." *And Still I Rise: A Book of Poems*. Random House, 1978. 41–42.

Anwer, Megha. "Beyond the Photograph: A Graphic History of Lynching." *Journal of Graphic Novels and Comics* 5.1 (2014): 15–28.

Apel, Dora. *Imagery of Lynching: Black Men, White Women, and the Mob*. Rutgers University Press, 2004.

Apel, Dora, and Shawn Michelle Smith. *Lynching Photographs*. University of California Press, 2007.

Appadurai, Arjun. "Archive and Aspiration." *Information Is Alive: Art and Theory on Archiving and Retrieving Data*, ed. Joke Brouwer and Arjen Mulder. V2/NAi, 2003. 14–25.

Araujo, Ana Lucia. *Slavery in the Age of Memory: Engaging the Past*. Bloomsbury, 2020.

Aretha, David, *The Story of Rosa Parks and the Montgomery Bus Boycott in Photographs*. Enslow, 2014.

Armah, Ayi Kwei. *Two Thousand Seasons*. 1973. Heinemann, 1979.

Armstrong, Julie Buckner. "Afterword: Hidden Memories." *Elegy for Mary Turner: An Illustrated Account of a Lynching*, by Rachel Marie-Crane Williams. Verso, 2021. 51–53.

Armstrong, Julie Buckner. *Mary Turner and the Memory of Lynching*. University of Georgia Press, 2011.

Armstrong, Julie Buckner. "Stay Woke: Teaching the Civil Rights Movement Through Literature." *Understanding and Teaching the Civil Rights Movement*, ed. Hasan Kwame Jeffries. University of Wisconsin Press, 2019. 261–75.

Armstrong, Julie Buckner, Susan Hult Edwards, Houston Bryan Roberson, and Rhonda Y. Williams, eds. *Teaching the American Civil Rights Movement: Freedom's Bittersweet Song*. Routledge, 2002.

Arnold, Edwin T. *What Virtue There Is in Fire: Cultural Memory and the Lynching of Sam Hose*. University of Georgia Press, 2009.

Arsenault, Raymond. *Freedom Riders: 1961 and the Struggle for Racial Justice*. Oxford University Press, 2006.

Ashe, Bertram D., and Ilka Saal, eds. *Slavery and the Post-Black Imagination*. University of Washington Press, 2020.

Asma, Stephen T. *On Monsters: An Unnatural History of Our Worst Fears*. Oxford University Press, 2009.

Assmann, Aleida. "Canon and Archive." *Cultural Memory Studies: An International and Interdisciplinary Handbook*, ed. Astrid Erll and Ansgar Nünning. De Gruyter, 2008. 97–107.

Assmann, Aleida. *Cultural Memory and Western Civilization: Functions, Media, Archives*. 1999. Cambridge University Press, 2011.

Austin, Allan W., and Patrick L. Hamilton. *All New, All Different? A History of Race and the American Superhero*. University of Texas Press, 2019.

Azoulay, Ariella Aïsha. *Civil Contract of Photography*. Trans. Rela Mazali and Ruvik Danieli. Zone, 2008.

Azoulay, Ariella Aïsha. *Civil Imagination: A Political Ontology of Photography*. 2012. Trans. Louise Bethlehem. Verso, 2015.

Bailey, Amy Kate, and Stewart E. Tolnay. *Lynched: The Victims of Southern Mob Violence*. University of North Carolina Press, 2015.

Baker, Christina N. "Introduction: Embracing Black Feminist Joy and Pleasure in Communication Studies." *Women's Studies in Communication* 44.4 (2021): 459–62.

Baker, Courtney R. *Humane Insight: Looking at Images of African American Suffering and Death*. University of Illinois Press, 2015.

Baker, Kyle. *Nat Turner*. Abrams, 2008.

Baldwin, James. "Come Out the Wilderness." 1958. *Going to Meet the Man*. Dell, 1965. 170–97.

Baldwin, James. "Going to Meet the Man." *Going to Meet the Man*. Dell, 1965. 198–218.

Ball, Alverne, and Stacey Robinson. *Across the Tracks: Remembering Greenwood, Black Wall Street, and the Tulsa Race Massacre*. Abrams ComicArts Megascope, 2021.

Bambara, Toni Cade. "On the Issue of Roles." *The Black Woman: An Anthology*, ed. Toni Cade Bambara. Signet, 1970. 101–10.

Bambara, Toni Cade. *The Salt Eaters*. Random House, 1980.

Banks, Ingrid. *Hair Matters: Beauty, Power, and Black Women's Consciousness*. New York University Press, 2000.

Baraka, Amiri [LeRoi Jones]. *It's Nation Time: African Visionary Music*. Black Forum/Motown, 1972.

Baraka, Amiri [LeRoi Jones]. *Slave Ship: An Historical Pageant*. 1967. *The Motion of History and Other Plays*. Morrow, 1978. 131–50.

Barber, Tiffany. "From Dark Water to Dark Matter: An Interview with John Jennings." 2018. *John Jennings: Conversations*, ed. Donna-lyn Washington. University Press of Mississippi, 2020. 54–62.

Barnes, Rodney, Jason Shawn Alexander, Luis Nct, and Marshall Dillon. *Sins of the Father*. Killadelphia, vol. 1. Image Comics, 2020.

Barnes, Rodney, Jason Shawn Alexander, Luis Nct, Marshall Dillon, and Bill Sienkiewicz. *Burn Baby Burn*. Killadelphia, vol. 2. Image Comics, 2021.

Barnes, Rodney, Jason Shawn Alexander, Luis Nct, Marshall Dillon, and Chris Mitten. *Home Is Where the Hatred Is*. Killadelphia, vol. 3. Image Comics, 2021.

Barnes, Rodney, Jason Shawn Alexander, Luis Nct, and Marshall Dillon. *The End of All*. Killadelphia, vol. 4. Image Comics, 2022.

Barnes, Rodney, Jason Shawn Alexander, German Erramouspe, and Lee Loughridge. *There's No Place Like Home*. Killadelphia, vol. 5. Image Comics, 2023.

Barnes, Rodney, Jason Shawn Alexander, German Erramouspe, and Lee Loughridge. *Death Be Not Proud*. Killadelphia, vol. 6. Image Comics, 2024.

Barnes, Rodney, David Brame, and Hector Negrete. *Shook! A Black Horror Anthology*. Dark Horse Comics, 2024.

Barrett, Lindon. *Racial Blackness and the Discontinuity of Western Modernity*, ed. Justin A. Joyce, Dwight A. McBride, and John Carlos Rowe. University of Illinois Press, 2014.

Bellino, Michelle J., and Darin Stockdill. *March, Book One: Reading Guide for University Level Student Discussions*. University of Michigan LSA International Institute/Center for Education Design, Evaluation, and Research, 2017.

Bendis, Brian Michael, Oscar Bazaldua, Nico Leon, and Sara Pichelli. *Spider-Man: Miles Morales*. Marvel Comics, 2019.

Bendis, Brian Michael, Jonathan Hickman, Nick Spencer, Sara Pichelli, Salvador Larroca, and Clayton Crain. *Ultimate Comics: Fallout 4*. Marvel Comics, October 2011.

Benson, Josef, and Doug Singsen. *Bandits, Misfits, and Superheroes: Whiteness and Its Borderlands in American Comics and Graphic Novels*. University Press of Mississippi, 2022.

Berg, Manfred. *Popular Justice: A History of Lynching in America*. Dee, 2011.

Berger, Martin A. *Seeing Through Race: A Reinterpretation of Civil Rights Photography*. University of California Press, 2011.

Berlatsky, Noah. "'I Wasn't Writing About the Work I Find Most Valuable': An Interview with Marc Singer." *The Comics Journal*, 13 March 2019. https://www.tcj.com/an-interview-with-marc-singer/.

Bernier, Celeste-Marie. *Stick to the Skin: African American and Black British Art, 1965–2015*. University of California Press, 2019.

Bernier, Celeste-Marie, and Nicole Wilson. "We Were Brave, We Were Strong, We Survived: Acts and Arts of Liberation in the African Atlantic Imaginary." *Slavery & Abolition* 41.1 (2020): 1–13.

Bernstein, Patricia. *The First Waco Horror: The Lynching of Jesse Washington and the Rise of the NAACP*. Texas A&M University Press, 2006.

Bernstein, Robin. *Racial Innocence: Performing American Childhood from Slavery to Civil Rights*. New York University Press, 2011.

Berry, Daina Ramey, and Kali Nicole Gross. *A Black Women's History of the United States*. Beacon, 2020.

Best, Stephen. "Neither Lost nor Found: Slavery and the Visual Archive." *Representations* 113.1 (2011): 150–63.

Bibb, Henry. *The Life and Adventures of Henry Bibb: An American Slave*. 1849. University of Wisconsin Press, 2000.

The Birth of a Nation. Dir. D. W. Griffith. Epoch, 1915.

The Birth of a Nation. Dir. Nate Parker. Fox Searchlight, 2016.

Black Panther. Dir. Ryan Coogler. Marvel Studios, 2018.

Black Panther: Wakanda Forever. Dir. Ryan Coogler. Marvel Studios, 2022.

Blaser, Thomas M. "Africa and the Future." Interview with Achille Mbembe. *Africa Is a Country*, 20 November 2013. https://africasacountry.com/2013/11/africa-and-the-future-an-interview-with-achille-mbembe/.

Blassingame, John W. *The Slave Community: Plantation Life in the Antebellum South*. Oxford University Press, 1972.

Blaufarb, Rafe, and Liz Clarke. *Inhuman Traffick: The International Struggle Against the Transatlantic Slave Trade: A Graphic History*. Oxford University Press, 2015.

Bodroghkozy, Aniko. *Equal Time: Television and the Civil Rights Movement*. University of Illinois Press, 2012.

Body of George Hughes Hanging from a Tree, Sherman, Texas. 9 May 1930. International Center of Photography, www.icp.org/browse/archive/objects/body-of-george-hughes-hanging-from-a-tree-sherman-texas.

Boonin-Vail, Eli. "'The Body of the Nation': Ta-Nehisi Coates' *Black Panther* and the Black Literary Tradition." *Inks: The Journal of the Comics Studies Society* 4.2 (2020): 135–55.

Boykin, Jessica. "Filling in the Gutters: Graphic Biographies Disrupting Dominant Narratives of the Civil Rights Movement." *Journal of Multimodal Rhetorics* 3.1 (2019): 68–85.

Braham, Persephone. "The Monstrous Caribbean." *The Ashgate Research Companion to Monsters and the Monstrous*, ed. Asa Simon Mittman, with Peter J. Dendle. Ashgate, 2012. 17–47.

Brand, Dionne. *A Map to the Door of No Return: Notes to Belonging*. Random House Canada, 2001.

Brand, Dionne. "On Narrative, Reckoning and the Calculus of Living and Dying." *Toronto Star*, 4 July 2020.

Brathwaite, Kamau. *Middle Passages*. Bloodaxe, 1992.

Breckenridge, Janis, and Madelyn Peterson. "Lila Quintero Weaver's 'Darkroom: A Memoir in Black and White': Envisioning Equality." *Confluencia* 29.1 (2013): 109–25.

Bright, Sheila Pree. *#1960Now: Photographs of Civil Rights Activists and Black Lives Matter Protests*. Chronicle, 2018.

"The *Brookes*—Visualising the Transatlantic Slave Trade." *1807 Commemorated: The Abolition of the Slave Trade*, 2007, https://archives.history.ac.uk/1807commemorated/exhibitions/museums/brookes.html.

Brooks, Kinitra D. "The Root of the Matter: Rootwork and Conjure in Black Popular Culture." *Bitter Root Omnibus: Book One*, by David F. Walker, Chuck Brown, and Sanford Greene. Image Comics, 2023. 141.

Brooks, Kinitra D. *Searching for Sycorax: Black Women's Hauntings of Contemporary Horror*. Rutgers University Press, 2018.

Brooks, Maegan Parker. *A Voice That Could Stir an Army: Fannie Lou Hamer and the Rhetoric of the Black Freedom Movement*. University Press of Mississippi, 2014.

Brooks, Tim. *The Blackface Minstrel Show in Mass Media: 20th Century Performances on Radio, Records, Film and Television*. McFarland, 2019.

Broonzy, Big Bill. "Mississippi River Blues." Bluebird Records, 1934.

Brown, Chuck, Prenzy, and Clayton Cowles. *On the Stump*. Image Comics, 2020.

Brown, Jeffrey A. *Black Superheroes, Milestone Comics, and Their Fans*. University Press of Mississippi, 2001.

Brown, Jeffrey A. "Panthers and Vixens: Black Superheroines, Sexuality, and Stereotypes in Contemporary Comic Books." *Black Comics: Politics of Race and Representation*, ed. Sheena C. Howard and Ronald L. Jackson II. Bloomsbury, 2013. 133–49.

Brown, Kimberly Juanita. *Mortevivum: Photography and the Politics of the Visual*. MIT Press, 2024.

Brown, Kimberly Juanita. *The Repeating Body: Slavery's Visual Resonance in the Contemporary*. Duke University Press, 2015.

Brown, Sterling. "Bitter Fruit of the Tree." 1939. *The Norton Anthology of American Literature, 1914–1945*, ed. Nina Baym et al., vol. D. Norton, 2012. 869.

Brown, Vincent. "Mapping a Slave Revolt: Visualizing Spatial History Through the Archives of Slavery." *Social Text* 125.33 (2015): 134–41.

Browne, Simone. *Dark Matters: On the Surveillance of Blackness*. Duke University Press, 2015.

Brown-Guillory, Elizabeth, ed. *Middle Passages and the Healing Place of History: Migration and Identity in Black Women's Literature*. Ohio State University Press, 2006.

Bruce, La Marr Jurelle. *How to Go Mad Without Losing Your Mind: Madness and Black Radical Creativity*. Duke University Press, 2021.
Brundage, W. Fitzhugh, ed. *Under Sentence of Death: Lynching in the South*. University of North Carolina Press, 1997.
Bruno, Tim. "Nat Turner After 9/11: Kyle Baker's *Nat Turner*." *Journal of American Studies* 50.4 (2016): 923–51.
Bukatman, Scott. *Black Panther*. University of Texas Press, 2022.
Bukatman, Scott. *Hellboy's World: Comics and Monsters on the Margins*. University of California Press, 2016.
Bukatman, Scott. *Matters of Gravity: Special Effects and Supermen in the 20th Century*. Duke University Press, 2003.
Burger, Alissa, ed. *Teaching Graphic Novels in the English Classroom: Pedagogical Possibilities of Multimodal Literacy Engagement*. Palgrave Macmillan, 2018.
Burger, Bibi, and Laura Engels. "'A Nation Under Our Feet': *Black Panther*, Afrofuturism and the Potential of Thinking Through Political Structures." *Image & Text* 33 (2019): http://dx.doi.org/10.17159/2617-3255/2018/n33a2.
Burke, Chesya. *Hero Me Not: The Containment of the Most Powerful Black, Female Superhero*. Rutgers University Press, 2023.
Burroughs, Todd Steven. *Marvel's Black Panther: A Comic Book Biography, from Stan Lee to Ta-Nehisi Coates*. Diasporic Africa Press, 2018.
Burton, Antoinette. *Archive Stories: Facts, Fictions, and the Writing of History*. Duke University Press, 2005.
Byrd, Ayana D., and Lori L. Tharps. *Hair Story: Untangling the Roots of Black Hair in America*. St. Martin's, 2001.
Cameron, James. *A Time of Terror: A Survivor's Story*. 1994. Rev. ed. Lifewrites, 2016.
Camp, Stephanie M. H. *Closer to Freedom: Enslaved Women and Everyday Resistance in the Plantation South*. University of North Carolina Press, 2004.
Campbell, Bill, and Bizhan Khodabandeh. *The Day the Klan Came to Town*. PM, 2021.
Campt, Tina M. *A Black Gaze: Artists Changing How We See*. MIT Press, 2021.
Campt, Tina M. *Listening to Images*. Duke University Press, 2017.
Canot, Theodore. *Captain Canot; or, Twenty Years of an African Slaver*, ed. Brantz Mayer. Appleton, 1854.
Canuto, Hugo. *Tales of the Orishas*, trans. Victor Dias and Tony Soares. Abrams ComicArts Megascope, 2023.
Capshaw, Katharine. "Photography and Dissent in John Lewis's Graphic Novel *March*." *Landscapes of Realism: Rethinking Literary Realism in Comparative Perspectives*, vol. 2, *Pathways Through Realism*, ed. Svend Erik Larsen, Steen Bille Jørgensen, and Margaret R. Higonnet. Benjamins, 2022. 535–48.
Carbonell, Bettina M. "The Afterlife of Lynching: Exhibitions and Re-Composition of Human Suffering." *Mississippi Quarterly* 61.1–2 (2008): 197–215.
Carby, Hazel V. *Reconstructing Womanhood: The Emergence of the Afro-American Woman Novelist*. Oxford University Press, 1987.
"[Caricature of an African American Child Drinking Ink]." *Library of Congress*, https://www.loc.gov/resource/cph.3g04296/. Accessed 26 May 2025.
Carlson, Peter. "In Arbery's Death, an Echo of the 'Sundown Towns' That Banned and Threatened Black People." *Washington Post*, 23 November 2021.

Caron, Tim. "'Black and White and Red All Over': Representing Race in Mat Johnson and Warren Pleece's *Incognegro: A Graphic Mystery*." *Comics and the U.S. South*, ed. Brannon Costello and Qiana J. Whitted. University Press of Mississippi, 2012. 138–60.

Carpenter, Stanford W. "Opening the Box." *Box of Bones: Book One*, by Ayize Jama-Everett and John Jennings. Rosarium, 2021.

Carpenter, Stanford W. "Truth Be Told: Authorship and the Creation of the Black Captain America." *Comics as Philosophy*, ed. Jeff McLaughlin. University Press of Mississippi, 2005. 46–62.

Carr, Cynthia. *Our Town: A Heartland Lynching, a Haunted Town, and the Hidden History of White America*. Crown, 2006.

Carroll, Noël. *The Philosophy of Horror; or, Paradoxes of the Heart*. 1990. Routledge, 2004.

Caruth, Cathy, ed. *Trauma: Explorations in Memory*. Johns Hopkins University Press, 1995.

Caruth, Cathy. *Unclaimed Experience: Trauma, Narrative, and History*. Johns Hopkins University Press, 1996.

Chamberlin, Barbara. "Patterns Beneath the Grid: The Haunted Spaces of Folk Horror Comics." *The Routledge Companion to Folk Horror*, ed. Robert Edgar and Wayne Johnson. Routledge, 2023. 331–41.

Chambliss, Julian C. "A Different Nation: Continuing a Legacy of Decolonization in *Black Panther*." *The Ages of the Black Panther: Essays on the King of Wakanda in Comic Books*, ed. Joseph J. Darowski. McFarland, 2020. 204–19.

Chambliss, Julian C. "The Soul of Black Comics: An Interview with John Jennings." 2017. *John Jennings: Conversations*, ed. Donna-lyn Washington. University Press of Mississippi, 2020. 50–53.

Chambliss, Julian C. "Black Kirby Now: An Interview with John Jennings." 2014. *John Jennings: Conversations*, ed. Donna-lyn Washington. University Press of Mississippi, 2020. 21–25.

Chaney, Michael A. "Drawing on History in Recent African American Graphic Novels." *MELUS* 32.3 (2007): 175–200.

Chaney, Michael A. "Is There an African American Graphic Novel?" *Teaching the Graphic Novel*, ed. Stephen E. Tabachnik. MLA, 2009. 69–75.

Chaney, Michael A. "Misreading with the President: Re-Reading the Covers of John Lewis's *March*." *International Journal of Comic Art* 20.1 (2018): 25–42.

Chaney, Michael A. "On the Nature of the Boundary in Comics Memoir: The Case of *March*." *Comics an der Grenze: Sub/Versionen von Form und Inhalt*, ed. Matthias Harbeck, Linda-Rabea Heyden, and Marie Schröer. Bachmann, 2017. 49–58.

Chaney, Michael A. *Reading Lessons in Seeing: Mirrors, Masks, and Mazes in the Autobiographical Graphic Novel*. University Press of Mississippi, 2016.

Chaney, Michael A. "Slave Memory Without Words in Kyle Baker's *Nat Turner*." *Callaloo* 36.2 (2013): 279–97.

Charras, Françoise. "Landings: Robert Hayden's and Kamau Brathwaite's Poetic Renderings of the Middle Passage in Comparative Perspective." *Black Imagination and the Middle Passage*, ed. Maria Diedrich, Henry Louis Gates Jr., and Carl Pedersen. Oxford University Press, 1999. 57–69.

Chassot, Joanne. *Ghosts of the African Diaspora: Re-Visioning History, Memory, and Identity*. Dartmouth College Press, 2018.

Chesnutt, Charles W. *The Conjure Woman*. 1899. *Charles W. Chesnutt: Stories, Novels, and Essays*, ed. Werner Sollors. Library of America, 2002. 5–95.

Chireau, Yvonne P. *Black Magic: Religion and the African American Conjuring Tradition.* University of California Press, 2003.

Chireau, Yvonne P. "From Horror to Heroes: Mythologies of Graphic Voodoo in Comics." *A New Gnosis: Comic Books, Comparative Mythology, and Depth Psychology*, ed. David M. Odorisio. Palgrave Macmillan, 2023. 27–57.

Chireau, Yvonne P. "Looking for Black Religions in 20th Century Comics, 1931–1993." *Religion* 10.6 (2019): https://doi.org/10.3390/rel10060400.

Chute, Hillary L. *Disaster Drawn: Visual Witness, Comics, and Documentary Form.* Belknap Press of Harvard University Press, 2016.

Chute, Hillary L., and Marianne DeKoven. "Introduction: Graphic Narrative." *MFS Modern Fiction Studies* 52.4 (2006): 767–82.

Clarke, John Henrik, ed. *William Styron's Nat Turner: Ten Black Writers Respond.* Beacon, 1968.

Clarke, Matthew, and Nigel Lynch. *Hardears.* Abrams ComicArts Megascope, 2021.

Clifford, Carrie Williams. "Little Mother (Upon the Lynching of Mary Turner[)]." 1922. *African American Poetry: A Digital Anthology*, by Amardeep Singh. https://scalar.lehigh.edu/african-american-poetry-a-digital-anthology/carrie-williams-clifford-little-mother-upon-the-lynching-of-mary-turner-1922. Accessed 25 June 2025.

Clifton, Lucille. "The Photograph: A Lynching." *Blessing the Boats: New and Selected Poems, 1988–2000.* BOA Editions, 2000. 19.

Clifton, Lucille. "Slaveships." *Blessing the Boats: New and Selected Poems, 1988–2000.* BOA Editions, 2000. 121.

Cloutier, Jean-Christophe. *Shadow Archives: The Lifecycles of African American Literature.* Columbia University Press, 2019.

Coates, Ta-Nehisi. *The Beautiful Struggle.* 2008. Verso, 2016.

Coates, Ta-Nehisi. *Between the World and Me.* Spiegel & Grau, 2015.

Coates, Ta-Nehisi. "The Case for Reparations." *The Atlantic*, June 2014. Rpt. *We Were Eight Years in Power: An American Tragedy.* Hamilton, 2017. 163–208.

Coates, Ta-Nehisi. "The Return of the Black Panther." *The Atlantic*, April 2016.

Coates, Ta-Nehisi. "Wakanda and the Black Aesthetic." *The Atlantic*, 29 June 2016.

Coates, Ta-Nehisi. *The Water Dancer.* One World/Random House, 2019.

Coates, Ta-Nehisi. *We Were Eight Years in Power: An American Tragedy.* Hamilton, 2017.

Coates, Ta-Nehisi. "Why I'm Writing *Captain America* and Why It Scares the Hell Out of Me." *The Atlantic*, 28 February 2018.

Coates, Ta-Nehisi, et al. *Black Panther: A Nation Under Our Feet.* Books 1–3. Marvel Comics, 2016–17.

Coates, Ta-Nehisi, et al. *Black Panther: Avengers of the New World.* Parts 1–2 [Books 4–5]. Marvel Comics, 2017–18.

Coates, Ta-Nehisi, et al. *Black Panther: The Intergalactic Empire of Wakanda.* Parts 1–3 [Books 6–8]. Marvel Comics, 2018–19.

Coates, Ta-Nehisi, Yona Harvey, et al. *Black Panther & The Crew: We Are the Streets.* Marvel Comics, 2017.

Cohen, Jeffrey Jerome. "Monster Culture (Seven Theses)." 1996. *The Monster Theory Reader*, ed. Jeffrey Andrew Weinstock. University of Minnesota Press, 2020. 37–56.

Cohen, Jeffrey Jerome. "Preface: In a Time of Monsters." *Monster Theory: Reading Culture*, ed. Jeffrey Jerome Cohen. University of Minnesota Press, 1996. vii–xiv.

Cole, Teju. "On the Blackness of the Panther." *Medium.com*, 6 March 2018. https://medium.com/s/story/on-the-blackness-of-the-panther-f76d771b0e80.

Cole, Teju. "A Photograph Never Stands Alone." *New York Times Magazine*, 14 March 2017.

Cole, Teju. "The Superhero Photographs of the Black Lives Matter Movement." *New York Times Magazine*, 26 July 2016.

Coleman, Robin R. Means. *Horror Noire: A History of Black American Horror from the 1890s to Present*. 2nd ed. Routledge, 2023.

Collier-Thomas, Bettye, and V. P. Franklin, eds. *Sisters in the Struggle: African American Women in the Civil Rights–Black Power Movement*. New York University Press, 2001.

Collins, Patricia Hill. "The Tie That Binds: Race, Gender and US Violence." *Ethnic and Racial Studies* 21.5 (1998): 917–38.

Colomba, Elizabeth, and Aurélie Levy. *Queenie: Godmother of Harlem*. 2021. Abrams ComicArts Megascope, 2023.

Cone, James H. *The Cross and the Lynching Tree*. 2011. Orbis, 2021.

Connor, Julia Johnson. "'The Textbooks Never Said Anything About . . .': Adolescents Respond to *The Middle Passage: White Ships/Black Cargo*." *Journal of Adolescent & Adult Literacy* 47.3 (2003): 240–46.

Costello, Brannon, and Qiana J. Whitted, eds. *Comics and the U.S. South*. University Press of Mississippi, 2012.

Cowan, William Tynes. *The Slave in the Swamp: Disrupting the Plantation Narrative*. Routledge, 2005.

Cox, Ida. "Mojo Hand Blues." Paramount, 1927.

Crawford, Dustin. "The Lynching of George Hughes." *East Texas History*, https://easttexashistory.org/items/show/367. Accessed 7 September 2023.

Crawford, Vicki L., Jacqueline Anne Rouse, and Barbara Woods, eds. *Women in the Civil Rights Movement: Trailblazers and Torchbearers, 1941–1965*. 1990. Indiana University Press, 1993.

Crenshaw, Kimberlé. "Demarginalizing the Intersection of Race and Sex: A Black Feminist Critique of Antidiscrimination Doctrine, Feminist Theory and Antiracist Politics." *University of Chicago Legal Forum* 1 (1989): 139–67.

Crownson, David, Courtland Ellis, Joey Vazquez, et al. *Harriet Tubman: Demon Slayer*. 2017–.

Crucifix, Benoît. *Drawing from the Archives: Comics Memory in the Contemporary Graphic Novel*. Cambridge University Press, 2023.

Cruse, Howard. *Stuck Rubber Baby*. 1995. DC Comics, 2010.

Cugoano, Quobna Ottobah. *Thoughts and Sentiments on the Evil of Slavery*, ed. Vincent Carretta. Penguin, 1999.

Cunningham, Phillip Lamarr. "The Absence of Black Supervillains in Mainstream Comics." *Journal of Graphic Novels and Comics* 1.1 (2010): 51–62.

Cussans, John. *Undead Uprising: Haiti, Horror and the Zombie Complex*. MIT Press, 2017.

Cutter, Martha J. "Redrawing Race: Renovations of the Graphic and Narrative History of Racial Passing in Mat Johnson and Warren Pleece's *Incognegro*." *Redrawing the Historical Past: History, Memory, and Multiethnic Graphic Novels*, ed. Martha J. Cutter and Cathy J. Schlund-Vials. University of Georgia Press, 2018. 18–40.

Dabiri, Emma. *Don't Touch My Hair*. Penguin, 2019.

Dando, Michael Norton. "To the Griot in Times of Terror." *Bitter Root Omnibus: Book One*, by David F. Walker, Chuck Brown, and Sanford Greene. Image Comics, 2023. 331–32.

Darowski, Joseph J. *The Ages of the Black Panther: Essays on the King of Wakanda in Comic Books*. McFarland, 2020.

Daughters of the Dust. Dir. Julie Dash. Kino International, 1991.

Davis, Blair. "*All-Negro Comics* and the Birth of Lion Man, the First African American Superhero." *Inks: The Journal of the Comics Studies Society* 3.3 (2019): 273–97.

Davis-McElligatt, Joanna C. "On Being the First Black Woman." *Narratives of Marginalized Identities in Higher Education: Inside and Outside the Academy*, ed. Santosh Khadka, Joanna Davis-McElligatt, and Keith Dorwick. Routledge, 2018. 42–54.

Davis-McElligatt, Joanna C. "Rebellious Affects: Black Joy, Pleasure, and Happiness as Counterabjection." Call for Papers, MLA 2024, 24 February 2023. https://call-for-papers.sas.upenn.edu/cfp/2023/02/24/rebellious-affects-black-joy-pleasure-and-happiness-as-counterabjection.

Davis-McElligatt, Joanna C. "'Walk Together, Children': The Function and Interplay of Comics, History, and Memory in *Martin Luther King and the Montgomery Story* and John Lewis's *March: Book One*." *Graphic Novels for Children and Young Adults: A Collection of Critical Essays*, ed. Michelle Ann Abate and Gwen Athene Tarbox. University Press of Mississippi, 2017. 298–311.

Davis-McElligatt, Joanna C. "White Black Men and Black White Men: Reading Race as Violence in Mat Johnson and Warren Pleece's *Incognegro: A Graphic Mystery*." *BOOM! SPLAT! Comics and Violence*, ed. Jim Coby and Joanna Davis-McElligatt. University Press of Mississippi, 2024. 83–99.

Dawes, Kwame. *Requiem: A Lament for the Dead*. Peepal Tree, 1996.

Dawson, Kevin. *Undercurrents of Power: Aquatic Culture in the African Diaspora*. University of Pennsylvania Press, 2018.

de Bruin-Molé, Megen. *Gothic Remixed: Monster Mashups and Frankenfictions in 21st-Century Culture*. Bloomsbury, 2019.

The Defiant Ones. Dir. Stanley Kramer. United Artists, 1958.

De Kosnik, Abigail. *Rogue Archives: Digital Cultural Memory and Media Fandom*. MIT Press, 2016.

Delaney, Martin R. *Blake; or, the Huts of America: A Corrected Edition*, ed. Jerome McGann. Harvard University Press, 2017.

Denson, Shane, Christina Meyer, and Daniel Stein, eds. *Transnational Perspectives on Graphic Narratives: Comics at the Crossroads*. Bloomsbury, 2013.

Derrida, Jacques. "Archive Fever: A Freudian Impression," trans. Eric Prenowitz. *Diacritics* 25.2 (1995): 9–63.

DeviantArt.com, https://www.deviantart.com/search?q=black+panther. Accessed 25 May 2025.

Diedrich, Maria, Henry Louis Gates Jr., and Carl Pedersen, eds. *Black Imagination and the Middle Passage*. Oxford University Press, 1999.

Diouf, Sylviane A. *Slavery's Exiles: The Story of the American Maroons*. New York University Press, 2014.

Dittmer, Jason. *Captain America and the Nationalist Superhero: Metaphors, Narratives, and Geopolitics*. Temple University Press, 2012.

Dittmer, Jason, and Daniel Bos. *Popular Culture, Geopolitics, and Identity*. 2nd ed. Rowman & Littlefield, 2019.

Dixon, Thomas, Jr. *The Clansman: An Historical Romance of the Ku Klux Klan*. 1905. University Press of Kentucky, 1970.

Dong, Lan, ed. *Teaching Comics and Graphic Narratives: Essays on Theory, Strategy and Practice*. McFarland, 2012.

Douglass, Frederick. *Narrative of the Life of Frederick Douglass, an American Slave, Written by Himself*. 1845. Ed. William L. Andrews and William S. McFeely. Norton, 1997.

Drake, Frederick C., ed. "Secret History of the Slave Trade to Cuba Written by an American Naval Officer, Robert Wilson Schufeldt." 1861. *Journal of Negro History* 55.3 (1970): 218–35.

D'Salete, Marcelo. *Angola Janga: Kingdom of Runaway Slaves*. 2017. Trans. Andrea Rosenberg. Fantagraphics, 2019.

D'Salete, Marcelo. *Run for It: Stories of Slaves Who Fought for Their Freedom*. 2014. Trans. Andrea Rosenberg. Fantagraphics, 2017.

Du Bois, W. E. B. *Dusk of Dawn*. 1940. Oxford University Press, 2014.

Du Bois, W. E. B. *The Souls of Black Folk*. 1903. *The Oxford W. E. B. Du Bois Reader*, ed. Eric J. Sundquist. Oxford University Press, 1996. 97–240.

Due, Tananarive. *The Between*. HarperCollins, 1995.

Due, Tananarive. *The Good House*. Atria, 2003.

Due, Tananarive. "Healing Our Histories Through the Lens of Horror: Guest of Honor Plenary Address Online at VICFA 2022, 'The Global Fantastic.'" *Journal of the Fantastic in the Arts* 33.3 (2022): 132–51.

Due, Tananarive. *Joplin's Ghost*. Atria, 2005.

Due, Tananarive, Steven Barnes, and Marco Finnegan. *The Keeper*. Abrams ComicArts Megascope, 2022.

Duffy, Damian. "The Appetite for Hunger." *The Hole: Consumer Culture*, vol. 1, *Open*, by Damian Duffy and John Jennings. Front Forty, 2008. 153–55.

Duffy, Damian. "Deep Structures: Technosocial Meanings of the Bitter Root Logo." *Bitter Root Omnibus: Book One*, by David F. Walker, Chuck Brown, and Sanford Greene. Image Comics, 2023. 324–25.

Duffy, Damian, and John Jennings. *The Hole: Consumer Culture*, vol. 1, *Open*. Front Forty, 2008.

Dumas, Henry. "Rootsong." *Poetry for My People*, ed. Hale Chatfield and Eugene Redmond. Southern Illinois University Press, 1970. 24–25.

Dunning, Stefanie K. *Black to Nature: Pastoral Return and African American Culture*. University Press of Mississippi, 2021.

Durham, Michael S. *Powerful Days: The Civil Rights Photography of Charles Moore*. Stewart, Tabori & Chan, 1991.

Earle, Monalesia. *Writing Queer Women of Color: Representation and Misdirection in Contemporary Fiction and Graphic Narratives*. McFarland, 2019.

Ellison, Ralph. *Invisible Man*. 1952. Random House, 1982.

Elmer, Jonathan. "The Black Atlantic Archive." *American Literary History* 17.1 (2005): 160–70.

Elysee, Greg Anderson. "Diversifying Comics with John Jennings." 2015. *John Jennings: Conversations*, ed. Donna-lyn Washington. University Press of Mississippi, 2020. 33–45.

Emanuel, James A. "The Middle Passage Blues." *Black Imagination and the Middle Passage*, ed. Maria Diedrich, Henry Louis Gates Jr., and Carl Pedersen. Oxford University Press, 1999. 3–4.

Emerson, Ralph Waldo. *Nature*. Munroe, 1836.

Entman, Robert M. "Framing: Toward Clarification of a Fractured Paradigm." *Journal of Communication* 43.4 (1993): 51–58.

Equal Justice Initiative. *Lynching in America: Confronting the Legacy of Racial Terror*. 3rd ed. Montgomery: Equal Justice Initiative, 2017.

Equiano, Olaudah. *The Interesting Narrative and Other Writings*, ed. Vincent Carretta. Penguin, 2003.

Erikson, Peter. "The Black Atlantic in the Twenty-First Century: Artistic Passages, Circulations, Revisions." *Nka: Journal of Contemporary African Art* 24 (2009): 56–71.

Evans, Becca. "Conversations at the Cohen Center: Episode Two." 2018. *John Jennings: Conversations*, ed. Donna-lyn Washington. University Press of Mississippi, 2020. 109–21.

Ewing, Eve L., Luciano Vecchio, Kevin Libranda, et al. *Ironheart: Meant to Fly*. Marvel Comics, 2020.

Eyerman, Ron. *Cultural Trauma: Slavery and the Formation of African American Identity*. Cambridge University Press, 2001.

Eyes on the Prize. Parts 1–2. Prod. Henry Hampton. Public Broadcasting Service, 1987, 1990.

Fanon, Frantz. *The Wretched of the Earth*. 1961. Trans. Richard Philcox. Grove, 2004.

Fawaz, Ramzi. *The New Mutants: Superheroes and the Radical Imagination of American Comics*. New York University Press, 2016.

Fear, David. "'The Water Dancer': Ta-Nehisi Coates' American Odyssey." *Rolling Stone*, 24 September 2019.

Feelings, Tom. *The Middle Passage: White Ships/Black Cargo*. Dial, 1995.

Feelings, Tom. *Tommy Traveler in the World of Black History*. 1958–59. Black Butterfly, 1991.

Feelings, Tom, Joan Bacchus, and Ezra Jackson. *Crispus Attucks and the Minutemen*. Golden Legacy Magazine, vol. 3. Fitzgerald, 1967.

Feldman, Allen. *Archives of the Insensible: Of War, Photopolitics, and Dead Memory*. University of Chicago Press, 2015.

Fellowship of Reconciliation. *Martin Luther King and the Montgomery Story*. 1957. Top Shelf, 2014.

Fine, Theresa A. "*Incognegro* and Portrayals of Lynching." *Graphic History: Essays on Graphic Novels and/as History*, ed. Richard Iadonisi. Cambridge Scholars, 2012. 109–20.

Finley, Cheryl. *Committed to Memory: The Art of the Slave Ship Icon*. Princeton University Press, 2018.

Fisher, Craig. "Provocation Through Polyphony: Kyle Baker's *Nat Turner*." *The Blacker the Ink: Constructions of Black Identity in Comics and Sequential Art*, ed. Frances Gateward and John Jennings. Rutgers University Press, 2015. 255–73.

FitzMaurice, Hollie. "Gender in Wakanda: Exploring Intersectionality and Hyper-Sexualization in Princess Shuri's Tenure as Black Panther." *The Ages of the Black Panther: Essays on the King of Wakanda in Comic Books*, ed. Joseph J. Darowski. McFarland, 2020. 182–92.

Flowers, Arthur, Manu Chitrakar, and Guglielmo Rossi. *I See the Promised Land: A Life of Martin Luther King, Jr.* 2010. Tara, 2013.

Flowers, Ebony. *Hot Comb*. Drawn & Quarterly, 2019.

Flowers, Jonathan. "African Diaspora and Black Bodies: X-Men's Storm." *Immigrants and Comics: Graphic Spaces of Remembrance, Transaction, and Mimesis*, ed. Nhora Lucía Serrano. Routledge, 2021. 225–38.

Foucault, Michel. *The Archaeology of Knowledge and The Discourse on Language*. 1969. Trans. A. M. Sheridan Smith. Pantheon, 1972.

Francis, Consuela. "Drawing the Unspeakable: Kyle Baker's Slave Narrative." *Comics and the U.S. South*, ed. Brannon Costello and Qiana J. Whitted. University Press of Mississippi, 2012. 113–37.

Franklin, Aretha. "Respect." *I Never Loved a Man the Way I Love You*. Atlantic, 1967.

Freeland, Gregory. "Music and the Civil Rights Movement, 1954–1968: A Classroom Approach." *Teaching the American Civil Rights Movement: Freedom's Bittersweet Song*, ed. Julie Buckner Armstrong, Susan Hult Edwards, Houston Bryan Roberson, and Rhonda Y. Williams. Routledge, 2002. 125–40.

Freud, Sigmund. *Beyond the Pleasure Principle*. 1920. *The Standard Edition of the Complete Psychological Works of Sigmund Freud*, vol. 18, 1920–25, trans. James Strachey, Anna Freud, Alix Strachey, and Alan Tyson. Hogarth, 1955.

Fuentes, Marisa J. *Dispossessed Lives: Enslaved Women, Violence, and the Archive*. University of Pennsylvania Press, 2016.

Garber, Marjorie. *Vested Interests: Cross-Dressing and Cultural Anxiety*. Routledge, 1992.

Gardner, Jared. *Projections: Comics and the History of Twenty-First-Century Storytelling*. Stanford University Press, 2012.

Gardner, Sarah E. "Coming of Age in the Movement: Teaching with Personal Narratives." *Teaching the American Civil Rights Movement: Freedom's Bittersweet Song*, ed. Julie Buckner Armstrong, Susan Hult Edwards, Houston Bryan Roberson, and Rhonda Y. Williams. Routledge, 2002. 97–110.

Gates, Eddie Faye. *Riot on Greenwood: The Total Destruction of Black Wall Street*. Eakin, 2003.

Gates, Henry Louis, Jr. *The Signifying Monkey: A Theory of African-American Literary Criticism*. Oxford University Press, 1988.

Gates, Henry Louis, Jr. *Tradition and the Black Atlantic: Critical Theory in the African Diaspora*. Basic Civitas, 2010.

Gateward, Frances, and John Jennings, eds. *The Blacker the Ink: Constructions of Black Identity in Comics and Sequential Art*. Rutgers University Press, 2015.

Gavaler, Chris. "The Ku Klux Klan and the Birth of the Superhero." *Journal of Graphic Novels and Comics* 4.2 (2013): 191–208.

Gay, Roxane. "The Charge to Be Fair: Ta-Nehisi Coates and Roxane Gay in Conversation." *B&N Reads*, 10 August 2015. https://www.barnesandnoble.com/review/the-charge-to-be-fair-ta-nehisi-coates-and-roxane-gay-in-conversation.

Gay, Roxane, Ta-Nehisi Coates, et al. *Black Panther: World of Wakanda*. Marvel Comics, 2017.

Genette, Gérard. *Paratexts: Thresholds of Interpretation*. 1987. Trans. Jane E. Lewin. Cambridge University Press, 1997.

Getz, Trevor R., and Liz Clarke. *Abina and the Important Men: A Graphic History*. Oxford University Press, 2012.

Giannachi, Gabriella. *Archive Everything: Mapping the Everyday*. MIT Press, 2016.

Gibbs, Shawnelle, Shawneé Gibbs, and Emily Cannon. *Ghost Roast*. Versify/HarperCollins, 2024.

Gikandi, Simon. "Rethinking the Archive of Enslavement." *Early American Literature* 50.1 (2015): 81–102.

Gill, Joel Christian. *Bass Reeves. Tales of the Talented Tenth*, vol. 1. Chicago Review Press, 2014.

Gill, Joel Christian. *Bessie Stringfield. Tales of the Talented Tenth*, vol. 2. Fulcrum, 2016.

Gill, Joel Christian. *More Uncelebrated Narratives from Black History. Strange Fruit*, vol. 2. Fulcrum, 2018.

Gill, Joel Christian. *Robert Smalls. Tales of the Talented Tenth*, vol. 3. Chicago Review Press, 2021.

Gill, Joel Christian. *Uncelebrated Narratives from Black History. Strange Fruit*, vol. 1. Fulcrum, 2014.

Gill, Joel Christian. "Why Strange Fruit?" *Uncelebrated Narratives from Black History. Strange Fruit*, vol. 1. Fulcrum, 2014. 2–3.

Gilmore, David D. *Monsters: Evil Beings, Mythical Beasts, and All Manner of Imaginary Terrors*. University of Pennsylvania Press, 2003.

Gilroy, Paul. *The Black Atlantic: Modernity and Double Consciousness*. Verso, 1993.

Gilson, Dave. "These Racist Collectibles Will Make Your Skin Crawl: And They're Still Being Made." *Mother Jones*, March–April 2016.

Giovanni, Nikki. "Alabama Poem." 1976. *Poems, 1968–2020*. Penguin/Random House, 2024. 64–65.

Godfrey, Mollie. "Getting Graphic with *Kindred*: The Neo-Slave Narrative of the Black Lives Matter Movement." *Slavery and the Post-Black Imagination*, ed. Bertram D. Ashe and Ilka Saal. University of Washington Press, 2020. 83–105.

Goldsby, Jacqueline. *A Spectacular Secret: Lynching in American Life and Literature*. University of Chicago Press, 2006.

Goldstein, Nancy. *Jackie Ormes: The First African American Woman Cartoonist*. University of Michigan Press, 2008.

Gonzales, Aston. *Visualizing Equality: African American Rights and Visual Culture in the Nineteenth Century*. University of North Carolina Press, 2020.

Gonzales-Day, Ken. "Erased Lynchings." *Ken Gonzales-Day*, https://kengonzalesday.com/projects/erased-lynchings/. Accessed 29 April 2025.

Gonzales-Day, Ken. *Lynching in the West, 1850–1935*. Duke University Press, 2006.

Gordon, Avery F. *Ghostly Matters: Haunting and the Sociological Imagination*. 1997. University of Minnesota Press, 2008.

Goyal, Yogita. *Romance, Diaspora, and Black Atlantic Literature*. Cambridge University Press, 2010.

Goyal, Yogita. *Runaway Genres: The Global Afterlives of Slavery*. New York University Press, 2019.

Graff, Gilda. "The Intergenerational Trauma of Slavery and Its Aftermath." *Journal of Psychohistory* 41.3 (2014): 181–97.

Gray, Jonathan W. "'Commence the Great Work': The Historical Archive and Unspeakable Violence in Kyle Baker's *Nat Turner*." *Afterimages of Slavery: Essays on Appearances in Recent American Films, Literature, Television and Other Media*, ed. Marlene D. Allen and Seretha D. Williams. McFarland, 2012. 183–200.

Gray, Jonathan W. "A Conflicted Man: An Interview with Ta-Nehisi Coates About *Black Panther*." *New Republic*, 4 April 2016.

Green, Tara T. *Reimagining the Middle Passage: Black Resistance in Literature, Television, and Song*. Ohio State University Press, 2018.

Greenberg, Kenneth S., ed. *Nat Turner: A Slave Rebellion in History and Memory*. Oxford University Press, 2003.

Green's Dictionary of Slang, https://greensdictofslang.com/. Accessed 4 May 2025.

Griaule, Marcel. *Conversations with Ogotemmêli: An Introduction to Dogon Religious Ideas*. 1948. International African Institute, 1965.

Griffin, Farah Jasmine. *"Who Set You Flowin'?" The African-American Migration Narrative*. Oxford University Press, 1995.

Grimké, Angelina Weld. "Goldie." *Selected Works of Angelina Weld Grimké*, ed. Carolivia Herron. Oxford University Press, 1991. 282–306.

Groensteen, Thierry. *The System of Comics*. 1999. Trans. Bart Beaty and Nick Nguyen. University Press of Mississippi, 2007.

Guillory, Monique. "Black Bodies Swingin': Race, Gender, and Jazz." *Soul: Black Power, Politics, and Pleasure*, ed. Monique Guillory and Richard C. Green. New York University Press, 1998. 191–215.

Guillory, Rob. *Reap What Was Sown*. Farmhand, vol. 1. Image Comics, 2019.

Guillory, Rob. *Roots of All Evil*. Farmhand, vol. 3. Image Comics, 2020.

Guillory, Rob. *The Seed*. Farmhand, vol. 4. Image Comics, 2022.

Guillory, Rob. *Thorne in the Flesh*. Farmhand, vol. 2. Image Comics, 2019.

Gunkel, Henriette, and Kara Lynch, eds. *We Travel the Space Ways: Black Imagination, Fragments, and Diffractions*. Transcript, 2019.

Gustines, George Gene. "Ta-Nehisi Coates to Write Black Panther Comic for Marvel." *New York Times*, 22 September 2015.

Gutierrez, Peter. *A Teacher's Guide to March Book One*. Top Shelf, 2015. http://cdn.topshelfcomix.com/guides/march-book-one-teachers-guide.pdf.

Guynes, Sean, and Martin Lund. "Introduction: Not to Interpret, but to Abolish: Whiteness Studies and American Superhero Comics." *Unstable Masks: Whiteness and American Superhero Comics*, ed. Sean Guynes and Martin Lund. Ohio State University Press, 2020. 1–16.

Gyasi, Yaa. *Homecoming*. Penguin/Random House, 2016.

Haddad, Vincent. "#BlackLivesMatter and Cartooning Racial Violence." *BOOM! SPLAT! Comics and Violence*, ed. Jim Coby and Joanna Davis-McElligatt. University Press of Mississippi, 2024. 173–84.

Haensell, Dominique. *Making Black History: Diasporic Fiction in the Moment of Afropolitanism*. De Gruyter, 2021.

Hagood, Taylor. "Nostalgic Realism: Fantasy, History, and Brer Rabbit–Trickster Ambiguity in Jeremy Love's *Bayou*." *Redrawing the Historical Past: History, Memory, and Multiethnic Graphic Novels*, ed. Martha J. Cutter and Cathy J. Schlund-Vials. University of Georgia Press, 2018. 41–60.

Halberstam, Jack [Judith]. *Skin Shows: Gothic Horror and the Technology of Monsters*. Duke University Press, 1995.

Hall, Jacquelyn Dowd. "The Long Civil Rights Movement and the Political Uses of the Past." *Journal of American History* 91.4 (2005): 1233–63.

Hall, Jacquelyn Dowd. *Revolt Against Chivalry: Jessie Daniel Ames and the Women's Campaign Against Lynching*. Columbia University Press, 1993.

Hall, Rebecca, Hugo Martínez, and Sarula Bao. *Wake: The Hidden History of Women-Led Slave Revolts*. Simon & Schuster, 2021.

Hall, Stuart, and Mark Sealy. *Different: A Historical Context*. Phaïdon, 2001.

Hamer, Fannie Lou. "Testimony Before the Credentials Committee, Democratic National Convention—Aug. 22, 1964." *Archives of Women's Political Communication, Iowa State University*, https://awpc.cattcenter.iastate.edu/2017/03/09/testimony-before-the-credentials-committee-democratic-national-convention-aug-22-1964/.

Hamlin, Françoise N., and Charles W. McKinney Jr., eds. *From Rights to Lives: The Evolution of the Black Freedom Struggle*. Vanderbilt University Press, 2024.

Hannah-Jones, Nikole, Renée Watson, and Nikkolas Smith. *The 1619 Project: Born on the Water*. Kolila, 2021.

Haqq, Abuqadim, et al. *The Book of Drexciya*. 2 vols. Drexciyan Empire, 2020–21.

Hardt, Michael, and Antonio Negri. *Empire*. 2000. Harvard University Press, 2001.

Harris, Christopher Paul. *To Build a Black Future: The Radical Politics of Joy, Pain, and Care*. Princeton University Press, 2023.

Harris, Michael D. *Colored Pictures: Race and Visual Representation*. University of North Carolina Press, 2003.

Harris, Trudier. *Exorcising Blackness: Historical and Literary Lynching and Burning Rituals*. Indiana University Press, 1984.

Hartman, Saidiya. "The Dead Book Revisited." *History of the Present* 6.2 (2016): 208–15.

Hartman, Saidiya. *Lose Your Mother: A Journey Along the Atlantic Slave Route*. Farrar, Straus and Giroux, 2007.

Hartman, Saidiya. *Scenes of Subjection: Terror, Slavery, and Self-Making in Nineteenth-Century America*. Rev. and updated ed. Norton, 2022.

Hartman, Saidiya. "The Time of Slavery." *South Atlantic Quarterly* 101.4 (2002): 757–77.

Hartman, Saidiya. "Venus in Two Acts." *Small Axe* 12.2 (2008): 1–14.

Haskins, Jim, and Kathleen Benson. *John Lewis in the Lead: A Story of the Civil Rights Movement: Teacher's Guide*, illus. Benny Andrews. Lee & Low, 2019. https://www.leeandlow.com/wp-content/uploads/2025/01/John-Lewis-in-the-Lead-Teachers-Guide.pdf.

Hayden, Robert. "Middle Passage." 1945. *Collected Poems*, ed. Frederick Glaysher. Liveright/Norton, 2013. 48–54.

Haywood, Harry, and Milton Howard. *Lynching: A Weapon of National Oppression*. Union Labor, 1932.

Heaney, Christopher. "March: Interview with Nate Powell and Andrew Aydin." *The Appendix* 1.4 (2013): http://theappendix.net/issues/2013/10/march-interview-with-nate-powell-and-andrew-aydin.

Helfer, Andrew, and Randy DuBurke. *Malcolm X: A Graphic Biography*. Hill & Wang/Farrar, Straus and Giroux, 2006.

Helmreich, Stefan. "Kinship, Nation, and Paul Gilroy's Concept of Diaspora." *Diaspora: A Journal of Transnational Studies* 2.2 (1992): 243–49.

Helton, Laura, Justin Leroy, Max A. Mishler, Samantha Seeley, and Shauna Sweeney. "The Question of Recovery: An Introduction." *Social Text* 33.4/125 (2015): 1–18.

Hiatt, Brian. "Does the Hooded Justice Twist in 'Watchmen' Honor the Comic Books?" *Rolling Stone*, 25 November 2019.

Higginbotham, Evelyn Brooks. "Beyond the Sound of Silence: Afro-American Women in History." *Gender & History* 1.1 (1989): 50–67.

Hill, Karlos K., and David Dodson. *The Murder of Emmett Till: A Graphic History*. Oxford University Press, 2021.

Hillstrom, Laurie Collier. *Black Lives Matter: From a Moment to a Movement*. Greenwood, 2018.

Hinds, Rickerby. "John Jennings: Creating Social Change with Comics." 2018. *John Jennings: Conversations*, ed. Donna-lyn Washington. University Press of Mississippi, 2020. 94–108.

Hine, Darlene Clark. "Rape and the Inner Lives of Black Women in the Middle West." *Signs: Journal of Women in Culture and Society* 14.4 (1989): 912–20.

Hine, Darlene Clark, and Kathleen Thompson. *A Shining Thread of Hope: The History of Black Women in America*. 1998. Broadway, 1999.

Hirsch, Marianne. "The Generation of Postmemory." *Poetics Today* 29.1 (2008): 103–28.

Hirsch, Marianne, and Diana Taylor. "The Archive in Transit." *emisférica* 9.1–2 (2012): https://hemisphericinstitute.org/en/emisferica-91/91-editorial-remarks.

Hoeness-Krupsaw, Susanna. "Teaching *March* in the Borderlands Between Social Justice and Pop Culture." *Teaching Graphic Novels in the English Classroom: Pedagogical Possibilities of Multimodal Literacy Engagement*, ed. Alissa Burger. Palgrave Macmillan, 2017. 135–47.

Hogle, Jerrold E. "Introduction: The Gothic in Western Culture." *The Cambridge Companion to Gothic Fiction*, ed. Jerrold E. Hogle. Cambridge University Press, 2002. 1–20.

Holden, Vanessa M. *Surviving Southampton: African American Women and Resistance in Nat Turner's Community*. University of Illinois Press, 2021.

Holiday, Billie. "Strange Fruit." Commodore, 1939.

Hooker, Juliet. *Black Grief/White Grievance: The Politics of Loss*. Princeton University Press, 2023.

hooks, bell. *Ain't I a Woman? Black Women and Feminism*. South End, 1981.

hooks, bell. *Black Looks: Race and Representation*. South End, 1992.

hooks, bell. *Teaching to Transgress: Education as the Practice of Freedom*. Routledge, 1994.

hooks, bell. *We Real Cool: Black Men and Masculinity*. Routledge, 2004.

Houck, Davis W., and David E. Dixon, eds. *Women and the Civil Rights Movement, 1954–1965*. University Press of Mississippi, 2009.

Houck, Davis W., and Matthew A. Grindy. *Emmett Till and the Mississippi Press*. University Press of Mississippi, 2008.

Howard, Sheena C., ed. *Why Wakanda Matters: What Black Panther Reveals About Psychology, Identity, and Communication*. Smart Pop/BenBella, 2021.

Howard, Sheena C., and Ronald L. Jackson II, eds. *Black Comics: Politics of Race and Representation*. Bloomsbury, 2013.

Hudlin, Reginald, et al. *Black Panther: The Complete Collection*. 3 vols. Marvel Comics, 2017–18.

Hudson, Laura. "The Civil Rights Legend Who's Inspiring a New Generation with Comic Books." *Wired*, 21 January 2015.

Hughes, Charles L. "Freedom Songs: Building a Civil Rights Playlist." *Understanding and Teaching the Civil Rights Movement*, ed. Hasan Kwame Jeffries. University of Wisconsin Press, 2019. 209–23.

Hughes, Henry. *Treatise on Sociology, Theoretical and Practical*. Lippincott, 1854.

Hughes, Joseph. "Congressman John Lewis and Andrew Aydin Talk Inspiring the 'Children of the Movement' with 'March' [Interview]." *Comics Alliance*, 16 September 2013. https://comicsalliance.com/congressman-john-lewis-interview-march-andrew-aydin-top-shelf/.

Hughes, Langston. "The Bitter River." *The Collected Works of Langston Hughes*, vol. 2, *The Poems, 1921–1940*, ed. Arnold Rampersad. University of Missouri Press, 2001. 81–84.

Hurston, Zora Neale. *Barracoon: The Story of the Last "Black Cargo,"* ed. Deborah G. Plant. Amistad/HarperCollins, 2018.

Hurston, Zora Neale. *Every Tongue Got to Confess*, ed. Carla Kaplan. HarperCollins, 2001.

Hylton, Najah-Amatullah, Quraysh Ali Lansana, and Skipp Hill. *Opal's Greenwood Oasis.* Calliope Group, 2021.

Imani, Blair. *Making Our Way Home: The Great Migration and the Black American Dream*, illus. Rachelle Baker. Ten Speed Press/Penguin Random House, 2020.

Iton, Richard. *In Search of the Black Fantastic: Politics and Popular Culture in the Post–Civil Rights Era.* Oxford University Press, 2008.

Jackson, Cassandra. *Violence, Visual Culture, and the Black Male Body.* Routledge, 2011.

Jacobs, Dale. "Ho Che Anderson Interview." *International Journal of Comic Art* 8.2 (2006): 363–86.

Jacobs, Harriet Ann. *Incidents in the Life of a Slave Girl, Written by Herself.* 1861, ed. Lydia Maria Child. *Slave Narratives*, ed. William L. Andrews and Henry Louis Gates Jr. Library of America, 2000. 743–947.

Jaffe, Meryl. "Using Graphic Novels in Education: *King*." *Comic Book Legal Defense Fund*, 28 February 2014, https://cbldf.org/2014/02/using-graphic-novels-in-education-king/.

Jaffe, Sarah. "John Lewis' Advice for Young Activists: March." *In These Times*, 13 August 2013, https://inthesetimes.com/article/john-lewis-advice-for-young-activists-march.

Jama-Everett, Ayize, and John Jennings. *Box of Bones: Book One.* Rosarium, 2021.

Janken, Kenneth Robert. "Introduction to the New Edition." *Rope and Faggot: A Biography of Judge Lynch*, by Walter White. University of Notre Dame Press, 2001. vii–xxv.

Jefferson, Blind Lemon. "Lockstep Blues/Hangman's Blues." Paramount, 1928.

Jefferson, Thomas. *Notes on the State of Virginia: An Annotated Edition*, ed. Robert Pierce Forbes. Yale University Press, 2022.

Jeffries, Hasan Kwame, ed. *Understanding and Teaching the Civil Rights Movement.* University of Wisconsin Press, 2019.

Jenkins, Henry. *Comics and Stuff.* New York University Press, 2020.

Jenkins, Jerry Rafiki. *The Paradox of Blackness in African American Vampire Fiction.* Ohio State University Press, 2019.

Jennings, John. *Blue Hand Mojo: Hard Times Road.* Rosarium, 2017.

Jennings, John, and David Brame. *The Mighty Struggle: A Town Called Miracle.* Rosarium, forthcoming.

Jennings, John, and Damian Duffy. *Octavia E. Butler's Kindred.* Abrams ComicArts, 2017.

Jennings, John, and Damian Duffy. *Octavia E. Butler's Parable of the Sower.* Abrams ComicArts, 2020.

Jennings, John, and Damian Duffy. *Octavia E. Butler's Parable of the Talents.* Abrams ComicArts, 2025.

Johnson, Charles. *Being and Race: Black Writing Since 1970.* Serpent's Tail, 1988.

Johnson, Charles. "Foreword: A Capsule History of Blacks in Comics." *Still I Rise: A Graphic History of African Americans*, by Roland Laird with Taneshia Nash Laird, illus. Elihu "Adofo" Bey. Rev. ed. Sterling, 2009. vii–xviii.

Johnson, Charles. *Middle Passage.* 1990. Scribner/Simon & Schuster, 1998.

Johnson, Hannibal B. *Black Wall Street 100: An American City Grapples with Its Historical Racial Trauma.* Eakin, 2020.

Johnson, Javon. "Black Joy in the Time of Ferguson." *QED: A Journal in GLBTQ Worldmaking* 2.2 (2015): 177–83.

Johnson, Mat, Tony Akins, Dan Green, et al. *John Constantine Hellblazer: Papa Midnite.* Vertigo/DC Comics, 2006.

Johnson, Mat, and Warren Pleece. *Incognegro: A Graphic Mystery*. 2008. Berger Books/Dark Horse Comics, 2018.

"Jolly N*g*er Piggy Bank (No Hat)." *Black Archives*, https://collection.theblackarchives.nl/items/show/3454. Accessed 4 May 2025.

Jones, Patrick D. "Place Matters: The Indispensable Story of Civil Rights Activism Beyond Dixie." *Understanding and Teaching the Civil Rights Movement*, ed. Hasan Kwame Jeffries. University of Wisconsin Press, 2019. 95–110.

Jones, Stacy Holman, and Anne Harris. "Monsters, Desire and the Creative Queer Body." *Continuum: Journal of Media and Cultural Studies* 30.5 (2016): 518–30.

Kane, Bob, and Bill Finger. "The Legend of the Batman—Who He Is and How He Came to Be!" *Batman*, no. 1. DC Comics, Spring 1940.

Kaplan, Sara Clarke. "Souls at the Crossroads, Africans on the Water: The Politics of Diasporic Melancholia." *Callaloo* 30.2 (2007): 511–26.

"Kara Walker: Virginia's Lynch Mob and Other Works." *Montclair Art Museum*, 15 September 2018–6 January 2019, https://www.montclairartmuseum.org/exhibition/kara-walker-virginias-lynch-mob-and-other-works.

Karbassian, Malihe. "The Meaning and Etymology of *Barzakh* in Illuminationist Philosophy." *Illuminationist Texts and Textual Studies: Essays in Memory of Hossein Ziai*, ed. Ali Gheissari, Ahmed Alwishah, and John Wallbridge. Brill, 2017. 86–95.

Keizer, Arlene R. *Black Subjects: Identity Formation in the Contemporary Narrative of Slavery*. Cornell University Press, 2004.

Kendi, Ibram X. *Stamped from the Beginning: A Graphic History of Racist Ideas in America*. Adapted and illustrated by Joel Christian Gill. Ten Speed Press/Penguin Random House, 2023.

Kenyatta, Matthew Jordan-Miller. "'Need Black Joy?' Mapping an Afrotechtonics of Gathering in Los Angeles." *The Black Geographic: Praxis, Resistance, Futurity*, ed. Camilla Hawthorne and Jovan Scott Lewis. Duke University Press, 2023. 213–45.

King, Martin Luther, Jr. "I Have a Dream," *A Testament of Hope: The Essential Writings and Speeches of Martin Luther King, Jr*, ed. James Melvin Washington. HarperCollins, 2003. 217–20.

King, Martin Luther, Jr. "Loving Your Enemies." 17 November 1957. *Martin Luther King, Jr. Research and Education Institute, Stanford University*, https://kinginstitute.stanford.edu/king-papers/documents/loving-your-enemies-sermon-delivered-dexter-avenue-baptist-church.

King, Martin Luther, Jr. "The Negro Is Your Brother: Letter from Birmingham Jail." 1963. *The Atlantic Presents: King*, spring 2018, 74–81.

King, Shannon. "Walking in Their Shoes: Using #BlackLivesMatter to Teach the Civil Rights Movement." *Understanding and Teaching the Civil Rights Movement*, ed. Hasan Kwame Jeffries. University of Wisconsin Press, 2019. 300–312.

Koh, Adeline. "Inspecting the Nineteenth-Century Literary Digital Archive: Omissions of Empire." *Journal of Victorian Culture* 19.3 (2014): 385–95.

Kunert-Graf, Rachel. "Lynching Iconography: Looking in Graphic Narrative." *Inks: The Journal of the Comics Studies Society* 2.3 (2018): 312–33.

Kunka, Andrew J. "Intertextuality and the Historical Graphic Narrative: Kyle Baker's *Nat Turner* and the Styron Controversy." *College Literature* 38.3 (2011): 168–93.

Kuumba, M. Bahati. "Dismantling the Master's Narrative: Teaching Gender, Race, and Class in the Civil Rights Movement." *Teaching the American Civil Rights Movement: Freedom's Bittersweet Song*, ed. Julie Buckner Armstrong, Susan Hult Edwards, Houston Bryan Roberson, and Rhonda Y. Williams. Routledge, 2002. 175–91.

Kristeva, Julia. *Powers of Horror: An Essay on Abjection*. 1980. Columbia University Press, 1982.

Laird, Roland, with Taneshia Nash Laird. *Still I Rise: A Graphic History of African Americans*, illus. Elihu "Adofo" Bey. Rev. ed. Sterling, 2009.

Lambert, Raphaël. "The Slave Trade as Memory and History: James A. Emanuel's 'The Middle Passage Blues' and Robert Hayden's 'Middle Passage.'" *African American Review* 47.2–3 (2014): 327–38.

The Late Show with Stephen Colbert. "Congressman John Lewis: 'Get in Trouble: Good Trouble.'" 1 September 2016. *YouTube*, https://www.youtube.com/watch?v=6ATwisIrtfg.

Lauro, Sarah Juliet. *The Transatlantic Zombie: Slavery, Rebellion, and Living Death*. Rutgers University Press, 2015.

Lavender, Isiah, III. *Afrofuturism Rising: The Literary Prehistory of a Movement*. Ohio State University Press, 2019.

Lavender, Isiah, III, and Lisa Yaszek, eds. *Literary Afrofuturism in the Twenty-First Century*. Ohio State University Press, 2020.

Lee, Stan, and Jack Kirby. *Fantastic Four*, no. 52. Marvel Comics, July 1966.

Legman, Gershon. "The Comic Books and the Public." *American Journal of Psychotherapy* 2 (1948): 473–77.

Lester, Julius. *To Be a Slave*. Paintings by Tom Feelings. 1968. Puffin/Penguin Putnam, 2000.

Levina, Marina, and Diem-My T. Bui, eds. *Monster Culture in the 21st Century: A Reader*. Bloomsbury, 2013.

Lewis, John, Andrew Aydin, and Nate Powell. *March: Book One*. Top Shelf, 2013.

Lewis, John, Andrew Aydin, and Nate Powell. *March: Book Two*. Top Shelf, 2015.

Lewis, John, Andrew Aydin, and Nate Powell. *March: Book Three*. Top Shelf, 2016.

Lewis, John, Andrew Aydin, L. Fury, and Nate Powell. *Run: Book One*. Abrams ComicArts, 2021.

Lewis, John, with Michael D'Orso. *Walking with the Wind: A Memoir of the Movement*. Simon & Schuster, 1998.

Lewis, John, with Michael D'Orso. *Walking with the Wind: A Memoir of the Movement*. Harcourt Brace, 1999.

Lockard, Joe. "Nat Turner, Slave Revolts, and Child-Killing in U.S. Graphic Novels." *Cultures of War in Graphic Novels: Violence, Trauma, and Memory*, ed. Tatiana Prorokova and Nimrod Tal. Rutgers University Press, 2018. 105–22.

Loewen, James W. *Sundown Towns: A Hidden Dimension of American Racism*. New Press, 2005.

Long, Mark, Jim Demonakos, and Nate Powell. *The Silence of Our Friends*. First Second/Roaring Brook, 2012.

Lorde, Audrey. "The Master's Tools Will Never Dismantle the Master's House." 1984. *Sister Outsider: Essays and Speeches*. Crossing, 2007. 110–13.

Lorde, Audrey. "Afterimages." 1987. *The Collected Poems of Audre Lorde*. Norton, 1997. https://www.poetryfoundation.org/poems/42582/afterimages.

Lorde, Audrey. "A Litany for Survival." 1978. *The Collected Poems of Audre Lorde*. Norton, 1997. https://www.poetryfoundation.org/poems/147275/a-litany-for-survival.

Love, Jeremy, and Patrick Morgan. *Bayou*. Vols. 1–2. DC Comics, 2009–10.

Lowe, Lisa. "History Hesitant." *Social Text* 33.4/125 (2015): 85–107.

Lund, Martin. "'Introducing the Sensational Black Panther!' *Fantastic Four* #52–53, the Cold War, and Marvel's Imagined Africa." *The Comics Grid: Journal of Comics Scholarship* 6 (2016): http://dx.doi.org/10.16995/cg.80.

Lyon, Danny. *Memories of the Southern Civil Rights Movement*. 1992. Twin Palms, 2010.

Madison, James H. *A Lynching in the Heartland: Race and Memory in America*. Palgrave Macmillan, 2001.

Magruder, Nilah *M.F.K.* Insight Comics, 2017.

Mambrol, Nasrullah. "Trauma Studies." *Literary Theory and Criticism*, 19 December 2018, https://literariness.org/2018/12/19/trauma-studies/.

Mandel, Naomi. *Against the Unspeakable: Complicity, the Holocaust, and Slavery in America*. University of Virginia Press, 2006.

Mannion, Connor. "Ta-Nehisi Coates Begins Run as Writer of 'Black Panther.'" *NBCNews.com*, 13 April 2016. https://www.nbcnews.com/news/nbcblk/ta-nehisi-coates-begins-run-writer-black-panther-n550421.

"March: Book One." *Anti-Defamation League*, https://www.adl.org/march-book-one. Accessed 26 April 2025.

"March: Book Two." *Anti-Defamation League*, https://www.adl.org/march-book-two. Accessed 26 April 2025.

"March: Book Three." *Anti-Defamation League*, https://www.adl.org/march-book-three. Accessed 26 April 2025.

Margolick, David. *Strange Fruit: The Biography of a Song*. Ecco/HarperCollins, 2001.

Markovitz, Jonathan. *Legacies of Lynching: Racial Violence and Memory*. University of Minnesota Press, 2004.

Marouan, Maha. *Witches, Goddesses, and Angry Spirits: The Politics of Spiritual Liberation in African Diaspora Women's Fiction*. Ohio State University Press. 2013.

Marshall, Paule. *Praisesong for the Widow*. Plume/Penguin, 1983.

Martin, Kameelah L. *Conjuring Moments in African American Literature: Women, Spirit Work, and Other Such Hoodoo*. Palgrave Macmillan, 2012.

Martin Luther King Jr. Golden Legacy Magazine, vol. 13. Fitzgerald, 1972.

Martin, Waldo E., Jr., and Patricia A. Sullivan. Introduction. *Teaching the American Civil Rights Movement: Freedom's Bittersweet Song*, ed. Julie Buckner Armstrong, Susan Hult Edwards, Houston Bryan Roberson, and Rhonda Y. Williams. Routledge, 2002. xi–xviii.

Mayer, Ruth. "'Africa as an Alien Future': The Middle Passage, Afrofuturism, and Postcolonial Waterworlds." *Amerikastudien/American Studies* 45.4 (2000): 555–66.

Mbembe, Achille. *Critique of Black Reason*. Trans. Laurent Dubois. Duke University Press, 2017.

Mbiti, John S. *African Religions and Philosophy*. 1969. Heinemann, 1990.

McCloud, Scott. *Understanding Comics: The Invisible Art*. 1993. HarperCollins, 1994.

McCulloch, Derek, Shepherd Hendrix, et al. *Stagger Lee*. Image Comics, 2006.

McDowell, Deborah E. *Leaving Pipe Shop: Memories of Kin*. Scribner, 1996.

McGovern, James R. *Anatomy of a Lynching: The Killing of Claude Neal*. 1982. Louisiana State University Press, 2013.

McGregor, Don, and Billy Graham. "A Cross Burning Darkly Blackening the Night!" *Jungle Action*, no. 21. Marvel Comics, May 1976.

McGurk, Caitlin. "Ho Che Anderson Collection Donated to Ohio State." *Billy Ireland Cartoon Library & Museum Blog*, 1 April 2021, https://library.osu.edu/site/cartoons/tag/ho-che-anderson/.

McKay, Nellie. "An Interview with Toni Morrison." *Conversations with Toni Morrison*, ed. Danille Taylor-Guthrie. University Press of Mississippi, 1994. 138–55.

McKinney, L. L., and Robyn Smith. *Nubia: Real One*. DC Comics, 2021.

McKittrick, Katherine. *Demonic Grounds: Black Women and the Cartographies of Struggle*. University Minnesota Press, 2006.

McLaughlin, Eliott C. "America's Legacy of Lynching Isn't All History: Many Say It's Still Happening Today." *CNN.com*, 3 June 2020. https://edition.cnn.com/2020/06/03/us/lynching-america-george-floyd-ahmaud-arbery-breonna-taylor/index.html.

McSweeney, Terence. *Black Panther: Interrogating a Cultural Phenomenon*. University Press of Mississippi, 2021.

Medina, Tony, Stacey Robinson, and John Jennings. *I Am Alfonso Jones*. Tu/Lee & Low, 2017.

Meeropol, Abel. "Bitter Fruit." *New York Teacher*, January 1937.

Méon, Jean-Matthieu. "Sons and Grandsons of Origins: Narrative Memory in Marvel Superhero Comics." *Comics Memory: Archives and Styles*, ed. Maaheen Ahmed and Benoît Crucifix. Palgrave Macmillan, 2018. 189–209.

Messer, Chris M., and Patricia A. Bell. "Mass Media and Governmental Framing of Riots: The Case of Tulsa, 1921." *Journal of Black Studies* 40.5 (2010): 851–70.

Messer, Chris M., Thomas E. Shriver, and Alison E. Adams. "The Destruction of Black Wall Street: Tulsa's 1921 Riot and the Eradication of Accumulated Wealth." *American Journal of Economics and Sociology* 77.3–4 (2018): 789–819.

Métraux, Alfred. *Voodoo in Haiti*. Trans. Hugo Charteris. Oxford University Press, 1959.

Metress, Christopher, ed. *The Lynching of Emmett Till: A Documentary Narrative*. University of Virginia Press, 2002.

Michel, Claudine, and Patrick Bellegarde-Smith, eds. *Vodou in Haitian Life and Culture: Invisible Powers*. Palgrave Macmillan, 2006.

Miles, Tiya. *Tales from the Haunted South: Dark Tourism and Memories of Slavery from the Civil War Era*. University of North Carolina Press, 2015.

Miller, Joseph C. *Way of Death: Merchant Capitalism and the Angolan Slave Trade, 1730–1830*. University of Wisconsin Press, 1988.

Miller, Mark. *Jazz in Canada: Fourteen Lives*. University of Toronto Press, 1982.

Miller, W. Jason. "Langston Hughes's 'The Bitter River': American Lynching Culture and WWII." *Langston Hughes Review* 23 (Fall 2009): 32–41.

Milne, Leah. "Radical Empathy in *March*." *BOOM! SPLAT! Comics and Violence*, ed. Jim Coby and Joanna Davis-McElligatt. University Press of Mississippi, 2024. 185–95.

Misrahi-Barak, Judith. "Post-*Beloved* Writing: Review, Revitalize, Recalculate." *Black Studies Papers* 1.1 (2014): 37–55.

Mitchell, Koritha. *Living with Lynching: African American Lynching Plays, Performance, and Citizenship, 1890–1930*. University of Illinois Press, 2011.

Mitchell, Michele. "Silences Broken, Silences Kept: Gender and Sexuality in African-American History." *Gender & History* 11.3 (1999): 433–44.

Mitchell, W. J. T. *Picture Theory: Essays on Verbal and Visual Representation*. University of Chicago Press, 1994.

Mittman, Asa Simon. "Introduction: The Impact of Monsters and Monster Studies." *The Ashgate Companion to Monsters and the Monstrous*, ed. Asa Simon Mittman with Peter J. Dendle. Ashgate, 2012. 1–14.

Moody, Anne. *Coming of Age in Mississippi*. Dial, 1968.
Morales, Robert, Kyle Baker, et al. *Captain America: Truth*. Marvel Comics, 2009.
Morgan, Edmund S. *American Slavery, American Freedom: The Ordeal of Colonial Virginia*. Norton, 1975.
Morgan, Jennifer L. *Reckoning with Slavery: Gender, Kinship and Capitalism in the Early Black Atlantic*. Duke University Press, 2021.
Morgan, Jennifer L. "'Some Could Suckle over Their Shoulder': Male Travelers, Female Bodies, and the Gendering of Racial Ideology, 1500–1770." *William and Mary Quarterly* 54.1 (1997): 167–92.
Morrison, Toni. *Beloved*. Knopf, 1987.
Morrison, Toni. *The Bluest Eye*. Holt, Rinehart and Winston, 1970.
Morrison, Toni. "City Limits, Village Values: Concepts of the Neighborhood in Black Fiction." *Literature and the Urban Experience: Essays on the City and Literature*, ed. Michael C. Jaye and Ann Chalmers Watts. Rutgers University Press, 1981. 35–43.
Morrison, Toni. "Home." *The House That Race Built: Black Americans, U.S. Terrain*, ed. Wahneema Lubiano. Pantheon, 1997. 3–13.
Morrison, Toni. *The Origins of Others*. Harvard University Press, 2017.
Morrison, Toni. *Playing in the Dark: Whiteness and the Literary Imagination*. Harvard University Press, 1992.
Morrison, Toni. "Rootedness: The Ancestor as Foundation." *Black Women Writers (1950–1980): A Critical Evaluation*, ed. Mari Evans. Anchor/Doubleday, 1984. 339–45.
Morrison, Toni. *The Source of Self-Regard: Selected Essays, Speeches, and Meditations*. Knopf, 2019.
Morrison, Toni. "Unspeakable Things Unspoken: The Afro-American Presence in American Literature." *Michigan Quarterly Review* 28.1 (1989): 1–34.
Mosley, Walter. *Gone Fishin'*. Black Classic, 1997.
Moten, Fred. *In the Break: The Aesthetics of the Black Radical Tradition*. University of Minnesota Press, 2003.
"Movement Photographs of Danny Lyon, Cairo, IL., 1962." *Civil Rights Movement Archive*, https://www.crmvet.org/images/plyon.htm. Accessed 26 May 2025.
Moynihan, Sinéad. "'Watch Me Go Invisible': Representing Racial Passing in Mat Johnson and Warren Pleece's *Incognegro*." *South Central Review* 32.3 (2015): 45–69.
Murakawa, Naomi. *The First Civil Right: How Liberals Built Prison America*. Oxford University Press, 2014.
Murillo, John, III. *Impossible Stories: On the Space and Time of Black Destructive Creation*. Ohio State University Press, 2021.
Murray, Albert. *Stomping the Blues*. 1976, ed. Paul Devlin. University of Minnesota Press, 2017.
Murray, Christopher. *Champions of the Oppressed? Superhero Comics, Popular Culture, and Propaganda in America During World War II*. Hampton, 2011.
Murray, William. "Reimagining Terror in the Graphic Novel: Kyle Baker's *Nat Turner* and the Cultural Imagination." *CEA Critic* 77.3 (2015): 329–38.
Mustakeem, Sowande' M. *Slavery at Sea: Terror, Sex, and Sickness in the Middle Passage*. University of Illinois Press, 2016.
Nama, Adilifu. *Super Black: American Pop Culture and Black Superheroes*. University of Texas Press, 2011.

Narcisse, Evan. "Ta-Nehisi Coates Explains How He's Turning Black Panther into a Superhero Again." *Gizmodo.com*, 14 September 2016, https://io9.gizmodo.com/ta-nehisi-coates-explains-how-hes-turning-black-panther-1786632598.

Naylor, Gloria. *Mama Day*. Ticknor & Fields, 1988.

Neary, Janet. *Fugitive Testimony: On the Visual Logic of Slave Narratives*. Fordham University Press, 2017.

"Negro Hanged and Burned at Terre Haute." *New York Times*, 27 February 1901.

"Nigeria's Literary Lion Flies Home from Exile." *New York Times*, 15 October 1998.

"1921 Tulsa Race Massacre." *Tulsa Historical Society and Museum*, https://www.tulsahistory.org/exhibit/1921-tulsa-race-massacre. Accessed 7 May 2025.

Noble, Marianne. *The Masochistic Pleasures of Sentimental Literature*. Princeton University Press, 2000.

Noguchi, Isamu. "Birth and Death." 1934. *Noguchi Museum*, 2017, https://www.noguchi.org/museum/exhibitions/view/birth-and-death/.

North, Sterling. "A National Disgrace (and a Challenge to American Parents)." *Chicago Daily News*, 8 May 1940.

Oates, Stephen B. *The Fires of Jubilee: Nat Turner's Fierce Rebellion*. 1975. Harper Perennial, 2016.

Obenland, Frank, Nele Sawallisch, Johanna Seibert, and Pia Wiegmink, eds. *Special Forum: Transnational Black Politics and Resistance: From Enslavement to Obama. Journal of Transnational American Studies* 10.1 (2019).

Oboe, Annalisa, and Anna Scacchi, eds. *Recharting the Black Atlantic: Modern Cultures, Local Communities, Global Connections*. Routledge, 2008.

Okorafor, Nnedi, Vita Ayala, Paul Davidson, Rachael Scott, et al. *Shuri: 24/7 Vibranium*. Marvel Comics, 2019.

Okorafor, Nnedi, Aaron Covington, André Lima Araújo, Mario del Pennino, Tana Ford, et al. *Black Panther: Long Live the King*. Marvel Comics, 2018.

Okorafor, Nnedi, Tana Ford, and James Devlin. *LaGuardia*. Dark Horse Comics, 2019.

Okorafor, Nnedi, Leonardo Romero, Jordie Bellaire, et al. *Shuri: The Search for Black Panther*. Marvel Comics, 2019.

Omanga, Duncan, and Pamela C. Mainye. "More Than Just a Homecoming: The Reception of *Black Panther* in Kenya." *Safundi: The Journal of South African and American Comparative Studies* 20.1 (2019): 18–21.

"One-Way Ticket: Jacob Lawrence's Migration Series." MoMA, 2015, https://www.moma.org/interactives/exhibitions/2015/onewayticket/.

Oppolzer, Markus. "John Lewis's *March*: Promoting Social Action Through Comics." *Geschichte im Comic*, ed. Bernd Dolle-Weinkauff. Bachmann, 2017. 225–37.

Osei, Elisabeth Abena. "Wakanda Africa Do You See? Reading Black Panther as a Decolonial Film Through the Lens of the Sankofa Theory." *Critical Studies in Media Communication* 37.4 (2020): 378–90.

Oshinsky, David M. *"Worse Than Slavery": Parchman Farm and the Ordeal of Jim Crow Justice*. 1996. Free Press/Simon & Schuster, 1997.

Osminski, Joel. "Black Panther." *Pinterest*, https://de.pinterest.com/joelosminski/black-panther/. Accessed 3 May 2025.

Owusu, Portia. *Spectres from the Past: Slavery and the Politics of History in West African and African-American Literature*. Routledge, 2020.

Pande, Rukmini, ed. *Fandom, Now in Color: A Collection of Voices*. University of Iowa Press, 2020.

Pande, Rukmini. *Squee from the Margins: Fandom and Race*. University of Iowa Press, 2018.

Patterson, Orlando. *Slavery and Social Death: A Comparative Study*. Harvard University Press, 1982.

Patton, Charlie. "High Water Everywhere, Part 1 and 2." Paramount, 1930.

Peart-Smith, Paul. *W. E. B. Du Bois: Souls of Black Folk: A Graphic Interpretation*, ed. Paul Buhle and Herb Boyd. Rutgers University Press, 2023.

"Pedagogy." *Merriam-Webster*, https://www.merriam-webster.com/dictionary/pedagogy. Accessed 3 May 2025.

Peppard, Anna F. "'A Cross Burning Darkly, Blackening the Night': Reading Racialized Spectacles of Conflict and Bondage in Marvel's Early Black Panther Comics." *Studies in Comics* 9.1 (2018): 59–85.

Perry, Imani. "Racism Is Terrible: Blackness Is Not." *The Atlantic*, 15 June 2020.

Peterson, James Braxton. "Graphic Black Nationalism: Visualizing Political Narratives in the Graphic Novel." *The Rise and Reason of Comics and Graphic Literature: Critical Essays on the Form*, ed. Joyce Goggin and Dan A. Hassler-Forest. McFarland, 2010. 202–21.

Pfeifer, Michael J. *Rough Justice: Lynching and American Society, 1874–1947*. University of Illinois Press, 2004.

Pierrot, Grégory. *The Black Avenger in Atlantic Culture*. University of Georgia Press, 2019.

Pieterse, Jan Nederveen. *White on Black: Images of Africa and Blacks in Western Popular Culture*. Yale University Press, 1992.

Pinto, Samantha. *Difficult Diasporas: The Transnational Feminist Aesthetic of the Black Atlantic*. New York University Press, 2013.

Plasa, Carl. "Doing the Slave Trade in Different Voices: Poetics and Politics in Robert Hayden's First 'Middle Passage.'" *African American Review* 45.4 (2012): 557–73.

Polak, Kate. *Ethics in the Gutter: Empathy and Historical Fiction in Comics*. Ohio State University Press, 2017.

Pratt, Robert A. *Selma's Bloody Sunday: Protest, Voting Rights, and the Struggle for Racial Equality*. Johns Hopkins University Press, 2017.

Quattro, Ken. *Invisible Men: The Trailblazing Black Artists of Comic Books*. IDW, 2020.

Rabaka, Reiland. *Civil Rights Music: The Soundtracks of the Civil Rights Movement*. Lexington, 2016.

Raiford, Leigh. "'Come Let Us Build a New World Together': SNCC and Photography of the Civil Rights Movement." *American Quarterly* 59.4 (2007): 1129–57.

Raiford, Leigh. *Imprisoned in a Luminous Glare: Photography and the African American Freedom Struggle*. University of North Carolina Press, 2011.

Raiford, Leigh, and Heike Raphael-Hernandez. Introduction. *Migrating the Black Body: The African Diaspora and Visual Culture*, ed. Leigh Raiford and Heike Raphael-Hernandez. University of Washington Press, 2017. 3–9.

Raiford, Leigh, and Heike Raphael-Hernandez, eds. *Migrating the Black Body: The African Diaspora and Visual Culture*. University of Washington Press, 2017.

Rambsy, Howard, II. "Reading Kyle Baker's *Nat Turner* with a Group of Collegiate Black Men." *Contemporary African American Literature: The Living Canon*, ed. Lovalerie King and Shirley Moody-Turner. Indiana University Press, 2013. 285–301.

Rankine, Claudia. *Citizen: An American Lyric*. Graywolf, 2014.

Rankine, Claudia. "The Condition of Black Life Is One of Mourning." *New York Times Magazine*, 22 June 2015.

Rediker, Marcus. "History from Below the Water Line: Sharks and the Atlantic Slave Trade." *Atlantic Studies* 5.2 (2008): 285–97.

Rediker, Marcus. *The Slave Ship: A Human History*. Murry, 2007.

Reed, Ishmael. *Mumbo Jumbo*. Doubleday, 1972.

Regalado, Aldo. "Modernity, Race, and the American Superhero." *Comics as Philosophy*, ed. Jeff McLaughlin. University Press of Mississippi, 2005. 84–99.

"Rep. John Lewis Undergoing Cancer Treatment" (press release). *Association for the Study of African American Life & History*, 29 December 2019, https://asalh.org/rep-john-lewis-undergoing-cancer-treatment/.

"Rep John Lewis' Speech at March on Washington." *YouTube*, https://www.youtube.com/watch?v=tFs1eTsokJg. Accessed 23 May 2025.

Rice, Alan. *Creating Memorials, Building Identities: The Politics of Memory in the Black Atlantic*. Liverpool University Press, 2010.

Rice, Alan. *Radical Narratives of the Black Atlantic*. Continuum, 2003.

Rifkind, Candida. "Immigration, Photography, and the Color Line in Lila Quintero Weaver's *Darkroom: A Memoir in Black & White*." *Immigrants and Comics: Graphic Spaces of Remembrance, Transaction, and Mimesis*, ed. Nhora Lucía Serrano. Routledge, 2021. 204–24.

Ringgold, Faith. *If a Bus Could Talk: The Story of Rosa Parks*. Simon & Shuster, 1999.

Roberts, Gene, and Hank Klibanoff. *The Race Beat: The Press, the Civil Rights Struggle, and the Awakening of a Nation*. Knopf, 2006.

Roberts, Marcus H., Jamal Williams Jr., Iwan Joko Triyono, and Hector Negrete. *Hell to Pay. Shook! A Black Horror Anthology*. Dark Horse Comics, 2024.

Romano, Renee C., and Leigh Raiford, eds. *The Civil Rights Movement in American Memory*. University of Georgia Press, 2006.

Round, Julia. *Gothic in Comics and Graphic Novels: A Critical Approach*. McFarland, 2014.

Rowe, John Carlos. Introduction. *Racial Blackness and the Discontinuity of Western Modernity*, by Lindon Barrett, ed. Justin A. Joyce, Dwight A. McBride, and John Carlos Rowe. University of Illinois Press, 2014. vii–xx.

Royal, Derek Parker. "Introduction: Coloring America: Multi-Ethnic Engagements with Graphic Narrative." *MELUS* 32.3 (2007): 7–22.

Rusert, Britt. "New World: The Impact of Digitization on the Study of Slavery." *American Literary History* 29.9 (2017): 267–86.

Rushdy, Ashraf H. A. *The End of American Lynching*. Rutgers University Press, 2012.

Rushdy, Ashraf H. A. *Neo-Slave Narratives: Studies in the Social Logic of a Literary Form*. Oxford University Press, 1999.

Russworm, TreaAndrea M. *Blackness Is Burning: Civil Rights, Popular Culture, and the Problem of Recognition*. Wayne State University Press, 2016.

Ryan, Jennifer D. "Truth Made Visible: Crises of Cultural Expression in *Truth: Red, White, and Black*." *College Literature* 38.3 (2011): 66–96.

Saal, Ilka. *Collusions of Fact and Fiction: Performing Slavery in the Works of Suzan Lori Parks and Kara Walker*. University of Iowa Press, 2021.

Saguisag, Lara. *Incorrigibles and Innocents: Constructing Childhood and Citizenship in Progressive Era Comics*. Rutgers University Press, 2019.

Sanchez-Taylor, Joy. *Diverse Futures: Science Fiction and Authors of Color*. Ohio State University Press, 2021.

Santana, Aderivaldo Ramos de. "The Spanish Slave Ship Carlotta 'Denounced' by a Shark." *Black Perspectives*, 22 June 2022. https://www.aaihs.org/the-spanish-slave-ship-carlotta-denounced-by-a-shark-1894/.

Santiago, Tony. "Black Panther—T'Challa." *Tony Santiago Art*, https://www.tonysantiagoart.com/marvel-art/black-panther-tchalla. Accessed 3 May 2025.

Santos, Jorge J., Jr. *Graphic Memories of the Civil Rights Movement: Reframing History in Comics*. University of Texas Press, 2019.

Santos, Jorge J., Jr. "Talented Tensions and Revisions: The Narrative Double Consciousness of Miles Morales." *Mixed-Race Superheroes*, ed. Sika A. Dagbovie-Mullins and Eric L. Berlatsky. Rutgers University Press, 2021. 179–98.

Saro-Wiwa, Ken. *A Month and a Day: A Detention Diary*. Penguin, 1995.

Schmid, Johannes C. P. "American History, Civil Rights, and Protest in Graphic Nonfiction." ComFor, 13 December 2023.

Schmid, Johannes C. P. *Frames and Framing in Documentary Comics*. Palgrave Macmillan, 2021.

Schmid, Johannes C. P. "Graphic Nonviolence: Framing 'Good Trouble' in John Lewis' March." *European Journal of American Studies* 13.4 (2018): https://journals.openedition.org/ejas/13922.

Schneider, Nicole A. *Visual Protest, Viral Images, and Virtual Participation: Protest and Photography in the Contemporary Movement for Black Lives*. De Gruyter, 2025.

Scott, Anna Beatrice. "Superpower vs Supernatural: Black Superheroes and the Quest for a Mutant Reality." *Journal of Visual Culture* 5.3 (2006): 295–314.

Scott, Darieck. *Keeping It Unreal: Black Queer Fantasy and Superhero Comics*. New York University Press, 2022.

Scott, Darieck. "The Not-Yet Justice League: Fantasy, Redress, and Transatlantic Black History on the Comic Book Page." *Migrating the Black Body: The African Diaspora and Visual Culture*, ed. Leigh Raiford and Heike Raphael-Hernandez. University of Washington Press, 2017. 329–48.

Sears, Harry Luther. "The Burning of Sam Hose." *New York Times*, 27 April 1899.

Sekora, John. "Black Message/White Envelope: Genre, Authenticity, and Authority in the Antebellum Slave Narrative." *Callaloo* 32 (Summer 1987): 482–515.

Selma. Dir. Ava DuVernay. Paramount, 2014.

Selma Online. www.selmaonline.org. Accessed 23 May 2025.

Sewchurran, Anusharani. "Black Panther: A Reception Analysis." *Image & Text* 36 (2022): http://dx.doi.org/10.17159/2617-3255/2022/n36a5.

Sexton, Jared. "The Social Life of Social Death: On Afro-Pessimism and Black Optimism." *InTensions* 5 (Fall–Winter 2011): 1–47.

Sharpe, Christina. *In the Wake: On Blackness and Being*. Duke University Press, 2016.

Sharpe, Christina. *Monstrous Intimacies: Making Post-Slavery Subjects*. Duke University Press, 2010.

Sharpe, Jenny. *Immaterial Archives: An African Diaspora Poetics of Loss*. Northwestern University Press, 2020.

Sheller, Mimi. *Consuming the Caribbean: From Arawaks to Zombies.* Routledge, 2003.

"Shuri (Marvel)." *Archive of Our Own,* 18 June 2025, https://archive.transformativeworks.org/tags/Shuri%20(Marvel)/works.

Simien, Evelyn M., ed. *Gender and Lynching: The Politics of Memory.* Palgrave Macmillan, 2011.

Singer, Marc. "'Black Skins' and White Masks: Comic Books and the Secret of Race." *African American Review* 36.1 (2002): 107–19.

Singer, Marc. *Breaking the Frames: Populism and Prestige in Comics Studies.* University of Texas Press, 2018.

"Sixteenth Street Baptist Church Bombing—Broken Window with Faceless Jesus." *Birmingham Public Library,* https://bplonline.contentdm.oclc.org/digital/collection/p4017coll6/id/110/. Accessed 25 June 2025.

"Slave Barracoon." *Illustrated London News,* 14 April 1849. *Slavery Images: A Visual Record of the African Slave Trade and Slave Life in the Early African Diaspora,* https://slaveryimages.org/database/image-result.php?objectid=744. Accessed 3 May 2025.

Smallwood, Stephanie E. *Saltwater Slavery: A Middle Passage from Africa to American Diaspora.* Harvard University Press, 2007.

Smith, Frank. "Big Black," Jared Reinmuth, and Améziane. *Big Black: Stand at Attica.* Archaia, 2020.

Smith, Shawn Michelle. *Photography on the Color Line: W. E. B. Du Bois, Race, and Visual Culture.* Duke University Press, 2004.

Smith, Tommie, Derrick Barnes, and Dawud Anyabwile. *Victory. Stand! Raising My Fist for Justice.* Norton, 2022.

Smith-Llera, Danielle. *TV Exposes Brutality on the Selma March: An Augmented Reading Experience.* Compass Point, 2019.

"SNCC Poster: 'Come Let Us Build a New World . . . ,'" 1963. *Digital Collections at the University of Southern Mississippi,* https://usm.access.preservica.com/uncategorized/IO_186357c0-8f0e-44f3-a4df-efb035c8dacf. Accessed 25 June 2025.

Song of the South. Dir. Harve Foster and Wilfred Jackson. Walt Disney, 1946.

Sontag, Susan. *Regarding the Pain of Others.* Farrar, Straus, 2003.

Soyinka, Wole. *You Must Set Forth at Dawn.* Random House, 2006.

Space Is the Place. Dir. John Coney. 1974. Plexifilm, 2003.

Spatzek, Samira. "Post-Slavery Negotiations? On (Slave) Narrative and Impossible Stories in Toni Morrison's *A Mercy.*" *Esclavages & Post-Esclavages* 4 (2021): https://doi.org/10.4000/slaveries.3994.

Speltz, Mark. *North of Dixie: Civil Rights Photography Beyond the South.* Getty, 2016.

Spiegelman, Art. *The Complete Maus: A Survivor's Tale.* Pantheon, 1996.

Spillers, Hortense J. "Mama's Baby, Papa's Maybe: An American Grammar Book." *Diacritics* 17.2 (1987): 65–81.

Steedman, Carolyn. *Dust.* Manchester University Press, 2001.

Stein, Daniel. *Authorizing Superhero Comics: On the Evolution of a Popular Serial Genre.* Ohio State University Press, 2021.

Stein, Daniel. "Black Bodies Swinging: Superheroes and the Shadow Archive of Lynching." *Closure: Kieler e-Journal für Comicforschung* 7.5 (2021): 54–78.

Stein, Daniel. "Breaking Out of Confinement: Black History in African American Picturebooks for Children." *Narratives of Confinement in American Literature*, ed. Firuze Güzel. De Gruyter, 2025. 159–80.

Stein, Daniel. "Der Comic, das Archiv und das Populäre: Zwei Erklärungsversuche." *Comics & Archive*, ed. Felix Giesa and Anna Stemmann. Bachmann, 2021. 15–70.

Stein, Daniel. "From *Uncle Remus* to *Song of the South*: Adapting American Plantation Fictions." *Southern Literary Journal* 47.2 (2015): 20–35.

Stein, Daniel. "Lynching und grafische Literatur: Zur Intersektionalität von Rachel Marie Crane Williams' *Elegy for Mary Turner* (2021)." *Race, Class, Gender & Beyond: Intersektionale Ansätze der Comicforschung*, ed. Anna Beckmann, Kalina Kupczynska, Marie Schröer, and Véronique Sina. De Gruyter, 2024. 29–51.

Stein, Daniel. "Racialines: Interrogating Stereotypes in Comics." *The Cambridge Companion to Comics*, ed. Maaheen Ahmed. Cambridge University Press, 2023. 204–24.

Stein, Daniel. "Teaching Poetry Through Song Adaptation: Abel Meeropol's and Billie Holiday's 'Strange Fruit.'" *Adaptation and American Studies: Perspectives on Research and Teaching*, ed. Nassim Winnie Balestrini. Winter, 2011. 171–94.

Stein, Daniel. "What's in an Archive? Cursory Observations and Serendipitous Reflections." *Anglia: Journal of English Philology* 138.3 (2020): 337–54.

Stein, Daniel. "Zu den Potentialen einer kulturwissenschaftlichen grafischen Literaturwissenschaft: Ein Analysevorschlag am Beispiel von Jeremy Loves Graphic Novel *Bayou*." *Closure: Kieler e-Journal für Comicforschung* 3 (2016): 4–22.

Stoler, Ann Laura. *Along the Archival Grain: Epistemic Anxieties and Colonial Common Sense*. Princeton University Press, 2009.

Stone, Albert E. *The Return of Nat Turner: History, Literature, and Cultural Politics in Sixties America*. University of Georgia Press, 1992.

Stowe, Harriet Beecher. *Uncle Tom's Cabin*. 1851–52. Ed. Elizabeth Ammons. Norton, 1994.

Strickland, Debra Higgs. "Monstrosity and Race in the Late Middle Ages." *The Ashgate Research Companion to Monsters and the Monstrous*, ed. Asa Simon Mittman, with Peter J. Dendle. Ashgate, 2012. 363–86.

Strickland, Debra Higgs. *Saracens, Demons, and Jews: Making Monsters in Medieval Art*. Princeton University Press, 2003.

Strömberg, Fredrik. *Black Images in the Comics: A Visual History*. Fantagraphics, 2003.

Styron, William. *The Confessions of Nat Turner*. Random House, 1967.

Tabachnik, Stephen E., ed. *Teaching the Graphic Novel*. MLA, 2009.

Taylor, Clarence. *Fight the Power: African Americans and the Long History of Police Brutality in New York City*. New York University Press, 2019.

Taylor, Diana. *The Archive and the Repertoire: Performing Cultural Memory in the Americas*. Duke University Press, 2003.

Taylor, Diana. "Save As . . . : Knowledge and Transmission in the Age of Digital Technologies." *Imagining America*, 2010, https://surface.syr.edu/cgi/viewcontent.cgi?article=1011&context=ia.

Taylor, Keeanga-Yamahtta. *From #BlackLivesMatter to Black Liberation*. Haymarket, 2016.

Taylor, Leila. *Darkly: Black History and America's Gothic Soul*. Repeater, 2019.

Taylor, Paul C. *Black Is Beautiful: A Philosophy of Black Aesthetics*. Wiley, 2016.

Taylor, Whit, and Kazimir Lee. *Harriet Tubman: Toward Freedom*. Little, Brown, 2021.

Teachers Pay Teachers. https://www.teacherspayteachers.com/Browse/Search:march%20by%20john%20lewis. Accessed 23 May 2025.

Teutsch, Matthew. "Layouts in Rebecca Hall and Hugo Martínez's 'Wake.'" *Medium.com*, 9 July 2021. https://interminablerambling.medium.com/layouts-in-rebecca-hall-and-hugo-mart%C3%ADnezs-wake-8990ca9d25a3.

Teutsch, Matthew. "On Racism and Racial Violence in the Comics." *Black Perspectives*, 4 April 2017. https://www.aaihs.org/on-racism-and-racial-violence-in-the-comics/.

Teutsch, Matthew. "Retrieving History in Rebecca Hall and Hugo Martínez's 'Wake.'" *Medium.com*, 12 July 2021. https://interminablerambling.medium.com/retrieving-history-in-rebecca-hall-and-hugo-mart%C3%ADnezs-wake-a5ece2073078.

"Texas: Lynching, 1908." *Alamy*, https://www.alamy.com/stock-photo-texas-lynching-1908-nfive-blacks-hanged-from-a-dogwood-tree-in-sabine-95409012.html. Accessed 19 May 2025.

Thomas, Cathy. "Afterword: Caribbean Comics: Out of Place, Out of Time, Out of Sight." *Hardears*, by Matthew Clarke and Nigel Lynch. Abrams ComicArts Megascope, 2021. 178–83.

Thomas, Ebony Elizabeth. *The Dark Fantastic: Race and the Imagination from Harry Potter to the Hunger Games*. New York University Press, 2019.

Thomas, Roy, ed. *Amazing Spider-Man*, no. 122. Marvel Comics, July 1973.

Thompson, Nolan. "Sherman Riot of 1930." *Handbook of Texas*, 10 February 2021, www.tshaonline.org/handbook/entries/sherman-riot-of-1930.

Thoreau, Henry David. "Civil Disobedience." 1849. https://blogs.law.columbia.edu/uprising1313/files/2017/10/Civil-Disobedience-by-Henry-David-Thoreau.pdf. Accessed 22 May 2025.

Tillet, Salamishah. *Sites of Slavery: Citizenship and Racial Democracy in the Post–Civil Rights Imagination*. Duke University Press, 2012.

Tompkins, Kyla Wazana. *Racial Indigestion: Eating Bodies in the 19th Century*. New York University Press, 2012.

Tooks, Lance. *Narcissa*. Doubleday, 2002.

Toomer, Jean. "Portrait in Georgia." *Modern Review*, January 1923.

Toomer, Jean. *Cane*. 1923. Ed. Darwin T. Turner. Norton, 1988.

Torres, Sasha. *Black, White, and in Color: Television and Black Civil Rights*. Princeton University Press, 2003.

Transnational Graphic Narratives. Special symposium of *International Journal of Comic Art*, ed. Daniel Stein, Lukas Etter, and Michael Chaney, 20.1 (2018).

"Troops Fire on Texas Mob, Wounding Two in Battle After Burning of Negro." *New York Times*, 10 May 1930.

Turner, Morrie. *Explore Black History with Wee Pals*. Just Us, 1998.

Turner, Nat. *The Confessions of Nat Turner, the Leader of the Late Insurrections in Southampton, VA*. 1831. *Slave Narratives*, ed. William L. Andrews and Henry Louis Gates Jr. Library of America, 2000. 243–66.

Twain, Mark. *The Adventures of Huckleberry Finn*. 1885. *A Case Study in Critical Controversy*, ed. Gerald Graff and James Phelan. Bedford/St. Martin's, 2004.

Upton, Florence K. *The Adventures of Two Dutch Dolls and a "Golliwogg."* Illus. Bertha Upton. Longmans, Green, 1885.

van Veen, tobias c. "The Armageddon Effect: Afrofuturism and the Chronopolitics of Alien Nation." *Afrofuturism 2.0: The Rise of Astro-Blackness*, ed. Reynaldo Anderson and Charles E. Jones. Lexington, 2015. 63–90.

Villanueva, Nicholas, Jr. *The Lynching of Mexicans in the Texas Borderlands*. University of New Mexico Press, 2017.

Walker, David F., and Marcus Kwame Anderson. *The Black Panther Party: A Graphic Novel History*. Ten Speed/Penguin Random House, 2021.

Walker, David F., Chuck Brown, and Sanford Greene. *Bitter Root Omnibus: Book One*. Image Comics, 2023.

Walker, David F., Damon Smyth, and Marissa Louise. *The Life of Frederick Douglass: A Graphic Narrative of a Slave's Journey from Bondage to Freedom*. Ten Speed/Penguin Random House, 2018.

Wallace, Maurice O. *King's Vibrato: Modernism, Blackness, and the Sonic Life of Martin Luther King Jr*. Duke University Press, 2022.

Wallace, Michele. *Dark Designs and Visual Culture*. Duke University Press, 2004.

Wallace, Michele. "Variations on Negation and the Heresy of Black Feminist Creativity." *Women, Creativity, and the Arts: Critical and Autobiographical Perspectives*, ed. Diane Apostolos-Cappadona and Lucinda Ebersole. Continuum, 1995. 124–38.

Walters, Wendy W. *Archives of the Black Atlantic: Reading Between Literature and History*. Routledge, 2013.

Wanzo, Rebecca. *The Content of Our Caricature: African American Comic Art and Political Belonging*. New York University Press, 2020.

Wanzo, Rebecca. "How Long, Not Long: A Take on Black Joy." *Film Quarterly* 74.4 (2021): 51–55.

Wanzo, Rebecca. "On Monstrosity." *Bitter Root Omnibus: Book One*, by David F. Walker, Chuck Brown, and Sanford Greene. Image Comics, 2023. 482–83.

Ward, Jonathan. "Wakanda Liberation Is This? Interrogating Black Panther's Relationship with Colonialism." *Slavery & Abolition* 41.1 (2020): 14–28.

Wardi, Anissa Janine. *Water and African American Memory: An Ecocritical Perspective*. University Press of Florida, 2011.

Washington, Booker T. *Up from Slavery*. 1901. Ed. William L. Andrews. Norton, 1995.

Washington, Donna-lyn, ed. *John Jennings: Conversations*. University Press of Mississippi, 2020.

Washington, Donna-lyn. "John Jennings Interview." 2019. *John Jennings: Conversations*, ed. Donna-lyn Washington. University Press of Mississippi, 2020. 139–46.

Watt, Brian. "King and Faith: Art and the Urgency of Now with John Jennings." 2018. *John Jennings: Conversations*, ed. Donna-lyn Washington. University Press of Mississippi, 2020. 63–83.

Weatherford, Carole Boston. Introduction. *Harriet Tubman: Toward Freedom*, by Whit Taylor and Kazimir Lee. Little, Brown, 2021.

Weatherford, Carole Boston, and Floyd Cooper. *Unspeakable: The Tulsa Race Massacre*. Carolrhoda, 2021.

Weaver, Lila Quintero. *Darkroom: A Memoir in Black and White*. University of Alabama Press, 2012.

Weheliye, Alexander G. *Habeas Viscus: Racializing Assemblages, Biopolitics, and Black Feminist Theories of the Human*. Duke University Press, 2014.

Weier, Sebastian. "Forum: Consider Afro-Pessimism." *Amerikastudien/American Studies* 59.3 (2014): 419–45.

Weinstock, Jeffrey Andrew. "Introduction: A Genealogy of Monster Theory." *The Monster Theory Reader*, ed. Jeffrey Andrew Weinstock. University of Minnesota Press, 2020. 1–36.

Weinstock, Jeffrey Andrew. "Invisible Monsters: Vision, Horror, and Contemporary Culture." *The Ashgate Research Companion to Monsters and the Monstrous*, ed. Asa Simon Mittman, with Peter J. Dendle. Ashgate, 2012. 275–89.

Weiss, Allen S. "Ten Theses on Monsters and Monstrosity." *TDR: The Drama Review* 48.1 (2004): 124–25.

Wells, Ida B. *Southern Horrors: Lynch Law in All Its Phases*. New York Age, 1892.

Wells-Oghoghomeh, Alexis. *The Souls of Womenfolk: The Religious Cultures of Enslaved Women in the Lower South*. University of North Carolina Press, 2021.

Werness, Hope B. *The Continuum Encyclopedia of Animal Symbolism in Art*. Continuum, 2006.

Wertham, Fredric. *Seduction of the Innocent: The Influence of Comic Books on Today's Youth*. Rinehart, 1954.

Wester, Maisha L. *African American Gothic: Screams from Shadowed Places*. Palgrave Macmillan, 2012.

Wester, Maisha L. "Southern Horrors and the Black Gothic." *Box of Bones: Book One*, by Ayize Jama-Everett and John Jennings. Rosarium, 2021.

Whaley, Deborah Elizabeth. *Black Women in Sequence: Re-Inking Comics, Graphic Novels, and Anime*. University of Washington Press, 2016.

Whitaker, Ronell, and Eric Kallenborn. *March: Teacher's Guide*. https://globaljews.org/wp-content/uploads/2020/07/March-Teachers-Guide.pdf. Accessed 3 May 2025.

White, Hayden. *Metahistory: The Historical Imagination in Nineteenth-Century Europe*. 1973. Johns Hopkins University Press, 2014.

White, Renée T., and Karen A. Ritzenhoff, eds. *Afrofuturism in Black Panther: Gender, Identity, and the Re-Making of Blackness*. Lexington, 2021.

White, Walter. *A Man Called White: The Autobiography of Walter White*. 1948. University of Georgia Press, 1995.

White, Walter. *Rope and Faggot: A Biography of Judge Lynch*. 1929. University of Norte Dame Press, 2001.

White, Walter. "The Work of a Mob." *The Crisis* 16.5 (1918): 221–23.

Whitehead, Anne. *Trauma Fiction*. Edinburgh University Press, 2004.

Whitfield, Stephen J. *A Death in the Delta: The Story of Emmett Till*. Johns Hopkins University Press, 1991.

Whitman, James Q. *Hitler's American Model: The United States and the Making of Nazi Race Law*. Princeton University Press, 2017.

Whitted, Qiana J. "'And the Negro Thinks in Hieroglyphics': Comics, Visual Metonymy, and the Spectacle of Blackness." *Journal of Graphic Novels and Comics* 5.1 (2014): 79–100.

Whitted, Qiana J. "The Blues Tragicomic: Constructing the Black Folk Subject in McCulloch and Hendrix's *Stagger Lee*." *The Blacker the Ink: Constructions of Black Identity in Comics and Sequential Art*, ed. Frances Gateward and John Jennings. Rutgers University Press, 2015. 235–54.

Whitted, Qiana J. "Comics and Emmett Till." *Picturing Childhood: Youth in Transnational Comics*, ed. Mark Heimermann and Brittany Tullis. University of Texas Press, 2017. 70–91.

Whitted, Qiana J., ed. *Desegregating Comics: Debating Blackness in the Golden Age of American Comics*. Rutgers University Press, 2023.

Whitted, Qiana J. "Intertextual Journeys: Black Culture, Speculative Fiction and the Past as Text in Jeremy Love's *Bayou*." *Class, Please Open Your Comics: Essays on Teaching with Graphic Narratives*, ed. Matthew L. Miller. McFarland, 2015. 195–213.

Whitted, Qiana J. "Of Slaves and Other Swamp Things: Black Southern History as Comic Book Horror." *Comics and the U.S. South*, ed. Brannon Costello and Qiana J. Whitted. University Press of Mississippi, 2012. 187–213.

Wiegman, Robyn. *American Anatomies: Theorizing Race and Gender*. Duke University Press, 1995.

Williams, Patricia J. "Gathering the Ghosts." *The A-Line: A Journal of Progressive Thought* 1.3–4 (2018): https://alinejournal.com/vol-1-no-3-4/gathering-the-ghosts/.

Williams, Rachel Marie-Crane. *Elegy for Mary Turner: An Illustrated Account of a Lynching*. Verso, 2021.

Winant, Howard. "The Dark Matter." *Ethnic and Racial Studies* 35.4 (2012): 600–607.

Womack, Ytasha L. *Afrofuturism: The World of Black Sci-Fi and Fantasy Culture*. Chicago Review Press, 2013.

Womack, Ytasha L. *Black Panther: A Cultural Exploration*. Epic Ink/Quarto, 2023.

Wood, Amy Louise. *Lynching and Spectacle: Witnessing Racial Violence in America, 1890–1940*. University of North Carolina Press, 2011.

Wood, Amy Louise. "'Somebody Do Something!' Lynching Photographs, Historical Memory, and the Possibility of Sympathetic Spectatorship." *European Journal of American Studies* 14.4 (2019): DOI: 10.4000/ejas.15512.

Wood, Amy Louise, and Susan V. Donaldson, eds. *Lynching and American Culture*, special issue of *Mississippi Quarterly* 61.1–2 (2008).

Woodward, Frank H. "Film Sense: Afrofuturism and the Ethno-Gothic." 2019. *John Jennings: Conversations*, ed. Donna-lyn Washington. University Press of Mississippi, 2020. 122–38.

Work, Frederick J. *New Jubilee Songs, as Sung by the Fisk Jubilee Singers of Fisk University*. Collected and harmonized by Frederick J. Work. 2nd ed. Fisk University, 1904.

Wright, Alexa. *Monstrosity: The Human Monster in Visual Culture*. Tauris, 2013.

Wright, Michelle M. *Becoming Black: Creating Identity in the African Diaspora*. Duke University Press, 2004.

Wright, Michelle M. *Physics of Blackness: Beyond the Middle Passage Epistemology*. University of Minnesota Press. 2015.

Wright, Richard. *Native Son*. 1940. Harper Perennial, 1998.

Wright, Richard. *12 Million Black Voices: A Folk History of the Negro in the United States*. 1941. Arno, 1969.

Wyman, Sarah. "Imaging Separation in Tom Feelings' *The Middle Passage: White Ships/Black Cargo* and Toni Morrison's *Beloved*." *Comparative American Studies* 7.4 (2009): 298–318.

Yancy, George. "Ahmaud Arbery and the Ghosts of Lynchings Past." *New York Times*, 12 May 2020.

Yeats, William Butler. "The Second Coming." 1920. *The Collected Poems of W. B. Yeats*, ed. Richard J. Finneran. Collier, 1989. 187.

Young, Harvey. *Embodying Black Experience: Stillness, Critical Memory, and the Black Body*. University of Michigan Press, 2010.

Young, Hershini Bhana. "Performance Geography: Making Space in Jeremy Love's *Bayou*, Volume 1." *The Blacker the Ink: Constructions of Black Identity in Comics and Sequential Art*, ed. Frances Gateward and John Jennings. Rutgers University Press, 2015. 274–91.

Zuck, Rochelle Raineri. "Rethinking the Black Atlantic: Gallows Literature, Slave Narratives, and Visual Culture." *Early American Literature* 51.3 (2016): 683–96.

INDEX

Africa, 22, 29–30, 36, 47–48, 80, 137–39, 147, 154, 162, 167, 187, 232, 234, 251, 255–56, 260

Afrofuturism, 11–12, 135, 138, 155–56, 230, 253, 257, 262. *See also* Wakanda

agency, 3, 69, 79, 86, 92, 143–44, 146, 149, 186, 205, 252

Anderson, Ho Che, 15, 17, 24, 59, 81, 93, 95, 97–98, 108, 110–11, 113–15, 119, 121, 128–29, 132–33, 223–24, 241, 245–50. See also *King* (Anderson)

Angelou, Maya, 49, 237, 243

anti-Black violence, 7, 11–12, 15, 18, 20, 22, 56, 59, 69, 89, 93, 95, 156, 170–71, 175, 179, 183, 203–4, 213, 214, 218, 225, 229, 245, 262

archive, 3, 5–6, 8–11, 14–15, 17–18, 20–21, 24, 26–27, 30–31, 33–34, 36, 41–42, 45–46, 48–51, 54–56, 59–62, 66–68, 72, 74, 77–78, 80–81, 86–88, 91–93, 99–101, 103, 108, 110, 113, 115, 119–20, 129, 131, 134, 136–37, 139–57, 165, 167, 177, 183, 185, 190, 205, 218–19, 224–26, 230, 232, 235, 237, 239, 251–55, 259; archival absence, 51, 55; colonial archive, 27, 141–42, 153; diasporic archive, 11, 15, 17, 136, 139, 141, 252; graphic archive, 6, 9, 14; historical archive, 49, 51, 67, 101, 144, 146–47, 165, 167; photographic archive, 68, 72, 81, 86–87, 131; political archive, 144, 146–47, 149; rogue archive (De Kosnik), 143, 153, 155

Assmann, Aleida, 92, 139, 141–42, 146–47

Atlantic slave trade, 7, 14, 16, 19, 33, 79, 153, 174, 187, 223, 230, 259. *See also* Africa; Middle Passage

Aydin, Andrew, 15, 17, 59, 75, 93–95, 97, 99, 101, 110, 116–17, 125, 128–29, 220, 229, 243

Baker, Kyle, 9–10, 14–16, 20, 22–23, 25, 27–29, 31–48, 53, 55–56, 59, 61, 64, 77, 79–84, 91, 137, 168, 187, 190, 219, 222–24, 227, 231, 234–37, 243, 247, 249–51, 255, 264

Baraka, Amiri, 19, 23, 106, 232

Barnes, Steven, 15, 216, 256, 263

Batman, 49, 58, 70, 80

Bayou (Love, Morgan), 9, 14–16, 18, 59, 61, 68–78, 90–91, 168, 171, 175, 178, 190–91, 194, 199, 201–4, 206–7, 211, 219–20, 222, 225, 240, 241–42, 243–45, 247, 252, 256–58, 262; Billy, 68–70, 72–78, 91, 190–91, 202–3, 207, 220, 242–43 (*see also* Till, Emmett); butterflies, 72–73, 75, 201–2; Mother Sista, 75–76, 201, 203, 207–8

Beitler, Lawrence, 5, 81, 83, 180

Bitter Root (Walker, Brown, Greene), 9, 11, 13–15, 18, 22, 59, 142, 168, 171–73, 183–84, 186, 188–90, 192, 194, 198–201, 204, 206, 208–16, 222–25, 237, 239, 245, 250, 254, 256, 259–63; Sangerye family, 22, 59, 142, 172, 183–84, 186, 189, 192, 199–200, 206, 208, 210, 213, 222–23, 225, 237, 250, 258, 261

Black body, 13, 18, 21, 28, 31, 43, 59–61, 63–69, 71–73, 75–78, 80–81, 85–86, 90–92, 180, 196, 218, 220–22, 241–45, 247, 260–61; overdetermination, 65

Black joy, 205, 221–22, 224, 264; spaces of pleasure, 222–23, 225

Black Lives Matter (BLM), 4, 31, 50, 91, 94, 156, 177, 196, 213, 229, 245

black/Black magic, 188, 211. *See also* conjuring

Black Panther, 11, 15, 17–18, 58, 61, 135–49, 151, 153–59, 161–62, 164–67, 185, 189, 219, 223–24, 230, 244, 250–55; Hudlin, 136–37,

299

158, 161–62, 251; Lee/Kirby, 154, 254; vibranium, 144, 149, 152, 159, 167. *See also* Djalia; Shuri (*Shuri/Black Panther*)

Black Panther Party: A Graphic Novel History, The (Walker, Anderson), 16, 241

Black superhero, 58, 80, 83, 85, 87, 136, 154, 239, 243, 250

Bloody Sunday, 95, 102–3, 122–23, 247

Blue Hand Mojo (Jennings), 9, 14–15, 18, 22, 168, 171, 186, 188–89, 192, 194–95, 201, 204, 206, 211, 214, 223–25, 239, 259, 261, 263; Half-Dead Johnson, 14, 22, 186, 188–89, 192, 194–95, 208, 211, 223–24, 259, 262

Box of Bones (Jama-Everett, Jennings), 15, 18, 168, 170–71, 177–83, 188, 192, 194, 204–6, 212, 219, 224, 231, 239, 244, 258, 263; gorilla tree, 179–80. *See also* lynching: tree

branding, 20, 133, 231, 264

Brathwaite, Kamau, 19, 23

Brown, Kimberly Juanita, 47, 55, 73, 90, 239, 245, 256; *mortevivum*, 90

Brown, Sterling, 23

Browne, Simone, 6, 8, 153, 231, 234, 240; surveillance, 65, 153, 240

Bukatman, Scott, 60–61, 90, 93, 169, 254, 263

Campt, Tina M., 9–10, 157, 230, 240, 242, 245, 261, 264

Captain America, 12, 137, 243, 245, 250, 251, 255

Caruth, Cathy, 171–72, 184

castration, 61, 78, 83

Chaney, Michael A., 3, 29, 31, 37, 39, 41–42, 55, 67–68, 75, 77, 83, 94, 96, 98, 101, 104–7, 109, 111, 115, 117, 119, 132, 235, 241, 247, 249–50

chattel slavery, 36, 48, 53, 61, 174–75, 177, 236, 257

Chicago, 22, 96, 121, 192, 194, 213, 247

civil rights movement, 17, 68, 93–111, 113–25, 128–29, 132–35, 177, 220, 223, 245–50; nonviolent resistance, 94, 96, 101–2, 109, 113–14, 121, 247; photography, 86, 97, 99, 124 (*see also* photography); speeches, 101–3, 105, 108–9, 113–15, 118, 130–32, 247–48, 250

Clifton, Lucille, 19, 23, 238, 240

closure (McCloud), 104, 109, 122–24, 135, 167, 176, 183, 187, 218

Coates, Ta-Nehisi, 15, 17, 18, 96, 134, 136–44, 146–47, 149–50, 152–59, 165–67, 185, 223, 231, 250–55, 260. *See also* Black Panther; Shuri (*Shuri/Black Panther*)

colonialism, 32, 137–38, 150

Confessions of Nat Turner, The, 25, 28, 33, 35–36, 40–43, 79–80, 233, 235–36

conjuring, 13, 18, 22, 59, 174, 183, 186, 188–89, 192, 198, 205–9, 211, 223–24, 259, 261–63

Cugoano, Ottobah, 27–28

cultural memory, 10, 92, 141, 144, 147, 154, 173

dark matter (Winant/Browne), 6–8, 10–11, 13

Darkroom: A Memoir in Black and White (Weaver), 17, 96, 120

Dawes, Kwame, 19, 23, 33, 39, 53

DC, 69, 75

decolonization, 167, 255

Demonakos, Jim, 17, 96, 103, 120

diaspora, 6, 9–11, 14–15, 17–18, 20, 25, 27, 29, 36, 42, 49, 52–53, 55, 137, 139–41, 143–44, 146, 150, 152–53, 155, 166–68, 170–72, 174–75, 183, 185–86, 189, 192, 205–6, 220–21, 226, 230–31, 251–54, 256–59, 261, 263

didactics, 17, 93, 95–132, 134–35, 230, 246; critical engagement, 97, 118; media literacy, 122; resources, 98, 123. *See also King* (Anderson); *March* (Lewis, Aydin, Powell)

Djalia, 18, 140, 145–49, 158, 165, 185, 189, 253; as archival space, 145–49. *See also* archive

Douglass, Frederick, 22–23, 149, 155, 230, 232, 236, 244, 254

drowning, 53, 191, 198. *See also* suicide; water

Du Bois, W. E. B., 16, 63, 155, 239

Due, Tananarive, 15, 216, 256, 263

Ellison, Ralph, 26, 54, 55, 67, 155, 211

Emanuel, James A., 19, 23, 232–33

Emerson, Ralph Waldo, 186

enslaved women, 21, 43, 167, 176, 231–33, 237–38

epistemology (Wright), 15–16, 19, 25, 42, 205
Equiano, Olaudah, 27
ethnogothic, 174, 192–94, 199, 201, 204, 207

family, 13–14, 21–23, 27, 29, 31, 36–41, 43–45, 47–50, 55, 59, 84, 98, 102, 115, 120, 129, 142, 172, 179–86, 189, 192, 195–98, 205, 207–11, 213–14, 223–26, 230, 235–37, 244, 250–52, 258–61, 263–64; ancestry, 13, 22–23, 36, 47, 49, 55, 198, 245
fan art, 144, 157, 166
Farmhand (Guillory), 9, 11, 13, 15, 18, 168, 173, 187, 194, 197–98, 201, 203–4, 207, 223–24, 239, 261–62
Fawaz, Ramzi, 60–61, 84, 139. See also flux
Finnegan, Marco, 15, 216, 256, 263
flux, 60–62, 80, 84, 90
framing, 10, 56, 61, 94, 101, 107, 121–25, 129–30, 132, 230, 249; frame theory, 121; reframing, 7, 10, 24, 65, 115, 116
freedom rides, 114, 119, 128, 129, 133, 243

Gates, Henry Louis, Jr., 34, 48, 67–68, 231
Gay, Roxane, 15, 18, 137, 159, 166–67
gender oppression, 121
gender representation, 154, 166
gendered violence, 4. See also sexual violence
ghost, 21, 31, 69, 92, 169–70, 174, 184, 187, 191, 194, 196, 202, 205, 214, 256, 258, 263
Gill, Joel Christian, 16, 18, 24, 217–19, 226, 235, 239, 241, 257
Gilroy, Paul, 13, 21, 231, 233, 256
gothic, 169, 171, 174, 180, 183, 192–94, 257, 260. See also ethnogothic; Southern gothic
graphic biography, 17, 22, 93, 97, 99, 103, 110, 114–15, 117, 128, 133, 224, 247, 248, 249, 250, 263
graphic memoir, 94, 96–101, 120, 123
Griffith, D. W., 37, 58, 70, 79, 175; *The Birth of a Nation*, 37, 58, 70, 79, 175, 235
grotesque, 61, 69, 72–73, 82, 90, 177–78, 180, 194, 207, 212, 256
Guillory, Rob, 9, 11, 13, 15, 18, 168, 173, 187, 196–98, 207, 223, 239. See also *Farmhand* (Guillory)

Hall, Rebecca, 3–4, 10, 14–16, 20, 22, 25–28, 30–35, 43, 46, 48–56, 152, 168, 184, 190, 213, 220, 223–24, 229, 233–34, 237, 243, 246, 254. See also *Wake* (Hall, Martínez, Bao)
Hartman, Saidiya, 10, 19, 20, 24, 27, 46–48, 50–51, 55, 66, 140–41, 149, 152, 172, 183, 231–32, 234–35, 251, 253, 256; afterlife of slavery, 4, 50, 55, 172; critical fabulation, 27, 48, 50, 54, 140, 152, 251
Harvey, Yona, 15, 137–38, 167, 250
haunting, 3–4, 8, 14, 21, 30–31, 49, 54, 57, 64, 69, 97, 143, 149, 152–53, 167–74, 177, 180, 184, 188, 191–94, 196, 198, 201, 205, 219, 226, 233, 244, 256, 260. See also ghost
Hayden, Robert, 19, 23, 38, 47, 234, 236, 239
historiography, 25, 35, 39, 42, 110–11, 115, 117, 120–21, 134, 135
Hole: Consumer Culture, The (Duffy, Jennings), 189, 245
Holiday, Billie, 12–13, 23, 92, 219, 225
Holocaust, 55, 133–34, 243, 250
hooks, bell, 37, 48, 119, 196, 231, 236, 248, 259, 261
Hughes, George, 86, 88–89, 91, 244
Hughes, Henry, 175–76
Hughes, Langston, 14, 239; "The Bitter River," 14

iconography, 7, 10, 39, 46, 60, 68–69, 78, 87, 103, 106, 119, 121, 156, 220, 238, 242
Incognegro (Johnson, Pleece), 9, 16, 59, 71, 82–84, 241
infanticide, 36–37, 39, 41, 45
interpictoriality, 39, 87, 155
intertextuality, 14, 39, 119, 146, 159
invisibility, 26–27
Inzondo, 183–84, 186, 189, 199, 208, 213–15, 222, 258
Iron Man, 138

Jefferson, Thomas, 4–5, 13, 262
Jennings, John, 6, 9, 12–16, 18, 22, 27, 59, 168–70, 172–74, 177, 183, 189, 193–94, 196, 214, 219, 222–23, 231, 239, 244–45, 250, 253–55, 257–58, 261. See also *Blue Hand*

302 INDEX

Mojo (Jennings); *Box of Bones* (Jama-Everett, Jennings)
Jim Crow, 15, 17, 23, 70, 73, 133–34, 139, 177, 180, 192, 194, 198, 201, 203, 223, 248, 259
Jinoo, 173, 183–84, 186, 189, 199–200, 208, 210, 213, 256, 258, 261
Johnson, Charles, 19, 21, 28–29, 39, 43, 46, 54, 73, 193
Johnson, Lyndon B., 102, 114, 264
Johnson, Mat, 9, 16, 56, 59, 61, 63, 71, 82–83, 176, 229–30, 235, 237, 244–45
journalism, 62, 83–84, 125, 137–38, 140, 147, 152, 159, 241, 251

Keeper, The (Due, Barnes, Finnegan), 15, 216, 256, 263
Kendi, Ibram X., 16, 226, 241, 257, 264
King (Anderson), 15, 17, 24, 59, 81, 93, 95, 96–98, 110–16, 119, 121–22, 128–33, 135, 223, 243, 247–50; witnesses, 110–13, 120, 123, 128, 129, 131, 133, 193, 233, 247
Ku Klux Klan, 37, 58, 62, 83, 129, 132, 135, 196, 198–200, 204, 207, 222–23, 244–45, 247–48, 250, 261

landownership, 203. *See also* sharecropping
Lewis, John, 15, 17, 36, 44, 59, 75, 93–103, 105, 107–8, 110, 116–19, 122, 124–29, 132–34, 220, 223, 229, 233–35, 243, 246, 248. *See also March* (Lewis, Aydin, Powell)
liminal space, 188–89. *See also* Djalia
literacy, 35–36, 42, 123
living dead, 174, 177, 185, 187, 189–90, 192
Long, Mark, 17, 96, 103, 120, 246. *See also Silence of Our Friends, The* (Long, Demonakes, Powell)
Lorde, Audre, 50, 155, 172
Love, Jeremy, 9, 14–16, 18, 56, 59, 61, 63, 68–79, 81, 90–91, 134, 168, 190–91, 201, 220, 222, 225, 242–45, 247, 252, 258
lynching, 5, 9, 12–18, 22–23, 32, 36, 41, 43, 50, 56–93, 132, 171, 173, 176, 178–82, 184–85, 188–89, 192, 194–99, 201, 203–4, 206–7, 218–25, 229–30, 232, 238–45, 247–48, 258–62, 264; afterlife of lynching, 65, 68, 73; feet, 5, 32, 70–75, 78, 85, 243, 247, 259; tree, 5, 13–14, 18, 23, 59, 62, 70–71, 75, 77, 82–83, 177, 179, 180, 184–85, 195–99, 202, 204, 207, 218–19, 230, 243–45, 258–61; mob, 5, 57, 59, 61–64, 70–71, 77, 81, 83, 85, 88–91, 109, 129, 135, 194, 207, 238, 241–42, 244, 261–62; onlookers, 5, 32, 65, 71–72, 75, 77, 81, 90, 123, 242–43. *See also* noose
lynching photography, 12–13, 17, 59, 61, 63–68, 71, 73–77, 80–82, 84, 87, 90, 178, 184, 198, 218–19, 222, 240, 244–45, 248

Making Our Way Home (Imani), 16, 218
March (Lewis, Aydin, Powell), 15, 17, 59, 75, 83, 93–110, 114–28, 132–35, 220, 223, 243, 246–49, 264; Book One, 59, 99, 102–4, 107–9, 117, 243, 248; Book Three, 102, 106, 108, 117–18, 122–24, 126–27, 248, 264; Book Two, 99–100, 102, 105, 107–9, 117–19, 132–35, 248; cover images, 103–6; intended audience, 117
March on Washington, 101–3, 105, 114, 116, 118, 128, 132, 247
Marvel, 42, 86–87, 90–91, 136–37, 139, 144, 147, 153–54, 156–58, 251, 254
Mbiti, John S., 185–87, 190; *African Religions and Philosophy*, 185
mediation, 17, 62, 67, 84, 93, 96, 97, 99, 100, 101, 107, 115, 118, 120, 132
Meeropol, Abel, 12–14, 23, 62, 92, 180, 198, 219, 233
memorialization, 96–98, 100, 115, 119, 122, 125, 134
Middle Passage, 3, 7, 10, 14–16, 19, 20, 22, 24–30, 32, 34, 37, 39–40, 42, 46–48, 53–56, 79, 80, 167, 175, 177, 187–98, 190–92, 207, 219–20, 227, 231–38, 243, 248, 253
"Middle Passage" (Hayden), 19, 38, 47, 234, 236
Middle Passage (Johnson), 19, 21, 28, 39, 43, 46, 54
"Middle Passage Blues, The" (Emanuel), 19, 232–33
Middle Passage: White Ships/Black Cargo, The (Feelings), 11, 16, 19, 20, 25, 26, 29, 30,

31, 32, 34, 36, 39, 43–48, 55–56, 149, 168, 176, 187, 219, 224, 227, 231–32, 234, 237, 243

Middle Passages (Brathwaite), 19

Mighty Struggle: A Town Called Miracle, The (Jennings, Brame), 13, 18, 168, 207, 253, 258, 261

monsters, 14, 18, 35, 142, 168–77, 179, 183, 191–93, 198–99, 201, 204, 208, 211–16, 223, 256–59, 261–63; monster theory, 174, 175. *See also* ghost; zombie

Morrison, Toni, 6–7, 9, 16, 19, 21, 23–26, 37, 48, 51, 55, 75, 136, 159, 168–70, 177, 188, 205, 219, 256, 259–60; *Beloved*, 21–22, 37, 51, 169, 231, 256, 259; Morrison's paradox/ perfect dilemma, 7, 9, 16, 25, 168, 177, 219; rememory, 75; unspeakability, 27, 56

mothers, 21–23, 35–37, 42–43, 45, 47, 51, 68–69, 76, 145, 157, 162, 165, 180, 186, 190–91, 202–3, 207, 211, 218–19, 222, 235–37, 241, 253–54, 258, 260, 263. *See also Bayou* (Love, Morgan): Mother Sista; family

mourning, 53, 183, 198, 242

music, 12, 108–9, 133, 155, 194, 202, 206, 222, 225, 238, 247, 260, 264

Nat Turner (Baker), 9–10, 14–16, 20, 23, 25, 26, 29, 32, 34–43, 45–47, 55–56, 59, 64, 77, 79–82, 84, 91, 168, 187, 190, 212, 219, 222–24, 227, 231, 233–37, 243, 247, 249, 255, 259. See also *Confessions of Nat Turner, The*

Nation Under Our Feet, The (Coates), 136, 251, 253

Native Son (Wright), 46

nature, 13, 194, 199, 201, 203–4, 206, 260

Noguchi, Isamu, *Death*, 86, 88, 90–91

Noir, The, 188–89, 211, 259, 263

noose, 50, 59, 73, 177–80, 198–99, 202, 218–21, 263–64; rope, 18, 73, 78, 80, 88, 91, 196, 218–20, 239, 244, 264

Obama, Barack, 95–96, 102, 109, 132, 135, 245

Okorafor, Nnedi, 15, 18, 137–38, 141, 155–56, 159, 161–62, 165–67, 216, 224, 253–57. *See also* Shuri (*Shuri/Black Panther*)

paratext (Genette), 42, 101–2, 106–7, 150, 156, 189, 254, 255

pedagogy, 15, 17, 55, 97–98, 102–3, 116–17, 128, 246. *See also* didactics

photography, 5, 9, 13, 16, 56, 62–65, 67, 69, 71–74, 81, 83–84, 86–87, 90–91, 97, 99–100, 102, 111, 113, 115, 120, 122, 124–25, 132–33, 183, 205, 218, 229, 240–41, 243–44, 246–47, 263–65; postcards, 13, 62, 75–77, 84, 91, 239

plantation, 23, 35–36, 65, 152, 175, 187, 190, 206, 235–36, 242, 259, 263. *See also* sharecropping

plundering, 137–38, 141, 144, 150, 152, 154, 252. *See also* archive: rogue archive (De Kosnik)

police, 4, 12, 50, 65, 92, 94, 108, 113–14, 119–20, 123, 129, 133–35, 150, 156, 206, 243–45, 247, 250

Powell, Nate, 15, 17, 59, 75, 93–97, 99, 100–101, 103, 107–10, 120, 124–25, 128–29, 132–33, 220, 229, 243, 246

pregnancy, 46–48, 60, 224, 257. *See also* mothers

recuperation, 3, 10, 12, 15–16, 20, 24–25, 27, 43, 48, 55–56, 92, 108, 135, 145, 218

"Requiem" (Dawes), 19, 33, 39, 53

revolt, 33, 48, 50–51, 53–55, 115, 219, 233, 235, 237, 260

roots, 6, 13–14, 17, 24, 26, 58–59, 105, 122, 155, 197–99, 203–4, 206–8, 211, 239, 246, 249, 261

Sankofa, 12, 230

Selma, Alabama, 95, 101–2, 120, 122–24, 126–27

sentimental depiction, 29, 41, 134, 235

sexual difference, 61

sexual violence, 21, 27–28, 43, 47, 49, 61, 74, 159, 176, 199, 231, 233, 258, 261

sharecropping, 13, 14, 23, 203

Sharpe, Christina, 50, 53, 172, 176, 185, 188, 190, 231–32, 234, 236, 241, 258; wake of slavery, 26, 50, 53, 65, 172, 184, 190, 232

Shuri (*Shuri/Black Panther*), 11, 15, 18, 136–38, 144–46, 154–67, 185, 251, 253–55; ancestral figures, 161, 165, 205, 255; Vita Ayala, 156

Silence of Our Friends, The (Long, Demonakes, Powell), 17, 96, 103, 108, 120

slave narrative, 21, 22, 24, 29, 34, 41, 176, 232, 252

slave ship, 22, 28–29, 33–34, 45, 152, 233–36, 259; Brookes, 33–34, 45, 234; rats, 46, 236; *Unity*, 39, 44, 50, 53–55

Slave Ship: An Historical Pageant (Baraka), 19

"Slaveships" (Clifton), 19, 238

Song of the South (Disney), 70, 180

sound words, 35, 37, 78, 127

Southern gothic, 69, 241

Spider-Man, 17, 78, 83, 86–88, 90–92, 156–57, 161; Miles Morales, 17, 86–91, 137, 156, 243, 254 (*see also* Black superhero); Peter Parker, 78, 83, 87, 91, 157

Spillers, Hortense J., 11, 31, 37, 47, 77, 192, 234; *American Grammar Book*, 11

spin-off series, 18, 137–38, 154, 156–57, 159

splash page/panel, 3–4, 44, 49, 50, 53–54, 70, 73, 83, 91, 118, 132, 134, 142, 155, 177, 178, 183, 190, 198–99, 213, 220, 225, 235, 241, 245, 261

Stagger Lee, 61, 77, 85–86

Stagger Lee (Hendrix, McCulloch), 9, 16, 59, 61, 84–86, 225

Stamped from the Beginning (Kendi), 16, 226, 257

Still I Rise (Laird, Laird, Bey), 15–16, 46, 73, 218, 237

"Strange Fruit," 6, 12–14, 18, 23, 62, 92, 180, 201, 218–19, 261. *See also* Holiday, Billie; Meeropol, Abel

Strange Fruit (Gill), 16, 18, 24, 217; *Tales of the Talented Tenth*, 16; vol. 1, 16, 24, 217; vol. 2, 16, 24

Student Nonviolent Coordinating Committee (SNCC), 95, 98–100, 103, 107, 114, 118, 119, 122, 246

suicide, 31, 37–39, 45–46, 52, 54, 77, 79, 233, 235, 238; Flora (*The Birth of a Nation*), 37, 79

superhero, 16–18, 28, 41–42, 56–60, 62, 67, 69–70, 73, 78–80, 82–85, 87–88, 90–93, 136–42, 147, 149, 153–54, 156–59, 162, 165, 167, 169, 207, 238, 251, 254–55; decolonization, 167; superhero body, 60, 138. *See also* Black superhero

superhero comics, 17–18, 28, 41–42, 59, 73, 78–79, 93, 137, 139, 149, 153, 158, 167, 169, 254; fight scenes, 73, 79, 91–92

Taylor, Diana, 140–41, 143, 153

Taylor, Leila, 176, 183, 191–92, 256–60

television, 75, 97, 99, 107–8, 110, 115–16, 120, 122–24, 126, 129–30, 238, 255

temporality, 29, 31, 50, 53, 75, 77, 105, 170, 190; captive time, 29. *See also* Middle Passage

Till, Emmett, 68–69, 72, 75–78, 81, 172–73, 226, 230, 232, 240–42, 256; *Afterimages* (Lorde), 172; funeral, 68–69, 75, 241, 256

Tooks, Lance, 7

transatlantic slavery, 24, 27, 44, 153. *See also* Atlantic slave trade

trauma, 7, 13, 15, 19, 21, 29, 56, 69–70, 75, 80, 167–76, 179, 181, 183–84, 186–90, 192–94, 196, 198, 201–2, 204–8, 211–12, 218–19, 225, 231, 235, 242, 245, 256–59, 262–63; traumatic echo, 170–71, 189–90, 198; racial trauma, 167, 172, 177, 179, 181, 183–84, 187, 189, 206, 208; site of trauma (Caruth), 171, 184; survivors, 196, 207; transgenerational trauma, 173, 184, 189, 198

Tubman, Harriet, 16, 213, 216, 230, 263

Tulsa Race Massacre, 5, 91, 171, 184, 213–15, 220, 229, 232, 238, 245, 249

visual culture, 7, 24, 27, 34, 64, 86–87, 218–19, 229, 256

voyeursim, 62, 77, 107, 158, 256. *See also* lynching: onlookers

Wakanda, 18, 138, 140–41, 143–51, 155–66, 185, 251, 252–55; Wakandan women, 156, 159, 162–64; *World of Wakanda* (Gay, Coates, et al.) 18, 137, 154, 158–59, 166

Wake (Hall, Martínez, Bao), 3–6, 10, 14–16, 20, 25–26, 30–31, 33–35, 39, 43–46, 48–56, 152, 167–68, 184, 187, 190, 213, 219–20, 223–24, 237, 243, 259, 264; diving warrior woman, 52, 54, 55, 245

Walker, David F., 9, 11, 13–16, 18, 22–23, 59, 142, 168, 184, 186, 214, 222, 236–37, 239, 241–42, 244–46, 248, 250, 254, 259
Washington, Booker T., 22, 35, 102, 143, 232, 264
Washington, Donna-lyn, 12, 194
water, 14, 30, 38–39, 46, 51–54, 73, 77, 175, 189–91, 198, 202, 203, 219, 225, 233, 238, 242–43, 251, 260; sharks, 38–39, 45–46, 190, 233–35, 238
Weaver, Lila Quintero, 17, 96, 103, 120, 249
White, Walter, 62, 82, 192, 204, 239, 241, 243, 261; *Rope and Faggot*, 62, 204, 244
white supremacy, 4, 20, 66, 68, 74, 80, 90, 132, 176, 179, 184, 192, 201, 204, 212, 219, 221, 231, 246, 259, 264
Whitted, Qiana J., 8, 31, 35, 41, 69, 75–76, 84–85, 193, 235–36, 240, 242, 244, 256
Wright, Michelle M., 15–16, 25, 68, 231
Wright, Richard, 46, 203, 260, 262

Young, Harvey, 65

zombie, 173, 185–87, 189, 198–99, 259, 261

ABOUT THE AUTHOR

Photo by the author

DANIEL STEIN is professor of North American literary and cultural studies and dean of the Faculty of Arts and Humanities at the University of Siegen, Germany. He is the author of *Music Is My Life: Louis Armstrong, Autobiography, and American Jazz* (2012) and *Authorizing Superhero Comics: On the Evolution of a Popular Serial Genre* (2021) as well as coeditor of numerous essay collections and journal issues on US literature, graphic narratives, nineteenth-century serial literature, and popular culture. His work has appeared in *Amerikastudien/American Studies, Journal of American Studies, European Journal of American Studies, Journal of Graphic Novels and Comics, Southern Literary Journal*, and *Popular Music & Society*. He is one of the editors of *Anglia: Journal of English Philology* and since 2021 has been a principal investigator in the collaborative research center Transformations of the Popular funded by the German Research Foundation.

www.ingramcontent.com/pod-product-compliance
Lightning Source LLC
Chambersburg PA
CBHW021833220426
43663CB00005B/232